D0097750

Erratum

Please note: from page 14 onwards page numbers in the Index are out by one
page (e.g. for 180 read 179).

THE PROTEAN SCOT

1 *THE JOURNALIST. With a View of Auckinleck—or the Land of Stones.*
'I am, I flatter myself compleatly a Citizen of the World. In my Travels through Holland, Germany, Switzerland, Italy, Corsica, France, I never felt myself from home, and I sincerely love every kindred and tongue and people and nation'. p. 11
'My great grandfather the Husband of Countess Veronica, was Alexander Earl of Kincardine—From him the blood of Bruce flows in my Veins, of such Ancestry who would not be proud & glad to seize a fair opportunity to let it be known?' Vide Journal p. 16

THE PROTEAN SCOT

The Crisis of Identity in Eighteenth Century Scottish Literature

KENNETH SIMPSON

ABERDEEN UNIVERSITY PRESS

First published 1988
Aberdeen University Press
A member of the Pergamon Group

© Kenneth Simpson 1988

British Library Cataloguing in Publication Data

Simpson, Kenneth
    The protean Scot: multiple voice in
    eighteenth century Scottish Literature.
    1. English literature. Scottish writers,
    1702–1800—Critical studies
    I. Title
    820.9′9411

    ISBN 0 08 036401 2

PRINTED IN GREAT BRITAIN
THE UNIVERSITY PRESS
ABERDEEN

For David Simpson

Contents

List of Illustrations

Jacket illustration:

THE VISION
'I had a most elegant Room, but there was a Fire in it that blazed, And the Sea to which my Windows looked roared, & the Pillows were made of some Sea Fowls feathers which had to me a disagreeable Smell, So that by all these Causes I was kept awake a good-time. I saw in imagination Lord Errol's Father, Lord Kilmarnock (who was beheaded on Towerhill in 1746) & I was somewhat dreary, but the thought did not last long and I fell asleep.' Vide Journal, p. 110

The above illustrations are all reproduced by kind permission of the National Library of Scotland from *Picturesque Beauties of Boswell* by Rowlandson.

Preface

This book grew out of a general interest in the extent to which sentiment and satiric reduction co-exist in Scottish literature. Focusing increasingly on the eighteenth century, and guided by two definitive studies, David Daiches, *The Paradox of Scottish Culture* and Thomas Crawford, *Burns: A Study of the Poems and Songs*, I was struck by the range of voices—some of them contradictory— in the work of such writers as Smollett, Boswell, and Burns. If the tension between increasing Anglicisation and native Scottish forms could sometimes result in bathos or doggerel, it was also productive of writing of the highest order, as the example of Burns demonstrates (the recognition of Burns as sophisticated literary artist and master of modes and *personae* has advanced considerably with Carol McGuirk's excellent study, *Robert Burns and the Sentimental Era*).

That Scottish writers of the eighteenth century seem to have been par- ticularly prone to adopt personae and project self-images may well reflect a crisis of Scottish identity in the century after the Union. Those same writers responded early to the European vogue of primitivism, and the recurrence of the voice of feeling in the literature of the second half of the century suggests that, at least temporarily, an identity had been found. But Scotland's rôle in the quest for noble savagery and the contribution of her writers to the sentimental movement were prime factors in ensuring that the Scottish experience of Romanticism was partial or even flawed.

It is, then, to the eighteenth century that we must look to find the factors which have largely determined the nature of Scottish literature thereafter. In the chameleon nature of eighteenth-century Scottish writers there is, I suggest, one of the prototypes of modern alienation.

Chapters 1 and 7 have appeared in print, though with some alteration, in, respectively, *Tobias Smollett: Author of the First Distinction*, edited by Alan Bold (Vision Press/Barnes and Noble, 1982), and *The Art of Robert Burns*, edited by R D S Jack and Andrew Noble (Vision Press/Barnes and Noble, 1982). Part of Chapter 4 was published under the title, 'Rationalism and Romanticism: the Case of Home's *Douglas*', in *Scottish Literary Journal*, IX, i (May, 1983), and for permission to reprint, I am grateful to the Association for Scottish Literary Studies.

Acknowledgements

My debts of gratitude are many and considerable. Colin MacCabe encouraged me to write this book; Patricia J Wilson, Douglas H MacAllister and Douglas Gifford readily shared their extensive knowledge of Scottish literature; Andrew Noble offered invaluable help throughout; Andrew Hook's guidance was both wise and kindly; and David B Hutchison acquainted me with the drama of the period and maintained a friendly interest in the book's progress. Donald Gordon and Christopher Whatley advised on, respectively, philosophical and historical aspects, while the scientific viewpoint of Tony Watson led me to question some of my general assumptions. At the University of Massachusetts, Amherst, discussions with Morris Golden, Alex Page, Bob Smith and John C Weston were as thought-provoking as they were pleasant. Of the many authorities on Scottish literature from whose expertise I have benefited, Thomas Crawford and Donald Low warrant especial mention. For help with illustrations and titles I am indebted to the staff of the Language and Literature Section of the Mitchell Library, Frank Paterson, and Jack Sloss. To Aileen Hunter, Jean Leithead, Allison MacDonald, and Margaret Philips thanks are warmly proffered for help and guidance on many occasions. And I am particularly grateful to Marjorie Leith and Colin MacLean for their kindness in advising me in the preparation of the manuscript and seeing the book through press.

The staffs of the following libraries have been particularly helpful: Andersonian Library, University of Strathclyde; Glasgow University Library; Mitchell Library, Glasgow; National Library of Scotland; Houghton Library, Harvard; Pierpont Morgan Library, New York.

I acknowledge with gratitude an award from the Carnegie Trust which helped me to visit the Morgan Library in New York.

Above all, I would thank my wife, son, and parents for the interest and encouragement which have sustained me through the writing of this book.

Introduction

Rôle-playing and the projection of self-images are commonplace in modern life. Protean man is often regarded as a twentieth-century phenomenon. In fact, one of his prototypes is the eighteenth-century Scot. This is the self-characterisation with which Burns thought fit to preface his own commonplace book:

> Observations, Hints, Songs, Scraps of Poetry &c. by Robt Burness; a man who had little art in making money, and still less in keeping it; but was, however, a man of some sense, a great deal of honesty, and unbounded good-will to every creature rational or irrational.—As he was but little indebted to scholastic education, and bred at a plough-tail, his performances must be strongly tinctured with his unpolished, rustic way of life; but as I believe, they are really his own, it may be some entertainment to a curious observer of human-nature to see how a plough-man thinks, and feels, under the pressure of Love, Ambition, Anxiety, Grief with the like cares and passions, which, however diversified by the Modes, and Manners of life, operate pretty much alike I believe, in all the Species.[1]

In polished Augustan prose Burns claims that he lacked formal education. In fact the reality was something other than the untutored rustic that Burns projected for the benefit of an admiring world.

For James Boswell, rôle-playing was second nature. It seems to have come easily also to Lord Monboddo, one of the most eminent of the Edinburgh *literati*. Here is part of Boswell's account of the visit which Dr Johnson and he paid to Lord Monboddo:

> His lordship was drest in a rustick suit, and wore a little round hat; he told us, we now saw him as *Farmer Burnet*, and we should have his family dinner, a farmer's dinner. He said, 'I should not have forgiven Mr. Boswell, had he not brought you here, Dr. Johnson.' He produced a very long stalk of corn, as a specimen of his crop, and said, 'You see here the *laetas segetes*': he added, That Virgil seemed to be as enthusiastick a farmer as he, and was certainly a practical one. —Johnson: 'It does not always follow, my lord, that a man who has written a good poem on an art, has practised it.'[2]

When Johnson later expressed his disapproval of a judge's calling himself *Farmer* Burnett and 'laughed heartily at his lordship's saying he was an *enthusiastical* farmer, "for . . . what can he do in farming by his enthusiasm?",' Boswell was quick to defend keenness 'in all the occupations or diversions of life'.[3] Energy seeking a focus, an object, an ideal, is one of the recurrent characteristics of Scottish literature.

Many of the great European writers of the eighteenth century had complex personalities and expressed contradictory views. Of such unions of contraries Paul Hazard has written, 'You would have thought, about many and many a writer, that he was two men rolled into one . . . There were two Montesquieus; one of them wrote a grave treatise about laws, the other made fun of them.'[4] Multiplicity of voice and complexity of personality are not exclusive to Scottish writers in the eighteenth century. George Santayana's comment that Rousseau's *Confessions* demonstrated, in equal measure, candour and ignorance of self might be applied just as readily to Boswell's *London Journal*.

But in eighteenth-century Scottish literature multiplicity of voice, fragmentation of personality, and the projection of self-images recur with a frequency and an intensity that are quite remarkable. The purpose of this study is to identify the conflicting voices within individual Scottish writers of the eighteenth century and to account for the nature, the range, and the recurrence of them. This will involve consideration of the ways in which the Scottish literary tradition, with its own distinctive features, responded under the pressure of ever-increasing Anglicisation. The further concerns of the study are to estimate the significance of the chameleon quality of Scottish writers in respect of the Scottish experience of the movement from Rationalism to Romanticism, and, finally, to look at the implications of this for the future of Scottish literature. In his compulsive rôle-playing, it will be suggested, the eighteenth-century Scottish writer anticipates the modern condition.

The older Scottish tradition was characterised by a diversity of elements.[5] Its recurrent poetic types were lyrics, ballads, satires and poems of social realism. The characteristic strengths were anecdotal ability and expressive energy (typified at its most extreme in 'The Flyting of Dunbar and Kennedy' which John Speirs terms 'a *tour de force* of sheer language').[6] The representation of communal life co-existed with a propensity to fantasy; poignant emotionalism, which was especially evident in the song-culture (Boswell suggested that the tenderly melancholic note derived in part from Rizzio's influence on the music of Mary's court),[7] kept company with vigorous satiric reduction.

In the reductive strain in Scottish literature is the source of one of the voices of eighteenth-century Scottish writers. Habitual reduction almost inevitably comes to encompass self-reduction. In Scottish literature there is a tradition of ironic self-revelation from the Makars through Ramsay to Burns and Galt. Burns is unequalled in the ironic use of voice, a technique in which Scottish writers excelled. In part, this is a result of the fact that the Scottish intellect had limited scope for the exchange of ideas in the (numerically) limited Scottish environment. In the small communities which comprised most of Scotland, thinking Scots, after exhausting all possibilities of discussing with one another what they actually believed, proceeded to propound with apparently absolute conviction views which they did not personally hold. The alternative to falling foul of parochialism was (arguably still is) to play devil's advocate. One of the explanations of Burns's ability in the ironic use of voice lies in precisely this need to play devil's advocate for social and intellectual amusement in the self-contained community that Ayrshire (and it was not atypical) then was.

Another source of the range of voices and projections of self-images may well reside in Presbyterianism's discouragement of drama. Boswell's prose rendering of the drama of London intellectual life and Burns's command of a wide range of voices (in letters and behaviour, as well as poems) may be seen as expressions of a dramatic impulse which had to be either restrained or redirected. The rôle-playing to which a range of Scottish writers from Macpherson to Byron were so prone may be similarly explained. Such rôle-playing was stimulated further by another aspect of the Presbyterian legacy, namely the fatalism which predetermination fostered: if the individual is a passive subject rather than an active agent (as both Boswell and Burns claim on occasions)[8] then rôle-playing, gesturing, and fantasising have compensatory attractions.

Both the talent and the need for the assumption of voices are most apparent in Scottish writing from roughly 1740 onwards, precisely the years when the social and cultural effects of the Union were beginning to catalyse a crisis of identity among Scots. George Davie has identified as follows the problems of accommodating European Enlightenment thought within the new status of junior partnership in the Union:

> . . . the impact of the European Enlightenment on Scotland coincided precisely with the difficult post-Union decades, when Scotland was struggling to adapt to the exigencies of the new political partnership with England, a native inheritance of institutions which had been conceived on Continental lines, partly through the Franco-Scottish connection, partly through contacts with the Netherlands. It was, one might say, this practical experience of adapting un-English institutions to the Union that made the Scots so very reserved in their recognition of the glowing promise of the Enlightenment. In this way, *la crise de conscience Européenne* (as Paul Hazard called it), the all-out intellectual revolt against the Baroque legacy of the seventeenth century, was limited and modified in its impact on Scotland by the counter-experience of a sort of *crisis of national existence*, in which the threat of reality of assimilation to England brought home, to the Scots, the value of their native inheritance of institutions, legal, ecclesiastical, educational.[9]

In literary terms the clearest manifestation of this crisis of identity is in the vernacular revival. But that was an attempt to stem the unstoppable, and it had about it a hint of artificiality. By 1764 Boswell was admitting, 'the Scottish language is being lost every day and in a short time will be quite unintelligible'.[10]

Scottish literature of the eighteenth century is informed by paradox, as David Daiches has demonstrated in his seminal study.[11] It is also characterised by dualities and anomalies. Of these, the most immediately apparent is the linguistic. The *literati* were well versed in Latin and Greek, wrote in polite standard English, and spoke in Scots vernacular. The tradition of writing Latin poetry, which had endured in Scotland for several centuries, continued well through the eighteenth. Lord Hailes, described by Boswell as 'one of the best philologists in Great Britain, who has written . . . a variety of other works in prose and in verse, both Latin and English', pleased Johnson greatly.[12]

Paradoxically, while classical studies thrived in academic circles and schools, the Scots vernacular itself was under pressure. The Scots language had been in a state of declining use in the century prior to the Union of 1707. T S Eliot commented,

> It is precisely in the years when English literature was acquiring the power of a world literature that the Scottish language was beginning to decay or to be abandoned. Gawain Douglas, in Tudor times, is perhaps the last great Scotch poet to write Scots with the same feeling toward the language, the same conviction, as an Englishman writing English. A hundred years later, a Scot unquestionably Scottish, one of the greatest prose writers of his time, Sir Thomas Urquhart, translated Rabelais into a language which is English.[13]

The Union accelerated the decline and exacerbated the problem of the language duality. In his *History of Scotland* William Robertson ('a nervous man, who talks broad Scotch', according to Boswell)[14] contemplated what the linguistic situation might have been had there been no Union:

> If the two nations had continued distinct, each might have retained idioms and forms of speech peculiar to itself; and these, rendered fashionable by the example of a court, and supported by the authority of writers of reputation, might have been considered in the same light with the varieties occasioned by the different dialects in the Greek tongue; might have been considered as beauties; and, in many cases, might have been used promiscuously by the authors of both nations. But, by the accession, the English naturally became the sole judges and lawgivers in Language, and rejected, as solecisms, every form of speech to which their ear was not accustomed.[15]

In actual fact the process of linguistic and cultural assimilation had been in progress for over a century. Of the Scottish situation early in the second half of the eighteenth century Henry Mackenzie was later to observe, 'There was a pure classical *Scots* spoken by genteel people, which I thought very agreeable; it had nothing of the vulgar *patois* of the lower orders of the people.'[16] The former was spoken in Edinburgh, but in London it immediately betrayed the quaintly provincial, and many educated Scots tried to lose all traces of it there (though Mackenzie records that one at least, Dundas (Lord Melville), continued to speak broad Scots, with the result that Scotticisms were for a time part of the parlance of the House of Commons).[17]

Increasingly the vernacular of Mackenzie's 'lower orders' had come to be associated with comic subjects. Here, in an essay in the *Mirror* (1780), no. 83 entitled 'Enquiry into the Causes of the Scarcity of Humorous Writers in Scotland', William Craig accounts for this:

> The circumstances of a Scottish author not writing his own natural dialect must have a considerable influence upon the nature of his literary productions. When he is employed in any grave dignified composition, when he writes history,

politics, or poetry, the pains he must take to write, in a manner different from that in which he speaks, will not much affect his productions; the language of such compositions is, in every case, raised above that of common life; and, therefore, the deviation which a Scottish author is obliged to make from the common language of the country, can be of little prejudice to him. But if a writer is to descend to common and ludicrous pictures of life; if, in short, he is to deal in humorous composition, his language must be, as nearly as possible, that of common life, that of the bulk of the people; but a Scotsman who wishes to write English cannot easily do this. He neither speaks the English dialect, nor is it spoken by those around him: any knowledge he has acquired of the language is got from books, not from conversation. . .

. . . In confirmation of these remarks, it may be observed, that almost the only works of humour which we have in this country, are in the Scottish dialect, and most of them were written before the union of the kingdoms, when the Scotch was the written, as well as the spoken language of the country. . . If there have been lately any publications of humour in this country, written in good English, they have been mostly of the graver sort, called *irony*.[18]

This process was already in evidence in the works of Allan Ramsay. Noting that what Ramsay inherited was an already-bilingual tradition, Kinghorn and Law observe that it was unfortunate that *The Gentle Shepherd* (1725), in distinguishing 'peasant life' from 'gentle life', highlighted the association of the Scots language with the former.[19] While the collections the *Ever Green* and the *Tea-Table Miscellany* (1724) were, as Kinghorn and Law point out, 'inspired by the will to re-assert a national identity',[20] the situation was already irrecoverable in that Scots was well on the way to being associated with a limited range of subjects of a predominantly comic or satiric nature; and this despite Ramsay's undeniable degree of success in employing Scots to serious purpose in 'Keitha: a Pastoral' and combining Scots and formal English in 'Wealth, or the Woody' and 'The Prospect of Plenty'.

In fact Ramsay is a forerunner of that multiplicity of voice which was to characterise Scottish writers later in the century. To set 'The Morning Interview' alongside 'Lucky Spence' is to hear both the imitative Augustan voice and the revived vernacular voice in Ramsay.[21] Another, and obvious, indication of the dichotomy within Ramsay is in the pseudonyms which he assumed during his membership of the Easy Club—'Isaac Bickerstaff' (after the character in the *Tatler*) and 'Gavin Douglas'.

The alternative was to adopt wholeheartedly the voice and the manner of the English poet. This was the course favoured by James Thomson. Now it may be true that some of his descriptions of landscape were inspired by his early life in Scotland; and this harmony of rural and mercantile bliss seems to anticipate (while rendering in a stylised manner) one of the ideals of the Scottish Enlightenment:

> . . . thy Valleys float
> With golden Waves; and on thy Mountains Flocks
> Bleat numberless; while, roving round their Sides,
> Bellow the blackening Herds in lusty Droves.
> Beneath, thy Meadows glow, and rise unquell'd,

> Against the Mower's Scythe. On every Hand,
> Thy Villas shine. The Country teems with Wealth;
> And Property assures it to the Swain,
> Pleas'd, and unweary'd, in his guarded Toil.[22]

But there is little to support the recent attempt to find Scottish language in the poetry of Thomson.[23] Study of Thomson's language reveals his thorough knowledge of classical poetry, Spenser, and Milton, and the indebtedness of his diction to the two English poets. 'The Castle of Indolence', containing diction such as 'Ymolten with his syren melody', 'Depeinten was the patriarchal age', and epic similes such as that involving 'a shepherd of the Hebrid isles' suggests that any residual Scottish elements have been submerged beneath the orthodoxies of classicism. Thomson typifies a feature of much of the Scottish attempt in the eighteenth century to mimic English poetry, namely the reversion to the poetry of several centuries earlier in the search for models. In fairness to Thomson, it should be acknowledged that he was aware of the anomalous aspect of this, as the advertisement to 'The Castle of Indolence' testifies:

> This poem being writ in the manner of Spenser, the obsolete words, and a simplicity of diction in some of the lines which borders on the ludicrous, were necessary to make the imitation more perfect. And the style of that admirable poet, as well as the measure in which he wrote, are as it were appropriated by custom to all allegorical poems writ in our language. . .[24]

The linguistic turmoil is one manifestation of the Scottish crisis of identity in the eighteenth century. Dr Johnson observed that 'languages are the pedigree of nations'.[25] For the reason that 'books and public discourse in Scotland are in the English tongue', Boswell found that 'although an Englishman often does not understand a Scot, it is rare that a Scot has trouble in understanding what an Englishman says'.[26] For the Scot the optimum ought to have been dual nationality and the advantages thereof; the reality was a kind of statelessness. To understand readily, but to have to work at being understood, induced self-consciousness and a cleft identity. For instance, Smollett, according to G S Rousseau, experienced an identity crisis at some point in the seventeen-fifties, when he was already successful. Rousseau regards the self-dedication of *Ferdinand Count Fathom* in terms of a 'bifurcation of personality' which is symptomatic of the Scottish condition and adds, 'the narrator's command that the *alter ego* take charge of itself points to Smollett's most serious indictment of himself: an inability to feel whole'.[27]

David Hume also experienced problems of identity. Here he writes to John Home of Ninewells on the question of where the latter's son should be educated:

> There are several Advantages of a Scots Education; but the Question is whether that of the Language does not counterballance them, and determine the Preference to the English. He is now of an Age to learn it perfectly; but if a few Years elapse, he may acquire such an Accent, as he will never be able to cure of. It is

not yet determin'd what Profession he shall be of; but it must always be of great Advantage to speak properly; especially, if it shou'd prove, as we have reason to hope, that his good Parts will open him the Road of Ambition. The only Inconvenience is, that few Scotsmen, that have had an English Education, have ever settled cordially in their own Country, and they have been commonly lost ever after to their Friends.[28]

For many years Hume himself was vexed by the questions of where to live—Edinburgh, Paris, or London. He presented the problem of identity in these terms to Gilbert Eliot of Minto:

I do not believe there is one Englishman in fifty, who, if he heard that I had broke my Neck to night, would not be rejoic'd with it. Some hate me because I am not a Tory, some because I am not a Whig, some because I am not a Christian, and all because I am a Scotsman. Can you seriously talk of my continuing an Englishman? Am I, or are you, an Englishman? Will they allow us to be so?[29]

And to Benjamin Franklin he complained,

I expected, in entering on my literary course, that all the Christians, all the Whigs, and all the Tories, should be my enemies. But it is hard that all the English, Irish and Welsh, should be also against me. The Scotch likewise cannot be much my friends, as no man is a prophet in his own country.[30]

To this he added his belief that he 'must have recourse to America for justice'. It might be suggested that Hume the philosopher's abiding concern with identity (like that of Smith and Hutcheson) is a reflection at least in part of the national crisis of identity.

Boswell's response to the problem was to set out to acquire a London identity. Here he sees a threat in the arrival of the family of his friend, Andrew Erskine:

As I was therefore pursuing this laudable plan, I was vexed at the arrival of the Kellie family, with whom when in Scotland I had been in the greatest familiarity. Had they not come for a twelvemonth, I should have been somewhat established in my address, but as I had been a fortnight from them, I could not without the appearance of strong affectation appear much different from what they had seen me.[31]

His hold on his new identity was precarious. He avoided the Kellie family for over a week since, as he said, 'I wanted to have nothing but English ideas, and to be as manly as possible.'[32] In Boswell's case, the sense of displacement became acute. Having acquired, as he believed, the identity of a London sophisticate, he experienced difficulties of adjustment on returning to Scotland. 'It required some philosophy', he wrote, 'to bear the change from England to Scotland. The unpleasing tone, the rude familiarity, the barren conversation of those whom I found here, in comparison with what I had left, really hurt my feelings.'[33] When, on his father's death, his brother

suggested that he settle in Scotland Boswell protested that the 'narrow pro-
vinciality'[34] of Scottish life would be intolerable.

In the case of Burns it was the social and regional divisions *within* Scottish
life that exacerbated the tendency to dichotomy. Having projected the image
of the untutored rustic and having been fêted by literary Edinburgh for his
achievement, Burns then experienced disillusionment. He compensated by
means of an intensification of the rôle-playing at which he had always been
adept. This was to lead ultimately to a fragmentation of the personality. On
his return from Edinburgh he wrote of his own insignificance to the great
world which he had so recently left, and on a later visit to the capital he was
to confess to Mrs Dunlop in a letter of 21 February 1789, 'I am here more
unhappy than I ever experienced before in Edinburgh.'[35] Having tasted celebrity he found it difficult to settle to life in rural Ayrshire or, later, Dumfries.
Burns wrote, 'I was placed by Fortune among a class of men to whom my
ideas would have been nonsense'; this helps explain his desire to, as he said,
'Write myself out [of the] M.S.S. of my early years.'[36] The sense of cultural
division became more acute the longer he lived. The preparation of old Scots
songs for a potential English readership exemplified the need to compromise.
'I'll rather write a new song altogether, than make this English', he proclaimed
defiantly on one occasion, but then, with an eye to the market, added, 'The
sprinkling of Scotch in it, while it is but a sprinkling, gives it an air of rustic
naïveté, which time will rather increase than diminish.'[37]

How did it come about that the voices which Scottish writers of the second
half of the eighteenth century so successfully projected were those of 'rustic
naïveté' and purity of feeling? The answer lies in a remarkable concatenation
of events, a curious accident of cultural history.

In European thought in the middle of the eighteenth century certain trends
can be identified. The signs of dissatisfaction with rationalism were increasingly evident. In the foremost expression of this reaction—Rousseau's view
of the original nature of man—lay the basis of the Romantic concern with
the worth of the individual. This coincided with the emergence of a strong
cultural nationalism in various parts of Europe as the mainly French-domi-
nated neo-classicism found itself increasingly under pressure. Of that period
Paul Hazard commented,

> An attempt was made to re-create a European mind. Even the peoples on the
> outer limits, whose remoteness, whose very distinct kind of language, and whose
> marked individualism seemed to exclude them from the general movement,
> gradually came to throw in their lot with it.[38]

As examples he cites Sweden, Hungary, and Poland. What of Scotland's part
in this? Hazard acknowledges the growing cultural influence of the example
of England in the mid eighteenth century, but he makes no mention of a
recognisably Scottish contribution. Yet the work of Hutcheson, Hume, Smith,
Ferguson, and Robertson formed a distinctly Scottish body of material which
made a major impact on European thought.

Around the middle of the eighteenth century the conditions which determined the future of Scottish culture reached their culmination. It is to that period that we must look for an account of much that has happened since. In particular, the origins of our subsequent cultural parochialism and self-obsession may be found there. To Hugh MacDiarmid's eyes in 1927, 'the tendency inherent in the Union, to assimilate Scotland to England, and ultimately to provincialize the former . . . has not yet been effectively countered by the emergence of any principle demanding a reversed tendency'.[39] Over half a century later it seems realistic to accept that such a principle is unlikely ever to appear.

The fate of Scottish culture is inseparable from Scotland's experience of Romanticism, an experience that was quite singular among the countries of Europe. At first glance the potential for Romanticism in Scotland seems considerable. Celtic emotionalism; both a record and a love of heroic achievement; scenic grandeur; a folk-tradition and a vernacular—these seem the very breeding-grounds of Romanticism. However, consideration of the last-named begins to cast some light on one of the factors that thwarted the progress of Romanticism in Scotland: by the mid eighteenth century the folk-tradition and the use of the vernacular were already neglected or else had been refined by the arbiters of cultural values. (The title of Allan Ramsay's collection of older Scottish poetry, *Tea-Table Miscellany*, gives some indication of the 'civilising' process well under way.)

With justification Jacques Barzun has claimed,

> The romantics' nationalism is cultural nationalism. They spoke less of nations than of 'peoples', whom they considered the creators and repositories of distinct cultures.[40]

Now when the first stirrings of Romanticism began to be felt Scotland was no longer a nation, and as a people she was already preoccupied with an image of herself that was rooted in a distant and largely unreal past. Ironically, Romanticism did much to encourage just such sentimental nationalism. Only in Scotland did Romanticism help to guide a people along the way to, not self-realisation and self-advancement, but a predominantly self-willed stereo-typing. A combination of circumstances and national characteristics determined the way in which Romanticism was to influence Scottish values. The crisis of identity which Scotland underwent after the Union of 1707, a crisis rekindled by the 'Forty-Five and its aftermath, converted Scottish national sentiment into an acute nostalgia for a remote and noble past. In Scotland insecurity, allied to that austerity and self-restraint which are part of the legacy of Presbyterianism, led to the distortion of the Romantic impulse, so that it found expression in extreme form as sentimentalising and nostalgia, the source of what David Daiches has designated the subsequent 'torrent of tartanry'.[41]

That dualism of aspect which informs so much of the Scottish experience was already apparent. David Hume wrote in 1770: 'I believe this is the historical Age and this the historical Nation';[42] with justification in the light of his and Robertson's work as historians (and to a lesser extent that of

Smollett). The burgeoning of historical interest was a direct result of the nature of the philosophical activities. If, as was claimed, man's nature was innately benevolent and differences amongst races, generations, and cultures were explicable in terms of different circumstances, then it became the task of historians to identify those circumstances. Yet this genuine historical investigation was contemporaneous with sentimentalising of Scotland's past. The post-Union crisis of identity expressed itself in another, quite distinct, manner: the rationalist and realistic sense which was the moving spirit of the Scottish Enlightenment manifested itself in imaginative literature as that persistent Scottish talent for reduction. These two extremes—of sentiment and satiric reduction—co-exist in Burns, the embodiment of several of the paradoxes of the Scottish cultural situation.

Here the crucial question is that posed by Francis Russell Hart: 'Are such rapidly alternating responses to experience to be explained as cultural distinctiveness or cultural dissociation?'[43] Need the question resolve into these alternatives? Sadly, is it not possibly the case that central to Scottish cultural distinctiveness was a potential, increasingly present, for cultural dissociation; and that this was brought to fruition by a process set in motion by the Union of the Crowns, accelerated by the Authorised Version, and finalised in the after-effects of the Union of the Parliaments?

The culmination of this process in Scotland coincided with increasing dissatisfaction, across Europe, with rationalism. Enlightenment confidence gave way to what Paul Hazard calls 'revulsion of sentiment'.[44] Concomitant with the growth of nationalism in Europe was, paradoxically, the Rousseauistic return to nature and the vogue of the original natural goodness of man. Enlightened Europe longed to shed the burden of its more recent heritage and return to its origins. Civilised European man saw in the Scottish Highlander perhaps not the noble savage, but certainly the closest approximation to him that was then extant. Hume wrote to John Wilkes on 8 October 1754,

> If your time had permitted, you shoud have gone into the Highlands. You woud there have seen human Nature in the golden Age, or rather, indeed, in the Silver: For the Highlanders have degenerated somewhat from the primitive Simplicity of Mankind. But perhaps you have so corrupted a Taste as to prefer your Iron Age, to be met with in London & the south of England; where Luxury & Vice of every kind so much abound.[45]

The identification of the clansman with the descendant of natural man served to heighten the existing Highland-Lowland division in Scottish attitudes. The safe return of Boswell and Johnson from the Hebrides was celebrated as a triumph in Edinburgh. Dr Johnson commented, 'I am really ashamed of the congratulations which we receive. We are addressed as if we had made a voyage to Nova Zembla, and suffered five persecutions in Japan.'[46] The response of the Lowlanders to the Highlanders seems to have been an odd amalgam of sentimental pride and fear. Paradox has continued to inform that attitude. Recently Malcolm Chapman has observed,

> Since the eighteenth century . . . the Scottish people have increasingly looked to
> the Highlands to provide a location for an autonomy in which they could lodge
> their own political, literary, and historical aspirations. They have thereby been
> allowed to reap all the benefits of the Union, while at the same time retaining a
> location for all the virtues of sturdy independence.[47]

The mood of Europe was caught by James Macpherson, and his Ossian poems
met its need. Macpherson's 'epics', *Fingal* and *Temora*, were precisely what
was sought by the widespread reaction against the practical, rationalist,
communal optimism of the European Enlightenment. Part of the preparatory
work had been done by James Thomson whose poem *The Seasons* had, as
G Gregory Smith notes, 'directed European taste to the "matter" of the
North';[48] Robert Blair's *The Grave* (1743) accorded with the post-Enlighten-
ment vogue of melancholy; and John Home's tragedy *Douglas* (1756) did
much to pave the way for Macpherson. The representative significance of
the Ossian poems should not be under-rated. Boswell records that Thomas
Sheridan

> thought [Ossian] excelled Homer in the Sublime and Virgil in the Pathetic. He
> said Mrs Sheridan and he had fixed it as a standard of feeling, made it like a
> thermometer by which they could judge of the warmth of everybody's heart.[49]

Of the significance of that moment when Macpherson entrusted his forgeries
to the avid John Home, John Wain does not exaggerate when he asserts,
'European literature crossed one of those frontiers that mark off one era of
sensibility from another.'[50]

For a time, then, from 1760 onwards, the predominant voice among the
range of Scottish voices was that of feeling. But it was not the pure feeling of
the kind that endured in the song-culture; rather, it was that which Scottish
writers had learned to project to meet the needs of European sensibility. The
possession of sensibility became the index to taste. The arbiters of taste were
the *literati*, the circle of intellectuals that centred around David Hume. The
majority were lawyers (Elibank, Hailes, Kames, Monboddo) and not imaginative writers. Paradoxes abound. For instance, those who as literary critics
held sensibility to be the foremost criterion were sometimes less than humane
in their practice as judges (tales of the coarse humour of Braxfield, Kames,
and Auchinleck are legion and do not need repeating here). The most telling
irony was that an intellectual élite of non-creative writers was dictating
the criteria for imaginative literature. And Hume, whose philosophy was
empiricist, was, as a critic, a slavish adherent to a strict neo-classicism. His
protégés, Wilkie and Blacklock, readily adopted his aesthetic stance. In *Douglas*
John Home presented potentially Romantic subject-matter according to the
neo-classical dictates of Hume. And, as J S Smart has noted,[51] Macpherson's
critical bias was decidedly neo-classical though his material was to contribute
to the growth of Romanticism.

There is one further important aspect of the domination of Edinburgh
cultural life by the law lords. In the course of his professional training each

had been schooled in the techniques and procedures of pleading a case. For each, presentation, style, and rhetoric came to take precedence over fact. Not substance but presentation was of cardinal importance. When Dr Johnson visited the Court of Session in Edinburgh 'He thought the mode of pleading there too vehement, and too much addressed to the passions of the judges'.[52] And this is Boswell's description of his activities as advocate:

> No doubt the practice of law here is sometimes irksome to me, but it is often a kind of amusement; I have to consider and illustrate *quicquid agunt homines*; I have to treat of characters, of the history of families, of trade and manufactures, as contracts concerning them are the foundations of many lawsuits; in short, the variety of subjects of which fragments pass through my mind, as a pleader, engages my attention; and, as upon most occasions, I become warmly desirous of my client's success. There is the agitation of contest, and sometimes, in a certain degree, the triumph of victory; but there is also sometimes the discouragement of defeat.[53]

In literary terms the effects were two-fold: a further impetus towards rôle-playing (so paralleling on the level of 'polite' literature the tradition of ironic voice in the older culture); and an emphasis on the supreme importance of rhetoric.

There remains to be considered one major contributor to the rôle-playing that characterises so much Scottish literature. It is in the nature of the concerns and the activities of the Scottish philosophers. The Scottish Enlightenment thinkers were concerned above all with man in society. Paradoxically, that focusing on the individual in terms of his relations with his fellow human-beings bred a self-consciousness in which are the origins of the divided self. In his dissertation, 'Of the Passions', Hume treats of mental flux and the momentary impression of sorrow and joy and contends that 'as the understanding, in probable questions, is divided betwixt the contrary points of view, the heart must in the same manner be devided betwixt opposite emotions'.[54] It becomes evident too from Adam Smith's *The Theory of Moral Sentiments* that his theory of sympathy is something of a compromise and indeed encourages self-observation and rôle-playing. According to Smith the sympathiser can indulge his feelings because he knows the limits of the sympathetic capacity, while the sufferer in triumphing over his griefs 'seems to exult over the victory he thus gains over his misfortunes'.[55] And here, in his consideration 'Of the Sense of Duty' is a section in which Smith conceives of the self as two persons:

> When I endeavour to examine my own conduct, when I endeavour to pass sentence upon it, and either to approve or condemn it, it is evident that, in all such cases, I divide myself, as it were, into two persons; and that I, the examiner and judge, represent a different character from that other I, the person whose conduct is examined into and judged of. The first is the spectator, whose sentiments with regard to my own conduct I endeavour to enter into, by placing myself in his situation, and by considering how it would appear to me, when seen from that particular point of view. The second is the agent, the person whom

I properly call myself, and of whose conduct, under the character of a spectator, I was endeavouring to form some opinion. The first is the judge; the second the person judged of. But that the judge should, in every respect, be the same with the person judged of, is as impossible, as that the cause should, in every respect, be the same with the effect.[56]

Here, it may be claimed, is the philosophical background to the divided nature of the Scottish personality.

CHAPTER 1

The Scot as English Novelist: Tobias Smollett

Smollett brought to the novel in English certain distinctive features of the Scots literary tradition. Moreover, with his range of voices, he is a key figure in the particular Scottish experience of the Europe-wide movement of ideas and taste in the eighteenth century from rationalism by way of sensibility and the Gothic to Romanticism.

The following is the judgement of Keats:

> You ask me what degrees there are between Scott's Novels and those of Smollet. They appear to me to be quite distinct in every particular—more especially in their aim—Scott endeavours to throw so interesting and romantic a colouring into common and low Characters as to give them a touch of the Sublime— Smollet on the contrary pulls down and levels what other Men would continue Romance.[1]

This can be substantiated by contrasting the battle scenes in *Roderick Random* with Scott's romanticising of warfare. Keats's comment may be employed to illuminate the change in Scottish literary values in the half century which separated Scott from Smollett.[2] It is salutary, therefore, to remember that Smollett was a Scot, and that if he wrote in standard English he did so very much as a Scot.

Smollett's fictional technique is characterised by range and pace, and by a concomitant lack of depth. The effect is that of watching a succession of crowded slides—some very vivid—with a few ubiquitous characters, but so depicted that there is little to convey individuality of response or development of values. The point of view remains firmly external: the reader is shown people in situations but sees little of their responses beyond the most obviously physical. Energy and inventiveness, rather than any interest in the mind and its workings, inform Smollett's novels. Scott, comparing Smollett's genius with that of Rubens, commented:

> His pictures are often deficient in grace; sometimes coarse, and even vulgar in conception; deficient in keeping, and in the due subordination of parts to each other; and intimating too much carelessness on the part of the artist. But these faults are redeemed by such richness and brilliancy of colours; such a profusion of imagination—now bodying forth the grand and terrible—now the natural, the easy, and the ludicrous; there is so much of life, action, and bustle, in every group he has painted; so much force and individuality of character—that we readily grant to Smollett an equal rank with his great rival Fielding, while

we place both far above any of their successors in the same line of fictitious composition.[3]

That Scott, with his consuming interest in Scottish culture, should have failed to relate such qualities in Smollett to a distinctly Scottish tradition, preferring instead to get involved in comparisons with Fielding, is indicative of the extent to which the competitive cultural impulse induced by the Union of 1707 had, by the end of the eighteenth century, turned some Scots into self-conscious and self-distorting North Britons.

The analogy with Rubens, however, is valid. Smollett excels, like earlier Scottish writers, in the vivid depiction of bustling communal life. Roderick and Strap descend into an ordinary, and with stylistic gusto Smollett draws a picture of London lower life centred around the farcical misadventure of Strap's fall. But after the inspired invention of this scene it is dropped with considerable haste and some contrivance. The imaginative energy subsides as readily as it has arisen. The scene remains a vivid scene, but it has led to nothing. Such episodes endorse Coleridge's evaluation of Smollett's method: 'We find that a number of things are put together to counterfeit humour, but there is no growth from within.'[4] In the main when Smollett has time for depiction of emotions they are comically heightened, melodramatised, sensationalised, and, as a result, reduced. Chapter 89 of *Peregrine Pickle*, for instance, is largely concerned with a prank played by Peregrine and accomplices on a gallant. Here the emotional changes are rung frantically:

> The gallant, whose passions were exalted to a pitch of enthusiasm, as susceptible of religious horror as of love, seeing such an apparition, when he was at the point of indulging a criminal appetite, and hearing the dreadful cry, accompanied with the terrible word *damnation*, which Pipes, in his peculiar tone, exclaimed from the alcove, when the animal made its escape; he was seized with consternation and remorse, and falling upon his face, lay in all the agonies of terror, believing himself warned by a particular message from above.[5]

The effect of the over-writing and the pace is comic reduction, which was presumably the intention. The trouble is that Smollett can rarely treat emotion in any other way.

The customary explanations of this stunting of Smollett are these: he was by nature restless and impulsive and 'stuck at nothing'[6] (in the pejorative sense of J H Millar's phrase); out of sheer economic necessity he wrote at great speed and carelessly; or, according to Scott, he wrote thus by virtue of 'unlimited confidence in his own powers'.[7] These may be part, but are certainly far from all, of the explanation. Much more important is the fact that Smollett writes as a Scot. His characteristic range and pace relate him to the medieval vision, which endured longer in Scotland than elsewhere, and which was distinguished by its plenitude. The lack of depth and the disinterest in the individual mind may be explained likewise. But both these aspects gain further impetus from the post-Union crisis of cultural identity in Scotland. The stylistic *mélange* of Smollett is regarded conventionally as readiness to experiment. It is; but it is also the response of a creative talent that has suffered enforced dislocation from its cultural roots; hence the sudden shifts of tone, the pace, the multiple voices. Similarly, the medieval plenitude of vision, which does nothing to encourage exploration of the individual mind, is reinforced by the post-Union reluctance of the Scot to embark on investigation of identity. Poised thus, Smollett occupies a quite distinctive place in Scottish literature: he looks back to the Makars and forwards, via the conflicting notes within Burns and Scott, to that modern alienation which Scotland, severed by the Union from its cultural traditions and denied, or impervious to, the fullest benefits of Romantic idealism, experienced well before the rest of Europe.

Breadth of social vision and stylistic energy are features of earlier Scottish poetry which are present also in Smollett. That primitive vigour of life which informs Dunbar's 'The Dance of the Sevin Deidly Sinnis' is captured by Smollett. In Dunbar, stylistic energy is set to the service of a realistic and comprehensive rendering of community life, as, for instance, in 'The Satire on Edinburgh'. This sense of communal life endures in Fergusson and Burns (e.g. Fergusson's 'Auld Reekie' and 'Leith Races', and Burns's 'The Holy Fair'). It says much for Smollett that he succeeded in communicating this sense in his descriptions, in standard English and in a different genre, of English communal life. Thus Matt Bramble's accounts of social life in Bath and London are more than the conventional unmasking of hypocrisy or revelation of the truth beneath the appearance: they fall within a tradition of the full recording of community life, as it is apprehended by the senses. The obsession with smells and bodily functions is part of Smollett's social realism; the 'man without a skin' (Jery's description of Matt) masks the unflinching social observer. Similarly, the amorous exploits of Smollett's heroes, and the accounts thereof, have a vitality comparable to 'that tremendous principle of life' which John Speirs found exemplified in 'The Twa Mariit Wemen and the Wedo'.[8]

In Smollett there is more than a trace of that coarseness and brutality of humour with which Lyndsay's *Ane Satyre of the Thrie Estaitis* is imbued. Smollett's farce has an edge to it and involves physical pain to an extent not found in any English writer of the period. In *Roderick Random* the fairly stock farcical exploits (principally of Strap) are prefaced by the physical maltreatment of the young Roderick and the equally physical revenge that is taken on the tyrannical schoolmaster. The farce in *Peregrine Pickle* approximates to the grotesque (e.g. Peregrine's exploit with the chamber-pot), and to the brutal (in pursuit of revenge, Gam and Mr Sackbut, the curate, plan 'to sally upon [Peregrine] when he should be altogether unprovided against such an attack, cut off his ears, and otherwise mutilate him in such a manner, that he should have no cause to be vain of his person for the future' [*PP*, p. 160]). Even the mellower work of Smollett's later years, *Humphry Clinker*, contains pranks, of which Lismahago is the prime target, and an account of atrocities perpetrated upon the lieutenant and his companion by the American Indians, in a sequence which is almost certainly offered as ironic comment on the vogue of the travel adventure.

There is, then, evidence of a dualism within Smollett's fictional practice: realism and social concern are made to co-exist with a talent, or even a need, for the grotesque and the fantastic. George Kahrl concludes his article, 'Smollett as a Caricaturist', by adducing Martin Foss as follows:

> In times of chaos men return to a magic form of art, using the demoniac aspects of life for their stories and plays: sickness, insanity, death; but they turn them into grotesque means for laughter in order to regain their inner balance. . . The grotesque will always appear and take hold of those ages which are under the strain of disaster, feeling the sinister and chaotic aspects of life, but advanced enough to appease the mind by laughter.[9]

The use of the demoniac and the grotesque was innate within the Scots tradition. How natural, then, that they should be prominent features of Smollett's writing during the crisis of values which Scotland underwent in the decades after the Union.

The expressive force of Smollett's satire is reminiscent of that linguistic energy which is characteristic of much earlier Scottish poetry and the flyting in particular. Edwin Muir commented,

> Scottish poetry at its best has never run to sweetness or magnificence like English, but to a sort of wild play with imagination and technique, coming from an excess of energy which expends itself both recklessly and surely. It is seen at its most characteristic in Dunbar, the greatest craftsman in Scottish poetry; but it is seen in Burns too, although he was only an apprentice in his craft compared with the older poet.[10]

Smollett was denied, or in part denied himself, the rich and varied linguistic resources that were available to Dunbar or, to a lesser degree, Burns, but in his writing he managed to preserve something of that 'excess of energy which expends itself both recklessly and surely'. Here Matt Bramble demolishes a distant relative with a succession of verbal blows:

> He is not only a sordid miser in his disposition, but his avarice is mingled with a spirit of despotism, which is truly diabolical.—He is a brutal husband, an unnatural parent, a harsh master, an oppressive landlord, a litigious neighbour, and a partial magistrate.—Friends he has none; and in point of hospitality and good breeding, our cousin Burdock is a prince in comparison of this ungracious miscreant, whose house is the lively representation of a gaol. (HC, p. 171).

In this there is the expressive force, but little of the humour, of the flyting; and, as often happens, Smollett succumbs to overkill. It is undeniable that he employed such literary energy as a kind of personal therapy: compare the aggressive self-justification of his heroes (e.g. Roderick Random, pp. 5–7) with similar passages in his own letters where he directs to personal purposes the vituperation that was part of the convention of the flyting.[11]

But Smollett's concern extended far beyond himself, as is evident from his claim: 'I have such a natural Horror of Cruelty that I cannot without uncommon Warmth relate any Instance of Inhumanity.'[12] Some of his most expressive writing results from the union of that stylistic vitality and his responsiveness to inhumanity. From precisely this the naval scenes in *Roderick Random* derive a force and urgency lacking in the remainder of the book. In Roderick's account of his first inspection of the sick-bay on the *Thunder*, realistic observation forms the basis of forceful expressions of outrage, as it does in the accounts of the conduct of the battle, the disposal of the dead, and the effects of the fever epidemic. Like a true child of the Enlightenment, Smollett is committed to the amelioration of the living-conditions of his fellow-men. Despite Matt Bramble's fulminations against the monster which is mass society (again expressed with similar energy) and his hankering after the social discrimination attendant upon the medieval social hierarchy, by the end of *Humphry Clinker* he has shed the mask of the irascible valetudinarian and, in guiding Baynard towards the restoration of his farm after the ravages of his wife's vanity, has become practical Englightenment man (one is reminded of the agricultural interests of Lord Kames, one of the foremost of the *literati*, to whom tributes are paid in the novel). This practical, social concern of Smollett's should not be forgotten, and Matt's vehement denunciations of the lack of hygiene among the *beau monde* should not be dismissed as the rantings of 'Smelfungus'.

Smollett's concern with the physical derives jointly from the medieval plenitude of vision and his Enlightenment social concern. At his best the energetic expression of the former subserves the latter: vigorous rendering of the grotesque subserves social satire. Smollett has the Scot's capacity to discern and render through language the physical in its grotesque extremes. In one of his last letters he wrote:

> I am already so dry and emaciated that I may pass for an Egyptian mummy without any other preparation than some pitch and painted linen, unless you think I may deserve the denomination of a curiosity in my own character.[13]

Vivid representation of the physical is part of the earlier Scots tradition, as in part of the description of Saturn in Henryson's 'Testament of Cresseid':

> His face (fronsit), his lyre was lyke the Leid,
> His teith chatterit, and cheverit with the Chin,
> His Ene drowpit, how sonkin in his heid,
> Out of his Nois the Meldrop fast can rin,
> With lippis bla and cheikis leine and thin;
> The Iceschoklis that fra his hair doun hang
> Was wonder greit, and as ane speir als lang.

With justification G Gregory Smith remarked of much of the poetry of the Makars that 'the completed effect of the piling up of details is one of movement, suggesting the action of a concerted dance or the canter of a squadron'.[14] Such writing is not the product of bland recording of neutral observation. The mind's purpose directs the eye as to what it will choose to discern; the mind's expressive capacity invests the rendering of it with a dynamism of its own. Stevenson described the process succinctly as that of 'the sentiment assimilating the facts of natural congruity'.[15] The finest of Smollett has this very quality suggestive of the momentary arrest of energy, so that, paradoxically, a vividly pictorial impact is achieved without any diminution of the verbal dynamism. (Again, the analogy is with a rapid succession of vivid slides, and the method is comparable to that employed by Burns in 'Tam o' Shanter'). The great advantages of a predominantly pictorial method are force of impact, and economy and range of effect. Thus E H Gombrich could claim that Hogarth's *Marriage à la Mode* 'is equivalent to at least two volumes of Richardson's novels'. If, as Gombrich asserts, Hogarth 'accepted the idea of art as a language',[16] the converse is true of Smollett. In employing language in the service of visual art, Smollett has to pay the price of sacrificing depth, as the contrast with Richardson suggests.

Smollett's work, then, falls within a tradition, which endured longer in Scotland than in England, of that mode of the picturesque which, as Hazlitt observed, 'depends chiefly on the principle of discrimination and contrast' and 'runs imperceptibly into the fantastical and the grotesque'.[17] The combination of picturesque strength and freedom of movement pervades Smollett's novels from misadventures at inns early in *Roderick Random* to the Scarborough bathing accident in *Humphry Clinker*. Smollett's last novel offers acknowledgement of the mind-body relationship which has been implied in his earlier novels. Matt Bramble both evinces and admits to a reciprocity of spirits and health. His acute sensibility, feelingly responsive to the grotesque and unjust aspects of life, affects his health. Smollett is close to Matt in this equation of feeling with responsiveness to the grotesque in life. Social concern is allied to the eye of the caricaturist which, as John Butt noted, 'by grossly exaggerating a feature or two converts the human form into a gargoyle'.[18] Discussing the freedom of movement from mood to mood that is a feature of Scottish literature, Gregory Smith commented: 'It takes some people more time than they can spare to see the absolute propriety of a gargoyle's grinning at the elbow of a kneeling saint'.[19]

Smollett offers excellent examples of the deployment of this sense of incongruity in the interests of social satire. In *Peregrine Pickle* a nun, abandoned by her lover, is described thus:

> No tygress robbed of her young was ever exalted to an higher pitch of fury than this nun, when she found herself abandoned by her lover, and insulted in this mortifying explanation. She darted upon her antagonist, like a hawk upon a partridge, and with her nails disfigured that fair face which had defrauded her of her highest expectation. (*PP*, p. 330)

Habitually with Smollett, physical deformity accompanies (or in his descriptions heralds) mental eccentricity. Here is Peregrine's aunt, Mrs Grizzle:

> Exclusive of a very wan (not to call it a sallow) complexion, which perhaps was the effect of her virginity and mortification, she had a cast in her eyes that was

not at all engaging, and such an extent of mouth, as no art or affectation could contract into any proportionable dimension: then her piety was rather peevish than resigned, and did not in the least diminish a certain stateliness in her demeanour and conversation, that delighted in communicating the importance and honour of her family, which, by the bye, was not to be traced two generations back, by all the power of heraldry or tradition. (*PP*, pp. 2–3)

The emphasis on deformity is a feature of the Scots tradition. Noting the differences between Chaucer's 'Troilus and Criseyde' and Henryson's 'Testament of Cresseid', John Speirs says of the latter:

The moral horror at the 'uncleanness' of the 'fleshly lusts' that have 'changed in filth' Cresseid's 'femininitie' merges into the purely physical horror of the 'uncleanness' of the leprosy that devours her beauty and youth. When the 'Court and Convocation' that inflicts the poetic justice has

> Vanishchit away, than rais scho up and tuik
> Ane poleist glas, and hir schaddow culd luik:
> And quhen scho saw hir face sa deformait
> Gif scho in hart was wa aneuch God wait.

There is no such grim moment in Chaucer.[20]

In precisely such passages are the antecedents for Smollett's concern with grotesque physicality, to which there is nothing comparable in Fielding or in Scott, by whose time this grimness and coarseness had been refined out of much of Scottish literature.

Smollett's caricatures function by means of selection and heightening of physical blemish as an index to character and values. Here is Mr Launcelot Crab as he first appears to Roderick:

This member of the faculty was aged fifty, about five foot high, and ten round the belly; his face was capacious as a full moon, and much of the complexion of a mulberry: his nose resembling a powder-horn, was swelled to an enormous size, and studded all over with carbuncles; and his little grey eyes reflected the rays in such an oblique manner, that while he looked a person full in the face, one would have imagined he was admiring the buckle of his shoe. (*RR*, p. 26)

Under the guise of observation the highly selective use of detail works to produce the desired effect of extravagance. Such caricature aims at uniting the illusion of resemblance with mockery.

Of the figures in Rowlandson's illustrations of Smollett, V S Pritchett remarked, 'They are not human beings. They are lumps of animal horror or stupidity'.[21] In earlier Scots poetry—the *Fables* of Henryson, for instance— animals and birds bear resemblance to humans and enact human behaviour. In the manner of the caricaturist Smollett employs extravagant animal analogies to reductive effect in his caricatures.[22] Captain Weazel

was about five foot and three inches high, sixteen inches of which went to his face and long scraggy neck; his thighs were about six inches in length, his legs resembling spindles or drum-sticks, two feet and an half, and his body, which put me in mind of extension without substance, engrossed the remainder;—so that on the whole, he appeared like a spider or grasshopper erect,—and was almost a *vox et praeterea nihil. (RR,* p. 50)

The effect here derives principally from the way in which specificity serves as the basis of imaginative heightening, and from the animal analogies—the former inflating, the latter diminishing. Detailed comparison with animals fulfils this function in almost every one of Smollett's caricatures. Lavement, the apothecary,

was a little old withered man, with a forehead about an inch high, a nose turned up at the end, large cheek bones that helped to form a pit for his little grey eyes, a great bag of loose skin hanging down on each side in wrinkles, like the alforjas of a baboon; and a mouth so accustomed to that contraction which produces grinning, that he could not pronounce a syllable without discovering the remains of his teeth, which consisted of four yellow fangs, not improperly by anatomists, called *canine. (RR,* p. 97)

In *Peregrine Pickle* Trunnion is described habitually in terms of animals. The first account of him is prefaced by this record of the sounds made by him and his companions as they approach Mr Pickle:

The composition of notes at first resembled the crying of quails, and croaking of bullfrogs; but, as it approached nearer, he could distinguish articulate sounds pronounced with great violence, in such a cadence as one would expect from a human creature scolding thro' the organs of an ass. It was neither speaking nor braying, but a surprising mixture of both, employed in the utterance of terms absolutely unintelligible to our wondering merchant . . . (*PP,* pp. 6–7)

Much of the comedy of the early chapters of the book springs from the enforced domestic containment of Trunnion's energy. Here animal analogy is structured by Smollett into a particularly effective sequence: Trunnion is 'like a lion roaring in the toil'; 'was committed to the care of Pipes, by whom he was led about the house like a blind bear growling for prey'; and 'seemed to retire within himself, like a tortoise when attacked, that shrinks within its shell, and silently endure the scourge of her reproaches, without seeming sensible of the smart' (pp. 45–7). Here the steady subjugation of the Commander in marriage is most tellingly conveyed.

As with Lavement, so with Trunnion and Hatchway; distinctive manner of speech, indicative, as conventionally in caricature, of class, occupation, or nationality, is used in conjunction with physical blemish to achieve the extravagant effect. In one of his earliest caricatures, Lieutenant Bowling, Smollett organises features into a significant sequence: distinctive physique (with animal analogy), distinctive attire, distinctive behaviour, distinctive speech. In the creation of peculiar personal idioms and distortions of language is one of Smollett's finest accomplishments; and invariably such idiosyncrasy of speech is a component of the caricature. Yet, as James Beattie was to observe less than forty years after Smollett began his career as novelist,

> We smile, when sailors use at land the language of the sea, when learned pedants interlard ordinary discourse with Greek and Latin idioms, when coxcombs bring abroad into the world the dialect and gesticulations of their own club, and, in general, when a man expresses himself on all subjects in figures of speech suggested by what belongs to his own profession only. Now what but habits contracted in a narrow society could produce these particularities? And does not this prove, that ludicrous qualities are incident to men who live detached in a narrow society, and, therefore, that the feudal, or any other, form of government, that tends to keep the different orders of men separate, must be favourable to wit and humour, and to enlarge the sphere of ludicrous writing?[23]

Here is another indication of the pace and the extent of the change which Scottish values underwent in the middle decades of the eighteenth century. Even allowing for individual differences between Smollett and Beattie, this helps to illuminate the extent to which post-Union Scotland was being drawn rapidly away from feudalism and towards the world of mass society. It is ironic that Smollett found a source of comedy, and at times mockery, in that kind of limiting individuality which was best fostered in the rigidly structured society whose demise he so lamented.

If Smollett was unaware of this particular tension, it is only right to acknowledge those tensions which are central to his technique as caricaturist and which he brings into equipoise, and those potential contradictions which he resolves into paradox. Indicative of his major achievement as caricaturist are that ambivalence of status with which he invests his caricatures and the ambivalence of response which he is able to elicit towards them. Like many Scottish writers, Smollett both inflates and reduces, celebrates and mocks; and we laugh at such figures, are somewhat in awe of them, and at the same time admire the imaginative and expressive skill of their creator. In, for instance, the description of Crabshaw at the start of *Sir Launcelot Greaves* the range of extravagant detail and analogy is remarkable, and unifying the mass of apparently disparate detail is the mind of the author, intent on identifying and vigorously rendering, or even celebrating, the grotesque in man. This imaginative adventurism is typical of Smollett and it locates him firmly within the Scottish tradition of dynamic plenitude.

To Scottish literature Smollett left, in his caricatures, a major legacy, with Scott and Galt the most immediate beneficiaries.[24] But in terms of caricature Smollett's most significant bequest may well have been to the English novel and one of its greatest practitioners, Dickens.[25] Smollett's achievements in finding the verbal equivalent to the pictorial, and the exact balance of action and fixity in literary caricature, should not be under-rated. E H Gombrich notes that in the visual arts

> decorum militated against experimenting with all varieties of human types and emotions. The noble neither laugh nor cry. Thus humorous art was left to be the testing ground of these discoveries.

In the experimentation of this kind attempted in the early novel in English, Smollett is arguably more adventurous and 'modern' than Fielding. The verve of Smollett's caricatures almost warrants the application to him of Gombrich's judgement that Picasso's humorous creations 'show that here is a man who has succumbed to the spell of making, unrestrained and unrestrainable by the mere descriptive functions of the image'.[26]

Smollett's characteristic plenitude permits of the coexistence of fact and heightened imaginative vision, social concern and comic or Gothic fantasy. Again, the important aspects of such a fictitional method are energy and flux. The opening of *Roderick Random* testifies to this. A paragraph of standard autobiographical introduction in the manner of Defoe rapidly gives way to Roderick's mother's dream in all its remarkable imaginative detail:

> She dreamed, she was delivered of a tennis-ball, which the devil (who to her great surprize, acted the part of a mid-wife) struck so forcibly with a racket, that it disappeared in an instant; and she was for some time inconsolable for the loss of her off-spring; when all of a sudden, she beheld it return with equal violence, and earth itself beneath her feet, whence immediately sprung up a goodly tree covered with blossoms, the scent of which operated so strongly on her nerves that she awoke. (*RR*, p. 1)

This immediately identifies Smollett's first novel in terms of the traditional propensity of the Scottish literary imagination to the unusual or grotesque.

Each of Smollett's novels is marked in its early stages by just such inspired imaginative flourishes. In *Peregrine Pickle* there are the riotous imaginative fertility of the approach of Trunnion and company to the inn; the splendidly idiosyncratic speech and behaviour of those characters; the bizarre whims of Mrs Pickle in pregnancy; the absurd prank played upon Trunnion; and, the climax of this opening sequence, the richly comic representation of Trunnion's ride to his wedding. In the light of such fecundity it is difficult to accept the judgement of Herbert Read, that Smollett 'is at the best but an arranger of the objective facts of existence'.[27] Rather, Smollett's novels reflect his dual role: that of social historian, and fantasist. The union of these qualities in such extreme form is distinctly Scottish. G Gregory Smith related to the Scottish character the coexistence of the prose of extravagance and the prose of experience in Scottish literature, and commented,

> There is more in the Scottish antithesis of the real and fantastic than is to be explained by the familiar rules of rhetoric. The sudden jostling of contraries seems to preclude any relationship by literary suggestion. The one invades the other without warning. They are the 'polar twins' of the Scottish Muse.[28]

Smollett's prose evinces this notion of antithesis within fictional flux.

Against such a background the concatenation of emotion and farce in Smollett's novels becomes more readily explicable. An emotional reunion between Roderick and Strap takes place as follows:

> At that instant recollecting his face, I flew into his arms, and in the transport of

> my joy, gave him back one half of the suds he had so lavishly bestowed on my
> countenance; so that we made a very ludicrous appearance . . . (RR, p. 32).

Strap serves as a particular embodiment of contraries held in juxtaposition:
the journeyman barber with a smattering of Greek rises to a position of some
eminence in France only to revert to being Roderick's servant and, latterly,
to demonstrate his joy in a manner so exuberant as to be deemed ludicrous.
The emotional flux and range of *Roderick Random* is demonstrated in chapter
58: Roderick, 'tortured with jealousy' over Narcissa, vents his fury on Strap
by violently pinching his ear, whereupon Strap 'could not help shedding some
tears at my unkindness'; this occasions 'unspeakable remorse' which sets all
his passions into a ferment:

> . . . I swore horrible oaths without meaning or application, I foamed at the mouth,
> kicked the chairs about the room, and played abundance of mad pranks, that
> frightened my friend almost out of his senses.—At any length my transport
> subsided, I became melancholy, and wept insensibly. (RR, p. 357)

Roderick is restored to the 'adorable creature', Narcissa, and this emotional
high is then undermined by a farcical encounter with Strap, whose presence
is betrayed by 'a noise like that of a baboon when he mows and chatters'.
For Smollett, truth is contained within these boundaries of the sublime and
the ludicrous, and each colours the other by virtue of their juxtaposition.
Smollett is detached equally from man at his sublimely emotional and pragmatic extremes. Their juxtaposition is often extremely telling; nowhere more
so than when Smollett interplays the physical and intellectual grotesquerie
of Narcissas's aunt with the romantic sensibility of Roderick which is blind
to all else but the attractions of Narcissa.

For Smollett such emotional self-binding, and the rapid transition of
emotions, are credibly human, and they are comic. The flux of emotions can
be so rapid and so extreme as to incapacitate temporarily. Here is the comment
in *Peregrine Pickle* on Jolter's response to surviving a squall on the Channel
crossing:

> Such a transition from fear to joy, occasioned a violent agitation both in his mind
> and body; and it was a full quarter of an hour before he recovered the right use
> of his organs. (PP, p. 188)

Man, for Smollett, is the victim of his own emotional extremes which render
him comically limited. In Smollett the Augustan satirist's concern with the
discrepancy between ideal and actual and with the mind-body relationship
is reinforced by a scepticism about the nature of the human condition. This
can be traced to his Calvinist background and it relates him to that Scottish
tradition of scepticism which arose as an antidote to Calvinism's certitude
and which was to culminate in Hume.

Peregrine Pickle is largely concerned with the discrepancy between abstrac-
tions and actuality. This is most obviously expressed in the discussions

between the Doctor and Pallet (which lead them into a physical duel), at the heart of which is the way in which the Doctor's sublime world of the imagination is invaded by Pallet; and throughout, Peregrine's vigorous amours provide ironic commentary. In *Peregrine Pickle* Smollett depicts man's condition as a battleground between reason and emotions. Of Peregrine he remarks, 'It would have been well for our hero, had he always acted with the same circumspection: but he had his unguarded moments, in which he fell prey to the unsuspecting integrity of his own heart' (*PP*, p. 612). Central to Smollett's view of life, and to his fictional expression of it, is his belief that the mind is constituted on a principle of energetic contradiction. Peregrine's immediate response to the warrant for his arrest is to beat the bailiff for his insolence, and, on receiving the latter's apology, he 'waked to all the horrors of reflection'. There follows this passage, which is central to Smollett's thought:

> All the glory of his youth was now eclipsed, all the blossoms of his hope were blasted, and he saw himself doomed to the miseries of a jail, without the least prospect of enlargement, except in the issue of his law-suit, of which he had, for some time past, grown less and less confident every day. What would become of the unfortunate, if the constitution of the mind did not permit them to bring one passion into the field against another? Passions that operate in the human breast, like poisons of a different nature, extinguishing each other's effect. (*PP*, p. 678)

For Smollett—and this is a definite legacy of the Scottish background—no emotional note may endure for long without being subject to transition.[29] After his release from the Fleet prison Peregrine feels 'all the extasy that must naturally be produced in a young man of his imagination from such a sudden transition, in point of circumstance' (*PP*, p. 765). The Calvinist Providence ensures such a flux of circumstance as to undermine any emotion that is prolonged beyond the moment. There is a splendid symbolic representation of this in the interruption of the audible progress of Hatchway to an emotional reunion with Peregrine by the breaking of the lieutenant's wooden leg. Here that peculiarly Scottish emphasis on the way in which the providential governance of life reduces it to the farcical-grotesque dimension becomes explicit in Smollett.

These ideas find fuller expression in *Ferdinand Count Fathom*. In his dedication Smollett acknowledges the importance of *Relief*[30] and writes of his attempts 'to subject folly to ridicule, and vice to indignation; to rouse the spirit of mirth, wake the soul of compassion, and touch the secret springs that move the heart' (*FCF*, p. 4). For Smollett there is no incongruity in such composite motivation, since life itself is incongruously complex. Contrast is recognised as the quintessence of life. After the caricature of the aged brothel-keeper Smollett observes,

> Yet there was something meritorious in her appearance, as it denoted her an indefatigable minister to the pleasure of mankind; and as it formed an agreeable contrast with the beauty and youth of the fair damsels that wantoned in her train. It resembled those discords in musick, which properly disposed, contribute to the harmony of the whole piece: or those horrible giants who in the world of

> romance, used to guard the gates of the castle, in which the inchanted damsel was confined. (*FCF*, p. 93)

The acknowledgement that discord is an essential component of the whole is central to Smollett's notion of the inherence of diversity, flux, and contradiction within the total vision.[31] With Smollett the totality of life is in its diversity, and within that totality everything, by virtue of its very presence, is subject to reductive juxtaposition. Thus in such a world the sudden *volte-face* is quite unexceptional. In rapid succession Count Trebasi can express his inveterate hostility to Renaldo by firing at him and removing part of his left eye-brow, and, in an agony of conscience, beg forgiveness for his past treatment of him.

Another manifestation of Smollett's mingling of contraries is his contrasting of manner and matter. In *Roderick Random* this is highly effective as a vehicle of social censure. Roderick's criticism of the society wherein, like Miss Williams, respectable lady can readily degenerate into prostitute is the more forceful by virtue of its expression through Roderick's refined prose; and the same applies to Miss Williams's account of her experiences in Bridewell. But the most striking use of this technique is in Roderick's reports on naval life and his experience of battle, where Roderick's horror is the more forcibly expressed because shockingly realistic details are contained within a carefully modulated prose syntax. In the same novel, however, the contrast of manner and matter is used for the purpose of comic reduction, and in particular those passages in which Roderick appears as romantic lover have an inflation of style which is often undermined by reductive detail.

In *Peregrine Pickle* a clearly identifiable comic-epic manner is employed intermittently. The example of *Tom Jones* possibly influenced Smollett, but his technique should be related also to the Scottish tradition of inflation and reduction. In what Wittig calls the 'dynamic vigour' of Dunbar's poem, 'The Twa Mariit Wemen and the Wedo' and in the mixture of aureate diction, extravagance, and vernacular of 'Colkelbie's Sow' are some of the antecedents of Smollett's comic-epic manner. Wittig notes that the Lowland Scot's 'mistrust of fine sentiment'[32] is reflected in mock-heroic poems such as the 'Justings' of Dunbar, Lyndsay, and Alexander Scott, and in Montgomerie's 'The Cherrie and the Slae'. The following passage, descriptive of Pipes's playing, may be related to that tradition:

> This musician accordingly, applied to his mouth the silver instrument that hung at a buttonhole of his jacket, by a chain of the same metal, and though not quite so ravishing as the pipe of Hermes, produced a sound so loud and shrill, that the stranger (as it were instinctively) stopped his ears, to preserve his organs of hearing from such a dangerous invasion. The prelude being thus executed, Pipes fixed his eyes upon the egg of an ostrich that depended from the ceiling, and without once moving them from that object, performed the whole cantata in a tone of voice that seemed to be the joint issue of an Irish bagpipe, and a sow-gelder's horn. (*PP*, p. 12)

Hatchway's descriptions of woman in nautical terms, his epitaph on

Trunnion, and his letter to Peregrine have all the vitality of the tradition of the mock-heroic;[33] and the courtship of Trunnion by Mrs Grizzle and the episode of Trunnion's progress to his wedding have the imaginative fertility and attention to comic detail endemic within the same tradition (qualities in the Scots tradition which were to endure in such poems of Burns as 'Tam o' Shanter' and 'The Jolly Beggars').

In *Ferdinand Count Fathom* the mock-heroic mode, and the tone thereof, are crucial to the overall meaning of the book. The narrative tone is established in the first chapter in the claim that 'by the time the reader shall have glanced over the subsequent sheets, I doubt not, but he will bless God, that the adventurer was not his own historian'; and then Ferdinand is described as 'this mirror of modern chivalry' (*FCF*, p. 6). The tone established, Smollett proceeds to make extravagant claims for his method. From the account of Ferdinand's birth in a waggon the comic-epic mode is sustained through the details of his being weaned from the brandy-flask of his mother, his mother's marriage, his progress through infancy, and his mother's participation in warfare and her death. Throughout, the comedy derives from the application of heroic formulae and the high style to low matter; from the undermining of that manner by telling linguistic detail; and from the reductive juxtaposition of world and individual, history and personal experience, which prefigures the use of such a stratagem by Burns and Galt.[34]

The effect of the irony is to distance author from subject and to identify Smollett's attitude to his material as one of realism of assessment. Thus when Fathom feigns the romantic lover to Wilhelmina, Smollett undermines his effusions by skilful use of detailed observation. The 'lover's' protestation is succeeded by the statement, 'So saying, he threw himself upon his knees, and seizing her plump hand, pressed it to his lips with all the violence of real transport' (*FCF*, p. 47). 'Plump hand' establishes beyond doubt the comic tone which informs the subsequent 'heroic' account of the courtship:

> the nymph's . . . heart began to thaw, and her face to hang out the flag of capitulation, which was no sooner perceived by our hero, than he renewed his attack with redoubled fervour . . .

Smollett distances himself as the ironic observer of human weaknesses and pretensions, and the comic-epic manner is instrumental in depicting the gap between illusion and actuality.

In the compound of values which Smollett's work evinces the predominant note is ultimately that of a rationalist realism. Smollett proffers forceful endorsement of reason and sounds warnings against fancy, imagination, and romance. The Preface to *Roderick Random* includes the claim that 'Romance, no doubt, owes its origin to ignorance, vanity, and superstition' (*RR*, p. xliii). The misfortunes of Miss Williams originate in her 'having more imagination than judgement' (*RR*, p. 118). In his youth Peregrine was 'a distinguished character, not only for his acuteness of apprehension, but also for that mischievous fertility of fancy . . .' (*PP*, p. 81); and in his early manhood, influenced by the young bucks whose company he keeps, Peregrine frequents 'a certain tavern, which might be properly stiled the temple of excess, where they left the choice of their fare to the discretion of the landlord, that they might save themselves the pains of exercising their own reason' (p. 582). (Significantly, here, and elsewhere, Smollett notes that Peregrine did not relish such riotous excess, indicating that he may yet be saved for the side of reason which could then direct his 'acuteness of apprehension' to good effect).

Habitually Smollett's rationalist sense manifests itself in the investigation of the reality beneath appearances, or in the confrontation of innocence and experience. When Rifle, the highwayman of whom Roderick, Strap, and others have been terrified, is captured, Roderick comments, 'I was amazed to see what a pitiful dejected fellow he now appeared, who had but a few hours ago filled me with such terror and confusion' (RR, p. 42). Captain Weazel is soon to be more farcically unmasked, and the landlord to whom Roderick warms because of his classical learning proves himself an uncompromising opportunist. Smollett employs virtually as a formula the encounter between his hero and the group of characters—be it *beau monde* or fellow-prisoners— where no-one is as he seems.

All of this might be regarded as conventional Augustan satire but for an edge to the censure which is characteristic of Smollett and which relates him to the Scottish tradition of sceptical rationalism typified in Hume and given imaginative expression in Burns's fondness for the unmasking of hypocrites. This sharpness is present, for instance, in Smollett's effective juxtaposition in *Ferdinand Count Fathom* of London life and that of the lunatic asylum and the prison. In Chapter 31 Ratchkali tells Ferdinand that 'this metropolis is a vast masquerade, in which a man of stratagem may wear a thousand different disguises, without danger of detection' (FCF, p. 146), and, fortified by this information, Ferdinand dismisses Ellenor who, distraught as a result, is 'conveyed into the hospital of Bethlem; where we shall leave her for the present, happily bereft of her reason' (p. 147). Himself committed to prison a little later, Ferdinand encounters other victims of the masquerade which is life in mass society, including Minikin, Macleaver, and Theodore, King of Corsica. Significantly, the same novel contains a little later the most unequivocal statement of Smollett's scepticism regarding human nature and achievement. A discourse on the fact that a lucky miscarriage has promoted Fathom's medical reputation leads to the following forthright admission:

> Success raised upon such a foundation, would, by a disciple of Plato, and some modern moralists, be ascribed to the innate virtue and generosity of the human heart, which naturally espouses the cause that needs protection: but I, whose notions of human excellence are not quite so sublime, am apt to believe it is owing to that spirit of self-conceit and contradiction, which is, at least, as universal, if not as natural, as the moral sense so warmly contended for by those ideal philosophers. (p. 263)

Here Smollett dissociates himself from Shaftesbury's belief that man is naturally predisposed to good (and, Damian Grant has suggested, from Fielding's fictional expression of this view),[35] and adopts a position that is close to

Humean scepticism. On the relationship between reputation and moral worth Smollett has no misgivings: 'The most infamous wretch often finds his account in these principles of malevolence and self-love'.

Like all good writers, Smollett exemplifies a congruence of values and technique. His rationalism finds expression by means of reductive devices and modes, and in this he typifies that innate propensity of Scots and Scottish literature towards diminution.

On one particularly comic occasion the progress of Peregrine's amours is thwarted by the entry to his apartment of Pallet on a reluctant ass. In the midst of Win Jenkins's account of her visit to London is the following:

> And I have seen the Park, and the paleass of Saint Gimses, and the king's and the queen's magisterial pursing, and the sweet young princes, and the hillyfents, and the pyebald ass, and all the rest of the royal family. (*HC*, p. 108)

Keats is quite right: Smollett does 'pull down and level what other Men would continue Romance'. He does so, in the manner he does, at least partly because he is a Scot. Such trenchant comic reduction can be found in Scottish literature from the Makars to Burns.

The Scottish characteristic of diminution is a direct legacy of the Calvinist emphasis on the omnipotence of Providence: if all is predetermined can illusions be cherished about the significance of the individual, the value of his actions, or the scope of his understanding? For Smollett all depends on 'the tossing up of a halfpenny'.[36] The world of his novels, where the fortunate last-ditch encounter habitually saves the beleaguered hero, would seem to be a fictional demonstration of Hume's thoughts on how 'the cause of events is concealed from us'.[37]

Herein too lies at least part of the explanation for the nature of Smollett's characterisation. From Smollett's first novel to his last more is promised than is ever fulfilled by way of character development. The effect of Miss Williams's tale on Roderick is to induce a pause for self-examination and an uncharacteristic consideration of the situation of another. This might imply the onset of a significant stage in Roderick's development, and the humanitarian sentiments which he voices in the naval sequence would appear to endorse this; but thereafter any suggestion of growth in personality or values is dropped. When, later, in the company of Miss Snapper Roderick meets his beloved Narcissa, love banishes instantly the opportunism which he has so vigorously practised. It is plainly providential, and there is not a hint of self-scrutiny. There is no need: Fortune has smiled, and it continues to smile on Roderick to the last. Here is the one major contradiction in Smollett which is never resolved (and, arguably, never could be): the Calvinist determinism runs counter to the satirist's humanitarian concern. Even in *Humphry Clinker* there is the same problem. The theme of understanding developing out of experience is broached but not convincingly treated: it is suggested that greater mutual understanding has arisen between Jery and Matt but Jery remains to the end a spectator at life's farce.

In Smollett's world, then, individuality is flattened out as being of no inherent interest. Should individuality persevere, against the grain as it were, it is necessarily driven to grotesquely idiosyncratic extremes. Thus V S Pritchett writes of Trunnion as 'a fantastic and maimed character'.[38] The Scottish Presbyterian background casts light on Smollett's reductive treatment of subjectivity and individual ways of seeing: these are but examples of human limitation. As the language of his caricatures shows, for Smollett individuality both characterises and limits in a way that is often comic. Smollett exemplifies that 'radical and violent subjectivity of vision'[39] which Francis Russell Hart, adducing Wittig, sees as distinctly Scottish; but, for all the energy, the subjectivity is ultimately a manifestation of limitation. Thus Smollett delights in stark and sudden juxtaposition of individual responses: contrast the respective letters of Peregrine and Trunnion, as indicative of character and values, on the occasion of the opposition of the commodore and his wife to Peregrine's interest in Emilia. *Sir Launcelot Greaves*, following the experiences of a cross-section of society on the move, is concerned with the limiting effects of subjectivity and anticipates the fuller treatment of this in *Humphry Clinker*, where the very form implies investigation of individual limitation.

The epistolary mode of fiction is naturally conducive to ironic self-revelation. Smollett had already achieved this effect by means of first-person narration in *Roderick Random*. For instance, Roderick warns Strap against being duped, by the pregnant widow, into marriage, only to proceed to pursue his own interest in Melinda. The irony is heightened here by virtue of Roderick's conviction, evident in his account of his subsequent rebuff by Melinda, that he is more worldly-wise and self-aware than Strap (for example, he speaks of the success of the 'finesse' of his 'affected passion' (*RR*, p. 296)). Similarly, after the encounter with Strutwell, Roderick feigns melancholy to disguise his joy and so affect Strap the more; Roderick, attempting to fool Strap, is much more seriously duped by Strutwell.

Ironic self-revelation is central to *Humphry Clinker*. Matt betrays his values in his first letter—the obsession with health, the veneer of irascibility, and the embarrassed generosity. 'What business have people to get children to plague their neighbours?' (*HC*, p. 5) he exclaims; and, in his penultimate letter and well after the revelation of his paternity of Humphry, he can remark of the latter's projected marriage,

> I would have wished that Mr Clinker had kept out of this scrape; but as the nymph's happiness is at stake, and she has had already some fits in the way of despondence, I, in order to prevent any tragical catastrophe, have given him leave to play the fool, in imitation of his betters; and I suppose we shall in time have a whole litter of his progeny at Brambleton-hall. (p. 345)

Underlining the irony here is the fact that, prior to this discourse on matrimony, Matt had referred to his natural son as 'Mr Clinker Loyd'. Matt's unwitting disclosure of contradiction within himself is achieved in masterly fashion. The fact that a doctor has offered a diagnosis of his condition which he finds unacceptable leads to his raging, 'I wish those impertinent fellows, with their ricketty understandings, would keep their advice for those that ask it', and the same letter to Dr Lewis ends with the postscript, 'I forgot to tell you, that my right ancle pits, a symptom, as I take it, of its being oedematous, not leucophlegmatic' (pp. 24–5). A lengthy harangue on the fashionable ball at Bath culminates in a heated denunciation of the odours of polite society; his storm at last over, Matt then remarks, 'But few words are best: I have taken my resolution' (p. 66).[40]

Each of the characters is subjected to ironic self-revelation. For instance, Tabitha's first letter displays her characteristics of vanity, meanness, and repressed physicality. Tabitha attempts to present herself as the devout religious convert; the reality is that of the repressed sexuality of the spinster— as the nature of her errors in vocabulary so often indicates—venting itself in such niggardliness as

> you will do well to keep a watchfull eye over the hind Villaims who is one of his (Dr Lewis's) amissories, and, I believe, no better than he should be at bottom. God forbid that I should lack christian charity; but charity begins at huom, and sure nothing can be a more charitable work than to rid the family of such vermine. (p. 156)

Here surely is one of the ancestors of 'Ye high, exalted, virtuous dames/Tied up in godly laces' of Burns's 'Address to the Unco Guid'; and it might almost have been with Tabitha in mind that James Beattie wrote, 'Mean sentiments, or expressions, in the mouth of those who assume airs of dignity, have the effect . . . of laughter.'[41]

Ironic self-revelation is a feature of Scottish literature. Wittig rightly discerns it in Dunbar's 'Testament of Mr Andro Kennedy',[42] and Burns was to employ it to great effect in 'Holy Willie's Prayer'. In fiction, Smollett's use of the technique almost certainly influenced Galt: *The Ayrshire Legatees* adopts the format of *Humphry Clinker*, and *Annals of the Parish* and *The Provost* are masterpieces of self-revelation. Writing of *Humphry Clinker*, Scott praised

> the finished and elaborate manner in which Smollett has, in the first place, identified his characters, and then fitted them with language, sentiments, and powers of observation, in exact correspondence with their talents, temper, condition, and disposition.[43]

Precisely such a capacity ought to have produced fine drama. The evidence of *The Regicide* and *The Reprisal* proves, regrettably, that it was late in his career that Smollett reached this peak of ability in imaginative delineation of character, while still commonly subjecting his characters to reductive (here self-reductive) treatment.

Multiple voices are characteristic of Scottish literature, and in this Smollett is no exception. Amongst the considerable range of moods and voices he adopts—those of sensibility, the sentimental, the melodramatic, the Gothic, the embryo Romantic—that of the rationalist is ultimately predominant. Diverse notes are sounded and have a temporary, and sometimes forcefully affective, validity, but in the end they are subordinated to Smollett's reductive rationalism. In designating it 'the rationalizing and sentimentalizing Enlightenment'[44] Morse Peckham has, rightly, identified the interfusion of elements within that complex intellectual movement. These elements coexist in Smollett, but the former has the upper hand. His first hero, Roderick, can display readily the sensibility of the man of feeling. When Miss Williams swoons in response to his concern for her wretched condition, he comments,

> Such extremity of distress must have waked the most obdurate heart to sympathy and compassion: What effect, then, must it have on mine, that was naturally prone to every tender passion? (*RR*, p. 116)

Here Roderick seems to anticipate Mackenzie's Harley. It is undeniable, as a letter praising Richardson shows, that Smollett appreciated the values of the tender heart, but he does not allow sensibility to exist in isolation: it is, like everything else, subject to the flux of experience. The overwrought prose in which Roderick's encounters with Narcissa are presented is clear evidence of the distance at which Smollett stands from his hero's conduct. Smollett's fiction substantiates Wittig's observation that 'when confronted by a parade of feeling that an Englishman might be tempted to handle somewhat cavalierly, it gives the Scot a malicious satisfaction to take it down by apparently taking seriously'.[45] In *Peregrine Pickle* in particular there is considerable satire of the romantic effusion: the letters of Gam Pickle and of Mrs Hornback contrast with the love-letters of Peregrine, and there is the splendid irony wherein Emila receives the *reductio ad absurdum* of this mode in the 'fustian' effusion in the name of Peregrine but revised by the clerk-schoolmaster (p. 105). Again, Smollett has taken care to distance himself from his hero when he notes of the earlier meeting with Emilia that Peregrine

> laid hold of the proper opportunities to express his admiration of her charms, had recourse to the silent rhetoric of tender looks, breathed divers insidious sighs, and attached himself wholly to her during the remaining part of the entertainment. (p. 95)

When he is later and understandably spurned by Emilia, he gives way to 'a violent fit of distraction, during which he raved like a Bedlamite, and acted a thousand extravagances which convinced the people of the house (a certain bagnio) that he had actually lost his wits' (p. 409)

The behaviour of Peregrine exemplifies a certain tenet of Smollett's thought, which finds expression in this novel in Crabtree's discovery that

> when the passions are concerned, howsoever cool, cautious and deliberate, the disposition may otherwise be, there is nothing so idle, frivolous, or absurd, to which they will not apply for gratification. (p. 564)

And in so doing they run the risk of absurdity. For Smollett, when the single passion is indulged to the neglect of all others the result is inevitably comic.

Such is the bias of Peregrine's passion that when he mistakenly believes that Emilia's heart has been won by a young officer his jealousy manifests itself in violently physical form that culminates in his fainting. The prospect of the ultimate fruition of such an all-consuming passion evokes a complex response from Emilia: Smollett records that 'Peregrine's heart was fired with inexpressible ardour and impatience; while the transports of the bride were mingled with a dash of diffidence and apprehension' (p. 777). Similarly, in *Ferdinand Count Fathom* Renaldo 'entered the apartment, and like a lion rushing on his prey, approached the nuptial bed where Serafina, surrounded by all the graces of beauty, softness, sentiment, and truth, lay trembling as a victim at the altar' (*FCF*, p. 351). The consummation of the single emotion gives rise to this remarkable concatenation of beauty and truth with the instinctive or animal passions.

It is important to consider the place of Smollett in the movement of emphasis in European literature in the eighteenth century towards the eliciting and the manifestation of emotion. This embraced emotion in both its sentimental and Gothic dimensions, and the Scottish contribution was considerable. Now it is undeniable that there are episodes in Smollett which prefigure the vogues of benevolism and sentimentality (e.g. the meeting between Peregrine and Gauntlet in the Fleet (*PP*, p. 751); the effect of Emilia's 'sympathizing regard' on Peregrine (*PP*, p. 758); the occasion when Monimia, being taken away by Ferdinand, meets Renaldo's dog (*FCF*, p. 221); Tom Clarke's sobbing and weeping plenteously 'from pure affection' (*LG*, p. 17); and the encounter at the smithy with the grief-striken widow who believes Clinker is her husband restored to her, an incident described as 'too pathetic to occasion mirth' (*HC*, p. 186)).

To Smollett's eyes, however, intense or extreme emotion exists—quite validly—as part of an emotional complex, and hence in a situation of flux; if it is prolonged or indulged this is unnatural and becomes comic or grotesque and fit matter for reduction. This is precisely what Scott missed or chose to ignore when he wrote of Smollett's soaring 'far above [Fielding] in his powers of exciting terror' and commented,

> Upon many other occasions Smollett's descriptions ascend to the sublime; and, in general, there is an air of romance in his writings, which raises his narratives above the level and easy course of ordinary life. He was, like a pre-eminent poet of our own day [Byron], a searcher of dark bosoms, and loves to paint characters under the strong agitation of fierce and stormy passions.[46]

In the half century which separates Scott from Smollett the taste of Europe had ensured that Gothicism and sentimentality were able to elude the control of reason.

A letter of Smollett's gives some indication of his place in this movement of values. He wrote of Nice, 'Here is no Learning, nor Taste of any kind. All is gothic pride, Ignorance, and Superstition.'[47] In his novels, with the qualified exception of *Ferdinand Count Fathom*, horror, fear, and superstition, as well as sentiment, are elicited, played upon, and almost invariably undermined rapidly (e.g. the encounter of Roderick and Strap with the raven and the 'ghost'; the suspicion of witchcraft that is maintained against the wise and kind Mrs Sagely; the bizarre prank with the speaking-trumpet and the whitings which exploits Trunnion's fear of the supernatural (such a union of the fear of the supernatural and the comic prefigures Burns and is typical of the Scottish tradition); Crabtree's assuming the part of magician and his exploits as fortune-teller continue the satire on superstition; and Win Jenkins's experience in 'the land of congyration' (*HC*, p. 261), and the episode of the 'ghost' who turns out to be Lismahago, do likewise).

In *Ferdinand Count Fathom*, though such emotions and subjects are under-mined ultimately and participate in a total context in which their significance is only relative, this is not done nearly as rapidly as in the other novels. Here the Gothic and sentimental elements are afforded much more forceful and sustained expression, though in the context of the whole novel they still fall beneath the aegis of Smollett's reductive rationalism. This has to be recog-nised, and when Damian Grant claims that 'what is original in *Fathom* is Smollett's willingness to accept the experience of terror without ironic reser-ve'[48] he is overlooking both those occasions when the 'terrors' are reduced and the nature of the conclusion. The experience of terror is 'genuine' for its—limited—duration, but it is only one of various emotional chords in what is for Smollett the compound and flux of experience.

What is significant in *Ferdinand Count Fathom* is the relationship which Smollett establishes thus between fear and his alleged didactic aim:

> Yet the same principle by which we rejoice at the remuneration of merit, will teach us to relish the disgrace and discomfiture of vice, which is always an example of extensive use and influence, because it leaves a deep impression of terror upon the minds of those who were not confirmed in the pursuit of morality and virtue, and while the balance wavers, enables the right scale to preponderate. (p. 3)

Furthermore, he claims, 'the impulses of fear which is the most violent and interesting of all the passions, remain longer than any other upon the memory'. This helps clarify the rationale of the 'Gothic interlude' in Chapters 20 and 21 (which Grant suggests may be 'partly the result of inadvertence, a casting about for something different, or simply something next, to do').[49] In fact, in this episode Smollett firmly and clearly relates the Gothic to the fantasising power of the imagination:

> the darkness of the night, the silence and solitude of the place, the indistinct images of the trees that appeared on every side, 'stretching their extravagant arms athwart the gloom', conspired with the dejection of spirits occasioned by his loss to disturb his fancy, and raise strange phantoms in his imagination. Although he was not naturally superstitious, his mind began to be invaded with an awful horror, that gradually prevailed over all the consolations of reason and philosophy: nor was his heart free from the terrors of assassination. (p. 83)

The fancy positively induces an increased receptivity to fear: after the sighing of the trees and the roar of the thunderstorms, Ferdinand 'had well nigh lost the use of his reflection, and was actually invaded to the skin' (p. 84). As generally in Smollett, the correlation of mental and physical is important: in the course of his struggle through the forest 'his skin suffered in a grievous manner, while every nerve quivered with eagerness of dismay' (pp. 84–5).

The point of this episode is to demonstrate that Ferdinand, for all the success of his rational opportunism, is subject, like any other human being, to fear, and in particular to that co-operation of the mind with circumstances in the creation of fear. Thus the episode follows the pattern of alternation between Gothic horror and reductive observation, and between Ferdinand's terror and his opportunism. In the house of the old woman who offers him shelter he finds 'the dead body of a man, still warm, who had been lately stabbed, and concealed beneath several bundles of straw' (p. 86). The terror which this induces is vividly described in terms, first of physical effect, then of its stimulus to his conscience. When the robbers return to finish off their victim Ferdinand 'remained in a trance that, in all probability, contributed to his safety; for, had he retained the use of his senses, he might have been discovered by the transports of his fear' (p. 86). His first use of his 'retrieved recollection' is to note the open door as a means of escape, but, ever the opportunist, Fathom stops long enough to rob the corpse. The fluctuation between terror and practicality corresponds with a game of cat and mouse, with the rôles changing, between Fathom and the old woman who, seeing the departing Fathom, 'accustomed as she was to the trade of blood . . . did not behold this apparition without giving signs of infinite terror and astonishment, believing it was no other than the spirit of her second guest who had been murdered' (p. 87).

The episode is an accomplished ironic study of human limitation as manifested in the mind's capacity to induce fear. Again traversing the wood, with 'every whisper of the wind . . . swelled into hoarse menaces of murder . . . [Fathom] felt what was infinitely more tormenting than the stab of a real dagger'. Smollett's point is that the effects of the imagination are far worse than any actuality (a point exploited by Burns in 'Tam o' Shanter'). The episode ends with a splendidly ironic sequence. Now safe, Fathom

> earnestly exhorted her to quit such an atrocious course of life, and attone for her past crimes, by sacrificing her associates to the demands of justice. She did not fail to vow a perfect reformation, and to prostrate herself before him, for the favour she had found; then she betook herself to her habitation, with full purpose of advising her fellow-murderers to repair with all dispatch to the village, and impeach our hero, who wisely distrusting her professions, staid no longer in the place . . . (p. 89)

After the interlude of horrors, devious scepticism has resumed its ascendancy.

It is once more indicative of what was to happen to Scottish values in the ensuing half-century that Scott's judgement of this episode should miss the counterpointing that is at the heart of Smollett's method and instead concentrate on his attainment to the sublime. For Scott,

> The horrible adventure in the hut of the robbers, is a tale of natural terror which
> rises into the sublime; and, though often imitated, has never yet been surpassed
> or perhaps equalled.[50]

In fact, Smollett's achievement here is an instance of that identifiably Scottish
strain which Hugh MacDiarmid described as 'tremendously idiosyncratic, full
of a wild humour which blends the actual and the apocalyptic in an incalculable fashion';[51] and Gregory Smith found a connection between the 'double
mood' inherent in much of Scottish literature and 'the easy passing . . .
between the natural and the supernatural, as if in challenge to the traditional
exclusiveness of certain subjects, each within its own caste'.[52]

There is a tradition of interest in the demonic in Scottish writers such as
Dunbar, Burns, Hogg, and Stevenson. Plainly Smollett can be included here,
but the crucial point is that the passing between the natural and the supernatural, between the actual and the apocalyptic, is subsumed within his
reductive vision. Fathom is a vividly realised individual (as Scott recognised,
contrasting him as 'a living and existing miscreant' with Jonathan Wild, 'a
cold personification of the abstract principle of evil').[53] However the novel
contains suggestions that Fathom is a demon-figure. Fathom's diabolism
resides in his ability to identify life in terms of its flux and interfusion of values
and to capitalise upon this by rôle-playing.

The extent to which seventeenth- and eighteenth-century Scotsmen were
concerned with the opposition between the instincts and the rational will has
been recognised.[54] It is precisely this opposition that Fathom appears to
resolve by uniting instincts and rational will in the common cause of self-
interest. At the outset Smollett identifies Ferdinand's 'insidious principle of
self-love' (p. 20); and his early plotting establishes that equation of intimacy
and self-advancement that characterises him. His first experience in the
demonic role is farcical: Wilhelmina believes that Fathom is the devil come
to earth as her lover, and 'while her imagination teemed with those horrible
ideas' he emerges soot-covered from his chimney hiding-place and is mistaken
'for Satan *in propria persona*' (p. 52). With the mother he adopts the postures
of pathos and romantic love for self-advancement. A succession of rôles
follows thereafter, with Fathom appearing as a one-eyed fiddler, the Young
Pretender, and a philosopher armed with a full confutation of Newton's
philosophy. Such petty deception is prelude to the more sinister diabolism of
his encounter with Celinda. Here Fathom's demonic qualities reach their
height. Fathom wants 'to banquet his vicious appetite with the spoils of her
beauty' (p. 158). Recognising her 'superstitious fear', he plays upon 'such
sensibility': by means of music he soothes her sense of hearing 'even to a
degree of ravishment, so as to extort from her an exclamation, importing, that
he was surely something supernatural' (pp. 158–9). The subtle modulation of
the prose shows how Fathom interplays emotion, senses, music, and the
supernatural in the interests of his diabolic purposes: by his virtuosity on the
Aeolian harp Fathom pours forth 'a stream of melody more ravishingly
delightful than the song of Philomel, the warbling brook, and all the concert
of the wood' which introduces 'a succession of melodies in the same pathetic

style'. All this achieves the desired effect on the sensations of Celinda which, 'naturally acute, were whetted to a most painful keenness, by her apprehension' (p. 161). In the manner of the Satanic tempter Fathom orchestrates her emotions and in particular he plays upon her fear and superstition, with the result that

> In her paroxysms of dismay, he did not forget to breathe the soft inspirations of his passion, to which she listened with more pleasure, as they diverted the gloomy ideas of her fear; and by this time his extraordinary accomplishments had made a conquest of her heart. (p. 163)

After Fathom's triumph, Smollett, in a most effective juxtaposition, transports him to Bristol where he 'formed the nucleus or kernel of the beau monde' (p. 165). The significance is clear: at the heart of society is the man of demonic accomplishments. This theme is maintained in his claim, 'that fire was the sole vivifying principle that pervaded all nature', and in his high medical reputation 'though the death of every patient had given the lie to his pretensions' (pp. 166–7). Having raised Fathom's status to this peak of diabolism, Smollett then proceeds to reduce it and to restore him to the level of the merely and patently human. In chapter 38 'the biter is bit': at the encounter with Renaldo, what the latter believes to be tears of love, gratitude, and joy in fact 'proceeded from conscious perfidy and fear' (p. 196); confronted by Monimia's pledge of vengeance, 'he was not so much affected by his bodily danger, as awestruck at the manner of her address, and the appearance of her aspect, which seemed to shine with something supernatural, and actually disordered his whole faculties' (p. 237) (a splendidly ironic reversal of rôles).

Significantly, just after Smollett's unequivocal statement of his realistic attitude to the human condition, Ferdinand's 'diabolism' is finally subsumed within Smollett's reductive realism by its being made to degenerate into its first condition—that of farce:

> Then was his chariot overturned with a hideous crash, and his face so much wounded with the shivers of the glass, which went to pieces in the fall, that he appeared in the coffee-house with half a dozen black patches upon his countenance, gave a most circumstantial detail of the risque he had run, and declared, that he did not believe that he should ever hazard himself again in any sort of wheel carriage. (p. 268)

Likewise, his grandiloquent repentance is undermined most effectively by the acknowledgement of the circumstances of its origin. In this there are obvious affinities with Burns's reduction of the Devil to the level of the human in 'Address to the Deil', and of Death in 'Death and Dr Hornbook' and 'Tam o' Shanter', where he is 'tousie tyke, black, grim, and large'—fearsome but also familiar. But the point of difference is that Smollett has first to inflate, to create his 'devil', before reducing. By the conclusion the Satan-substitute has been restored to the dimension of flawed human being. Any attempt to relate

Ferdinand Count Fathom directly to Romantic Satanism must of necessity overlook this distinctly Scottish reductive trait.

If Fathom is treated thus, at the same time Smollett establishes a comparable distance between himself and Renaldo, the melancholic and sentimental lover. Through the experiences of Renaldo Smollett reveals the often-grotesque effects upon the emotional compound that result from the pursuit and the indulgence of the single emotion. He exploits to the full the potential pathos of Renaldo's situation, but the nature and the sequence of the author's prose indicates that his own attitude is far from being unrelievedly pathetic. The effects on Renaldo of the loss of Monimia are presented first in terms of physical detail, and then Smollett offers an account of the effect of his condition on his mother and sister. It is a situation fraught with paradox: their joy on witnessing his apparent recovery is merely, for Renaldo, a protraction of his misery. His melancholy is nourished by attempts to counter it. Melancholy, revenge, love, and physical beauty are all interfused, and the recollection of Monimia in sensuous pastoral terms induces what is termed his 'pleasing anguish'. The midnight pilgrimage to Monimia's tomb displays sentiment overbalancing into the grotesque:

> As they approached this capital, Renaldo's grief seemed to regurgitate with redoubled violence. His memory was waked to the most minute and painful exertion of its faculties; his imagination teemed with the most afflicting images, and his impatience became so ardent, that never lover panted more eagerly for the consummation of his wishes, than Melvile for an opportunity of stretching himself upon the grave of the lost Monimia. (p. 315)

The Gothic accompaniment is appropriate to Renaldo's extreme version of the sentimental lover, in which

> the soul of Melvile was wound up to the highest pitch of enthusiastic sorrow. The uncommon darkness of the night, the solemn silence, and the lonely situation of the place, conspired with the occasion of his coming, and the dismal images of his fancy, to produce a real rapture of gloomy expectation, which the whole world would not have persuaded him to disappoint. (p. 317)

Such terms would seem to identify Smollett as one of the harbingers of the belief that painful emotions can be relished for their own sake and can be pleasurable. Yet, like everything else in Smollett, such passages cannot be extracted from context and considered apart from the total composite meaning of the book, a meaning which does nothing to suggest that Smollett's attitude is one of unequivocal endorsement of the joys of anguish. Renaldo's speech delivered prostrate on Monimia's tomb is deliberately over-wrought (on Smollett's part), and the recognition of the therapeutic effects of such an effusion is at least partly reductive:

> [Renaldo] frankly owned, that his mind was now more at ease than he had ever found it, since he first received the fatal intimation of his loss; that a few such

feasts would entirely moderate the keen appetite of his sorrow, which he would afterwards feed with less precipitation. (p. 319)

Far from this being so, he 'renews the rites of sorrow, and is entranced'. The reunion with Monimia, stage-managed by his 'friends . . . in consequence of his enthusiastic sorrow' (p. 327), allows Smollett to introduce most of the trappings of Gothicism, but once again the prose account of Renaldo's response becomes extravagant and self-deriding:

> In the midst of these ejaculations, he ravished a banquet from her glowing lips, that kindled in his heart a flame, which rushed thro' every vein, and glided to his marrow: this was a privilege he had never claimed before, and now permitted as a recompense for all the penance he had suffered. (p. 326)

As habitually in Smollett, such emotional extremes accompany (and in some cases are prompted or reinforced by) awareness of the pleasurably sensuous.

Towards the end of *Ferdinand Count Fathom* the theme of the pleasures of benevolism gains importance, but here again Smollett's attitude is far from being entirely unironical. Serafina pleads on behalf of Fathom, claiming to Renaldo, 'his present wretchedness . . . will move your compassion, as it hath already excited mine' (p. 341). In time Renaldo agrees to visit Fathom, 'not with a view to exult over his misery, but in order to contemplate the catastrophe of such a wicked life, that the moral might be the more deeply engraved on his remembrance', and, on entering, 'they beheld the wretched hero of these adventures stretched almost naked upon the straw, insensible, convulsed, and seemingly in the grasp of death' (p. 353). Fathom writes that he wishes to 'excite the compassion of the humane count de Melvile', and his confession, he hopes, 'may be a warning for him to avoid henceforth, a smiling villain, like the execrable Fathom' (p. 354). Fathom's situation may have evoked compassion in the reader, but this is qualified by the element of grovelling in his appeals.

However, the self-approving joy of Renaldo is then subjected to comparable qualification. Fathom's suitably overwrought plea ('ah murthered innocence! wilt thou not intercede for thy betrayer at the throne of grace?' [p. 359]) is interrupted by a lecture from Renaldo on the subject of Providence, the tone and nature of which are such as to suggest that Renaldo regards the benevolent as the Elect. Even more disturbing is the mixture of the motives claimed in the comment of the narrator:

> . . . the strange occurrence of the day . . . seemed to have been concerted by supernatural prescience, in order to satisfy the vengeance, and afford matter of triumph to the generosity of those who had been so grievously injured by the guilty Fathom. (p. 359)

Renaldo proceeds to relish the 'luxurious enjoyment of communicating happiness to his fellow creatures in distress' (p. 360), the first instalment of which is an annuity of £60 per annum and a promise of more if Fathom's behaviour warrants it.

For Sterne, 'there is nothing unmixed in this world'.[55] In Smollett too nothing—not benevolism, sentiment, or sensibility—remains unmixed. As Matt Bramble and his party travel further into the Highlands the use of such terms as 'romantic', 'picturesque' and 'sublime' increases, and this might be regarded as a forerunner of the Romantics' concern with such qualities. Jery notes that the country and the people are 'more wild and savage the further we advance' (HC, p. 238), and he goes on to enthuse over the antiquarian spirit and the Ossian poems. Such romanticising over tartanry is then undermined in the fine comic detail of the laird's 'invincible antipathy to the sound of the Highland bagpipe' (p. 241), and his unavailing attempt to dispense with the ritual morning recital thereon.

Perhaps the greatest reason for the neglect of Smollett by his countrymen now becomes plain. Sentiment and rationality coexist in Smollett's vision, but the latter holds the ascendancy. Smollett's values were formed before the Scottish dissociation of sensibility could have any significant effect on them. Underlying the diverse manifestations of his vision is a unity which derives from his reductive rationalism. By Burns's day, and certainly by Scott's, feeling had become polarised as sentiment and existed virtually independently of reason. Thus a nation whose taste dictated that they separate quite rigidly Burns's satiric voice from his sentimental could have little interest in a writer in whom these and many other voices intermingle. In this Smollett exemplifies the older Scottish literary tradition.

CHAPTER 2

The Joy of Grief: The Poetry of James Macpherson

The voice of feeling is, in the work of Smollett, one of a range of voices that is subsumed within a reductive rationalism. The poetry of James Macpherson reveals no such diversity. There is nothing ironical about the attitude to sensibility which Macpherson attributes to Ossian (though what is paradoxical is that an unknown but ambitious young poet should have created the identity and the voice of a morose and elderly bard living in times allegedly far-distant).

Central to the ethos of *The Poems of Ossian* is commitment to both action and the manifestation of feeling. Virtually every poem is characterised by a pattern of alternate heroic deed and emotional response. Every poem reveals as the principal values of this remote heroic age the capacity for brave deed and noble emotion (in terms of the ability to both feel and sympathise). The predominant note is that of 'the joy of grief'. As Larry L Stewart has pointed out, Macpherson uses the phrase (its first appearance in his poetry is in 'Carric-thura') almost exactly as Burke had done three years earlier in *A Philosophical Enquiry into the Origin of our Ideas of the Sublime and Beautiful*, to refer to 'the specific kind of pleasure which results from recalling and reliving the pleasures of the irretrievable past'.[1]

Fascinating subject as it is, the Ossian controversy is not in itself the concern of this study; neither is the relationship between Macpherson's poems and those of the Gaelic tradition, an area already carefully investigated in D S Thomson's *The Gaelic Sources of MacPherson's Ossian* (London and Edinburgh, 1951). Rather, the purpose of this chapter is to identify, and to account for, the distinctive features of Macpherson's writing, and to show how peculiarly Scottish characteristics were adapted to meet the needs of European taste. In a situation fecund in ironies not the least is in the scale of Macpherson's achievement: prompted by the Edinburgh *literati* he feigned the voice of heroic feeling and became as a result a celebrity across Europe, while at the same time he effectively ensured that the authentic voice of an earlier Scotland, as expressed in the genuine Gaelic poems of such writers as Alexander Macdonald, Duncan Macintyre, and Rob Donn, was ignored. As the examples of Chatterton, William Ireland, and Robert Surtees demonstrate, there were various attempts in the course of the eighteenth century to fake the poetry of a remote past. While it would be easy to overemphasise the Scottish dimension, the nature of Macpherson's achievement is a reflection of the way in which, by the middle of the eighteenth century in Scotland, considerable imaginative energies had to be diffused over a range of voices, including the false, for the want of the healthy survival of endemic modes. In Macpherson the Scottish talent for rôle-playing, given greater scope by the crisis of cultural identity which the Union exacerbated, reached both its zenith and its nadir: fame was won on the basis of deception. In modern literature (indeed in modern life) one of the authentic voices of the individual is that of the poseur or phoney. In Macpherson Scottish literature heralded this chilling paradox.

Yet to dismiss Macpherson as a hoaxer is to ignore the extent of his contribution to the age of sensibility. In his definitive account, Northrop Frye has identified the considerable part played by Macpherson in the 'concentration on the primitive process of writing [which] is projected in two directions, into nature and into history'. With justification he terms Macpherson's Ossian poems 'not simple hoaxes . . . [but] pseudepigrapha, like the book of Enoch, and like it they take what is psychologically primitive, the oracular process of composition, and project it as something primitive'.[2]

That Macpherson was responsive to the note of melancholy sounded in Young's *Night Thoughts*, Blair's *The Grave*, Hervey's *Meditations*, and Warton's *The Pleasures of Melancholy* is evident from his first poem, 'Death', written before he was twenty, which begins,

> Come melancholy, soul-o'erwhelming power!
> Woe's sable child! sweet meditation come;
> Come, pensive gaited, from thy hermit cell,
> Brood wide o'er life, and all its transient joys,
> The noisy follies, and corroding strifes:
> Shut the pleas'd ear from harmony and song;
> And from the heart ensnaring voice of fame.
> (II, 445)[3]

Replete with poetic diction, this poem has nothing to distinguish it as Macpherson's. In his notes to the edition of 1805 Malcolm Laing censures the poem as 'marked with the same extravagance of sentiment and diction that prevails in Ossian' (II, 445, n.1). This is to do less than justice to Macpherson's accomplishment in the Ossian poems, where the poetic diction is more thinly spread and where it is set to a specific use, with the result that those poems are, ironically, more obviously the product of an individual mind. Of comparable manner to 'Death' is 'To the Memory of an Officer Killed before Quebec' which begins,

> Ah me! what sorrow are we born to bear!
> How many causes claim the falling tear!
> In one sad tenor life's dark current flows,
> And every moment has its load of woes.
> (II, 592)

Macpherson had caught the popular note of romantic melancholy. As J S Smart notes,[4] Mme de Stael was to attribute its prevalence among English writers to the fact that liberty enabled meditation, which in turn terminated in melancholy. Macpherson, like many other Scots, was to lament his nation's loss of liberty. In the case of the Scottish version of romantic melancholy one of the sources lay in the loss of national liberty and the sentimental nationalism which this occasioned.

Melancholy, spontaneous emotion, and natural benevolence were held to be the principal characteristics of natural man, and it is to the vogue of the noble savage that one has to look to begin to understand why Macpherson came to write the *Poems of Ossian*. Rightly John MacQueen found the kindred to Fingal in Rousseau's *Emile*, which appeared in the same year as Macpherson's epic.[5] By the 1750s the process of questioning the effects of much-vaunted rationalism had led to a close scrutiny of the nature of society and the ways in which it had evolved. Civilisation, so much the product of man's reason and epitomised in the new urban society, came to be regarded as the means whereby man's original natural benevolence had been corrupted and his pristine emotionalism repressed. Hence spontaneity came to be of cardinal importance, spontaneity both of feeling and of literary expression. The search was initiated to find the people who approximated most closely to the last embodiment of such values. Who were the people who had been least tainted by rationalism's restraints and civilisation's corruption? It was a quest that was to lead Herder to identify the Caledonians with the North American Indians.[6]

The philosophical and the antiquarian interests proceeded in tandem. As Malcolm Chapman has noted,[7] the harbinger of the interest in antiquities, and especially Celtic antiquities, was Lhuyd's *Archaeologica Britannica* of 1707. The fuller flowering of that interest was to be delayed for over half a century until the publication of such collections as Percy's *Reliques* (1765). In the process, the work of William Stukely (*Stonehenge* (1740) and *Abury* (1743)) encouraged a merging of the interest in Celts with the interest in Druids. The result of this activity was that by mid century the general interest in primitive society and its values had come to focus upon the Celts. Gray's poem 'The Bard' (1757) is a typical reflection of this. At the same time the cry of that philosophical movement which is held to centre around Rousseau was for a return to nature. In the vanguard of this movement were Francis Hutcheson, who stressed the importance of the emotions, the value of beauty, and the original benignity of man, and Adam Smith, whose *Theory of Moral Sentiments* (1759) was described by James Wodrow as 'founded on sympathy, a very ingenious attempt to account for the principal phenomena in the moral world from this one general principle, like that of gravity in the natural world'.[8] Between Rousseau's natural emotionalism and Hobbesean materialism Smith serves as mediator.

By the English, and presently also by the Lowland Scots, the Highlands of Scotland came to be regarded as the last refuge of the remnants of intuitive emotionalism and nobility of action. In Collins's 'An Ode on the Popular Superstitions of the Highlands of Scotland' (1749) that region is presented as the home, in MacQueen's words, of 'internal natural truth, which in a scientific or philosophical sense may not be truth at all, but which convinces the imagination, and to which the achievement of Shakespeare and Tasso has given an authority equal to that of the scientific'.[9] The attitude of educated Lowland Scots to the Highlands was rather more complex. Confronted through the seventeenth and eighteenth centuries by an increasing and apparently inevitable process of Anglicisation, they tended to identify that process with progress and the Gaelic culture with decline. Chapman notes contempt for the Gaelic language being expressed as early as the Statutes of Iona of 1609.[10] A certain guilt at relinquishing the Gaelic tradition and an understandable insecurity in the face of Anglicisation seem to have been channelled together into, first, a hostility to the Highlands and its culture, only for that to give way, in the course of the eighteenth century, to an almost-compulsive sentimentalising.

Perhaps it is wrong to see this as a sequential process. In fact there is evidence that the two responses could be held simultaneously by the one individual. As MacQueen has observed, James Thomson's attitude, anticipating that of Scott, contradicted itself, in that

> On the one hand, he looked with approval for the rapid approximation of Scotland to England and Europe. Despite this, his verse kindled to its best when he celebrated the wildness, the natural, even heroic simplicities of Scottish life, and in particular the life of the Highlands and Islands.[11]

Thomson was not the sole exemplar of this contradiction. In 1724 Allan Ramsay's preface to *The Ever Green* included this comment:

> I have observed that *Readers* of the best and almost exquisite Discernment frequently complain of our *modern Writings*, as filled with affected Delicacies and studied Refinements, which they would gladly exchange for that natural Strength of Thought and Simplicity of Style our Forefathers practised: to such, I hope, the following *Collection of Poems* will not be displeasing. When these good old *Bards* wrote, we had not yet made Use of imported Trimmings upon our Cloaths, nor of Foreign Embroidery in our Writings. Their *Poetry* is the Product of their own Country, not pilfered and spoiled in the Transportation from abroad: Their *Images* are nature, and their *Landskips* domestick; copied from those Fields and Meadows we every Day behold.[12]

Ramsay went on to claim

> . . . such there are, who can vaunt of acquiring a tolerable perfection in the French or Italian Tongues, if they have been a fortnight in Paris or a Month in Rome: But shew them the most elegant Thought in a Scots Dress, they as disdainfully as stupidly condemn it as barbarous . . . for the most part of our Gentlemen, who are generally Masters of the most useful and politest Languages, can take Pleasure (for a Change) to speak and read their own.

The paradox wherein such a view came from the pen of a writer who mimicked Pope, quoted Prior, and sought in the columns of the *Spectator* a model life-style, has been well noted by David Daiches. Daiches remarks that it is 'a reflection of the impoverishment of Scottish Culture that the issue should have been between a native simplicity and an imported sophistication'.[13] The unfortunate irony is that Scottish culture was not by then impoverished; rather, it was experiencing a crisis of identity, direction and confidence.

Most of the literatures of western Europe in the eighteenth century reflect the debate between the rival claims of civilisation and primitivism. What especially distinguishes the Scottish situation is the number of individual writers who offer the two responses ambivalently. Nor is this purely an eighteenth-century phenomenon. Chapman comments astutely:

> Since the eighteenth century . . . the Scottish people have increasingly looked to the Highlands to provide a location for an autonomy in which they could lodge their own political, literary and historical aspirations. They have thereby been allowed to reap all the benefits of the Union, while at the same time retaining a location for all the virtues of sturdy independence.[14]

The close relationship between cultural and economic values was, in the Scottish context, a particularly potent factor. Anglicisation coincided with growing industrialisation. Alert to the limitingly materialist implications of industrialisation, Adam Ferguson was to write,

> Many mechanical arts, indeed, require no capacity; they succeed best under a total suppression of sentiment and reason; and ignorance is the mother of industry as well as of superstition . . . Manufactures, accordingly, prosper most, where the mind is least consulted, and where the workshop may, without any great effort of imagination, be considered as an engine, the parts of which are men.[15]

Now while the universal applicability of this prophetic statement endures, it can be said that it accorded with the Scottish impulse towards dichotomy (to which the geographical division within the country lent credence), to compartmentalise emotion and deed, to polarise the spiritual and the emotional. The legacy of the coincident growth of sensibility and economic materialism—and in each case Adam Smith was a progenitor—is with us to this day.

In consideration of the major determinants of the nature of Macpherson's *Poems of Ossian* one important factor remains—the sentimental nationalism which is not entirely unrelated to the growth of antiquarianism. There was a mounting urgency to record the remnants of the Gaelic tradition. In 1740, for instance, Adam Ferguson noted a poem from the recitation of a tailor at his father's house. The less readily accessible material was to be sought out and recorded for posterity. This impetus was accelerated by the 'Forty-Five and its aftermath. The punitive measures exacted of the Highland clans (some of the effects of which Macpherson had witnessed as a boy)[16] seemed to sound the death-knell for that primitive society of heroic values which the clans rapidly and conveniently came to symbolise. The loss of such a life-style was readily encompassed within the vogue of melancholy; and the need to find and preserve the remnants of its culture became the more pressing.

Among ethnic groups only the American Indians have been subjected to more immediate and more intense mythologising. No single event exemplifies better the dichotomies within the Scottish value-system—the polarising of fact and fantasy, of reason and sentiment, of deed and emotion. Loyal Unionists such as Smollett (in 'The Tears of Scotland') and Mackenzie (in 'The Exile' and the story of Albert Bane) found in sentimental Jacobitism a means of expressing a side of their personalities which otherwise had to be firmly checked. Later, Burns, Scott (most obviously in *Waverley*), and Stevenson (in *Kidnapped*) were to be induced by contemplation of the 'Forty-Five into effusion of ambivalent feelings. The realist side of the Scot recognised the inevitability of the historical process, while the sentimental could romanticise around what might have been. With justification Jacques Barzun has observed of neoclassicism, 'The pattern of conformity came to England with the restored Stuarts who had lived in exile at the French court; and everywhere in the following century it evolved into a cosmopolitan classicism, during which its ideals became less and less compelling or productive, until the ground was cleared for the romantic revival.'[17] The paradox wherein the Stuart dynasty both exerted an influence in the direction of the neoclassical and provided in Mary, Queen of Scots, and the Young Pretender focuses for nascent romanticising should not go unnoticed.

The occupation of Holyrood by the Young Pretender has been described by David Daiches as 'a deliberately histrionic act'.[18] There is a case for regarding the entire 'Forty-Five in this light. The histrionic tendency of a nation bereft of nationhood found expression in a grand and futile gesture, and the non-combatant Scots (the vast majority) could live vicariously through identification with the participants (just as Macpherson was shortly to encourage them to live vicariously through identification with his Celts). The 'Forty-Five may be said both to exemplify and to have further stimulated the existing tendency of Scots towards rôle-playing, while the crucial decision at Derby is one instance of that crisis of confidence by which Scots have been beleaguered for over two centuries. When confidence wavers it is comforting to turn from fact to fantasy. The 'Forty-Five rapidly came to fulfil that therapeutically symbolic function for Scots. It is as a non-Scot that Malcolm Chapman fails to appreciate the questionable advantages of the event when he writes,

> Celtic Ireland, Wales and Brittany do not in any clear sense have their Culloden. They do not have an apocalypse in which the threshold of the modern world was crossed. The drama that they can inject into their historical reconstruction of themselves is the poorer for the lack.[19]

To endow a national event with such symbolic significance and proceed to make it a focus for sentimentalising can be severely restrictive: contemplation of the apocalypse too readily becomes a substitute for constructive thought or action. What has to be acknowledged, in fairness to Macpherson, is that in the decades after the 'Forty-Five the histrionic tendency of the Scots was at its most extreme. That he himself should have accepted the rôle that was presented to him is thus more readily understood.

There are clear signs that Macpherson was responsive to, and capable of, sentimental nationalism. In the following lines from his poem 'On the Death of Marshal Keith' there is a significant claim for Scottish pre-eminence in sensibility, along with blatant sentimentalising of the nation, its people, and the hero whom they had—ironically—rejected:

> But Caledonia o'er the rest appears,
> And claims pre-eminence to mother-tears:
> In deeper gloom her tow'ring rocks arise,
> And from her vallies issue doleful sighs.
> Sadly she sits, and mourns her glory gone;
> He's fallen, her bravest, and her greatest son!
> While at her side her children all deplore
> The godlike hero they exiled before.
>   Sad from his native home the chief withdrew;
> But kindled Scotia's glory as he flew;
> ...   .
>
>   But chief, as relics of a dying race,
> The Keiths command, in woe, the foremost place;
> A name for ages through the world revered,
> By Scotia loved, by all her en'mies feared;
> Now falling, dying, lost to all but fame,
> And only living in the hero's name.
>   See! the proud halls they once possessed, decayed,
> The spiral tow'rs depend the lofty head;
> Wild ivy creeps along the mould'ring walls,
> And with each gust of wind a fragment falls;
> While birds obscene at noon of night deplore,
> Where mighty heroes kept the watch before.
>   (II, 588–9)

Here, surely, is the prototype of the Ossianic lament for past glories and nobility of action and deed which can never be recovered.

Typical of the way in which classical forms were employed by eighteenth-century Scots to celebrate Scottish achievements is Macpherson's Pindaric ode, 'The Earl Marischal's Welcome to his Native Country' (published in the *Scots Magazine* for September 1760) which includes these words of 'Melanthus':

> Now my youthful heat returns,
> My breast with youthful vigour burns:
> Methinks I see that glorious day,
>   When, to hunt the fallow-deer,
> Three thousand march'd in grand array:
>   Three thousand march'd with bow and spear,—
> All in the light and healthy dress
>   Our brave forefathers wore,
> In Kenneth's wars, and Bruce's days,
> And when the Romans fled their dreadful wrath of yore.
>   (II, 597)

Similarly, the early poem, 'The Hunter', contains many of the elements later, and more successfully, employed in the Ossian poems. In his attempt to render 'Highland' experience Macpherson uses stock poetic diction and the heroic couplet throughout the ten cantos. Banal, and sometimes utterly incongruous, effect is the result. The poem opens thus:

> Once on a time, when Liberty was seen
> To sport and revel on the northern plain,
> Immortal fair! and was supremely kind
> On Scotia's hills to snuff the northern wind;
> There lived a youth, and DONALD was his name.
> To chance the flying stag his highest aim;
> A gun, a plaid, a dog, his humble store;
> In these thrice happy, as he wants no more.
> (II, 465)

But after twenty lines Donald is discarded—temporarily—in favour of the following:

> I chanced the Fairie's king and daughter had,
> A beautious, blooming, and a sportive maid.
> She took delight, upon the flowery lawn
> To frisk, transported, round a female fawn.
> The hunter aims the tube: the powder flies;
> The fawn falls, roars, and shakes her limbs, and dies.
> The blooming Flavia saw her play-thing die;
> Sighs rend her breast, and tears bedew her eye,
> Wrath, sorrow, rage, her tender fabrick rock,
> And thus, indignant, she the silence broke.
> (II, 466)

This is far from being an isolated instance of the co-existence of Scottish rustics and the figures of classical poetry. 'The Cerulean sky and zephyrs' give way to this description of eighteenth-century Edinburgh:

> On rocks a city stands, high-tower'd, unwall'd,
> And from its scite the hill of Edin call'd,
> Once the proud seat of royalty and state,
> Of kings and heroes, and of all that's great;
> But these are flown, and Edin's only stores
> Are fops, and scriveners, and English'd whores.
> Here blooming Xanthe slopingly descends,
> And, softly lighting, all her journey ends.
> Invisible; for Fergus' Scottish line,
> Disdain'd not yet on barren fields to reign.
> (II, 469)

Some of Macpherson's excursions into poetic diction (often sub-Miltonic) are far from happy ('He snored aloud; the palace thundered round/And repercussive walls repel the sound'; and (of 'the faithful hound') 'But once let loose, he snuffs the gelid wind,/And leaves the winged blast to puff behind'). Too often the ascent to the grand manner ends in bathos (witness the Scottish king's rallying-cry to repel the English—'Rise, Caledonian chiefs! ye heroes, rise!/Your bleeding country for your succour cries').

'The Hunter' is directed at both national pride and sensibility. Inspired by Liberty, the Scots vanquish the English, with Donald meeting Prince Henry in single combat; the description of the return of the triumphant army to Edinburgh includes

> Amidst the crowd the fond maternal eye
> Seeks out her son, her young and only joy:
> Sometimes she hopes, and then she trembling fears,
> And down the furrowed cheeks descend the tears;
>
> (II, 491)

and the minstrel sings at length of previous Scottish victories. Exemplifying the principle of contrast which was to be integral to *Fingal* and *Temora*, Macpherson devotes Canto VI to an account of the king's daughter's falling in love with Donald, the hunter, and in Canto VII he is shown to be torn between the rival claims of his loved one, at court in Edinburgh, and the mountains of his home. In what may be an echo of Home's *Douglas* the hunter is found to be the grandson and heir of a lord; thus, as 'No horrid herdsman, no indecent hind/Of clownish manners or rapacious mind' (II, 522), he is fit husband for the princess Egidia. All in all, the poem is a strange mixture of proto-Ossianic features and some of the tritest elements of diction and plot.

'The Highlander' is rather more successful, though it has clear traces of the same weaknesses—bombast, bathos, and repetitive diction (here the favourite term is 'sable'). Once again, as these lines show, the marriage of Scottish subject-matter and stock poetic diction and forms is not always a happy one:

> Heaven's opening portals shot the beam of day;
> Earth changed her sable robe to sprightly grey;
> To west's dark goal the humid night is fled;
> The sun o'er ocean rears his beamy head;
> The splendid gleam from Scottish steel returns,
> And all the light reflexive mountains burns.
> Deep-sounding bag-pipes, gaining on the air,
> With lofty voice awake the Scottish war.
>
> ...   .
>
> Each clan their standards from the beam unbind;
> They float along, and clap upon the wind:
> The hieroglyphic honours of the brave
> Acquire a double horror as they wave.
>
> (II, 536)

The poem—actually concerned with the Caledonians and their hero, Alpin, fighting the Danes—begins with this obvious glance in the direction of the Young Pretender:

> The youth I sing, who, to himself unknown,
> Lost he the world, and CALEDONIA'S throne,
> Sprung o'er his mountains to the arms of Fame,
> And, winged by Fate, his sire's avenger came;
> That knowledge learn'd so long deny'd by Fate,
> And found that blood, as merit, made him great.
>
> (II, 527)

Clearly implied is the identification of the Jacobite cause with the heroic ethos as exemplified in the Scottish-Danish War (Haco, a Danish warrior, enjoins Alpin, 'Accept, brave man, the friendship of a Dane,/Who hates the Scot, but yet can love the man' (II, 534)). Such sentiments, rarefied still further, were to be transposed to an even remoter Scottish past as part of the ethos of the world of Ossian. And as if to balance the Jacobite sentiments of the early part of the poem, Macpherson shrewdly incorporates later a hermit's vision of Caledonia's history which concludes with an endorsement of the Union (II, 570).

Macpherson's poems, and 'The Highlander' in particular, were not received with the favour which he believed they merited. Laing's preface includes contemporary testimony that

> Mr Macpherson had declared . . . that having given an exceeding good poem to the public, which passed unnoticed, he then published as ancient, some fragments of his own, which were so much applauded, that henceforth he resolved to give the world enough of such ancient poetry. (I, xxi)

Personal disappointment should be recognised as another of the factors that led to his offering his own compositions as the poems of Ossian.

The importance of the meeting on the bowling-green at Moffat between Macpherson and John Home, the latter already avidly interested in Celtic antiquities, has been widely noted; and there is no need to retell the tale of Macpherson's rise to eminence. Suffice it to say that Macpherson cleverly whetted an existing appetite with his *Fragments of Ancient Poetry*, only to strengthen and satisfy it with the subsequent publication of the *Poems of Ossian*. In the preface Blair, writing from Macpherson's information, designated the *Fragments* 'the genuine remains of ancient Scottish poetry' (II, 381). The poems were held to 'abound with those ideas, and paint those manners, that belong to the most early state of society'. Since there is no mention of clanship it is held that they must predate that institution; and Ossian's disdainful response to the Culdee, or monk, suggests they are 'coeval with the very infancy of Christianity in Scotland'. It is confidently asserted that 'these poems are to be ascribed to the bards'.

Fragment VII, the first specimen of Celtic poetry which Macpherson produced, begins with this lament of Ossian:

> Why openest thou afresh the spring of my grief, O son of Alpin, inquiring how Oscur fell? My eyes are blind with tears; but memory beams on my heart. How can I relate the mournful death of the head of the people? Prince of the warriors, Oscur, my son, shall I see thee no more! (II, 393–4)

Macpherson so created the ethos of the distant heroic age that it would appeal immediately and strongly to the age of sensibility. Ossian tells in this fragment of the warriors Oscur and Dermid whose friendship 'was strong as their steel'. Each fell in love with the daughter of Dargo who 'was fair as the moon; mild as the beam of night. Her eyes, like two stars in a shower: her breath, the gale of spring: her breasts, as the new fallen snow floating on the moving heath' (there seems a clear link between this and the *blason* of the courtly-love tradition). 'Each loved her as his fame', the poet tells us, 'each must possess her or die'. Here is the description of the inevitable combat:

> They fought by the brook of the mountain, by the streams of Branno. Blood tinged the silvery stream, and curdled round the mossy stones. Dermid the graceful fell; fell, and smiled in death.

Oscur, grieving over his loss of renown and honour, contrives 'to be slain by his mistress'. She, desolate with grief, kills herself (with Macpherson claiming this is manifestly an interpolation since suicide was unknown to the people of that heroic age). Ossian ends the account thus:

> By the brook of the hill their graves are laid; a birch's unequal shade covers their tomb. Often on their green earthy tombs the branchy sons of the mountain feed, when mid-day is all in flames, and silence is over all the hills.

This fragment exemplifies most of what were to be the major components of the *Poems of Ossian*: the predominant note of melancholy; the evocative use of landscape; the close relationship between man and natural world (this is reinforced by the propensity to man-nature analogies and similes), and in particular the attempt to suggest that such a relationship was an integral and natural part of such a people's way of seeing; the heroic deeds and noble emotions; the love interest, including the pleasingly sensuous description of the lady, and its termination in tragic irony; and the importance to such people of the heroic values of fame and honour.

Most of these features are variously present in each of the *Fragments*. Fragment I opens with these words of 'Vinvela', from which it is easy to see the nature of the appeal to the English and Lowland Scots readers at whom they were carefully aimed:

> My love is a son of the hill. He pursues the flying deer. His gray dogs are panting around him; his bow-string sounds in the wind. Whether by the fount of the rock, or by the stream of the mountain thou liest; when the rushes are nodding with the wind, and the mist is flying over thee, let me approach my love unperceived, and see him from the rock. Lovely I saw thee first by the aged oak of

Branno; thou wert returning tall from the chace; the fairest among thy friends.
(II, 385)

Macpherson was inviting the new bourgeoisie to live vicariously in terms of magnitude of deed and intensity of emotion. Here, for instance, the warrior Garve proclaims his might:

> He answered like a wave on the rock; who is like me here? The valiant live not with me; they go to the earth from my hand. The king of the desert of hills alone can fight with Garve. Once we wrestled on the hill. Our heels overturned the wood. Rocks fell from their place, and rivulets changed their course. Three days we strove together; heroes stood at a distance, and feared. On the fourth, the king saith that I fell; but Garve saith, he stood. Let Cuchulaid yield to him that is strong as a storm. (II, 409)

To an increasingly urban readership Macpherson played upon the attractions of wild landscape. Here, as on many occasions, landscape assumes a symbolic dimension:

> Raise high the stones; collect the earth: preserve the name of Fear-comhraic. Blow, winds, from all your hills; sigh on the grave of Muirnin.
> The dark rock hangs, with all its wood, above the calm dwelling of the heroes.
> The sea, with its foam-headed billow, murmurs at their side.
> Why sigh the woods, why roar the waves; They have no cause to mourn.
>
> (II, 405–6)

Undeniably, Macpherson anticipates the Romantics, and Wordsworth in particular, in such symbolic use of landscape, and in rendering a natural world which can reflect and embody the emotions of the human participants he formulates a version of what Ruskin was later to term 'the pathetic fallacy'. Here, for instance, is the opening of Fragment XV:

> Morna thou fairest of women, daughter of Cormac-Carbre; why in the circle of stones, in the cave of the rock, alone! The stream murmureth hoarsely. The blast groaneth in the aged tree. The lake is troubled before thee. Dark are the clouds of the sky. But thou art like snow on the heath. Thy hair like a thin cloud of gold on the top of Cromleach. Thy breasts like two smooth rocks on the hill, which is seen from the stream of Brannuin. Thy arms, as two white pillars in the hall of Fingal. (II, 409–10)

Common to each of the fragments are the pervasive mood of melancholy and the blatant appeals to the readers' emotions, especially that of pity. Fragment IX ends, 'Thou has heard this tale of grief, O fair daughter of the isles! Rivine was fair as thyself: shed on her grave a tear' (II, 399). Habitually Ossian laments the loss of long-dead friends and recounts their heroic deeds, always with the implication that heroic practices are themselves in decline. In Fragment VIII Ossian, having recalled both brave deeds and a beautiful maid, ends with this address to the long-dead Fingal:

> Such, Fingal! were thy words; but thy words I hear no more. Sightless I sit by
> thy tomb. I hear the wind in the wood; but no more I hear my friends. The cry
> of the hunter is over. The voice of war is ceased. (II, 397)

And in one of the poems there is explicit acknowledgement of the pleasures
of melancholy. Fragment XII includes these words of Ryno: 'Sweet are thy
murmurs, O stream! but more sweet is the voice I hear. It is the voice of Alpin,
the son of song, mourning for the dead' (II, 404).

In an age when melancholic sensibility was the rage of Europe Macpherson
played subtly upon Scottish patriotism by implying Scottish pre-eminence in
precisely this quality: to the ancient Scots it had come naturally, while
contemporary Scots would demonstrate that the race continued to exemplify
this capacity in their response to his translations. In his preface to the *Fragments*, after explaining that some had been handed down in manuscript
form while the majority formed part of the oral tradition, he observed that
'tradition, in a country so free from intermixture with foreigners, and among
a people so strongly attached to the memory of their ancestors, has preserved
many of them in a great measure uncorrupted to this day' (II, 383). Equally
astutely, he stated that there must be other such works extant and suggested
that one, 'an heroic poem, might be recovered and translated, if encouragement were given to such an undertaking', intimating also that the subject
of the poem was the invasion of Ireland by the Danes and their subsequent
expulsion by the Scots, under Fingal, who had come to the aid of Cuchulaid.

The response of the Scottish literary establishment, given their antiquarian
interests, their patriotic desire that a Scotland within the Union might boast,
as England did, of its own epic (but Scotland's would be older!), and their
pride in their sensibility, was all that Macpherson might have wished. Of the
joyful response of the *literati* Laing remarked, 'it appears that the ambiguity
of the fragments was implicitly admitted, because they teemed with the
sentimental cant which was then in vogue' (I, xiv). (That this comment was
made in 1805 indicates that the vogue of sensibility did not endure in every
Scottish quarter—not all were swept on an unbroken wave of sentiment
from Macpherson to the Kailyard). Blair actively set about a scheme for
'encouraging Mr Macpherson to apply himself to the making a further collection of Earse poetry, and particularly for recovering *our epic*' (I, xvi). While
wishing that Macpherson might find 'more of these wild flowers', Hume
voiced this doubt: 'If a regular epic poem, or even anything of that kind,
nearly regular, should also come from that rough climate, or uncivilised
people, it would appear to me a phenomenon altogether unaccountable.'[20]
Such misgivings were rare in Scottish circles, however, and, with a sub-
scription raised by the *literati*, Macpherson set out to search the Highlands
and Islands for Scotland's epic, already knowing well what he would find.

The result was the publication, in 1761, of *Fingal*, with Macpherson's
acknowledgement of 'the generosity of a certain noble person' (I, lviii), the
Prime Minister, Lord Bute. The material of the poem was a fusion of Celtic
ballads and lays and history of Scotland in the time of both the Roman and
the Danish invasions, while the style revealed Macpherson's extensive reading

of classical epics, the Bible, and a range of English and Scottish poets that included Milton, Pope, and Thomson. For various reasons Macpherson chose to write an epic: it was regarded as the pre-eminent poetic form, and Scotland must have its representative; its nobility of mode made it the perfect medium for rendering purity of emotion (Chapman has noted that in 1736 Thomas Blackwell observed of the age of Homer that it had 'natural and simple Manners: it is irresistible and inchanting; they best shew human Wants and Feelings; they give us back the emotions of an arteless Mind');[21] and although publicly he could acknowledge only the praise due to a translator he would have the private satisfaction of having mastered a major literary form.

As Macpherson was well aware (and he had Blair to remind him), the epic was subject to various rules. The preface to the first edition finds him remarking, 'How far it comes up to the rules of the epopaea, is the province of criticism to examine. It is only my business to lay it before the reader, as I have found it' (I, lxii). Both allusions to, and similarities with, classical epics abound. Macpherson takes care to ensure that the reader detects similarities by offering footnotes such as 'The reader may compare this passage with a similar one in Homer' (I, 35, n. 49). The epigraph—*Fortia facta patrum*—is from Virgil; epic similes are in abundance; and apostrophes appear with a frequency which is, in fact, more typical of neoclassical poetry. By analogy with the temporary removal of Achilles from the action of the *Iliad*, Macpherson diverts attention from Fingal for a time and notes, 'The poet, by an artifice, removes Fingal, that his return may be the more magnificent' (I, 113, n. 30). Blair compared favourably Ossian's aggrandising of Fingal with 'Homer's art in magnifying the character of Achilles' (I, 137, n. 23). In one particular respect Macpherson, with characteristic nerve, claims that Ossian has excelled beyond the achievement of other epic poets. *Fingal* ends thus: '"Spread the sail", said the king, "seize the winds as they pour from Lena." We rose on the wave with songs. We rushed, with joy, through the foam of the deep' (I, 206), and Macpherson comments approvingly,

> It is allowed by the best critics, that an epic poem ought to end happily. This rule, in its most material circumstances, is observed by the three most deservedly celebrated epic poets, Homer, Virgil and Milton; yet, I know not how it happens, the conclusions of their poems throw a melancholy damp on the mind. One leaves his reader at a funeral; another at the untimely death of a hero; and a third at the solitary scenes of an unpeopled world (I, 206, n. 26).

After the recurrent sadness of *Fingal* Macpherson opts to end on a note of qualified optimism.

Foremost among the 'best critics' in Macpherson's case was Blair, who pronounced as follows on *Fingal*: 'Examined even according to Aristotle's rules, it will be found to have all the essential requisites of a true and regular epic; and to have several of them in so high a degree, as at first view to raise our astonishment on finding Ossian's composition so agreeable to rules of which he was entirely ignorant.'[22] As John MacQueen has noted, the intention was that 'in the works of Ossian the resemblances were to be attributed to nature rather than to imitation or derivation'.[23]

Likewise, the heroic ethos was to be attributed to Nature. The people of the Ossian poems are characterised by their chivalry of deed, purity of morals, emotional integrity, and refinement of manners. Misfortune is the result not of the malign actions of others but of tragic irony of circumstances (plainly Macpherson was conversant with classical tragedy as well as classical epic). Friend and foe alike adhere to heroic codes of behaviour. The closest approximations to villains are those who are induced to rebel by imagined slight to their honour. The principal values of Macpherson's Celts are courage (as, for instance, in Cuthullin's speech of defiance in the face of Swaran's attack (I, 68), and his claim, 'Danger flies from the lifted sword. They best succeed who dare! (I, 97)); pride in one's fame (see, for example, the description of Cuthullin's mourning the loss of his fame (I, 174–5)); pride in one's honour (Fingal rebukes Connan for upbraiding Cuthullin with pusillanimity (I, 203–4)); and magnanimity towards the vanquished (see, for instance, the terms on which Fingal and Swaran part (I, 193–5)).

But what characterises the world of Macpherson's epic, and what especially distinguishes it from the classical epic, is the pervasive melancholy within which all else—heroism, love, honour—is subsumed. Macpherson misses no opportunity for pathos. In pursuit of the enemy, Fingal encounters Orla, a chief of Lochlin and already a casualty, whereupon the following exchange takes place:

> 'King of Morven', said the hero, 'lift thy sword and pierce my breast. Wounded and faint from battle, my friends have left me here. The mournful tale shall come to my love, on the banks of the streamy Lota; when she is alone in the wood; and the rustling blast in the leaves'! 'No'; said the king of Morven, 'I will never wound thee, Orla. On the banks of Lota let her see thee, escaped from the hands of war. Let thy grey-haired father who, perhaps, is blind with age. Let him hear the sound of thy voice, and brighten within his hall. With joy let the hero rise, and search for his son with his hands'! 'But never will he find him, Fingal'; said the youth of the streamy Lota. 'On Lena's heath I must die: foreign bards shall talk of me. My broad belt covers my wound of death. I give it to the wind'! (I, 161–2)

So moved is Fingal by the death of Orla that he orders the pursuit of the enemy to be halted. When his sons assemble he learns that the youngest, Ryno, has been killed, whereupon 'the tear is on the cheek of the king, for terrible was his son in war' (I, 164). What Macpherson is attempting in such episodes is to graft on to the heroism traditional to the epic the compulsive pathos of the age of sensibility. Now John MacQueen has pointed out that this distinguishes Macpherson's poems from the Gaelic bardic poetry of the seventeenth and eighteenth centuries (up to the 'Forty-Five) which is characterised 'by the confidence of the Gaels in the permanence, as well as the excellence, of the old order, even when it was visibly crumbling before their eyes'.[24] And Smart, remarking that 'Ossianic legend is free from that strain of overwrought melancholy which Macpherson sustains in unbroken monotone',[25] shows how the writers of the genuine ballads turn for relief to the grotesque, exaggerated claims, and jokes. Macpherson studiously avoids such elements in the older Scottish tradition as disruptive of the mood which he wishes to prevail.

One result of the transposition of sensibility to earlier times is that while many battles are mentioned the details given are fewer than in the accounts of Homer, Virgil, and Milton. Here, by way of partial exception, Ossian describes the first encounter between the armies of Fingal and Swaran:

> Ryno went on like a pillar of fire. Dark is the brow of Gaul. Fergus rushed forwards with feet of wind. Fillan, like the mist of the hill. Ossian, like a rock, came down. I exulted in the strength of the king. Many were the deaths of my arm! dismal the gleam of my sword! My locks were not then so grey; nor trembled my hands with age. My eyes were not closed in darkness; my feet failed not in the race!
> Who can relate the deaths of the people? Who the deeds of mighty heroes? when Fingal, burning in his wrath, consumed the sons of Lochlin? groans swelled on groans from hill to hill, till night had covered all. Pale, staring like a herd of deer, the sons of Lochlin convene on Lena. We sat and heard the sprightly harp, at Lubar's gentle stream. (I, 106–8)

As might be indicated by a description of battle that contains direct appeals to sensibility, Macpherson's main interest is in the pathos attendant upon the personal situation. The above account is followed by Fingal's anecdote of the tragic death of Fainasollis, whom he had guarded in his youth. The anecdote ends thus:

> The maid stood trembling by my side. He drew the bow. She fell. 'Unerring is thy hand', I said, 'but feeble was the foe'! We fought, nor weak the strife of death! He sunk beneath my sword. We laid them in two tombs of stone; the hapless lovers of youth! Such have I been in my youth, O Oscar; be thou like the age of Fingal. Never search thou for battle, nor shun it when it comes. (I, 112)

Thereupon Fillan and Oscar are despatched by Fingal to keep watch upon the enemy. This patterned alternation between anecdote (invariably both exemplary and pathetic) and present action, between creating pathos and arousing admiration for heroic achievement, characterises Macpherson's method. Before battle is joined once more, Ossian recounts his courtship of Evirallin and her death. She is the subject of a poignant conversation between Ossian and his son, Oscar, which is interrupted thus: 'Such were our words, when Gaul's loud voice came growing on the wind. He waved on high the sword of his father. We rushed to death and wounds . . .' (I, 133)

The appeal to sensibility takes precedence over narration of action, and often heroic deed seems of significance not primarily in its own right but rather in terms of the pathetic situation to which it will, sometimes inadvertently, give rise. This effect is compounded by the recurrence of Ossian's own habitual melancholy. The exuberant heroic activism, exemplified in the hunt, the combat, the feast, is offset by the regular appearance of the lugubrious narrator. Here Fingal's reassurance to Cuthullin that he will again be victorious and that he will recover his fame, and the ensuing feasting and singing, are qualified by the intrusion of Ossian's note of personal regret:

> We sat. We feasted. We sung. The soul of Cuthullin rose. The strength of his arm returned. Gladness brightened along his face. Ullin gave the song; Carril raised the voice. I joined the bards, and sung of battles of the spear. Battles! where I often fought. Now I fight no more! The fame of my former deeds is ceased. I sit forlorn at the tomb of my friends! (I, 205)

It is noticeable that Ossian seems relatively detached from the distant battles which he recalls from old age and is prone to objectify his participation in terms of 'Ossian did . . .', whereas the lamentation—for loss of friends, kin, honour, courage—in which he engages while narrating is immediate.

Macpherson's aim—in which he is at least partly successful—was the creation of a distinctive ethos and a way of seeing that might readily be associated with the ancient Celts. Such a *weltanschauung* had to be sufficiently discrete to be authentic but had still to be within the responsive compass of the eighteenth-century reader of taste and sensibility; and if, without being too blatant about it, it could catch the resonances of, and so stimulate further, the debate about the origins and development of society, so much the better. For this Macpherson carefully prepared the reader in the following passage in his preface to the first edition:

> If our fathers had not so much wealth, they had certainly fewer vices than the present age. Their tables, it is true, were not so well provided, neither were their beds so soft as those of modern times; and this, in the eyes of men, who place their ultimate happiness in those conveniences of life, gives us a great advantage over them. I shall not enter farther into this subject, but only observe, that the general poverty of a nation has not the same influence, that the indigence of individuals, in an opulent country, has upon the manners of the community. The idea of meanness, which is now connected with a narrow fortune, had its rise after commerce had thrown too much property into the hands of a few; for the poorer sort, imitating the vices of the rich, were obliged to have recourse to roguery and circumvention, in order to supply their extravagance, so that they were, not without reason, reckoned in more than one sense, the worst of the people. (I, lxi–lxii)

By his use of language Macpherson succeeds in conveying the distinctive values, experiences, and perspective of his ancient Celts. In this context a simple sentence such as 'He sent Ullin of songs to bid him to the feast of shells' (I, 103) can be highly effective; likewise 'the strength of the shells goes round. The souls of warriors brighten with joy' (I, 184). By repetition in episode after episode Macpherson makes credible a people whose prime concerns are valour, honour, fame, and a sense of transience. Without attributing to them any specific religious orthodoxy he succeeds in investing them with a rather vague awareness of a spiritual dimension to life. On one occasion Ossian states, 'Fingal, like a beam from heaven, shone in the midst of his people' (I,

139). Cuthullin offers this speech which is capable of a loosely religious interpretation:

> 'Blessed be her soul'; said Cuthullin, 'blessed be the mouth of the song! Strong was the youth of Fingal; strong is his arm of age. Lochlin shall fall again before the king echoing Morven. Shew thy face from a cloud, O moon; light his white sails on the wave: And if any strong spirit of heaven sits on that low-hung cloud; turn his dark ships from the rock, thou rider of the storm! (I, 95–6).

But Macpherson's commentary sounds this deliberately equivocal note:

> This is the only passage in the poem that has the appearance of religion. But Cuthullin's apostrophe to this spirit is accompanied with a doubt, so that it is not easy to determine whether the hero meant a superior being, or the ghosts of deceased warriors, who were supposed in those times to rule the storms, and to transport themselves in a gust of wind from one country to another. (I, 95, n. 7)

In an earlier note Macpherson suggests that his warriors 'thought the soul was material, something like the εἴδωλον of the ancient Greeks' (I, 62, n. 9). Such notes are intended to provide the reader with toe-holds on the ascent into the allegedly distant world.

It is especially in his rendering of the natural world that Macpherson expresses the particular perspective of his Celts. They are presented as people for whom the natural world plays a central part in both experience and the expression of it. Frequently, intensity of feeling is reflected in the sympathetic landscape. Landscape, animals, weather—these are important to such people, and since they loom large in their terms of reference they also provide the means of analogy or the basis of image. Grumal's flight before the army of Swaran is described as follows: 'He fled like the stag of Morven; his spear is a trembling beam of light behind him' (I, 74). This way of seeing and describing is not peculiar to Ossian the bard; others exemplify it in their speech. Here, for instance, Swaran addresses Fingal: ' "Blest be thy soul, thou king of shells", said Swaran of the dark-brown shield. "In peace thou art the gale of spring. In war the mountain-storm" ' (I, 194). Paradoxically, the repetitiveness of imagery serves to further define, and hence authenticate, the distinctive way of seeing.

Instrumental in the rendering of that way of seeing is the highly rhythmical prose, the creation of which is one of Macpherson's foremost achievements. Macpherson's rhythmical prose—evocative at times of the Old Testament—is emotive (generally poignantly so) and does much to convey the nature and perspective of the people. Here, for instance, the episode of Comal and Galvina is introduced:

> Comal was a son of Albion; the chief of an hundred hills! His deer drunk of a thousand streams. A thousand rocks replied to the voice of his dogs. His face was the mildness of youth. His hand the death of heroes. One was his love, and fair was she! The daughter of mighty Conloch. She appeared like a sun-beam among women. Her hair was the wing of the raven. Her dogs were taught to the chace.

Her bow-string sounded on the winds. Her soul was fixed on Comal. Often met their eyes of love. Their course in the chace was one. Happy were their words in secret. But Grumal loved the maid, the dark chief of the gloomy Ardven. He watched her lone steps in the heath; the foe of unhappy Comal! (I, 81–2)

The use of prose rhythms to convey rhythms of mood and emotion in such passages is masterly. In attempting to account for the continued popularity of the poems long after the deception had been publicised, Laing claimed, with some justification, that 'the secret consisted in the measured prose which the translator adopted, and brought to perfection; and from the novelty of which, the public was unable to recognize its own poetry when clothed in prose sublime, and transformed into bombast' (I, 207).

Sublimity and pathos are the aims of Macpherson's method which, allowing for the pace at which the epic was written, shows some artistry. Book IV, largely concerned with Ossian's recollection of his youthful heroism and courtship, is justified thus: 'The action of the poem being suspended by night, Ossian takes the opportunity to relate his own actions at the lake of Lego, and his courtship of Evirallin, who was the mother of Oscar, and had died some time before the expedition of Fingal into Ireland' (I, 119). This episode serves to offer personal exemplification of the main concerns of the poem, to characterise further the narrator, and to permit of typically Ossianic lamentation and nostalgia. Generally the *raison d'être* for the episode is its potential for emotional appeal. In a note, Macpherson claims that the story of the death of Orla 'is so beautiful and affecting in the original, that many are in possession of it in the north of Scotland, who never heard a syllable more of it in the poem' (I, 159, n. 10). No such original has ever been found; rather, Macpherson invented the story (and that of the death of Agandecca) in the interests of pathos. Similarly, that book (Book V) ends with an anecdote that evokes melancholy and poignant recollection in the narrator. Generally skilled in the structuring of material, Macpherson is particularly adept in the juxtaposition of events. Early in Book III is an exuberant account of a lively boar-hunt, in the course of which Starno's daughter warns Fingal that her father threatens his life (I, 93); and Book VI in its entirety is a model of this patterned structuring of material.

Macpherson was highly selective also in the use which he made of such source material as the *Agricola* of Tacitus and Toland's *History of the Druids*. He took liberties with dates and settings, as Laing noted (I, 166–7, n. 15; I, 193, n. 8), but it is worth recognising that anachronism is a feature of the genuine ballads also since, as Smart remarks, 'tradition knows nothing of dates'.[26] In particular, Macpherson invented the ancient kingdom of Morven and converted the Irish chief, Finn, into Fingal, its king. By claiming a whole body of Celtic mythology as Scotland's property Macpherson, as Smart points out, 'enlisted upon his own side the patriotism and partiality of his countrymen, and made his defence seem a national duty'.[27] Again, Macpherson selects from the ballads according to his purpose. A dialogue between Ossian and Saint Patrick is omitted, presumably because it would contradict Macpherson's claims for the dating of the poems. Celebrated in Ossianic legend is the tale of the slaying of the boar by Dermid, but Macpherson omits this entirely, probably because Fingal's part in the episode reveals him as less than perfect. Macpherson follows a note on Allad, a Druid, with this statement: 'From the druids, no doubt, came the ridiculous notion of the second sight, which prevailed in the Highland and Isles' (I, 169, n. 18). Quite ruthlessly, Macpherson takes what he wants from Highland lore and clothes his creations in a vague mystique, but, as a child of Enlightenment rationalism, he cannot allow his people to behave entirely irrationally and he demeans those in the ballads who do.

Fingal, then, is not epic in the classical tradition or reliable Celtic history or authentic Celtic literature: it is a creative conflation of aspects of each of these to meet the early needs of the vogue of sensibility (and, as such, it did much to strengthen that vogue). This is the explanation of melodramatic episodes such as the tale of Comal and Galbina, which concludes,

> He went to the deer of Mora. The daughter of Conloch would try his love. She cloathed her fair sides with his armour; she strode from the cave of Ronan! He thought it was his foe. His heart beat high. His colour changed, and darkness dimmed his eyes. He drew the bow. The arrow flew. Galbina fell in blood! He run with wildness in his steps: he called the daughter of Conloch. No answer in the lonely rock. 'Where art thou, O my love?' He saw, at length, her heaving heart, beating around the arrow he threw. 'O Conloch's daughter, is it thou?' He sunk upon her breast. (I, 83)

It is the explanation too of the sensuous descriptions of attractive maidens in their grief, such as 'She came with the red eye of tears. She came with loosely flowing locks. Her white breast heaved with broken sighs, like the foam of the streamy Lubar' (I, 94). So, too, Macpherson exploits the possibilities of landscape, mood, and superstition to play upon the emotions of fear and horror in such a way as to place him alongside Smollett, Mackenzie, and Burns (and, later, Scott, Hogg, and Stevenson) as contributors to what may be termed 'Scottish Gothic'. Despite his gibes at the ballads, it suits Macpherson to begin Book II by separating Connal from the rest of the army as prelude to his being visited by the ghost of Crugal. Macpherson approves thus of Ossian's stratagem: 'The scene here described will appear natural to those who have been in the Highlands of Scotland. The poet removes him (Connal) to a distance from the army, to add more horror to the description of Crugal's ghost, by the loneliness of the place' (I, 57, n. 1).

It is an ironic reflection of the entrepreneurial talents which the competitive stimulus of the Union seems to have fostered that it was a Scot who purveyed what was, *par excellence,* the age of sensibility's version of Celtic antiquity. If the Highland landscapes were unequalled in their potential for sublimity, there was in the Scottish character a reductive tendency which surfaces, presumably unintentionally, in Macpherson's writing and is reflected most frequently in a realist-materialist sense. This accounts for such incongruities as 'He half-assumed the spear' (I, 136), and for the disruption of mood and tone by the intrusion of the 'snorting horse' and 'hard polished bits' into the description of Cuthullin's war-chariot (I, 31–2).

Scottish attempts at sublimity have a habit of coming to grief in this way. The reductive strain served the comic talents of Smollett and Burns extremely well; it had no place in the lachrymose sublimity of Macpherson's scheme.

It was—and again there is perhaps a certain ironic appropriateness in this—a Scot who produced what is a *tour de force* of compromise. For Macpherson, the character of the Caledonians was 'happily compounded of what is noble in barbarity and virtuous and generous in a polished people'.[28] In Scott's view, Fingal united the bravery of Achilles with the courtesy, sentiment, and high-breeding of Sir Charles Grandison.[29] Himself averse to romance and, as Smart has noted, under the guidance of Blair 'pedantically attached to classical rules',[30] Macpherson yet presented proto-Romantic material. Subject-matter that by its nature was helping to bring down neoclassicism was presented in accordance with the practice of Homer and Virgil and the rules of Aristotle and Horace (and all interpreted by Blair).

One of the ironies is that if Macpherson, instead of offering his own verses as someone else's, had acknowledged them as his own he would not have enjoyed immediate and wide-ranging celebrity but the considerable merits of those verses would have been recognised. Macpherson's mistake was not in imitating. It is only since the Romantic movement's exemplification of individuality of vision and originality of expression that imitation has become in any sense reprehensible. It was common practice in the eighteenth century and earlier. Shakespeare's reworking of source material, and the extent to which his plays 'inspired' eighteenth-century dramatists offer obvious exemplification. In fairness to Macpherson it has to be recognised that some critics and editors (pre-eminently Laing) took to extremes the business of source-hunting, claiming derivation where the most everyday terms were involved.[31] Many of the terms which Laing deems deliberate borrowings are, rather, those which might reasonably have been retained in the mind of the intelligent and widely-read young man that Macpherson was. It should also be conceded that on many of the occasions where there is a specific and identifiable source of inspiration Macpherson does something with the borrowed material— builds upon it, adapts it, sets it to a new use, or achieves a different effect. Laing is much troubled by the recurrent whale-similes and finds the original in *Paradise Lost*, VII, 41, but in this description of Cuthullin, for instance, Macpherson develops it to significant effect: 'The chief, like a whale of ocean, whom all his billows pursue, poured valour forth, as a stream, rolling his might along the shore' (I, 28). Likewise, Cuthullin's injunction, 'Bid the king of Morven come. O let him come, like the sun in a storm, to lighten, to restore the isle' (I, 98), is traced by Laing to the line in *Troilus and Cressida*, I, i—'As when the sun doth light a storm'. If there is any debt at all here, Macpherson has more than repaid it by the vivid and moving effect he achieves.[32]

Of the *Poems of Ossian* Matthew Arnold commented, 'Make the part of what is forged, modern, tawdry, spurious, in the book as large as you please . . . But there will still be left in the book a residue with the very soul of the Celtic genius in it.'[33] Malcolm Chapman takes to task Arnold and like-minded critics, such as D M Stuart who found in Macpherson's work 'a curious quality, Celtic and crepuscular, elusive yet pervasive, not to be matched in any antecedent English prose or verse'.[34] Chapman's concern is with the illogicality of accepting that the poems are counterfeit but claiming that they epitomise Celtic qualities. A more valid judgement is reached by dropping the term, 'Celtic', from Arnold's and Stuart's claims, for the quality of the poems is distinctive and is much more than the sum of Macpherson's borrowings, as the following short extract shows:

> We gave the song to the kings. An hundred harps mixed their sound with our voice. The face of Swaran brightened, like the full moon of heaven, when the clouds vanish away, and leave her calm and broad, in the midst of the sky! (I, 196)

Along with *Fingal* and the later epic, *Temora* (1763), Macpherson published other poems allegedly by Ossian. Indeed there are signs that Macpherson thought in terms of the entire corpus as a composite record: 'The Death of Cuthullin' prepares the way for *Temora*, and 'Carthon' contains Macpherson's note that 'Fingal returns here, from an expedition against the Romans, which was celebrated by Ossian in a poem called "The Strife of Crona"' (I, 313, n. 7). Read singly, most of the poems are fairly impressive. Read collectively, they consolidate the sense of a distinct ethos—but a hybrid one—and highlight Macpherson's weaknesses and strengths. Foremost among the former are the formulaic alternation between heroic action and romantic complication, and the way in which the characters appear as people from the age of sensibility. In 'Carric-thura', for instance, is this:

> Gladness brightened in the hall. The voice of Ullin was heard; the harp of Selma was strung. Utha rejoiced in his presence, and demanded the song of grief; the big tear hung in her eye, when the soft Crimora spoke. Crimora, the daughter of Rinval, who dwelt at Lotha's roaring stream! The tale was long, but lovely; and pleased the blushing Utha. (I, 439)

Against this has to be set the occasional note of an increasing realism. Here, for instance, is part of a description of a battle in 'Lathmon' where the usual stylised appeal to sensibility has been abandoned:

> It was then the spear of Gaul flew in its strength; it was then his sword arose. Cremor fell; and mighty Leth. Dunthormo struggled in his blood. The steel rushed through Crotho's side, as he bent, he rose on his spear; the black stream poured from the wound, and hissed on the half-extinguished oak. Cathmin saw the steps of the hero behind him; he ascended a blasted tree; but the spear pierced him from behind. Shrieking, panting, he fell. Moss and withered branches pursue his fall, and strew the blue arms of Gaul. (I, 505–6)

Foremost among the strengths of Macpherson's technique are the highly effective use of prose rhythms and the greater modulation thereof (see, for example, I, 233, 242, 354–5), and the mastery of anecdote. The latter is, rather surprisingly, no less evident here than in the epics, with Clessamor's anecdote in 'Carthon' (I, 316–18) epitomising Macpherson's expertise.

In some of the shorter poems, too, are some of Macpherson's most successful evocations of the sublime, with the Address to the Sun in 'Carthon' pre-eminent. In several of the poems, also, Macpherson develops the sense of melancholy's informing and binding man and nature. This is well conveyed in this extract from *Dar-thula*:

> We sat that night in Selma, round the strength of the shell. The wind was abroad, in the oaks. The spirit of the mountain roared. The blast came rustling through the hall, and gently touched my harp. The sound was mournful and low, like the song of the tomb. Fingal heard it first. The crowded sighs of his bosom rose. (I, 401–2)

And throughout the poems there is Ossian as a unifying presence, while at the same time the characterisation of the narrator is consolidated and developed. In *Fingal*, as in several of the shorter poems, Ossian appears troubled by the deeds-words duality by which he is beset in that, as bard, he is at times a spectator rather than a participant (in 'Oina-morul' he remarks, 'I seize the tales, as they pass, and pour them forth in song' (II, 341–2)). When, in 'Calthon and Colmal', Fingal despatches Ossian on a war-mission he responds thus: 'I rejoiced in the words of the king. I took my rattling arms' (I, 479). That Ossian should feel the need to demonstrate his heroic prowess and should rejoice when he has the opportunity to do so is a neat piece of psychological realism on Macpherson's part. In 'Lathmon' Ossian's pleasure on being sent on a war-mission provides a base on which to build and make credible the suggestion of a spiritual dimension inherent within the heroic ethos, something which is present in Ossian's ensuing account, 'I saw Gaul in his arms; my soul was mixed with his . . .' (I, 498), and in the conversation between him and Gaul (I, 500–1).

Of all these poems it is 'Berrathon' that best exemplifies the conflation of elements, the compromise, which underlines Macpherson's method of achievement. Here there is an account of battle (though not as detailed and personalised as in 'Lathmon') where diction is well chosen and rhythms are well modulated to reinforce sense. This address of Ossian to Uthal, whom he has just killed in single combat, epitomises the idealised natural nobility which Macpherson's readership sought:

> But Uthal fell beneath my sword. The sons of Berrathon fled. It was then I saw him in his beauty, and the tear hung in my eye! 'Thou art fallen, young tree', I said, 'with all thy beauty round thee. Thou art fallen on thy plains, and the field is bare. The winds come from the desert! there is no sound in thy leaves! Lovely art thou in death, son of car-borne Larthmon'. (I, 567–8)

Nina-thoma, who is in love with Uthal, hears of his death as follows:

> She rose pale in her tears. She saw the bloody shield of Uthal. She saw it in Ossian's hand. Her steps were distracted on the heath. She flew. She found him.

> She fell. Her soul came forth in a sigh. Her hair is spread on her face. My bursting
> tears descend. A tomb arose on the unhappy. My song of woe was heard. (I, 568)

The emotional pitch achieved in the pathos attendant upon the distraught maid is reinforced by the spectacle of Ossian shedding sympathetic tears. The intention is that the reader should be moved to identify with him and shed tears also, thus sating his appetite for the joys of grief. Having ended his account, Ossian, in a speech that is both sad and proud, contemplates his past deeds and his approaching death. Macpherson's depiction of the flux and the complexity of emotions is a significant achievement and anticipates that of the Romantics. Here, in a passage that combines psychological credibility with overt appeal to sensibility, Ossian proposes a final song before his death:

> Bring me the harp, son of Alpin. Another song shall rise. My soul shall depart in
> the sound. My fathers shall hear it in their airy hall. Their dim faces shall hang,
> with joy, from their clouds; and their hands receive their son. The aged oak bends
> over the stream. It sighs with all its moss. The withered fern whistles near, and
> mixes, as it waves, with Ossian's hair. (I, 572)

The last song is addressed to his long-dead father, Fingal, whom he hears summoning him to join him in the clouds. The poem ends with Fingal's response, which embraces acceptance of the inevitability of death and affirmation of the enduring glory of life.

John MacQueen has suggested that 'a comparison of the earlier narratives with the later reveals a growing and impressive control over structure and tone'.[35] The increasing technical maturity is reflected in Macpherson's second epic, *Temora*, which was prompted by the success of *Fingal* and Macpherson's obsession, and that of the *literati*, with the epic mode. In the preface to *Temora* Macpherson explains the presence of the properties of the classical epic in the creation of a Celtic bard of the third century AD:

> The title of Epic was imposed on the poem by myself. The technical terms of
> criticism were totally unknown to Ossian. Born in a distant age, and in a country
> remote from the seats of learning, his knowledge did not extend to Greek and
> Roman literature. If, therefore, in the form of his poems, and in several passages
> of his diction, he resembles Homer, the similarity must proceed from nature, the
> original from which both drew their ideas.
>
> ...   .
>
> Though this poem of Ossian has not, perhaps, all the *minutiae* which Aristotle
> from Homer lays down as necessary to the conduct of an epic poem, yet, it is
> presumed, it has all the grand essentials of the epopoea. Unity of time, place, and
> action, is preserved throughout. The poem opens in the midst of things; what is
> necessary of preceding transactions to be known, is introduced by episodes
> afterwards; not formally brought in, but seemingly rising immediately from the
> situation of affairs. The circumstances are grand, and the diction animated;
> neither descending into a cold meanness, nor swelling into ridiculous bombast.
> (II, 6–7)

The subject of *Temora* is appropriate to the epic mode—Fingal's restoration of the Irish royal family after Cairbar has murdered Cormac and usurped the throne. Throughout, Macpherson's notes attest to the artistic integrity and historical accuracy of Ossian, in contrast with what he terms 'the extravagant fictions of the Irish bards' (II, 242, n. 14). Macpherson employs the traditional features of the epic (epic simile; lists of combatants; rigid adherence to time-scheme) and the alleged historical details in a mutually authenticating way. This combines with a stronger awareness of communal life than was evident in *Fingal* to produce a clear sense of a distinct society. And while the prose rhythms are as well modulated as in *Fingal*, Macpherson has refined further his sense of structural rhythm.

Along with the greater communal sense there is, too, a greater interest in the individual, as the increased number of soliloquies suggests. In, for instance, Ossian's soliloquy after the death of Fillan (II, 181–2) Macpherson is largely successful in employing staccato rhythms to convey mental agitation.

In *Temora* Macpherson continues to evince an acute sense of what the current taste demanded: the episode of Bran, Fillan's dog (II, 185–6) is of the essence of sentimentalism; and when Book III ends 'We bend towards the voice of the king. The moon looks abroad from her cloud. The grey-skirted mist is near: the dwelling of ghosts!' (II, 110) the tell-tale exclamation-mark alerts one to the realisation that warriors of the heroic age would be unlikely to respond in this way to the prospect of ghosts. Here, in fact, Macpherson, with the 'superior' attitude with which eighteenth-century rationalism invests him, is exploiting what he deems to be primitive man's response in order to titillate his readers. And, as in *Fingal*, the ever-present Ossian is employed to sustain the predominantly melancholic mood and to voice orthodox sentimentalism in such lines as 'The joy of grief belongs to Ossian, amidst his dark-brown years' (II, 220). The reader is required to—simultaneously—pity, identify, and admire.

Ironically, *Temora* was received less ecstatically than *Fingal*. Of this, Laing commented, 'As the imitations, perhaps, were less frequent, and as all ostentatious imitation of the classics was carefully avoided, the Temora was less pleasing and popular than Fingal' (II, 263–4). There is an important point here, in that part of the immediate popularity of *Fingal* derived from the reassuring echoes of the Bible, the *Iliad*, and Milton, that were to be found, apparently, in the Celtic epic. Eighteenth-century readers could respond to it on a basis of partial familiarity, and the echoes seemed to imply continuity in the literary rendering of human experience. Macpherson won widespread recognition because he assessed accurately what the reading-public wanted. His fame had its origin in a deliberate decision to make his considerable poetic talents subserve his ambition in alliance with his pragmatism. Ironically, the epic poem in which Macpherson emerged as a more independent poetic voice was not the success that *Fingal* had been.[36] Macpherson became caught in a trap which he himself had set. As the popularity of the *Poems of Ossian* spread he found it increasingly difficult to rest content with the reputation of a mere translator, and so to a number of friends and admirers he divulged the secret. And, at the instigation of enthusiasts, he had to proceed with the task of translation into Gaelic, a task for which he was not well equipped. Increasingly one comes to suspect that the habitual concern of Macpherson's Celts with fame and honour (and the loss thereof) and the habitual co-presence of the two terms have a certain psychological significance in terms of Macpherson himself.

Despite Macpherson's duplicity one inescapable fact emerges: he created a world. From the imaginative use of source material he created a world that has substance and appeal (analogies with the work of Tolkien and Peake in this respect are not amiss). The imaginative world was partly built on a lie, but that should not be allowed to overshadow the scale of the achievement.

Macpherson was largely successful in employing language and creating stylistic conventions to render a society with its own distinct values and way of seeing. Not dissimilar were the problems facing William Golding in his attempt in *The Inheritors* to represent neanderthal man.

Macpherson found fame as a literary entrepreneur purveying sentiment, and in, for instance, the later addition to 'Sul-malla of Lumon' of the sentence, 'The rustling sound gently spreads o'er the vale, softly-pleasing as it saddens the soul' (II, 290), there is evidence that he remained responsive to the dictates of taste. But it cannot be denied that he was largely responsible for consolidating the vogue of sensibility across Europe, and, as has been often noted, he influenced a wide range of European authors for half a century. Fraud as in one respect he was, Macpherson made a significant contribution to that major shift in ideas which characterises the latter half of the eighteenth century. Smart notes, 'In his essay *On the Sublime*, Schiller spoke of Ossian, declaring that a truer inspiration lay in the misty mountains and wild cataracts of Scotland than in the fairest of meadows and gardens.'[37] The mountain scenery had appeared, in Anglicised form, in the poetry of Thomson. Macpherson was to present it as follows:

> Autumn is dark on the mountains; grey mist rests on the hills. The whirlwind is heard on the heath. Dark rolls the river through the narrow plain. A tree stands alone on the hill, and marks the slumbering Connal. The leaves whirl round with the wind, and strew the grave of the dead. At times are seen here the ghosts of the departed, while the musing hunter alone stalks slowly over the heath. (I, 442)

By describing it in such evocatively rhythmical prose and by making it the home of his ancient Celts, Macpherson invests such scenery with a mystical grandeur.

In the use of scenery as a source of the sublime Macpherson was plainly a precursor of the Romantics, and of Wordsworth in particular (despite the ill-suppressed anger underlying Wordsworth's 'Written in a Blank Leaf of Macpherson's Ossian' (1827) it seems undeniable that he was influenced). There are, too, points of similarity between both the address to the moon with which 'Darthula' opens (II, 377–9) and the address to the evening star at the beginning of 'The Songs of Selma' and several of the poems of the English Romantics on such topics. Another significant legacy to the Romantics was the fact that Macpherson gave imaginative expression to the growing interest in things medieval. In the *Poems of Ossian* is the first clear indication that the primitive may serve as both repository of, and inspiration for, the spiritual and the visionary. But while, most notably, Coleridge and Keats were to develop this in their poetry, it has to be stressed that it is merely part, one constituent only, of the Romantic response. Wordsworth, Coleridge, and Keats were to recognise contemporary individual experience as the basis of such transcendent vision. And for Goethe (as George Steiner has noted),[38] Byron was the foremost talent of the age—neither classic nor romantic but the incarnation of the new harmony between the antique and the modern spirit.

Equally as important, though arguably less salutary, was Macpherson's influence on Scottish writers. There are Ossianic elements in the setting and the mood of Beattie's *The Minstrel*; and the following lines of Burns's 'Lament for James, Earl of Glencairn' proclaim its inspiration:

> 'I am a bending aged tree,
> That long has stood the wind and rain;
> But now has come a cruel blast
> And my last hold of earth is gane'
>
> . . .   .
>
> 'Awake thy last sad voice, my harp!
> The voice of woe and wild despair!
> Awake, resound thy latest lay,
> Then sleep is silence evermair!'

Byron, too, produced imitations of Ossian entitled 'Oscar of Alva' and 'The Death of Calmar and Orla'. As well as exerting specific influence, the *Poems of Ossian* also fulfilled an important general function in that, in the identity crisis which Scots experienced after the Union which had accelerated the rate of Anglicisation, they served to affirm the continuity of experience. In his *Critical Dissertation on the Poems of Ossian* (1763) Blair wrote,

> In every period of society, human manners are a curious spectacle; and the most natural pictures of antient manners are exhibited in the antient poems of nations. They present to us . . . the history of human imagination and passion. They make us acquainted with the notions and feelings of our fellow creatures in the most artless ages; before those refinements of society had taken place, which enlarge indeed, and diversify the transactions, but disguise the manners of mankind.[39]

If Scots of the mid eighteenth century were uncertain as to who they were they could at least look to *Ossian* for portraits of what they wished to believe were their ancestors.

It should be acknowledged, too, that Macpherson was the prototype of the successful Scottish sentimentalist, and he set an example that was followed eagerly by his contemporaries and descendants (soon Henry Mackenzie was extolling 'the joys of grief').[40] Now if Macpherson established beyond doubt the sentimentalist as one authentic Scottish voice, it might be argued that he

also confirmed another as equally authentic—that of the rôle-player. Soon
Burns was to be enthusing over *Ossian* as one 'of the glorious models after
which I endeavour to form my conduct'.[41] The discovery of Macpherson's
deception dimmed his literary reputation but did not damage his public career.
Writing for the press; political pamphleteering; serving as MP for Camelford;
amassing vast wealth as agent for the Nabob of Arcot; retiring to an Adam-
designed Italianate villa, which he named 'Belleville', at Badenoch—Macpherson's career epitomises the success which awaited a certain kind of
opportunism in the mid eighteenth century (and which, by testimony of their
unpopularity in London in the 1760s, Scots of the time seem to have possessed
in abundance).[42]

One of the unfortunate effects of the *Poems of Ossian* was that they helped
to drive still further the wedge which already existed in Scotland between
polite and popular culture. Macpherson's work sanctioned an élite of people
of taste. In numerous of his footnotes Macpherson makes it plain that only
people of superior intellect and taste will be capable of responding to his
depiction of sensibility amongst primitive people. Macpherson is prepared to
use myths and superstitions only to dismiss them as 'vulgar'. In a note to
'Conlath and Cuthona' he writes, 'It was long thought, in the north of
Scotland, that storms were raised by the ghosts of the deceased. This notion
is still entertained by the vulgar . . .' (I, 299, n. 1) (Laing counters neatly
with the assertion, 'This vulgar notion is to be found only in Macpherson's
"Hunter" '). Flattery is at the heart of Macpherson's designs on his readers,
as these extracts from the fourth edition (1773) make all too plain:

> In this country, men of genuine taste abound; but their still voice is drowned in
> the clamours of a multitude, who judge by fashion of poetry, as of dress. The
> truth is, to judge aright, requires almost as much genius as to write well; and
> good critics are as rare as great poets. Though two hundred thousand Romans
> stood up, when Virgil came into the theatre, Varius only could correct the
> AEneid . . . The following poems, it must be confessed, are more calculated to
> please persons of exquisite feelings of heart, than those who receive all their
> impressions by the ear. (I, lxvii)

Now precisely such a division between those who have taste and those who
lack it militates against that cultural wholeness upon which Romanticism was
to thrive. As Jacques Barzun has observed, Romanticism was emphatically
populist.[43] Moreover, the belief that man was perfectible—so dear to Rousseau—was to inspire early Romantic art, a point well made by George
Steiner.[44] In a society divided in terms of culture, or even of taste, such early
Romantic impulses could make little headway. It was an otherwise-suppressed
nationalist spirit that gave rise to the desire that Scotland should have its
epic. In a context in which nationalism could have found free and genuine
expression Romanticism might have flourished. But Scotland could not provide that context.

There is a further paradox in that the communal impulse of the Scottish
Enlightenment might otherwise have been expected to strike a chord in

the Romantic belief in, and desire for, man's perfectibility. Ironically, the concatenation of the vogue of sensibility and the obsession of educated Scots with proving that they were their neighbours' equals in taste meant that while the thrust of Scottish Enlightenment thinking was all towards the improvement of society the imaginative literature of the period (certainly as exemplified by Macpherson) was counter-productive in that it fostered divisions within that society. And in this respect Macpherson was, regrettably, a potent influence. To sophisticated eighteenth-century society Macpherson offered the voice of allegedly natural feeling as one of the shibboleths of the possessor of taste. Half a century later, in *Answer to Some Elegant Verses*, Byron was to write,

> For me, I fain would please the chosen few,
> Whose souls, to feeling and to nature true,
> Will spare the childish verse.[45]

CHAPTER 3

People of Taste: the Literati *and Scottish Poetry*

Increasingly in the second half of the eighteenth century Edinburgh came to be known as a centre of learning. Its university was for Thomas Jefferson in 1791 the finest in the world.[1] The Scottish Enlightenment thinkers made a major contribution to the study of man, and in particular the study of man in society. Yet the considerable intellectual achievement found no parallel in terms of imaginative literature. Now it may well be that there is no necessary relationship between intellectual advance and the flowering of imaginative literature, but there are certain peculiarities of the Scottish situation in the mid eighteenth century which help to explain why the Scottish Enlightenment did not generate literary activity of the highest quality. The purpose of this chapter is to account for the literary influence of the *literati*, identify the nature of that influence, and assess the accomplishment of those poets whom the *literati* sponsored.

It is strikingly paradoxical that the *literati*, committed as they were as philosophers and social theorists to the idea of progress, should, as literary critics, have been so predominantly retrospective. The philosophy of the Scottish Enlightenment was imbued strongly with the spirit of empiricism, while its literature was subjected to the critical dictates of the *literati*. While their concern, as philosophers and aestheticians, with such subjects as the development of society, the origins of language and the nature of sensory response did much to stimulate elsewhere the growth of what was to become Romanticism, the effect on Scottish literature of their practice as critics was, in contrast, decidedly restrictive. Their ambitions for the future of Scottish literature led Hume, for instance, and also Lord Monboddo to extol the virtues of classical and neo-classical models. As Scotland made her independent and original mark on the history of ideas, so, paradoxically, the *literati*, and Hume in particular, aimed for conformity in attempting to shape her literature on examples whose influence had already waned considerably. Scottish literature has never shaken itself free from the effects of this paradox. In the eighteenth century thought and imaginative literature took their separate ways in Scotland, and the lot of imaginative literature has been a difficult one ever since.

The nature of the effect of the *literati* on Scottish literature is explained in part by the fact that none was in his own right a poet, dramatist, or novelist. The cultural situation in Scotland had a lot to do with this. The departure of the king and the senior nobility in 1603 had removed the centres of patronage and literary orientation. After 1707 the institutions which remained in Scotland were those of the church and the law. Only the more liberal of the clergy were not inimical to the arts, while the professional training of the lawyers emphasised rhetoric, eloquence, and the principles and procedures of legislation. The power of churchmen and lawyers expanded to fill the void that resulted from the departures of court and parliament. Thus a small professional class became arbiters of taste in eighteenth-century Edinburgh, a class whose background and training were not conducive to imaginative creation. While Hume, Smith, and Kames in particular were to make important contributions to literary theory, none of them had experience of writing imaginative literature. It is tempting to suggest that such experience might have prevented some of their errors of critical judgement (Smith claimed that Swift 'is read with the same views and the same expectations as we read Tom Brown',[2] and his opinion of Gray was that 'nothing is wanting to render him, perhaps, the finest poet in the English language, but to have written a little more';[3] equally it might have tempered the enthusiasm of Hume's adoption of William Wilkie and Thomas Blacklock). It is ironic that, given their preoccupation with Taste, the *literati* should have been so deficient in discernment when it came to practical matters of evaluation.

The concern of the *literati* with taste was an aspect of their programme to justify Scotland's partnership in the Union in artistic terms. For them, the development of polite literature was both essential for, and an index to, the refinement of society. To Hume's eyes, the Union had brought at last to Scotland that stability upon which such progress could be based. In his *History*, in the account of the 'Affairs of Scotland' in the reign of Charles II, Hume writes,

> The Scottish nation, though they had never been subject to the arbitrary power of their prince, had but very imperfect notions of law and liberty; and scarcely in any age had they ever enjoyed an administration, which had confined itself within the proper boundaries. By their final union alone with England, their once hated adversary, they have happily attained the experience of a government perfectly regular, and exempt from all violence and injustice.[4]

And William Robertson, noting that the seventeenth century witnessed the refinement of language and taste in England and their debasement in Scotland, saw the advantages of the Union as follows:

> The Scots, after being placed, during a whole century, in a situation no less fatal to the liberty than to the taste and genius of the nation, were at once put in possession of privileges more valuable than those which their ancestors had formerly enjoyed; and every obstruction that had retarded their pursuit, or prevented their acquisition of literary fame, was totally removed.[5]

Pax Hanoveriana afforded the security essential to the progress of learning. For Hume, 'from law arises security: from security curiosity: and from curiosity knowledge'.[6] Furthermore, advancement in the arts is to the general benefit of society. In Hume's comprehensive social vision the refinement of the arts has an integral place:

The more these refined arts advance, the more sociable men become. . . So that, besides the improvements which they receive from knowledge and the liberal arts, it is impossible but they must feel an increase of humanity, from the very habit of conversing together, and contributing to each other's pleasure and entertainment. Thus *industry*, *knowledge*, and *humanity*, are linked together by an indissoluble chain, and are found, from experience as well as reason, to be peculiar to the more polished, and, what are commonly denominated, the more luxurious ages.[7]

In the close inter-relation of effort, knowledge, and man's concern for his fellow-man, this is a definitive formulation of the thinking that so characterised the Scottish Enlightenment and that arose partly out of the need to prove Scotland's right to partnership—intellectual and commercial—with England. In his *Lectures on Rhetoric and Belles Lettres*, first delivered in Edinburgh in 1748, Adam Smith made it quite plain that the cultivation of the arts, the refinement of manners, and the development of prose are inseparable from the rise of a mercantile class and an urban society. To explain the fact that poetry pre-dates prose in the development of society (and he cites the examples of Greece, Rome, England and Scotland) Smith identifies poetry with the ritual which follows the end of the day's work in primitive societies, whereas ''tis the introduction of commerce, or at least of the opulence that is commonly the attendant of commerce, that first brings on the improvement of prose'.[8] Commerce brings wealth and security, and 'wherever the inhabitants of a city are rich and opulent, where they enjoy the necessaries and conveniences of life in ease and security, there the arts will be cultivated, and refinement of manners a never-failing attendant'.[9]

Here theory and practice were in conflict. The Union had stimulated trade in Scotland certainly, but, unlike in England, the growth of prose that had accompanied it was for strictly historical, philosophical, sociological and altogether non-fictional purposes. Scotland may have acquired a merchant-class but it produced no Defoe to write the novel of the bourgeoisie. The Weber-Tawney thesis of a close inter-relationship between Calvinism and economic individualism, a thesis that underlies Ian Watt's account of the rise of the English novel, is definitely not borne out by the example of Scotland, as T C Smout has noted.[10] One main reason for this may well be that the *literati* were obsessed by the desire that Scotland be represented by the traditionally major and 'respectable' literary genres, and the kind of literary language which they encouraged was of a formality scarcely commensurate with the representation of ordinary human experience, which was increasingly the concern of novel. Given the relatively lowly status of the novel at that time there could be no place for it in the cultural ambitions of the *literati*. The interval between Smollett, who sometimes wrote of ordinary human experience, and Galt, who often did, is a long one. The major Scottish novelist of the intervening years was Scott who was largely concerned not with present social realities but a fictionalised Scottish past. Significantly, too, both Mackenzie and Galt went to some lengths to dissociate their fictions from the novel genre. In view of the conventional Scottish claims for egalitarianism it is a telling irony indeed that the literary form whose growth accompanied that of democratic individualism and whose principal subject was the experiences of the common man should have made such little headway in Scotland for most of the eighteenth century. At least part of the responsibility must lie with the *literati*.

It has already been indicated that the *literati* regarded as one of their foremost functions the task of hastening the cultivation of the arts and the refinement of manners. How was this to be accomplished? According to Hume the imitative nature of the human mind means that converse among men will induce a 'similitude of manners'.[11] In Edinburgh innate gregariousness combined with the desire for improvement to bring about the establishment of various literary and intellectual societies.[12] But Hume was also to detect a tendency to conformity amongst neighbouring states: 'Where several neighbouring nations have a very close communication together, either by policy, commerce, or travelling, they acquire a similitude of manners, proportioned to the communication.'[13] The degree of cultural influence depended of course to a large extent on the size of the population, the number and the activity of its institutions of learning, its publishing-houses, and the circulation of its publications. As very much the junior partners, the Scots sought guidance as to manners and tastes from such London periodicals as the *Spectator* and the *Tatler*.

These journals reflected the English character, and for Hume what was most striking about the English character was its multiplicity. He observed,

> We may often remark a wonderful mixture of manners and characters in the same nation, speaking the same language, and subject to the same government: and in this particular the English are the most remarkable of any people that perhaps ever were in the world. Nor is this to be ascribed to the mutability and uncertainty of their climate, or to any other physical causes; since all these causes take place in the neighbouring country of Scotland, without having the same effect.[14]

Noting the great social and professional range in England, he concludes, 'Hence the English, of any people in the universe, have the least of a national character: unless this very singularity may appear to pass for such.'[15] It may have been inferiority in numbers and a remoteness from continental Europe which made the Scots appear parochial in values and constrained in terms of range of personality in relation to the richness and diversity of the English character. Certainly the *literati* appear to have felt the limitations of Edinburgh life. Adam Smith wrote to the editor of the *Edinburgh Review* (which he had helped to establish in July 1755) recommending a widening of the scope of articles published and requesting the discussion of foreign literature; and the fact that Smith's reading in philosophy and literature was almost as extensive in foreign languages (especially French) as in English may reflect a deliberate attempt at avoiding parochialism.

The Scots, impressed by what Hume saw as the richness of the English character, may well have wished to try to mimic its genuine multiplicity. But it is questionable if a small nation, however determined, could succeed in acquiring such innate diversity of values. In any case, as Hume recognised, what Scotland required after centuries of faction was stability, and this could be best aided by the diffusion of uniformity from the centre. Thus, such diversity of voice as existed in Scotland came under threat from the pressure for standardisation, and imaginative individualism found itself competing with political realism. The attempt of the *literati* to unite Scottish culture around the banner of polite literature had two major effects: it placed regional literature under increasing threat, and, in requiring Scottish writers to master modes and styles which were not endemic, it served as a stimulus to rôle-playing and striking of attitudes.

Even within the responses of the *literati* to the cultural effects of the Union there was a measure of uncertainty or even ambivalence. While Hume was ready to acknowledge that the Union had brought the peace which made progress possible, yet signs of a nationalist strain recur in his writing. Intellectual commerce with one's neighbours has its benefits, but 'perhaps it may not be for the advantage of any nation to have the arts imported from their neighbours in too great perfection. This extinguishes emulation, and sinks the ardour of the generous youth.'[16] Hume cites the examples of the influx of Italian painting to England, the effect of Greek arts on Rome, and 'the multitude of polite productions in the French language, dispersed all over Germany and the North (which) hinder these nations from cultivating their own language, and keep them still dependent on their neighbours for those elegant entertainments'.[17]

It is here that the contradiction peculiar to the Scottish situation becomes especially evident. The Scots were not merely to annex English literature but by its example were to be stirred to emulation. But, unlike those emergent nations that were freeing themselves from the authority of French neo-classicism, the Scots were to adopt the very neo-classical values which its dominant cultural partner had favoured over half a century earlier. There is, then, a certain poignant irony in Hume's writing that

> nothing is more favourable to the rise of politeness and learning, than a number of neighbouring and independent states, connected together by commerce and policy. The emulation, which naturally arises among those neighbouring states, is an obvious source of improvement: but what I would chiefly insist on is the stop, which such limited territories give both to *power* and to *authority*.[18]

With reference to Scotland, this means, in effect, that the Union had saved the Scots from their own worst excesses. On such occasions Hume writes of 'neighbouring and independent states', but the crucial point is that Scotland was no longer independent and its writers could not proceed from an assumed basis of cultural equality. Examples abounded to substantiate Hume's contention that 'if we consider the matter in a proper light, we shall find, that a progress in the arts is rather favourable to liberty, and has a natural tendency to preserve, if not produce a free government'.[19] Scotland, it would seem, proved the converse. Independence was the price of peace and stability, and the arts which would be stimulated would be replicas, not originals.

There is a parallel in the way in which the moderating effect of English authority dulled the radical edge of Scottish Enlightenment thinking, at least in terms of its influence on British life. While Dupont might congratulate Adam Smith on his hastening the constitutional revolution in France,[20] there was little likelihood that Smith's thinking would have any comparable effect in Britain (nor is it probable that Smith would have wished it so). If the Jacobites had seemed to Londoners to offer a serious threat to the nation's security, there was no doubt that the activities of the London mob in the years 1768–71 represented, for Hume, a comparable danger; hence his repeated complaints that Wilkes and his supporters were abusing liberty. To Hume's eyes, periods of civil unrest were inseparable from decline in literature and the arts. Of the English he wrote to Smith on 6 February 1770,

> How can you so much as entertain a thought of publishing a Book (*The Wealth of Nations*) full of Reason, Sense, and Learning, to these wicked abandon'd Madmen? . . . Nothing but a Rebellion and Bloodshed will open the Eyes of that deluded People; tho' were they alone concerned I think it is no matter what becomes of them.[21]

It is a fine irony: to the civilised Scot it is the 'factious barbarians of London'[22] who threaten the cherished stability which the Union has brought to Scotland.

For the *literati* language, education, and polite literature were the agents of the civilising process. Mastery of the English language and its literary modes was counselled as a matter of urgency. Alexander Carlyle commented that

> to every man bred in Scotland the English language was in some respects a foreign tongue, the precise value and force of whose words and phrases he did not understand, and therefore was continually endeavouring to word his expressions by additional epithets or circumlocutions, which made his writings appear both stiff and redundant.[23]

To Charles Mackie, first Professor of History at Edinburgh, John Mitchell wrote,

> Give me leave to say that I wish some method might be fallen upon to teach Young Gentlemen the English, our chief Tongue, and that whereby any can make a figure in affairs at home, and the want of it is a very great loss to all who come, or are sent here.[24]

The self-consciousness of the Scots as regards their provincial speech grew, as Ernest Mossner has noted,[25] after the first sending of Scottish representatives to Westminster. Increasing contact with the English at every level exacerbated the Scots' feeling of inadequacy in the use of standard English. Yet their education had ensured that the *literati*, for instance, were conversant with a wide range of writers from the English literary tradition, and they could write from a basis of partnership within that tradition. In comparing Waller's poems with those of Horace, Hume wrote, 'we esteemed ourselves sufficiently happy, that our climate and language could produce but a faint copy of so excellent an original';[26] and at the start of his *Lectures on Rhetoric and Belles Lettres* Smith lamented the replacement of 'good old English words'[27] by terms derivative from French or Latin.

Undeniably, though, the Scottish writers were acutely conscious of the language which they spoke and the accent in which they spoke it. The paradox whereby such identifiable provincials were making a major contribution to the progress of ideas was not lost on Hume. On 2 July 1757 he wrote to Gilbert Eliot of Minto,

> . . . really it is admirable how many Men of Genius this Country produces at present. Is it not strange that, at a time when we have lost our Princes, our Parliaments, our independent Government, even the presence of our chief Nobility, are unhappy, in our Accent & Pronunciation, speak a very corrupt Dialect of the Tongue which we make use of; is it not strange, I say, that, in these Circumstances, we shou'd really be the People most distinguish'd for Literature in Europe?[28]

The peculiar circumstances of Scotland, and in particular the need to come to terms with the conditions which the Union had produced, had prompted social and philosophical thinking of the first order (and it is this that Hume terms 'Literature'). But such features of the written style as betrayed the author's provincial origins and limited the range of his readership were to be reformed on the model of standard English. On 16 October 1754 Hume sent Wilkes a copy of his *History* with this request:

> I know, that in many particulars, especially the Language, you wou'd be able, if you pleas'd to give me good Advice. I beg of you to remark, as you go along, such Words and Phrazes, as appear to you wrong or suspicious; and to inform me of them. You coul'd not do me a better Office: Notwithstanding all the Pains, which I have taken in the study of the English Language, I am still jealous of my Pen. As to my tongue, you have seen, that I regard it as totally desperate and irreclaimable.[29]

For Hume, 'the softness or force of their language' is one of the things 'of which men are vain'.[30] He remained hypersensitive as to the nature of his style, and employed David Malloch (who, on moving south, anglicised his name to Mallet) to identify and correct any usages which would seem singular to the London reader. In 1752 and again in 1760 Hume produced lists of 'Scotticisms', terms which the Scottish writer should avoid as betraying his origin (James Beattie did likewise in 1779).

To Adam Smith too, language was of the highest importance. Typical of the linguistic concern of the *literati* is Smith's prefacing his treatment of style in his *Lectures on Rhetoric and Belles Lettres* with a lengthy and detailed account 'Of the Origin and Process of Language'. This is informed by Smith's strong practical sense, and it develops from the categorical assertion that 'Our words must only be English and agreeable to the custom of the country, but likewise to the custom of some particular part of the nation. This part undoubtedly is formed of the men of rank and breeding.'[31] It is a social and intellectual élite that is to lead the mimicking of the English. Extolling the harmonious and sonorous pronunciation of the English, Smith observes,

> There is a certain singing in their manner of speaking which foreigners can never attain. Hence it is that this language, which when spoken by natives is allowed to be very melodious and agreeable, in the mouth of strangers is strangely harsh and grating.[32]

It is very much as the Scot that Smith writes,

> We in this country are most of us very sensible that the perfection of language is very different from that we commonly speak in. The idea we form of a good style is almost contrary to that which we generally hear. Hence it is that we conceive the further one's style is removed from the common manner, it is so much nearer to purity and the perfection we have in view.[33]

Now alongside the élitist direction of this line of thought has to be set a strong belief on the part of Smith that when style is functioning effectively it is expressing the whole man. He affirms,

> If . . . we find the first turn we give a sentence does not express our sentiment with suitable *aise*, we may reasonably imagine it is owing to some defect on the arrangement of the terms (that is to say if the words be proper English), and when we hit this, it is not only language but style, not only expresses the thought but also the spirit and mind of the author.[34]

But in the case of the Scot, given the language duality, the spirit and mind of the author were characterised by internal tensions and divisions. As the Scots had to work at acquiring an identity appropriate to the new situation in which they found themselves, so they had to work at shaping a style that would express that personality. Thus a measure of artificiality was inescapable.

The tension between individuality and authority which underlies so much of Scottish literature since 1707 gained force from the criteria of the *literati*. It is understandable that educated Scottish society should have been concerned to resolve as soon as possible the problems of cultural identity which it was experiencing, and which it had helped create, by becoming acceptable to English eyes in terms of polite literature. The intention of the members of the Select Society was 'by practice to improve themselves in reasoning and eloquence, and by the freedom of debate, to discover the most effectual methods of promoting the good of the country'.[35] In the belief that 'gentlemen educated in Scotland have long been sensible of the disadvantages under which they labour, from their imperfect knowledge of the ENGLISH tongue, and the impropriety with which they speak it',[36] the Select Society sought instruction in the proper reading and speaking of English. The man for the hour was Thomas Sheridan, father of the dramatist, and—a nice irony—an Irishman, whose *British Education* (1756) has as its sub-title a manifesto that might have been written with the needs and ideals of the *literati* in mind:

> The source of the disorder of Great Britain; being an Essay towards proving that the immorality, ignorance, and false taste, which so generally prevail, are the natural and necessary consequences of the present defective system of education; with an attempt to show that a revival of the Art of Speaking, and the Study of our own Language, might contribute, in a great measure, to the cure of those evils.[37]

Under the aegis of the Select Society, Sheridan gave lectures in Edinburgh in the summer of 1761 on Elocution and The English Tongue. All of this amounted, undeniably, to a manifestation of the practical spirit of the Scottish Enlightenment, a spirit which proved so beneficial in many other fields. The concern of the *literati* was entirely genuine, and they believed they were acting with the best interests of Scotland at heart. But in terms of imaginative literature the effect of their actions was to accelerate the disjunction from the older Scottish tradition.

It would be superfluous to labour the point already made in various studies of the period—that the desire for recognition as the equals of the English led the *literati* to neglect the Gaelic revival and the lowland vernacular tradition (and in particular the ballads, in which the embryonic Romantic spirit was soon to show an interest), and instead to enthuse over the spurious 'Celtic' literature. Suffice it to note that the programme of the *literati* lent strength to the division between popular and polite literature in Scotland. There has been a tendency among some writers on the period to overstress the contribution of the *literati* and to suggest that they were almost entirely responsible for this cultural dichotomy. Countering this, Thomas Crawford has argued cogently that the popular ballad found its way to the tea-table while the fine lyric was esteemed by all classes.[38] While this seems true, and while Crawford was right in redressing the balance of emphasis, it is undeniable that the values of the *literati* did hasten a process of cultural polarisation that was already under way. And a further effect was to encourage an emphasis in Scottish education (which endures to this day) on the written rather than the spoken. Possibly it was dissatisfaction with the Scottish accent that led to the suppression of spoken activity in the Scottish classroom. The overall result was that individuality became subjugated to grammatical and rhetorical regularity.

Another important aspect of their cultural programme was the concern of the *literati* with the cultivation of taste. The concept of Taste came to occupy European thinkers in the eighteenth century as the effects of the growth of empiricism came to be felt. If one had to experience things for oneself by what standards was one's experience to be evaluated? Were such standards relative purely to the individual, or could any general criteria be identified? Such questions were not confined to Scotland, of course, but they were asked with a frequency and an urgency in Scotland which resulted directly from the wish to match the English as writers and critics and the concomitant need for standards. In academic circles treatises on Taste were appearing in the 1730s and 1740s, and in 1755 the prize offered by the Select Society for the best essay on the subject was won by Alexander Gerard.

The Scottish philosophers were prompted to engage with questions of taste by the writings of Francis Hutcheson on beauty and the finer feelings. Hutcheson devoted the sixth section of *An Inquiry into the Original of our Ideas of Beauty and Virtue* (1725) to establishing 'the *Universality* of the *Sense of Beauty* among Men'. In Hutcheson's consideration of the extent of the agreement among men in 'their Sense of Beauty'[39] are the early signs of what was to become the preoccupation of eighteenth-century Scottish thinkers with matters of taste. Two aspects of Hutcheson's discussion of the universality of the sense of beauty are especially important: he stresses that 'our Sense of Beauty seems design'd to give us positive Pleasure, but not positive Pain or Disgust, any further than what arises from disappointment';[40] and he questions and qualifies the significance of the power of custom, education and example.

In the thirty or so years that divide Hutcheson's writings on taste from those of Smith and Hume there seems to have been a noticeable increase in the belief that the possession of taste is a distinction. In his *Theory of Moral Sentiments* (1759) Smith was to observe,

> As taste and good judgement . . . are supposed to imply a delicacy of sentiment and an acuteness of understanding not commonly to be met with; so the virtues of sensibility and self-command are not apprehended to consist in the ordinary, but in the uncommon degrees of those qualities. The amiable virtue of humanity requires, surely, a sensibility, much beyond what is possessed by the rude vulgar of mankind.[41]

That Smith mentions taste and sensibility in the same breath is revealing and confirms the exclusive drift of the above. Similarly, when Hume treats 'Of the Delicacy of Taste and Passion' he advocates the cultivation and refinement of taste by study of literature and the arts. His reasons are these:

> I: Nothing is so improving to the temper as the study of the beauties, either of poetry, eloquence, music or painting. They give a certain elegance of sentiment to which the rest of mankind are strangers. The emotions which they excite are soft and tender. They draw off the mind from the hurry of business and interest; cherish reflection; dispose to tranquility; and produce an agreeable melancholy, which, of all dispositions of the mind, is best suited to love and friendship.

> II: A delicacy of taste is favourable to love and friendship, by confining our choice to few people, and making us indifferent to the company and conversation of the greater part of men.[42]

The way in which various strands in Hume's thinking draw together here is noteworthy. From a basis of utilitarian improvement (as earlier he had argued that delicacy of passion can be 'cured' by cultivating delicacy of taste), Hume

relates delicacy of taste to the vogue of sensibility and the pleasures of melancholy. Possession of delicacy of taste leads to both a self-consciousness and
an awareness of being part of an élite. Hume writes,

> One that has well digested his knowledge both of books and men, has little
> enjoyment but in the company of a few select companions. He feels too sensibly,
> how much all the rest of mankind fall short of the notions which he has enter-
> tained. And, his affections being thus confined within a narrow circle, no wonder
> he carries them further, than if they were more general and undistinguished.[43]

What seems to be stressed here is the importance of quality and intensity
of experience rather than range of responsiveness and empathy. Clearly
anticipated here is the notion that delicacy of taste and sensibility are the
prerogative of the few. The gulf between this belief and that 'innate universality'[44] which Keats saw embodied in Shakespeare as the essence of the
great dramatic writer is striking. Hume seems to have failed to see that what
he was recommending might well serve to limit the imaginative writer.
The concentration of feeling breeds introversion and self-consciousness, from
which it is an easy, even inevitable, step to playing such rôles as the man of
feeling or the person of taste (as the example of Burns shows).

Hume's most extensive consideration of Taste is his Dissertation IV, 'Of the
Standard of Taste', in his *Four Dissertations* (1757). There the tensions
between his philosophical values and his aesthetic values become very apparent. Hume deals with that species of philosophy which denies the possibility
of establishing a standard of taste since 'a thousand different sentiments,
excited by the same object, are all right: Because no sentiment represents
what is really in the object. It only marks a certain conformity or relation
betwixt the object and the organs or faculties of the mind.'[45] Ultimately
subjective relativism of taste is confronted by the need for some sort of
standard by which to judge. Thus Hume concedes, 'It appears then, that
amidst all the variety and caprices of taste, there are certain general principles
of approbation or blame.'[46] He proceeds to offer this definition of the standard
of taste: 'Strong sense, united to delicate sentiment, improved by practice,
perfected by comparison, and cleared of all prejudice, can alone entitle critics
to this valuable character; and the joint verdict of such, wherever they are
to be found, is the true standard of taste and beauty.'[47] Here the practical bias
of Scottish Enlightenment thinking is decidedly at odds with that alleged
Scottish egalitarianism which was one of the notes that Burns was soon to
sound. Hume affirms,

> Though men of delicate taste are rare, they are easily to be distinguished in
> society, by the soundness of their understanding and the superiority of their
> qualities above the rest of mankind. The ascendant, which they acquire, gives a
> prevalence to that lively approbation, with which they receive any productions of
> genius, and renders it generally predominant. Many men, when left to themselves,
> have but a faint and dubious perception of beauty, who yet are capable of
> relishing any fine stroke, which is pointed out to them.[48]

The urgent need to determine standards of taste led directly to the elevation of the critic and the rhetorician to positions of prominence in Scottish cultural life. Yet the remainder of Hume's dissertation reveals his aesthetic values as neo-classical, archly conservative, and rigidly restrictive of the imagination (in marked contrast to his philosophical stance).

According to Hume,

> we are more pleased with pictures of characters, which resemble such as are found in our own age or country, than with those which describe a different set of customs. 'Tis not without some effort, that we reconcile ourselves to the simplicity of antient manners, and behold princesses drawing water from a spring, and kings and heroes dressing their own victuals. We may allow in general, that the representation of such manners is no fault in the author, nor deformity in the piece; but we are not so sensibly touched with them.[49]

This shows that while Hume could write of the extent of human sympathy as a philosopher, as a literary critic he had no comparable sense. It also helps explain why the people in Macpherson's *Ossian* have some of the characteristics of eighteenth-century ladies and gentlemen.

Without doubt it was a concern about the Scots' adequacy as arbiters of taste that exacerbated this conservative element in Hume. In his dissertation Hume recognises that national tastes are founded on national characteristics; yet one of the effects of the Union was to prompt the *literati* to encourage emulation of English and neo-classical modes. And Hume's own criteria are revealed as strict and narrow, as befits a rigorous conception of what is civilised and refined. Finding 'vicious manners' depicted in the works of some earlier writers, he observes,

> However I may excuse the poet, on account of the manners of his age, I never can relish the composition. The want of humanity and of decency, so conspicuous in the characters drawn by several of the antient poets, even sometimes by Homer and the Greek tragedians, diminishes considerably the merit of their noble performances, and gives modern authors a great advantage over them. We are not interested in the fortunes and sentiments of such rough heroes: We are displeased to find the limits of vice and virtue so confounded.[50]

How distant this is from the views of the Romantics on both the literature of remote times and the mingling of virtues and vice in characters. Though Hume's aesthetic was imbued with neo-classicism far beyond those of his colleagues, yet he was extremely influential; hence such comment as that above-quoted may be held to say much about the nature of enlightened Scotland's literary taste in the middle decades of the eighteenth century. With knowledge of this background it is possible to begin to appreciate why the *Ossian* poems are as they are; why Edinburgh reacted as it did to Burns; how the divisions within Scott came into being; and what the conditions were out of which the kailyard arose.

The obsession with taste led inevitably to the question of how the finer feelings of the reader were to be aroused. Eighteenth-century Scottish writing on this subject too is characterised by dichotomy. Tensions arise between rhetoric and the nature of the finer feelings; between rule-making and the evocation of the pathetic and the sublime; between the influence of Aristotle (or, more accurately, his seventeenth-century interpreters) and that of Longinus. At the centre was the question of whether it was possible to prescribe rules as to the arousal of spontaneous feelings.

For Hume, eloquence is of crucial importance since 'nothing is more capable of infusing any passion into the mind, than eloquence, by which objects are represented in the strongest and most lively colours'.[57] In his dissertation, 'Of the Standard of Taste' Hume argues that while there are fashions in philosophy and the sciences there is a permanence about both the beauties of eloquence and poetry and the recognition thereof. With his citing of examples it becomes apparent that for Hume a writer's substance may lose its relevance with the passage of time while his rhetoric may endure. 'The abstract philosophy of Cicero', asserts Hume, 'has lost its credit: The vehemence of his oratory is still the object of our admiration'.[52] In such claims Hume was endorsing a dichotomy of substance and technique.

When the *literati* compared the achievements of British orators with those of classical times there were grounds for concern: it was the classical orators who appealed most to the finer feelings. Noting the English tradition of composure and restraint and its implications for oratory, Smith remarked wryly, 'We are not then to expect that anything passionate or exaggerated will be admitted in the House of Lords.'[53] It is worth noting that on such matters Smith, like all the *literati*, writes very much as a North Briton, choosing to consider only the formal and professional rhetoric of the classical and English models and ignoring the chanting ritual eloquence of the Celtic tradition. Likewise Hume, recognising the modern age's inferiority to the ancient in respect of eloquence, comments that 'ancient eloquence, that is, the sublime and passionate, is of a much juster taste than the modern, or the argumentative and rational; and, if properly executed, will always have more command and authority over mankind'.[54] The irony is a telling one: the rhetorical fire, the absence of which Hume so laments in modern English eloquence, characterised the Celtic tradition which he opted to overlook. Thus when Hume and his circle aspired to the sublime their thinking was influenced by its classical proponent, Longinus, and the recent treatise by Burke,[55] and not by the Celtic tradition which most of them were largely unqualified to judge. When Macpherson dazzled with his version of the native sublime it is perhaps understandable that they were fooled. However it is only fair to note that the paradox of laying down elaborate rules as to how to attain the sublime did not obtain universally. In his *Elements of Criticism* (1762) Kames cited the example of *Genesis* where the sublime was achieved by means of linguistic economy and simplicity. Blair in his *Lectures on Rhetoric and Belles Lettres* noted that 'exact proportion of parts, though it enters often into the Beautiful, is much disregarded in the Sublime'.[56] Observing that 'the Sublime is a Species of Writing which depends less than any other on the artificial embellishments of Nature', Blair substantiated the point by showing how Pope's use of heroic couplets in his translation of Homer had reduced the scope for reproducing the sublimity of the original.[57]

As the example of Hume has shown, one of the effects of the desire to master standard English and English literary modes was a tendency to emphasise style to the detriment of substance. John Maclaurin in his *Apology for the Writers against the Tragedy of Douglas* attacked the Select Society's criterion of style as follows:

> Some years ago, a few gentlemen in this town assumed the character of being the only judges in all points of literature; they were and still are styled the *geniuses*, and lately erected what they called a *select society*, which usurps a kind of aristocratical government over all men and matters of learning. The first and fundamental maxim of this dictatorial club is, That a punctilious correctness of style is the *summum bonum* of all composition: though the greatest genius should shine throughout a work, yet if in it is found an unguarded expression, a slip in syntax, or a peccadillo in grammar, *ad piper et farras* with it.[58]

The origin of the obsession with correctness of style lay in the self-consciousness and feeling of inadequacy on the part of the *literati* in the use of standard English. With some justification J H Millar was to claim that one of 'the mischiefs which sprang from the painful and sedulous aping of southern writers [was that] a terrible standard of "eloquence" was set up, which dominated Scotland for a hundred years'.[59] Again the fact that many of the arbiters of taste in Edinburgh were churchmen or lawyers is relevant. Henry Mackenzie reported that the Moderate faction in the Church of Scotland, to which Adam Ferguson, John Home, and Alexander Carlyle belonged, 'cultivated classical literature, and began that study of refined composition which some of them afterwards carried to such a degree of excellence in this country'.[60] It is distinctly paradoxical that those who took such pride in the survival of an independent Scottish church and legislature should have been so instrumental in the anglicising of Scottish letters.

In fairness, however, it has to be recognised that what was to become an extensive and enduring concern with rhetoric in Scotland originated in what the *literati* saw to be the immediate circumstances and specific requirements of Scottish literature. They can scarcely be held entirely to blame for what they could not possibly foresee. And not all the *literati* echoed the narrowly conservative aesthetics of Hume. Smith applied his practical mind to matters of rhetoric. Traditional systems of rhetoric he dismissed as 'a very silly set of books and not at all instructive',[61] and he acknowledged, 'It is rather reverence for antiquity than any great regard for the beauty or usefulness of the thing itself which makes me mention the ancient division of rhetoric.'[62] Smith based in common sense his criteria for judging style:

> . . . the perfection of style consists in expressing in the most concise, proper, and precise manner the thought of the author, and that in the manner which best conveys the sentiment, passion, or affection with which it affects—or he pretends it does affect—him, and which he designs to communicate to his reader. This, you'll say, is no more than common sense: and indeed it is no more. But if you will attend to it, all the rules of criticism and morality, when traced to their foundation, turn out to be some principles of common sense which every one

assents to: all the business of those arts is to apply these rules to the different
subjects, and show what the conclusion is when they are so applied.[63]

As this shows, Smith's thinking is something of a compromise: rules have a
function, but it is the application of principles which are rooted firmly in
common sense.[64] Among Smith's specific judgements there is something of a
tension between the orthodox and the more modern. Though, as he notes,
Addison is pleased with such descriptions, Smith objects to the unusual, and
at times near-surreal, elements in Ovid's *Metamorphoses* since 'they shock us
by their incredibility'.[65] Among his general rules for the description of objects
is this: 'Where the chief design is to excite mirth and cheerfulness, nothing
should be brought in that is gloomy or horrible: and, on the other hand,
where one would raise awful, grand sentiments, the whole must tend that
way'.[66] Such emphasis on unity of effect is decidedly orthodox. Yet Smith
does point forward to the affective psychology that underlies Kames's *Elements*
when he observes that 'When Virgil describes the tumbling of a torrent down
a rock, he strengthens the picture by describing a traveller astonished and
surprising at hearing it below him'.[67]

In the case of Hume, the co-presence of dissonant elements is even more
obvious. The literary judgements which Hume offers in his *History* are those
of a narrow neo-classicism rigidly interpreted. The Roman authors who write
in 'the Asiatic manner' are guilty of 'tinsel eloquence'; Shakespeare and
Jonson 'were equally deficient in taste and elegance, in harmony and correctness'; the 'flashes of wit and ingenuity' in Donne's satires were 'totally
suffocated and buried by the hardest and most uncouth expression that is
anywhere to be met with'; and 'the great glory of literature in this island
during the reign of James, was Lord Bacon'.[68] On examining the epics of
Homer and Fénelon, Hume finds the former mixing heroism and ferocity in
his presentation of Achilles and prudence, fraud, and cunning in his character
of Ulysses; in contrast, 'his more scrupulous son in the French epic writer
exposes himself to the most imminent perils rather than depart from the
exactest line of truth and veracity'.[69] Almost despite himself, Hume has
recognised here the authentic human complexity of Homer's characters,
but it is of Fénelon's that he approves because of their morally exemplary
behaviour. At times Hume admits of complexity and aims for compromise or
a balanced view, as, for instance, in his comment,

> No advantages in this world are pure and unmixed. In like manner, as modern
> politeness, which is naturally so ornamental, runs often into affectation and
> foppery, disguise and insincerity; so the ancient simplicity, which is naturally so
> amiable and affecting, often degenerates into rusticity and abuse, scurrility and
> obscenity.[70]

And the scenery along the Rhine elicited this enthusiastic comment: 'Surely
there never was such an Assemblage of the wild & cultivated Beauties in one
Scene.'[71] Typical of the way in which many of his judgements are marked by
an uneasy union of conflicting elements is his back-handed compliment to

Tristram Shandy: 'The best Book, that has been writ by any Englishman these thirty years . . . is Tristram Shandy, bad as it is.'[72] There, if anywhere, what pleased the empirical philosopher must have appalled the classicist critic.

In view of the extent of the contradictions within Hume's aesthetic stance it is perhaps regrettable that he was so influential in shaping the cultural programme of the *literati*. Integral to it was the belief that cultural respectability could be won only by success in what had been regarded traditionally as the major forms: Scotland must have her epic, her lyrics, and her tragedy. Of the *literati*, Smith, at least, seems to have been well aware that the influence of the conventions of genre and decorum was on the wane. Concerning the belief that each sentiment has its appropriate diction and formal properties, Smith remarked, 'The experience of modern times . . . seems to contradict this principle . . . What is the burlesque verse in English, is the heroic verse in French.'[73] To such flexibility Hume seems to have been immune, however. Though the mood and tastes of Europe were becoming increasingly modern, the choice of forms by the *literati*, largely reflecting Hume's influence, was conservative. Possibly the underlying feeling was that Scottish writers had several centuries of achievement to make up rapidly before attempting to advance. Yet the middle decades of the eighteenth century had witnessed the virtual demise of the epic. Epic material was remote from modern concerns, while modern or recent material—as the example of Voltaire's *Henriade* made plain (a point well noted by Kames)[74]—was inappropriate to the traditional epic mode. At the same time tragedy was moving steadily towards melodrama. What this means is that Scotland's literary reputation was entrusted to modes that were well past their prime. Here G Gregory Smith's counsel is salutary: 'The wisest patriotism does not seek to force on new and changed generations, and certainly in literary matters, the rule of a tradition already outworn.'[75]

The mantle of Scotland's epic poet descended upon William Wilkie, whose *Epigoniad* Hume promoted strenuously.[76] Wilkie's preface reveals his critical values as strictly neo-classical to the point of pedantry:

> Were my judgment of sufficient authority in matters of criticism, I would have it understood as a rule, That the subjects of Epic poetry should be taken from tradition only: that Tragedy should keep within the limits of true history; and that Comedy, without meddling at all with historical facts, should expose vice and folly in recent instances and from living examples. (p. xiv)[77]

When the tradition of kinds was under assault from many quarters, such strict insistence on categorisation seems almost reactionary. It is tempting to suggest that the first-rate imagination would transcend such rules, while the third-rate would allow the rules to regulate its activities. To a critical approach such as Wilkie's, *Paradise Lost* presented problems of evaluation. Designating it 'a work altogether irregular', Wilkie informs the reader that 'the subject of it is not Epic, but Tragic; and that Adam and Eve are not designed to be objects of admiration, but of pity: it is Tragic in its plot, and Epic in its dress and machinery' (p. xxix), and he adds that Milton offends by 'presuming to represent the Divine Nature, and the mysteries of religion, according to the narrowness of human prejudice' (p. xxxi).

This is typical of the central theme of Wilkie's discourse on the epic: the material of the epic should be remote in time and such as will arouse wonder in the mere mortal who is its reader. Thus Wilkie chose as his subject a fairly obscure episode in the history of Thebes, as recounted in the *Iliad*, Bk. IV ('Theseus leads the youth of Greece to punish Thebes where their fathers bled'). The charge that this material might be inaccessible to many potential readers was rejected as follows: 'Neither is this knowledge of antient manners confined to the learned; the vulgar themselves, from the books of Moses, and other accounts of the first periods of the Jewish state, are sufficiently instructed in the customs of the earliest times, to be able to relish any work where these are justly represented' (p. iv). The logic which argues that a presbyterian grounding in the Old Testament is appropriate preparation for understanding an imitation of part of a classical epic is dubious, to say the least. Wilkie appears to have realised this since he ends his preface with an explanation of the title and the episode around which the poem centres, this information being offered for the benefit of those who lack classical knowledge. But, despite the appeal to sensibility, it would require considerable powers of empathy on the part of the eighteenth-century Scottish reader to respond significantly to this:

> Ye rural Goddesses, immortal fair!
> Who all my triumphs, all my sorrows share;
> I come, afflicted, from th'etherial tow'rs,
> Where Thebes is doom'd to fall by partial pow'rs.
>   (p. 4)

According to Wilkie,

> Subjects for Epic poetry ought always to be taken from periods too early to fall within the reach of true history . . . it will be found to be impossible that any subject proper for that kind of writing should have a connection with present affairs. The proper business of Epic poetry is to extend our ideas of human perfection, or, as the critics express it, to excite admiration. In order to do this in any tolerable degree, characters must be magnified, and accommodated, rather to our notions of heroic greatness, than the real state of human nature . . . admiration claims for its object something superior to mere humanity. (p. viii)

While this is largely the traditional view of the epic, it is symptomatic of Scottish nostalgia for a remote and aggrandised past that a Scot should write in such terms when other European nations had mostly discounted the epic form as being in any way appropriate to their needs. In Wilkie's view, 'great passions and high characters reject ordinary forms; and therefore must, upon every occasion, break through all the common modes both of speech and behaviour' (p. v). History and the lower literary forms relate the particularities of human experience and represent recognisable human responses, whereas epic eschews the particular since its concern is with human experience magnified in legend or fable, and it thrives upon the creation of the mystique of greatness. Thus epic, for Wilkie, aims to evoke 'high admiration' (p. xii), unlike tragedy which addresses itself to compassion. This would imply that the vogue of feeling would be unlikely to be accommodated by Wilkie's version of epic.

But here Wilkie's theory and his practice are at variance. He includes in his epic two long episodes, one in Bk. iv and one in Bk. vii, of which 'the first . . . is intended as an experiment in that kind of fiction which distinguishes Homer's Odyssey, and the other is an attempt to heroic Tragedy, after the manner of Sophocles' (p. xlv). The former in particular contains affecting speeches and descriptions blatantly aimed at the reader's sensibility, and so undermines Wilkie's demand that the epic avoid compassion. The following is typical:

> Thus as he (Creon) spoke, parental grief suppresst
> His voice, and swell'd within his lab'ring breast.
> Silent amidst th'assembled peers he stands,
> And wipes his falling tears with trembling hands;
> For great Leophron, once his country's boast,
> The glory and the bulwark of her host,
> Pierc'd by a foe and lifeless on the plain,
> Lay drench'd in gore and mix'd with vulgar slain:
> Silent he stood; the Theban lords around
> His grief partake, in streams of sorrow drown'd.
>
> (p. 60)

Presumably Wilkie's reasoning was that if epic is about great people their emotions, including grief, will be of commensurate greatness and will excite the reader's awe. Yet it remains questionable whether the eighteenth-century Scottish reader can sympathise with the bereaved Theban leader, whereas *Paradise Lost*, which broke most of Wilkie's rules, was as relevant then as now.

To all appearances Wilkie's theory of epic was at odds with the growing spirit of individualism in the eighteenth century. For instance, Wilkie offers the outmoded view that for the purpose of arousing admiration 'it is necessary . . . that a poet should give his heroes, not only those intrinsic qualities which make men admired, but that he should magnify them likewise by a skilful management of outward circumstances' (pp. xvii–xviii); and he adds that we are impressed by a person if it seems that the gods favour him. Mythology is essential to the epic, he claims, and he defends the presence of gods in the epic with the contention, 'It belongs to men to design and act, but to Heaven alone to determine events' (p. xx). This rebounds upon Wilkie, however, in that the corollary is that mere mortals are flawed, and recognisably human, beings (though that Wilkie succeeds in rendering them so is questionable). In a sense, then, Wilkie's theory of epic is so ultra-traditional as to be self-undermining and, in theory at least, he is in this respect 'modern' despite himself. And, with more than a glance in the direction of Rousseau, Wilkie distinguishes between 'natural character' ('all those feelings, passions,

desires, and opinions which men have from nature and common experience')
and 'artificial character' ('a habit of mind formed by discipline, according to
the cool and dispassionate dictates of reason').

Yet Wilkie follows with a reformulation of his initial thesis in terms of its
implications for characterisation. In defending his decision not to invent any
new characters, he pronounces, 'the wonders which Epic poetry relates, will
shock even the ignorant vulgar, and appear altogether ridiculous, if they are
not founded on something which has already gained a degree of credit' (p.
xxxviii). Wilkie's traditionalism is extreme and it minimises the scope and the
value of the individual imagination. 'Tradition', he writes, 'is the best ground
upon which fable can be built, not only because it gives the appearance of
reality to things that are merely fictitious, but likewise because it supplies a
poet with the most proper materials for his invention to work upon' (p. xl).
The task of the poet is simply to rework the legacy of fable since 'No man . . .
can pretend to invent fables that will please so universally, as those which
are formed by the progress of the popular tradition' (p. xlii). Thus Wilkie turns
his back on the infant Romantic imagination and at the same time deludes
himself into believing that the material of the classical epic remains part of
the popular tradition. To the absurdity of this irony is added a poignancy
with the realisation that all the while Wilkie and his sponsors were ignoring
what survived of the genuine popular tradition.

Of the *Epigoniad* Wilkie claimed, 'The language is simple and artless. This
I take to be an advantage, rather than a defect; for it gives an air of antiquity
to the work, and makes the style more suitable to the subject' (p. xlv).
Presumably part of the intention was to employ simple language to render
the condition of natural man. In this, Wilkie anticipates Macpherson, but
Wilkie's descriptions of landscape and combat appear stilted and awkward
by comparison with Macpherson's because of Wilkie's commitment to the
heroic couplet. This extract is representative:

> Pond'ring we stood; when on the roof above,
> The tread of feet descending thro' the grove
> Which crown'd the hollow cliff, amaz'd we heard;
> And straight before the cave a youth appear'd.
> A bleeding buck across his shoulders flung,
> Ty'd with a rope of twisted rushes, hung.
> He dropt his burden in the gate, and plac'd
> Against the pillar'd cliff, his bow unbrac'd.
>
> (p. 143)

The need for rhyme means that Wilkie's diction becomes rather repetitive.
The sustained use of the heroic couplet places a very considerable strain on
his limited ability as a poet. Moreover, he is less than successful in achieving
'simple and artless' diction since his syntax is at times modelled on the Latin,
and Latinate terms recur, as the following shows:

> She said; and having fix'd upon the bow
> A venom'd shaft, the cause of future woe:

> Then, with reverted aim, the subtile dart
> Dismiss'd and fix'd it in the hero's heart.
> Amaz'd he wak'd; and, on his arm reclin'd,
> With sighs, thus spoke the anguish of his mind.
>
> (p. 9)

That someone of the intellect of Hume could have believed for a moment that the establishment of Scotland's literary reputation could lie with such imitation Latin verses beggars belief. At times the combination of epic material and diction and forced simplicity produces bathos or outright doggerel. Such was the reviewers' hostility to the poem's diction that when the revised edition appeared in 1759 Hume thought fit to commend its improvements in the *Critical Review* and deliver this rebuke to its reviewer:

> The author of that article had surely been lying under strong prepossessions, when he spoke so negligently of a work which abounds in such sublime beauties, and could endeavour to discredit a poem, consisting of near six thousand lines, on account of a few mistakes in expression and prosody, proceeding entirely from the author's being a Scotchman, who had never been out of his own country.[78]

Sublimity and bulk are its merits, and its few blemishes are to be excused in terms of the author's nationality!

Hume's other poetic protégé was Thomas Blacklock. Early in 1754 Hume circulated amongst his friends his praise of Blacklock's poems. Hume had several reasons for championing Blacklock. For literary respectability Scotland required a body of lyrics, and in Hume's judgement Blacklock's were 'remarkable for correctness and propriety'[79] (the terms of approval are significant). Equally, the poet's blindness formed the basis of this appeal to taste and sensibility: 'Every man of taste, from the merit of the performance, would be inclined to purchase them: every benevolent man, from the situation of the author, would wish to encourage him.'[80] Unfortunately Hume undercuts this recommendation with his further comment that Blacklock's 'poetical, though very much to be admired, is the least part of his merit'. Arguably the major reason for Hume's interest in the blind poet is revealed first in a letter to Wilkes of 8 October 1754: 'He employs the Ideas of Light & Colors with great Propriety.'[81]

In common with many eighteenth-century philosophers Hume was fascinated by the nature of, and the relationships among, the various senses and the manifestation of emotions. When he recited Pope's 'Elegy to the Memory of an Unfortunate Lady' to Blacklock,

> it affected him extremely. His eyes, indeed, the great index of the mind, could express no passion: but his whole body was thrown into agitation. That poem was equally qualified to touch the delicacy of his taste, and the tenderness of his feelings.[82]

Blacklock assured Hume that he retained no trace of the ideas of light or colours. Recalling Locke's example of the blind man who likened scarlet to the sound of a trumpet, Hume

> asked him whether he had not formed associations of that kind, and whether he did not connect colour and sound together. He answered, that as he met so often, both in books and conversation, with the terms expressing colour, he had formed some false associations, which supported him when he read, wrote, or talked of colours: but that the associations were of the intellectual kind. The illumination of the sun, for instance, he supposed to resemble the presence of a friend; the cheerful colour of green, to be like an amiable sympathy, &c.[83]

While conceding that he did not easily understand Blacklock, Hume draws this conclusion from his example:

> I believe, in much of our own thinking, there will be found some species of association. 'Tis certain we always think in some language, viz. in that which is most familiar to us; and 'tis too frequent to substitute words instead of ideas.[84]

Here was the main interest of Blacklock for Hume, and he was to advise Joseph Spence to consider Blacklock in terms of the way in which mystics associate.

Sadly, the poems reflect none of this interest, being stock, and sometimes awkward, exercises in the most traditional of modes—hymn, ode, pastoral, and epistle. Occasionally Blacklock does attempt to represent his sensory experiences, but all that appears to be available to him is an overblown version of stock poetic diction. Here, in the last stanza of 'An Hymn to Divine Love, in Imitation of Spenser' (p. 14) the attempt becomes self-dramatized to the point of absurdity:

> It comes! It comes! I feel internal day;
> Transfusive warmth thro' all my bosom glows;
> My soul expanding gives the torrent way;
> Thro' all my veins it kindles as it flows.
> Thus, ravish'd from the scene of night and woes,
>   Oh! snatch me, bear me, to thy happy reign:
>   There teach my tongue thy praise in more exalted strain.

The regrettable effect of Blacklock's blindness on his poetry was that he mimicked the poets whom he read and had little imaginative originality of his own. 'The First Ode of Horace Imitated' (p. 1ff.) copies Latin syntax and includes Latinate terms. These lines are representative:

> There are who on th'Olympic plain
> Delight the chariot's speed to rein;
> Involv'd in glorious dust, to roll,
> To turn with glowing wheel the goal.

Similarly in the line 'And fled like birds obscene from light' ('An Hymn to

Fortitude') Blacklock uses the term 'obscene' in a way that would be understood only by classical scholars.

As with Wilkie, Blacklock finds it difficult to sustain a formal or grandiloquent manner without descent into bathos or doggerel, as these lines from 'The CIV Psalm Imitated' show:

> Wide o'er the heav'ns the various bow he bends,
> Its tinctures brightens, and its arch extends.
> At the glad sign the airy conduits flow,
> Soften the hills, and chear the meads below.
> By genial fervour, and prolific rain,
> Swift vegetation runs thro' all the plain:
> Nature, profusely good, with bliss o'erflows,
> And still is pregnant, though she still bestows.
> Here verdant pastures wide extended ly,
> And yield the grazing herd exuberant supply.

In 'An Hymn to Benevolence' he attempts the note of sentimental benevolism, but it too degenerates into bathos:

> By thee inspir'd, the gen'rous breast,
> In blessing mankind only bless'd,
>   With goodness largely free,
> Delights the widow's tears to stay,
> To teach the blind their smoothest way,
>   And aid the feeble knee.

Even in Blacklock's two anti-Jacobite poems the degree of stylization makes the true (and presumably strong) feeling underlying the poems hard to identify. Hume had recruited as Scotland's national lyric poet a writer who even on subjects of immediate or recent national concern could offer little more than vague and self-indulgent gesturing, of which this, the first stanza of 'An Ode, On the Surrender of Edinburgh', is typical:

> While on Edina's fate intent,
> In sighs my joyless soul I sent,
>   In tears my weeping heart;
> The weeping streams gave tear for tear,
> And echo'd every sigh sincere,
>   With sympathetic smart.

In 'an Ode on the present Rebellion' the poet indulges in wildly overdone rhetoric such as 'Hence, fraud unbars Edina's gate,/Hence, recent slaughter loads yon plain'. That Hume continued to sponsor such efforts for so long is a tribute to his benevolence but an indictment of his literary judgement.

Ironically, when Edinburgh produced a poet of real ability in Robert Fergusson the *literati* ignored him. Fergusson's earliest published poems, which appeared in Ruddiman's *Weekly Magazine* in 1771, were mainly English imitations, and Fergusson continued to write poems in English, including witty burlesques such as 'The Sow of Feeling', his response to Mackenzie. But such reputation as he had acquired before his wretchedly premature death in 1774 rested mainly on those poems in which he evinced a considerable talent for the expressive use of the vernacular. Yet he went unheeded by the *literati*. Why?

It has to be said that Fergusson did not write primarily for an English readership, and he made no concessions to such tastes as sentimentalism or the vogue of melancholy (though his own experiences were such as might have led him to question the truth of the fashionable belief in the joys of grief). With a linguistic verve equalled since the Makars only by Ramsay, Fergusson made satire and humorous writing his forte. Now humour had no place in the earnest programme of the *literati*. Thus Fergusson could not expect to be favoured by the arbiters of polite taste. Moreover the fact that, like Ramsay, he revived the poetic use of the Scots vernacular meant that the whole tenor of his poetry ran counter to the desire of the *literati* that Scots writers should prove their eminence in standard English.

Fergusson's language has been identified by Alexander M Kinghorn and Alexander Law as

> fundamentally the Scots of Edinburgh Old Town, which he enriched by importing words from other dialects, notably that of his Aberdeenshire parents, and also by creating new words upon the analogy of older ones. His idiom mingled urban with rural strains and reflected the persisting mediaeval identity of the crowded city and its hinterland.[85]

One of Fergusson's motives in employing Scots vernacular was patriotic. The use of Scots idiom reflects a nationalism that found expression in the poem 'The Ghaists' (p. 166, lines 29–33) and in these lines in 'Auld Reekie' (p. 148):

> For O, waes me! the thistle springs
> In domicile of ancient kings,
> Without a patriot to regrete
> Our palace, and our ancient state.

To his use of the vernacular Fergusson brought an expressive energy redolent of that of the Makars. The range of his diction is remarkably broad. John Butt showed that Fergusson was able to include Latinate terms alongside those of the vernacular, and also that he was successful in employing the vernacular for the expression of such features as personification which he borrowed from English poets. Citing these lines from 'The Daft Days' (p. 122)—

> Tho' Discord gie a canker'd snarl
> To spoil our glee,
> As lang's there's pith into the barrel
> We'll drink and gree.

—Butt comments,

Fergusson shows that he had already learned a lesson that Pope and Gray could have taught him. While they delight us with a well-placed vulgarism in a passage of otherwise elegantly familiar verse, Fergusson delights us by his skill in placing words from a wider British usage into a Lothian setting.[86]

Fergusson's originality in the use of language is matched by an originality in the use of poetic forms. Particularly impressive is the way in which he combines expressive use of Scots vernacular with an often-original and specific use of traditional forms. Often, rather than merely accepting the inherited form, Fergusson adapts it and employs it to his own particular purpose. In marked contrast with the vapid imitations of Blacklock is Fergusson's version of Horace's 'Ode XI, Lib. I' where the use of the vernacular is highly expressive and manages to avoid being reductive of its subject. In his 'Elegy on the Death of Scots Music' (p. 123) Fergusson takes a traditional mode and turns it to original use while employing the 'standart Habbie' measure for serious purposes. Fergusson's 'An Eclogue' is characterised by an especially effective use of Scots idiom, so much so that Matthew P McDiarmid, noting the poem's 'admirable keeping of decorum', deems it 'unique in the whole range of pastoral or rural poetry'.[87] Similarly, the success of 'The Farmer's Ingle' is partly the result of the way in which Fergusson adapts the Spenserian stanza in an original way to accommodate the vernacular expression of his subject.

Like Ramsay, Burns, and Smollett, Fergusson injects his own creative energies into inherited forms, turning them to original expressive purposes. Such a readiness to adapt traditional modes to serve the needs of the individual imagination, rather than merely submit to them, marks out the major talent. In contrast, Wilkie and Blacklock allowed adherence to rules to direct their writing.

Even in Fergusson's earliest poem in Scots, 'The Daft Days' there are clear indications of his innovative capacity. There he employs the pastoral mode in demonstrating its irrelevance to his description of Edinburgh during the New Year holidays:

> From naked groves nae birdie sings;
> To shepherd's pipe nae hillock rings;
> The breeze nae od'rous flavour brings
> From Borean cave;
> And dwyning Nature droops her wings,
> Wi' visage grave.
>
> (p. 121)

Fergusson addresses the city and such representative inhabitants as 'browster wives' and 'fiddlers' and ends on this characteristic note of humour:

> And thou, great god of *Aqua Vitae*!
> Wha sways the empire of this city,
> When fou we're sometimes capernoity,
> Be thou prepar'd

To hedge us frae that black banditti,
The City-Guard.

This is typical of the best of Fergusson's poetry in that he writes from close
knowledge of the richly diverse life of the urban community. In such poems
as 'The King's Birth-Day in Edinburgh', 'Caller Oysters', 'Hallow-Fair', 'Auld
Reekie', 'The Rising of the Session', 'The Sitting of the Session', and 'The
Election' Fergusson displays both a keen sense of the life of Edinburgh and
the true poet's capacity to detach himself and render that life using his
resources of language to the full. This stanza in 'Hallow-Fair' is illustrative of
the way in which Fergusson's richly expressive language mimics its subject:

> Without, the cuissers prance and nicker,
>   An' owr the ley-rig scud;
> In tents the carles bend the bicker,
>   An' rant an' roar like wud.
> Then there's sic yellowchin and din,
>   Wi' wives and wee-anes gablin,
> That ane might true they were a-kin
>   To a' the tongues at Babylon,
>   Confus'd that day.
>   (p. 134)

This same quality is abundantly present in 'Auld Reekie' in which the poet
offers a narrative account of his impressions of the events of a day and night
in the capital. The remarkable aspect of Fergusson's achievement in this poem
is the way in which he employs narrative in the service of representing a
succession of strongly visual and oral impressions. In this use of linguistic
energy for pictorial representation there are obvious affinities with the
Makars and, to an extent, with the vibrancy of Smollett's rendering of
urban life in standard English prose. No other Scottish writer could depict
Scottish urban life with the vividness of Fergusson. None of the *literati* or
their protégés had his expressive capacity. While the *literati* were familiar
with the scenes and events which Fergusson presented, it was in their view
inappropriate that the Athens of the North be known elsewhere in terms of a
social panorama of its harlots, merchants, errand-boys, and oyster-sellers,
all represented in the idiom of the place.

Fergusson's poetry embodied many of the features of the older Scottish
tradition, for which the arbiters of polite taste in Edinburgh saw no future
within the unified culture that was now theirs. The inventive and often wildly
humorous exaggeration of the Makars is frequently present in Fergusson's
poems.

In 'To the Principal and Professors of the University of St. Andrews, on
their superb treat to Dr. Samuel Johnson' the sustained expressive energy,
and in particular the hyperbole that is at once both wild and beautifully
modulated and the way in which the description of Scottish produce is turned
into a fierce attack on Dr Johnson, recalls, as Kinghorn and Law note, 'the
old Scots flyting tradition, which in style and character is quite different from

any convention that Johnson could have recognised' (p. xxiv). When Kinghorn and Law speak of Fergusson's possessing 'a Dunbar-like detachment' the quality alluded to is that capacity, typified at its most extreme in the flyting, to give vent to a linguistic fire while at the same time directing it to some over-riding expressive function. Since Burns this quality has been rare in Scottish poetry.

In other respects, too, Fergusson maintains the line of continuity in Scottish poetry from the Makars to Burns. 'On Seeing a Butterfly in the Street' (p. 169) is notable for the flux of attitude—apparently spontaneous, but actually carefully controlled—from the initial 'Daft gowk, in macaroni dress' to 'Kind Nature lent but for a day/Her wings to make ye sprush and gay'. This reflects an emotional complexity and movement which recall Dunbar, which Burns reproduces with some success, and which are decidedly at odds with the taste of the age of sensibility for polarisation and prolongation of emotion. At the same time, it is truer to human experience. This sense of emotional complexity is reflected in Fergusson's masterly modulation of tone. Rightly, Kinghorn and Law identify his 'ability to blend the lyrical with the satirical [as] Fergusson's most consistently perceptible poetic talent' (p. xxvii). In such a poem as 'Ode to the Gowdspink' (p. 179) he is, in his editors' terms, at once both 'sardonic and reflective' (p. xxviii).

The poets who were to find favour in literary Edinburgh were those who were able to prolong the single emotional note, and it mattered not if this led to gesturing, self-consciousness, and rôle-playing. Such awareness of emotional complexity and such balancing of voices against one another as Fergusson's poems evince were quite beyond them. One aspect of Fergusson's importance, then, is in providing a bridge in eighteenth-century Scottish poetry—and totally contrary to polite taste at that time—between the emotional realism of the older tradition and the emotional realism of our time. His other particular accomplishment was to revive the tradition in Scottish literature wherein the poet represented the life of the community; but, to an extent unequalled then or since, he expressed through poetry the life of a large and urban community. If, in this respect, his subject-matter is modern, in technique he is the descendent of the older Scottish tradition. No poem exemplifies this better than 'Leith Races'. Here the poet introduces the figure of Mirth in terms that recall the ballads:

> In July month, ae bonny morn,
>   Whan Nature's rokelay green
> Was spread o'er ilka rigg o'corn,
>   To charm our roving een;
> Glouring about I saw a quean,
>   The fairest 'neath the lift;
> Her een ware o' the siller sheen,
>   Her skin like snawy drift,
>   Sae white that day.
>   (p. 174)

But Fergusson proceeds to offer an account of the all-too-human activities of a whole range of Edinburgh citizens. Thus, without strain, ballad and social realism are linked and several centuries are spanned.

That the *literati* should have disregarded a poet who was so obviously integral to the Scottish literary tradition is probably the clearest indication of the artificiality of their cultural programme and the strongest indictment of their literary judgement. It is acutely paradoxical that Adam Smith and Adam Ferguson could foresee the problems of industrial urban life but were ready to ignore the poet of urban life. The most charitable construction that can be placed upon the neglect of Fergusson by the *literati* is that they were being realistic about the limitations inseparable from the use of the vernacular for the poet who would reach a British audience. Sadly, but perhaps almost inevitably, they overlooked a major Scottish poet while promoting minor versifiers in English.

Chapter 4

'Whaur's your Willie Shakespeare noo?': the Tragedies of John Home

Above all else, Scotland had to produce a tragedian for her claims for literary recognition to be taken seriously; or so the *literati* believed. Scottish achievements in the genre had been undistinguished. Arguably James Thomson was the most accomplished Scottish tragedian to that date, but he had headed south early in his career, written in a manner and on subjects which did nothing to proclaim his nationality, and died in 1748. The Select Society, and in particular those whom Ernest Mossner terms its 'literary triumvirate'[1] of Elibank, Kames, and Hume, set out to find a Scottish tragic writer who might work upon Scottish material.

Yet again, the interests of the Scottish philosophers lent support to the nature and the direction of the literary programme. The concern of the philosophers with the joys of melancholy led to examination of the nature of tragedy and the particular question of why we derive pleasure from the spectacle of tragedy. In his *Lectures on Rhetoric and Belles Lettres* Smith noted that

> The actions and perceptions which directly affect us and make the deepest impression on our minds, are those that are of the misfortunate kind, and give us in the perception a considerable degree of uneasiness. They are always found to be more interesting than others of the same degree of strength, if they are of a pleasant and agreeable nature.[2]

Confronted by such actions and perceptions, we become interested, Smith contends, in the connection between cause and effect. Where accidents befall human beings, these

> interest us greatly by the sympathetical affections they raise in us. We enter into their misfortunes, grieve when they grieve, rejoice when they rejoice, and in a word feel for them in some respects as if we ourselves were in the same condition.[3]

We not only share in the misfortune of the sufferer but long for his release from his suffering and rejoice with him if this is accomplished. Smith recognises all of these as components of our response to tragedy.

Stressing that it is the view of the situation rather than the view of the passion it has prompted in the sufferer that excites sympathy, Smith points out that 'we sometimes feel for another, a passion of which he himself seems to be altogether incapable; because, when we put ourselves in his case, that passion arises in our breast from the imagination, though it does not in his from the reality'.[4] Smith goes on to recognise the limitations of sympathy, noting that the sympathiser 'can never conceive, for what has befallen another, that degree of passion which naturally animates the person principally concerned'.[5] Smith accounts for this in these two main ways: firstly, 'that imaginary change of situation, upon which their sympathy is founded, is but momentary'; and, secondly, and more significantly in respect of the spectator at a tragedy, 'the thought of their own safety, the thought that they themselves are not really the sufferers, continually intrudes itself upon them; and though it does not hinder them from conceiving a passion somewhat analogous to what is felt by the sufferer, hinders them from conceiving anything that approaches to the same degree of violence'.[6]

In the philosophical background, then, is the basis of the conflict of sympathy and credulity in Smith's thinking. It is natural and also creditable to feel sympathy for the characters of tragedy, but there must necessarily be limits to that sympathy since, as Smith claims when discussing the unities,

> We know that we are in the playhouse, that the persons before us are actors, and that the thing represented either happened before, or perhaps never happened at all. The pleasure we have in a dramatical performance no more rises from deception than that which we have in looking at pictures. No one ever imagined that he saw the sacrifice of Iphigenia; no more did any one imagine that he saw King Richard the Third.[7]

The same duality informs his account of the rise of literature. According to Smith, the first writers played upon the wonder of 'a rude and ignorant people'. The growth of learning was accompanied by a decline in credulity. In place of the marvellous, writers then 'had recourse to that which they believed would please and interest most: that is, to represent such actions and passions as, being affecting in themselves, or displaying the delicate feelings of the human heart, were likely to be most interesting'.[8] That is to say, our ancestors marvelled, whereas we wish to be sufficiently involved emotionally to sympathise while at the same time, as sophisticated beings, we know all along that it is all a pretence.

About this notion of partial commitment, or rather a constant process of commitment giving way to detachment, there is something distinctly modern. With the disintegration of the self into a variety of rôles, total and sustained commitment is largely beyond modern man. For most western cultures this discovery has accompanied the recognition of the shortfall of Romantic idealism. It is typical of the way in which so many Scottish writers are the harbingers of the modern divided self that Smith should have identified this duality in the situation of the spectator of tragedy. It is very much as the Scot that he perceives that simultaneous involvement and detachment are integral to the human response. If we sympathise and then are conscious of being detached witnesses to a spectacle; if we partake of the emotions of the character, only to recall that we are sitting in the theatre; or even if we are involved

in both of these activities simultaneously—everything conduces to self-consciousness, awareness of the several rôles that we are, or have been, playing.
It is no accident that it was Scottish philosophers who were so concerned
with these matters. The underlying notion that identity is meaningful in
terms of flux has much to do with the eighteenth-century Scottish uncertainty
as to identity.

Hume, in considering how it is that spectators of tragedy can take pleasure
from the sorrow, terror, and anxiety they feel, offered the view that

> The whole art of the poet is employed, in rouzing and supporting the compassion
> or indignation, the anxiety or resentment of his audience. They are pleased in
> proportion as they are afflicted; and never so happy as when they employ tears,
> sobs, and cries to give vent to their sorrow and relieve their heart, swoln with
> the tenderest sympathy and compassion.[9]

Hume's explanation of the pleasure of sympathy suggests a close affinity with
living vicariously (he takes the example of how, at the gaming-tables, it is
high stakes, rather than skilful play, that draw the crowds). Citing Fontenelle
on how pleasure and pain 'differ not so much in their cause', and taking the
example of tickling which, according to degree, can be pleasant or painful,
Hume maintains,

> Hence it proceeds, that there is such a thing as a sorrow, soft and agreeable: It
> is a pain weakened and diminished. The heart likes naturally to be moved and
> affected.[10]

He then makes this clear delineation of the hybrid nature of the spectator's
response:

> We weep for the misfortune of a hero, to whom we are attached: In the same
> instant we comfort ourselves, by reflecting, that it is nothing but a fiction: And
> it is precisely that mixture of sentiments, which composes an agreeable sorrow,
> and tears that delight us.[11]

For Hume, it is imperative that the tragedian acknowledge and cater for such
complexity. He contends that the movements of the imagination must be
predominant over those of passion, and he argues against the unrelieved
representation of suffering since 'even the common sentiments of compassion
require to be softened by some agreeable affection, in order to give a thorough
satisfaction to the audience.'[12] In contrast with this, the advice of the *literati*
in real, practical terms tended to direct writers towards playing unrelievedly
upon the single melancholic note.

When Scottish writers and critics came to look beyond the theory of tragedy
to significant exemplification of the mode they were confronted time and
again by the figure of Shakespeare. Shakespeare impinged very considerably
on the consciousness of the eighteenth-century Scottish writer. This is
reflected in the extent and the nature of the contribution of Scots to the
increasing body of Shakespeare criticism. As criticism in general freed itself

from the restraining influence of neo-classical rules, so Shakespeare's richly individual and multi-faceted genius came to be appreciated. At the same time, evaluation of tragic dramatists became a European critical activity and assumed a national dimension, the more so after Voltaire's wild mis-representation of Shakespeare's achievement after his stay in England in the years 1726–9.

The focus for much of the critical activity in the first half of the eighteenth century was the question of Shakespeare's relation to Aristotelian criteria, and in particular to the requirements of the unities of action, place, and time. In 1709 Nicholas Rowe asserted that Shakespeare could not be judged on the basis of rules of which he knew nothing. Similarly Pope, in the Preface to his edition of 1725, affirmed that to evaluate Shakespeare on the basis of Aristotle's rules would be 'like trying a man by laws of one country who acted under those of another'.[13] Shakespearian drama was compared by Pope to 'an ancient majestic piece of Gothic architecture', whereas more orthodox drama was 'a neat modern building'. In 1751 came the strongest challenge to Aristotelian rules with Dr Johnson's item in *The Rambler*, No. 156 (14 September 1751), 'The laws of writing not always indisputable. A vindication of tragi-comedy.' The crux of this is Johnson's assertion, 'It ought to be the first endeavour of a writer to distinguish nature from custom.'[14] Johnson warns that 'the accidental prescriptions of authority, when time has procured them veneration, are often confounded with the laws of nature, and those rules are supposed coeval with reason, of which the first rise cannot be discovered'. The relevance of various rules to modern drama is questioned by Johnson. The rule that 'only three speaking personages should appear at once upon the stage' he traces to the origin of tragedy in monody, and he finds that 'the variety and intricacy of modern plays has made it impossible to be observed'. Likewise, he dismisses the law limiting the number of acts to five, and rejects the demands for unity of time. Tragi-comedy is vindicated, 'for what is there in the mingled drama which impartial reason can condemn?' Among those rules which he deems 'more fixed and obligatory' are: 'the chief action should be single', and 'tragedy must always have a hero, a person apparently and incontestably superior to the rest, upon whom the attention may be fixed, and the anxiety suspended'.[15] In his *Preface* of 1765 Johnson defended Shakespeare's disregard of the unities, the basis of the defence being the appeal to nature. For Johnson, the unities of time and place 'have given more trouble to the poet, than pleasure to the auditor'.[16] In his discussion of the unities Johnson stresses that theatrical representation is never taken by us for reality itself, and he adds that

> The delight of tragedy proceeds from our consciousness of fiction; if we thought murders and treasons real, they would please no more. Imitations produce pain or pleasure, not because they are mistaken for realities, but because they bring realities to mind.[17]

One further point on which Johnson takes care to distance himself from the French tragedians is in his claim that 'we still find that on our stage something must be done as well as said, and inactive declamation is very coldly heard, however musical or elegant, passionate or sublime'.[18] This leads on to Johnson's description of the work of a correct writer as a garden, whereas that of Shakespeare is a forest. Rules, according to Johnson, were 'to be sacrificed to the nobler beauties of variety and instruction'.

All of this demonstrates that in England neo-classical regularity was retreating under strong pressure. Scottish reactions range from those of the ultra-conservative Lord Monboddo to the views of Smith which run parallel to Johnson's at several points. For Monboddo, the English reverence of Shakespeare had been detrimental to English taste. He judged Shakespeare's tragedies failures because they lacked adequate fables, and this for the reason that Shakespeare believed a 'plain historical fact would make a poetic fable'.[19] Vital to the success of a tragedy, according to Monboddo, was the anagnorisis, or discovery; had Shakespeare been familiar with Aristotle he would have known this, but ignorance of this fact precluded his success.

Only marginally less unbending was Hume. To his eyes Shakespeare was possessed of genius but was deficient in learning. Hume deplores the deleterious effects of 'many irregularities and even absurdities' in Shakespeare's plays; he suspects that Shakespeare's genius is over-rated 'in the same manner as bodies often appear more gigantic, on account of their being disproportioned and misshapen'; and, above all, he regrets thus the influence of the 'rude genius' of Shakespeare on the English theatre:

> The English theatre has ever since taken a strong tincture of Shakespeare's spirit and character; and thence it has proceeded, that the nation has undergone, from all its neighbours, the reproach of barbarism, from which its valuable productions in some other parts of learning would otherwise have exempted it.[20]

In such judgements Hume writes as both the admirer of French elegance, order, and propriety and the civilised Scot who values the enlightening stability which the Union has brought and fears regression to the wrangling and bloodshed that had characterised so much of Scottish life.

In contrast, Adam Smith did not regard adherence to neo-classical rules as pre-requisite to dramatic success. In his *Lectures on Rhetoric and Belles Lettres* he notes that Shakespeare, unlike the French tragedians, does not observe the unity of time. Shakespeare, Smith points out, has gaps of several years in his accounts. But then Smith implicitly plays down the importance of this by stressing that we are never deceived in any case and always remember that we are in a playhouse. Similarly, after contrasting Shakespeare with Racine and Sophocles in terms of unity of place, Smith comments,

> But when this rule is not observed, we find the effect of the piece may still be very considerable which . . . shows that it is not deception which gives us the pleasure we find in these works, and, in fact, we never are deceived for one moment.[21]

In short, there is a certain ambivalence in Smith's thought on this matter: he begins by acknowledging that the unities retain some importance, but when he finds that their neglect can still result in effective drama his answer is that this demonstrates that we are never deceived by the theatrical illusion.

Of the *literati* it was Kames who made the most significant contribution to Shakespeare criticism. Much of Kames's thinking is progressive. He perceives the unities of time and place to be irrelevant to modern drama; if adhered to, they create absurd situations. Kames's attitude is realistic and his thought carefully measured. 'But though I have thus taken arms to rescue modern poets from the slavish fetters of modern critics', he writes, 'I would not be understood to justify liberty without any reserve';[22] and he goes on to emphasise that freedom from the unities of time and place should not be allowed to threaten unity of action. Like Smith and Johnson, Kames contends that the spectator is aware that the real time and place are not those of the representation, and he stresses that while adherence to the unities might be conducive to refinement freedom of action brings with it more substantial excellencies. This is the most important aspect of Kames's version of tragedy: the whole drift of his thinking is towards recognition of the primacy of substance over technique. He sees clearly the deficiences of the declamatory and descriptive style of Corneille and Racine, and identifies as the particular strength of Shakespeare his capacity to individualise characters in terms of actions, feelings and thoughts. When he examines technique—as in noting Shakespeare's use of blank verse and his modulation of verse and prose—his abiding concern is with the way in which technique is geared to psychological investigation of the individual. Observing that 'no passion beats always with equal pulse', Kames studies the complexity and the flux of the passions in *Othello* and appreciates the special function, in this context, of Shakespeare's soliloquies. Above all, Kames recognises that Shakespeare's knowledge of human nature enables him to represent human experience and human response across a wide range of characters. Thus, Kames's importance in the development of Shakespeare criticism is in giving impetus to the movement towards psychological study of the plays, a movement which was to reach new heights within half a century in the criticism of the Romantics.

It has become evident that Scottish thinking on the subject of tragedy encompassed a diversity of views. Not only was there a range of opinion amongst the critics, but in some cases there were conflicting elements within the individual. Thus it becomes plain that he who would bear the title of Scotland's tragedian would be subject to varied advice. The task fell to John Home, minister of Athelstaneford and a relation of David Hume. By 1749 John Home had to his credit a tragedy, *Agis*, which is a re-working of an episode in Spartan history as recounted by Plutarch. According to its author, 'the play breathes heroism and virtue'.[23] The trouble is that while the hero, Agis, radiates virtue his heroism is of the passive suffering kind and his death is not tragic but pathetic. A further problem is that Home added a sub-plot to sustain love-interest and he fails to inter-relate main plot and sub-plot sufficiently closely to one another. Possibly there is a connection between the failure on the part of Scottish writers to achieve imaginative integration of diverse elements and the fragmentation of the Scottish personality. Certainly Home is, in both personal and literary contexts, a conspicuous example of the eighteenth-century Scottish characteristic of division within.

But if Home and some of his sponsors reflect internal division, what united them all was a dedication to the cause of Scotland's literary reputation. Encouraged by all, Home completed *Douglas*, a tragedy based on Scottish material. For the *literati, Douglas* was a standard-bearer in the cause of Scottish cultural nationalism. After its rejection by Garrick, the play was revised and Home wrote a new prologue for the first performance at Edinburgh. That this prologue was strongly nationalistic in spirit reflects not only the author's resentment of Garrick's refusal but also his responsiveness to the play's rôle in the cultural ambitions of his circle; and it probably takes account also of fairly widespread grumbling about the way in which the Union was working out for Scotland, a dissatisfaction which centred in the particular thorn of the suppression of the Scottish militia. The Edinburgh prologue is carefully orchestrated to appeal to such sentiments. Ancient Athens is likened geographically to Caledonia. And implicit is the wish that the two countries may be further identified in terms of learning and, in particular, 'the Tragic Muse'. In the delineation of the features of the heroic age of Athens tragedy is associated with the finest of feelings; poets and heroes are related in the claim that they share the same reward—glory; and it is alleged that 'The Tragic Muse each glorious record kept/And, o'er the kings she conquer'd, Athens wept'.

That the response of compassionate tears should warrant especial admiration is significant. At an early stage Home caught the resonances of the vogue of pity and the pleasures of melancholy. Here Home's meeting with William Collins at Winchester in 1749 was certainly influential. At their meeting the two writers discussed their future plans. In Collins' 'Ode on the Popular Superstitions of the Highlands', composed shortly afterwards, Home is said to have lingered 'Mid those soft friends, whose hearts, some future day/Shall melt, perhaps, to hear thy tragic song'—a clear reference to the projected tragedy which became *Douglas*. Home is exhorted to find his subject in his native land:

> Fresh to that soil thou turn'st, whose very vale
> Shall prompt the poet, and his song demand:
> To thee thy copious subjects ne'er shall fail;
> Thou need'st but take the pencil to thy hand,
> And paint what all believe who won thy genial land.

After an account of the myths and legends of Scotland that are available to the writer, Home is further advised:

> Proceed, in forceful sounds and colours bold
> The native legends of thy land rehearse;
> To such adapt thy lyre and suit thy powerful verse.

Collins' endorsement of Home's interest in Scottish lore helped determine the subject-matter of the tragedy. In the Edinburgh prologue Home suggests that, if in the past the Scottish audience has shown 'soft compassion' to the woes of foreign heroes, they will respond with more than a 'common tear' to the experiences of a hero from their own nation. Thus the Edinburgh prologue is directed at both nationalism and sensibility.

Home derived specific inspiration from another, and quite different, source—the ballad, 'Gil Morrice'. What Home did with the ballad is typical of the values of the age in Scotland. Taking the central situation of the ballad—murder of son by husband in the mistaken belief that he is wife's lover—Home, with some slight alteration of detail, made it the climactic incident in a play about one of Scotland's most ancient and renowned families. The selection of an episode rich in its potential for pathos related Home's play to the tradition of pathetic tragedy developed by Otway and Rowe. At the same time, the choice of characters and the dating of the play's action reflected the playwright's interest in Scotland's distant past. This locates Home in the forefront of that concern with an earlier Scotland which grew steadily through the eighteenth century and culminated in Scott.

If the creation of a heroic past offered safe release for such feelings (as Andrew Hook has suggested, with reference to the Ossian poems),[24] it also lends a distinctive colouring to the Scottish version of the movement towards sensibility. It is in this light that *Douglas* is especially important; and the nature of the play may be regarded as an expression of the union of subject and personality of the writer. Such is Mackenzie's judgement, but he comments that 'Gil Morrice' 'happily suited the bent of [Home's] imagination, that loved to dwell amidst the heroic times of chivalry and romantic valour'.[25] This view fails to take account of the chill realism of the ballad's treatment of its subject-matter, of which the following is representative:

> Now he has drawn his trusty brand,
> And slaited in the strae;
> And thro' Gill Morrice' fair body
> He's gar cauld iron gae.
> And he has ta'in Gill Morrice' head
> And set it on a speir;
> The meanest man in a' his train
> Has gotten that head to bear.

None of this spirit survives in Home's version, where the treatment of the subject is, with the exception of the fate of Douglas, unrelievedly sentimental.

Of the literature produced under the aegis of David Hume and his circle *Douglas* was the most influential and best exemplifies the spirit of compromise that characterises the literature of the age in Scotland. It is worth recognising in *Douglas* the existence of features which might be described as proto-Romantic, or at least potentially Romantic. Such features are present a little later in the work of James Beattie, and in *The Minstrel* in particular. In a different cultural context they might well have heralded the fuller flowering of Romanticism.

Foremost among such elements in *Douglas* is the aura of the mysterious— with a hint of the transcendental—with which Home invests the experiences of his characters. Lady Randolph's first words suggest communion with the natural world—it both shares and evokes her mood—and with a spirit resident in nature and identified as that of her dead husband:

> Ye woods and wilds, whose melancholy gloom
> Accords with my soul's sadness, and draws forth
> The voice of sorrow from my bursting heart,
> Farewel a while: I will not leave you long;
> For in your shades I deem some spirit dwells,
> Who from the chiding stream, or groaning oak,
> Still hears, and answers to Matilda's moan.
>
> (I, 1–7)

The notion of nature's affording access to truth is made explicit in Douglas's address to the landscape with which the final act begins:

> This is the place, the centre of the grove.
> Here stands the oak, the monarch of the wood.
> How sweet and solemn is this mid-night scene!
> The silver moon, unclouded, holds her way
> Thro' skies where I could count each little star.
> The fanning west wind scarcely stirs the leaves;
> The river, rushing o'er its pebbly bed,
> Imposes silence with a stilly sound.
> In such a place as this, at such an hour,
> If ancestry can be in ought believ'd,
> Descending spirits have conversed with man,
> And told the secrets of the world unknown.
>
> (V, 1–12)

That the first and last acts begin in this vein is far from accidental, and the suggestion is of a power in nature which can induce man into a transcendental awareness of truth. Both this and the idea of the consonance of feelings and landscape anticipate Wordsworth; and the hermit, whose history is recounted (IV, 50–89) is the precursor of the hermit-sage in Beattie's *The Minstrel* and the solitary beings of Wordsworth's poems (and, possibly, of the bard in Burns's 'Lament for James, Earl of Glencairn').

Significant too is the recurrent imagery in which the characters in *Douglas* express themselves by means of analogy with the natural world. In the main this imagery is relatively unornate, and in its natural purity lies much of its effectiveness in communicating the values of a distant but heroic age. Implicit in the use of such imagery is the sense that these are people who relate in terms of the natural world, are close to nature, and are nearer to natural man than to modern man. Examples abound:

> Lord Randolph: These might contend with, and allay thy grief,
> As meeting tides and currents smooth our firth.
>
> (I, 75–6)

Lord Randolph: Emblem of me: affliction, like a storm,
                    Hath kill'd the forward blossom of my heart.
                                                    (II, 197–8)

Glenalvon: Darkly a project peers upon my mind,
                    Like the red moon when rising in the east,
                    Cross'd and divided by strange-colour'd clouds.
                                                    (II, 276–8)

Douglas: Eventful day! how hast thou chang'd my state!
                    Once on the cold, and winter shaded side
                    Of a bleak hill, mischance had rooted me,
                    Never to thrive, child of another soil:
                    Transplanted now to the gay sunny vale
                    Like the green thorn of May my fortune flowers.
                                                    (V, 87–92)

Such recurrent imagery relates the characters and their behaviour to forces and principles inherent in nature. At the heart of this is the assumption of a correspondence between intensity of emotion and proximity to nature; and this prefigures the Romantic equation of the sublime in nature and in man. Home was one of the first, especially in drama, to give expression to such ideas.

Against these hints at Romanticism have to be set those elements in the play which are firmly neo-classical. Both his education and profession encouraged Home to look back to the classical and neo-classical ages; and, in particular, the influence of David Hume directed the dramatist to neo-classical forms and modes. With justification, David Daiches has commented that David Hume's 'was not the kind of creative mind which could help to fertilize a national culture'; and of Hume and Adam Smith, Alexander Carlyle remarked that 'their taste was a rational act rather than the instantaneous effect of fine feeling'.[26]

The absolutist nature of French neo-classicism, which Hume so admired, is widely recognised. Moreover, as George Steiner points out, 'in his *Introduction à la poésie française* Thierry Maulnier argues that French poetry is more remote than any other from universal elements of folklore and vernacular'.[27] Hume, then, was extolling the virtues of a civilised, timeless, but often lifeless absolutism which was totally inimical to those very elements to which Romanticism was attracted. This was precisely at the time when other European nations, most notably Germany, were beginning to free themselves from the neo-classical authority of France and to develop their native languages to express their distinct cultural needs. (Significantly, in Germany this coincided with the first translations of Shakespeare, e.g. Wieland's in the 1760s). Within two years of Johnson's *Preface* Lessing was to suggest that the nature of French tragedy was the result of a mis-reading of Aristotle on the part of Corneille. Nowhere more than here is the contrast more striking: emergent cultural nationalism in Germany found expression by liberating itself from the French neo-classical example, whereas in Scotland, despite the fact that Blair and, even more so, Kames were less rigid in their interpretation of the unities than Hume, refuge was sought in just such authority.

George Steiner has remarked of Racine's *Phèdre*: 'All that happens, happens inside language. That is the special narrowness and grandeur of the French classic manner.'[28] This quality had to be achieved by Scottish tragedians in a language they were still striving to master. Explaining that he could never bring himself to like John Home's earlier play, *Agis*, Hume wrote,

> The author, I thought, had corrupted his taste by the imitation of Shakespeare, whom he ought only to have admired. But the same author has composed a new tragedy on a subject of invention; and here he appears a true disciple of Sophocles and Racine. I hope in time he will vindicate the English stage from the reproach of barbarism.[29]

In circumstances replete with paradox not the least was in Hume's ambitions for the play, which were based in a compound of aesthetic principles and national pride: the peculiar distinction of the Scottish contribution to the course of British drama was that it was to be non-Shakespearian and rigidly neo-classical. The subject-matter was to be Scottish, the language refined English, and the rules French neo-classical.

The effects of the guidance of the *literati*, and of Hume in particular, are evident in *Douglas*. Hume was able to commend the play thus to l'Abbé le Blanc:

> I am perswaded, that there is not any Tragedy in the English Language so well adapted to your Theatre, by reason of Elegance, Simplicity, & Decorum, which run through the whole of it. I would be much pleas'd to see it translated into French, and to find it successful with those good Critics who so much abound in Paris.[30]

And in a letter of 29 September 1757 he judged *Douglas* 'an admirable tragedy, comparable (to the ecce)llent pieces of the Good Age of Louis Quatorze'.[31] From both the language and the form of the play Home could take heart. As Gerald Parker has pointed out in the most recent edition of the play,[32] the versification is a model of Augustan order, and Home evinces a fondness for the poetic 'set speech'. These features might well suggest that Home's prime interest is in poetry rather than dramatic action, and that style is given priority over substance (precisely the accusation levelled against the Select Society by John Maclaurin in the *Apology for the Writers against the Tragedy of Douglas*).

Taken as a whole, *Douglas* is no more artificial in its diction, no more weighted down by rhetoric, than many eighteenth-century pathetic tragedies. In its day *Douglas* was held to mark something of an advance towards a greater degree of natural purity in diction.[33] Yet there are occasions, especially in the first and second acts, where declamation takes the place of action, be it physical or mental. Lady Randolph's 'complaints' have a habit of ending in high-flown abstraction. A lengthy speech of explanation to Anna ends thus:

> ... Sincerity,
> Thou first of virtues, let no mortal leave
> Thy onward path! altho' the earth should
> gape,
> And from the gulph of hell destruction cry
> To take dissimulation's winding way.
>
> (I, 212–16)

For the modern reader or audience, unlike their counterparts in the eighteenth century, the effect of rhetorical gesturing of this kind is to reduce the desired response of pity; and such declamatory passages slow down the action (Dr Johnson was soon to censure such practice, writing, 'We still find that on our stage something must be done as well as said, and inactive declamation is very coldly heard, however musical or elegant, passionate or sublime.'[34] The taste for declamation coincided with the increasing ascendancy of the actor and the concomitant decline in the status of the play itself. This was part of a general lowering of dramatic standards which Scott was to attribute to the fact that more and more the bourgeoise compromised the audience; and, as Steiner has observed, 'When the theatrical is allowed complete rule over the dramatic, we get melodrama.'[35] In *Douglas* the declamation of the first half of the play makes the subsequent action appear melodramatic by contrast. The extent of that declamation is a direct result of Home's adherence to the unities.

In *Douglas* Home observes the unities of action, time, and place. There is no sub-plot, thus avoiding the division of both mood and audience's interest which, as Mackenzie suggested, weakened Home's first play, *Agis*. Adherence to the unities means that the drama proceeds largely through interviews and the play is, as Gerald Parker noted, fairly static. Events important to the plot take place offstage ('Norval's' foiling of the attempt to murder Lord Randolph, described early in Act II), or have occurred long before the action of the play begins (family feud). Either way, one gets a report, not the action itself, and an element of contrivance surrounds the business of conveying information to the audience. While admiring the poetry of Lady Randolph's opening soliloquy, Henry Mackenzie pointed out that 'it tells a great part of Lady Randolph's story', which is less than true to the nature of soliloquy; and that Lady Randolph should after eighteen years break silence and offer a laborious account of her past life strained the credulity of David Hume—somewhat ironically, given that such an account resulted from adherence to the procedures which he advocated so strongly.[36]

Lady Randolph's proclamations of her grief establish a unity of mood. Mrs Siddons found this monotonous, a judgement that was for Mackenzie—and this is a clear indication of the values of the age of Sensibility—a tribute, 'because that sort of level tone, which is so difficult to support in scenic representations, is the very voice of nature in those situations of long-nourished settled sorrow, which had been for so many years the constant and cherished companion of Lady Randolph'.[37] The intended effect of the single unified plot is that the sustained melancholy of mood and theme should evoke the single, desired response of pity. One outcome of the predominance of reporting over action and the repeated appeals to the emotions of the spectator is, as Gerald Parker notes, that 'the Sophoclean and Aristotelian ideals of tragic action and tragic knowledge were constricted to the superficialities of tragic sensation'.[38] For the eighteenth-century spectator, however, such sensation was far from superficial. Paradoxically, the waning neo-classicism, in its emphasis on unity of mood, hastened the advent of sentimental melo-drama.

Examination of the nature of the appeals to the spectator's pity is important in revealing the direction which the play might have taken, had Home not been fettered by the unities. Initially the spectator is asked to pity Lady Randolph's situation in the present action of the play, a situation that derives from events now distant (death of husband and assumed death of child). A greater measure of poignancy results from the thwarting of what Mackenzie called 'parental tenderness and aspiring virtue'[39] in the observable drama. The point of having Lady Randolph brood over past experiences is to establish the dominant mood of melancholy in which any subsequent response or action of hers is rooted. Thus her reaction on meeting 'Norval' is a complex one, but common to each of its aspects is the potential for evoking pity:

> Lord Randolph: Ha! my Matilda! wherefore starts that tear?
> Lady Randolph: I cannot say: for various affections,
> And strangely mingled, in my bosom swell;
> Yet each of them may well command a tear.
> (II, 83–6)

Lady Randolph's gradual realisation of the identity of 'Norval' (culminating in III, 163–5) is extremely moving for an audience, such as the eighteenth-century one, which has been emotionally engaged in her plight. The anag-norisis (of which Blair deemed *Douglas* and Voltaire's *Mérope* 'great master-pieces')[40] forms the centre of the play. The tragedy inherent in Lady Ran-dolph's situation at the outset is compounded by the fact that she finds and loses her son within one day: only briefly can her maternal affection find its object. With this in mind, Home has her relish the slow revelation of her identity to her son (IV, 164–99), thus establishing an emotional pitch that is the prerequisite to the evocation of a commensurate intensity of pity.

A further and fruitful source of appeals to the spectator's pity is the clash between the heroic code and the maternal instinct, which is one of the recurrent themes of the play. If the play is relatively static and somewhat devoid of dramatic tension, there is a compensatory element in a measure of psychological interest, of which Home might have made much more if he had not been obliged to devote so much of the first half of the play to explanation and declamation. This psychological interest centres around Lady Randolph: for all her obsessive grief, her responses are not single but complex, and within her the conflict between honour and life is constantly enacted. When her son (now thus identified) states his ambition—'Declare my birth/And in the field I'll seek for fame and fortune' (IV, 234–5)—her reaction is a compound of concern for his safety and pride in his sense of honour (which proves him truly a Douglas): pride gives way to prudence concerning his safety (IV, 236–56), and then she thanks God for preserving in her son the 'sacred fire' of her forefathers (IV, 266–80).[41]

There is further considerable pathos in respect of how much is lost with Douglas's death, not only in terms of the suffering caused to Lady Randolph but also in terms of the admirable qualities which he embodies. 'Norval' blesses the hour when he was able to leave his 'father's' house and gain access to his true heritage—the arena of chivalric deeds (IV, 142–6). Faced with the prospect of such experience, he reacts immediately by romanticising war, but—and this is indicative of the balanced nature of his values and of how much is lost with his death—he very rapidly realises that he has been romanticising:

'Norval':   The setting sun,
            With yellow radiance lighten'd all the vale,
            And as the warrior mov'd, each polish'd helm,
            Corslet, or spear, glanc'd back his gild'd beams.
            The hill they climb'd, and halting at its top,
            Of more than mortal size, tow'ring, they seem'd
            An host angelic, clad in burning arms.
Glenalvon: Thou talk'st it well; no leader of our host,
            In sounds more lofty, speaks of glorious war.
'Norval':   If I shall e'er acquire a leader's name,
            My speech will be less ardent. Novelty
            Now prompts my tongue, and youthful admiration
            Vents itself freely; since no part is mine
            Of praise pertaining to the great in arms.

                                                    (IV, 349–62)

Douglas depicts an idealism (akin to the 'lofty and heroic ideas' which, Mackenzie tells us, so engaged Home)[42] reduced to nothing, aspirations rapidly and cruelly balked. Douglas seeks an opportunity to achieve in the arena of battle the 'wondrous deeds' of which he has only read in books (V, 154–5), but of which he has shown himself likely to be capable by his rescue of Lord Randolph (II, 10–22). The bitterest irony is that he dies, not according to the chivalric ideal on the battlefield, but stabbed in the back in a domestic feud of the kind which Lady Randolph had earlier deplored (I, 84–92); and, worse still, he dies in the full knowledge of the fact that valiant deeds and the fame which accompanies them have been denied him (V, 236–9). Lady Randolph's suicide is hastened by her awareness of how much was promised, after such misery, only to be snatched away (V, 289–93).

Melodrama thrived, as tragedy turned increasingly for its subject-matter from the public to the private sphere. *Douglas*, with the potentially great public career denied by the personal feud, points in that direction. In this it resembles *Othello*, but in this only: *Othello* is no melodrama; neither is it pathetic tragedy. For Aristotle the sufferings of an innocent or virtuous man are not tragic but pathetic. Possibly it could be argued that Lady Randolph is, at least in part, the victim of her own tragic obsession; but Douglas is both innocent and virtuous. The portrayal in *Douglas* of the victimisation of essentially good characters relates the play to the eighteenth-century debate about the nature of poetic justice and of natural morality. It also supports Andrew Hook's view that the central characters of *Douglas* 'prefigure the grand heroic protagonists of Ossian'.[43] The circumstances of Douglas's fate, where a heroic idealism is terminated by a petty personal feud, suggest that Home's primary intention was to wring the maximum of pathos from the situation of his hero. In that same situation, however, he expressed—probably without being fully conscious of so doing—a strong criticism of the idealising or romanticising of war, and this runs counter to the heroic spirit with which the preceding action of the play is imbued and which it has appeared to endorse.[44]

Ostensibly *Douglas* is about an episode in Scotland's distant past. But it is also about post-Union Scotland and reflects the complex responses which many Scots felt for their country. That ambivalence of attitude on the part of Lady Randolph—pride in honour and protection of life—is an expression of the ambivalence of Home's attitude towards Scotland.[45] Despite the apparent endorsement of the heroic ethos in most of the action of the play, a strong rationalist element has surfaced by the end. The attempt to idealise the heroic age from afar terminates in an unexpected note of realism. In himself Home never achieved that promising balance of romance and realism which characterises Douglas. Significantly, Douglas, thus endowed, is the most conspicuous victim. Arguably, his fate is the fate of Scotland: promise necessarily denied fulfilment. Thus the inevitability which, in encompassing the situations of good and evil characters alike, reduces the tragic to the level of the pathetic, equally informs the view of the Scottish situation. Francis Russell Hart has remarked of Mackenzie's *Julia de Roubigné* that 'it suggests the direction in which Mackenzie's fiction is moving: toward the compact, grim tale of tragic fatality'.[46] This was to be the characteristic of much post-Union Scottish literature, and the precedent is there in *Douglas*.

In *Douglas* the gap between ideal and experience, potential and actuality, is a telling one. Biographical evidence suggests a similarity with Home's own situation and confirms him as an extreme case of that dichotomy of values with which most Scottish writers of the eighteenth century were afflicted. In personality romantic and conservative, he was anti-Jacobite by virtue of both family and profession. Mackenzie observed that Home's 'temper was of that warm susceptible kind which is caught with the heroic and the tender, and which is more fitted to delight in the world of sentiment than to succeed in the bustle of ordinary life'. Home's experience of the events of 1745 can have offered little to satisfy 'that military ardour, that chivalrous spirit, which his natural temperament and favourite course of reading had produced and fostered'.[47] In the light of Home's personality there is a sense in which he found himself on the wrong side in the 'Forty-Five. For Home the romantic appeal was all on the Jacobite side. In particular, the Young Pretender had about him a certain mystique and glamour: Home wrote that from the moment when news of his landing was given to Cope 'every body spake of nothing but the young Pretender, though very few people knew what to believe about him'; whereas Sir John Cope 'was one of those ordinary men who are fitter for any thing than the chief command in war, especially when opposed, as he was, to a new and uncommon enemy'.[48]

Home's own conduct in the events of that year was in accord with the dictates of his romantic nature, but around the activities of the side to which he belonged there hangs a distinctly unheroic aura; of this he was not unaware, as his *History of the Rebellion in the Year 1745* indicates. The failure to find his heroic ideal matched by experience led Home to persist in maintaining it with increasing fervour throughout his long life in a world which attested to the equally increasing archaism and redundancy of such views. Amongst abundant evidence, this anecdote of Ramsay of Ochtertyre reveals the extent of contemporary recognition of the extreme nature of Home's views and behaviour:

> I heard Mr Solicitor Murray . . . tell the Assembly one day that any opposition it could make to the bill [the Catholic Relief Bill, 1778] would be treated with contempt. It was an unwise speech at best. Nobody wondered to see Mr John Home hold the same language. By that time this gentleman had accepted of a lieutenancy in the Duke of Buccleuch's Fencibles. Coming in dressed in his regimentals to the Assembly, a country minister exclaimed, 'Sure that is John Home the poet. What is the meaning of that dress?' 'Oh', said Mr Robert Walker of Edinburgh, 'it is only the farce after the play.'[49]

In earlier years the disparity between Home's values and those of the modern world led to his giving vicarious expression to his martial and heroic spirit in his plays. Latterly, his Quixotic pursuit of heroic values and a heroic past seems to have transformed Home himself into something like the prototype of the music-hall Scot; with the important difference that for Home it was for real.

Similarly Home's *History of the Rebellion*, begun in 1746/7, revived in 1778, and finally published in 1802, reflects the problems that arose from the need to try to accommodate within the one mind a romantic disposition and anti-Jacobite political views. Part of the reason for the difficulty and delay which Home encountered in writing his account of the Rebellion may lie in the fact that its subject-matter, like that of *Douglas*, brought into conflict the romantic and the rational elements in his personality. Underlying Home's account of the clan system, with which his *History* begins, is a sympathetic interest, and his attitude to Lochiel is one of thinly disguised admiration for the heroic qualities which he embodies. Despite this, the History, dedicated to the King, is a tactful whitewash: notwithstanding 'the impolitic, as well as ungenerous use which Mr Home conceived had been made of the victory of Culloden',[50] little reference is made to the activities of 'Butcher' Cumberland, the King's uncle. The compromise of values which informs *Douglas* is once more evident: here romantic inclinations give way to the rationalistic opportunism to which most Scots who would succeed in the south had to succumb.

In each of his other tragedies Home depicts both heroism and grief, and aims to elicit both admiration and sympathy. The recurrent types are the youthful idealist who is motivated by love of glory and who asserts that public honour and private virtue mean more than survival, and the mother whose love has turned to grief. In each play there is sustained appeal to the tender emotions of the spectator. In each there is at least one character who is beset by the rival claims of love and reason or the private and the public lives.

According to Mackenzie,[51] the next in contemporary popularity to *Douglas* was *Alonzo* (1773). That it was so successful is a clear indication of the extent to which the audience of the day responded to, and demanded, the stock formulae of pathetic tragedy. *Alonzo* is little more than a transposition of the events and situations of *Douglas* to the setting of Spain at the time of the Moorish invasions. The pathos centres upon the stricken maternal love of Ormisinda who, like Lady Randolph, has concealed her grief for eighteen years.

Of the remaining tragedies one has direct, and two have indirect, Scottish reference. By June 1761 Home had completed *Rivine*, which he later renamed *The Fatal Discovery*, but it was not performed until Garrick produced it at Drury Lane in February 1769; ironically, this was when anti-Scottish feeling was at its height in London. The play originated in Home's admiration for Macpherson's *Fragments of Ancient Poetry* and is based on 'Fragment IX'. After completing the play Home set off to the Highlands with Macpherson and on 3 August he was enthusing,

> the grave of Ronan and Rivine is still preserved and consequently it marks and determines the scene of my tragedy. With the greatest surprise and pleasure I found that the descriptions I have given are as if I had taken them from the place itself.[52]

Home was to the last a fervent believer in the authenticity of Macpherson's 'translations'.

In *The Fatal Discovery* Home takes a situation of which Macpherson was very fond—the love triangle where complications result from a false report. The manner is close to that of Macpherson, as this description of the heroine, Rivine, indicates:

> Like a wounded deer,
> Apart she stalks and seeks the darkest shade
> Of hanging rocks, and melancholy boughs,
> To hide and nourish her determin'd sorrow.
> (p. 5)[53]

Rivine addresses a fallen oak as the 'expressive emblem' (p. 6) of her state, and, typical of the Ossianic mode, landscape is often found to echo the mood or situation of the character. As in the *Ossian* poems, too, there is habitual juxtaposing of the private and the public realms, not least when Rivine, after a bout of madness in which she closely resembles Ophelia, encounters the hermit, Orellan, a once-proud warrior undone by jealousy. It is especially in the scenes involving Rivine and Orellan that Home spells out the play's significance for the age of sensibility. Rivine addresses Orellan as follows:

> Affliction's friend!
> Devoted vassal of eternal sorrow,
> Thanks for thy gentle sympathy, if thou
> Should'st give a tear to me or my sad story,
> Namora's memory would not be wrong'd.
> (p. 45)

In his reply Orellan compares her to a young oak torn from the mountain's brow and attempts to console her with the assurance,

> This cave, a while the mansion of thy woes,
> Those hoary cliffs, and yon resounding bay,
> Shall often echo thy lamented name.
> (p. 45)

Later, Kathul is made to identify for the audience the representative significance of Orellan:

> He is the judge who cannot be unjust;
> For his pure mind no partial passion knows;
> The sole affection of his breast is pity;
> The man of sorrow feels for human woes!
> (p. 56)

With the closing lines of the play Connan underlines the appeal to sensibility: 'The brave, the fair shall give the pleasing tear/Of nature, partial to the woes of love' (p. 76).

Commenting that the author wastes the potential for truly tragic effects in the situation of his heroine, James S Malek points out that Home 'opts for pity rather than pity and fear as the action develops'.[54] Rivine could be a more complex and psychologically interesting character than Home allows her to be. He limits her by stressing that she is the victim of the treachery of Durstan and her own error of judgement in the distant past. Robertson Davies remarked that Lady Randolph in *Douglas* is 'almost Byronic in the sense she gives of an introverted nature feeding upon itself'.[55] Ormisinda in *Alonzo* and Rivine share that characteristic.

That several of Home's heroines have this deeply brooding quality that culminates in self-destruction reflects that fatalism, Calvinist-inspired, that colours so much Scottish experience and also, perhaps, the sense that what is meaningful in terms of the Scottish destiny is already long over. With regard to the individual this serves to heighten the awareness of the roles that one has to play; if one's destiny is irreversible rôle-playing becomes the next-best thing. So Rivine's speeches are imbued with a sense of self-drama, as, for instance, when she insists, 'The part I've taken I must act alone' (p. 66).

In these plays Home writes with the self-consciousness and awareness of his national identity that seem to have been characteristic of many Scottish writers after the Union. An awareness of the political balance which is the Union surfaces in other plays besides *Douglas*. The events of *The Siege of Aquileia* (1760) derive from accounts of the siege of Berwick by Edward III in 1333. However Home chooses to relocate them in Roman times (Malek has dated the action in the year 238). Presumably it was political tact that led Home to avoid presenting an English king—however remote historically— leading a force of aggressors against the Scots. Despite the antiquity of the setting this is Home's most accomplished play in terms of both creation of dramatic interest and psychological realism of characterisation. Maximin, leader of the besieging army, has captured the two sons of Aemilius, governor of Aquileia, and is using them as bargaining-counters: Aemilius must surrender the city or his sons will die. Dialogue between Aemilius and his wife, Cornelia, in which he affirms the honour of dying for Rome and she pleads a mother's rights, genuinely arouses dramatic tension and allows the public-v.-private debate to be well aired. Aemilius is keenly aware of the division of loyalties within himself and has to remind himself, 'let not my duty yield/To the strong yearning of a father's heart' (p. 43). Each of the principal characters has a sense of the respective calls of identity and rôle. Sent by Maximin to apply pressure to Aemilius to surrender, Titus, his son, says that in fact he came to prevent 'strong affection, and a mothers's tears' (p. 46) weakening the consul's (i.e. his father's) resolve. That Home achieved his profoundest dramatic effects when writing of the conflicting demands of the private self and the public rôle should not pass unremarked.

The caution which Home thought fit to observe with regard to Anglo-Scottish relations is especially evident in his last play, *Alfred* (1778). Part of Home's motivation in writing this play was to pay tribute to the great English hero and the values he embodied. In the play the Earl of Devonshire refers thus to the conduct of Arthur after the Danish invasion:

> Much he endured;
> And much his people suffer'd. English virtue,
> Like England's oak, grew firmer from the storm.
> (p.3)

Home's best intentions rebounded, however, largely because he presented Alfred as not only a heroic leader but also a man in love. Fearing that his beloved Ethelswida is lost or dead, Alfred describes his grief in these terms:

> Sometimes, a broken scene of other woes
> My troubled fancy to her image joins,
> And adds the monarch's to the lover's grief.
> (p. 6)

Again it is noticeable that a Scottish writer creates characters possessed of an acute sense of the various aspects of their identity and the several roles they have to play. In this exchange Alfred, now a captive of the Danes, is reunited with Ethelswida:

Alfred: O, Ethelswida, do not pierce my heart,
             With looks so full of pity and of love!
Ethelswida: My soul looks thro' my eyes. My love, my lord,
             My king, my husband!

                                              (p. 51)

In the discussion that follows, much is made of the rival claims of the private life and the public life, and Home does achieve a degree of psychological realism. Instrumental in this is the quality of Home's language which, by the standards of eighteenth-century pathetic tragedy, is relatively free from bombast and needless ornament. And imagery is often put to good effect, as in Alfred's description of the disturbed mind of Ethelswida:

            Her mind's a burning fire,
        Where sudden thoughts, like wreaths of smoak arise,
        And, parting from the flame, disperse in air.
        Her shatter'd fancy, like a mirror broken,
        Reflects no single image just and true,
        But many false ones.

                                              (p. 27)

Despite Home's succeeding in contriving a happy ending out of an extremely tangled plot (doubtless he saw that it would be impolitic to involve either English hero or his beloved in a conclusion that was remotely tragic), the play appears to have offended English critics, and this largely for the reason that Home had succeeded in representing Alfred as a recognisable human being, rather than a figurehead. Responding to criticism, Home added a preface to the play on its publication. There he offered this defence of the author's right to exercise some imaginative power over historical material:

> In Tragedy, if the subject be Historical, an author is not permitted to introduce events, contrary to the great established facts of History; for instance, in the Tragedy of Alfred, the Hero must not be killed, nor driven out of England by the Danes; but preserving those ancient foundations, as the piers of his bridge, the Author may bend his arches, and finish the fabrick, according to his taste and fancy, for the poet is at liberty, and it is the essence of his art, to invent such intermediate circumstances, and incidents, as he thinks will produce the most arresting situations. In this department, the Poet's fancy is controuled by nothing, but probability and consistence of character, the barriers of dramatic truth.
> (p. vii)

Many ironies surround John Home. Not the least is this: that when he chose to 'bend his arches' a little when working over English history—and achieved a measure of psychological realism into the bargain—the censure which this occasioned drew from him a spirited defence of the imagination.

CHAPTER 5

The Chameleon Scot: James Boswell

Among Scottish writers of the eighteenth century it is James Boswell who presents the most extreme manifestation of fragmentation of personality. Boswell is plastic man; and he was well aware of the fact. The entry in the *London Journal* for 21 November 1762 includes this:

> Since I came up, I have begun to acquire a composed genteel character very different from a rattling uncultivated one which for some time past I have been fond of. I have discovered that we may be in some degree whatever character we choose. Besides, practice forms a man to anything. I was now happy to find myself cool, easy, and serene.[1]

Boswell's life was a search through a range of rôles and *personae* for an identity. This process involved inveterate parasitism on the lives and the personalities of others. 'The correspondence of distinguished men is very much to be valued', he observed, 'It gives a man a dignity that is very desirable' (*LJ*, p. 194). It gave more than dignity, however: it offered the opportunity to assume aspects of their identity. Boswell asked David Hume to correspond with him and promised, 'I should gladly endeavour to return you now and then something in your own style, which I am ambitious enough not to despair of doing' (*LJ*, p. 193). In the case of Boswell the line between an innate dramatic capacity and a deep-rooted psychological need to identify with others is difficult to discern. For him, Hume's quarrel with Rousseau was 'a literary tragi-comedy'; and he appended the revealing comment, 'I write verses in the character of each of them'.[2]

Boswell is a remarkable amalgam of vanity and self-consciousness, egotism and self-detachment. Experience is vital to him as a means of attempted self-identification, but, paradoxically, equally important is the rôle of self-observer. Instances of his behaviour are recounted only to be followed by such comments as 'I think this a very strong proof of my being agreeable' (*LJ*, p. 59). Of his presence at a party at Lady Northumberland's he proclaims, 'I could observe people looking at me with envy, as a man of some distinction and a favourite of my Lady's . . . There's conduct for you' (*Letters*, p. 71). That exclamation of triumph is as much for his own benefit as it is for Temple's or the reader's.

The degree of dichotomy of personality which Boswell reveals is striking. The first page of his *London Journal* contains this sentence:

> I was observing to my friend Erskine that a plan of this kind was dangerous, as

117

> a man might in the openness of his heart say many things and discover many facts that might do him great harm if the journal should fall into the hands of my enemies. (*LJ*, p. 39)

The shift of construction from 'a man' to 'my enemies' is more than a mere grammatical slip: it says much about the divided personality of the writer. A recurrent concern of the *London Journal* is the need to try to reconcile different elements of the personality, to achieve some sort of equilibrium between passion and judgement. And habitually Boswell identifies these qualities in terms of their presence in others. 'I am determined', he writes, 'to have a degree of Erskine's indifference, to make me easy when things go cross; and a degree of Macdonald's eagerness for real life, to make me relish things when they go well' (*LJ*, p. 79).

If the personality is fragmented the characteristics are a lack of fixity and a desire for some sort of stasis to arise out of flux. Here, typically of this paradox, Boswell sees the mind as a gallery:

> The mind of a young man (his gallery I mean) is often furnished in different ways. According to the scenes he is placed in, so are his pictures. They disappear, and he gets a new set in a moment. But as he grows up, he gets some substantial pieces which he always preserves, although he may alter his smaller paintings in a moment. (*LJ*, p. 204)

What is characteristic of Boswell in this is the sense both of the mind as receptor—rather than initiator—of experience and of the mind as self-observer. One of the recurrent features of Boswell's writing is his contemplation, sometimes even his relishing, of the multiplicity of his personality. Armed with diverse testimonials, he embarked for Holland, observing to Temple, 'I have been amused to see the different modes of treating that favourite subject *myself*' (*Letters*, p. 29). For Boswell, life becomes masquerade, with virtually unlimited potential for rôle-playing. Wherever possible he ensures that he acts as author and stage-manager as well as casting himself in various rôles. For instance, an occasion when he wished to buy a silver-hilted sword but lacked the requisite guineas was turned to good use as follows: 'I determined to make a trial of the civility of my fellow-creatures, and what effect my external appearance and address would have' (*LJ*, p. 60). Life in London society abounded with opportunities for that projection of self-images to which Boswell was so prone. His unremitting attempt to secure a commission was rebuffed at every turn. Here he writes of his most recent disappointment to Lady Northumberland in whose supposed efforts on his behalf he had placed great faith:

> I have received a letter from the Duke of Queensberry informing me that a commission in the Guards cannot be got for me. What does your Ladyship think of a man who, notwithstanding of such a disappointment, can cry *vive la bagatelle!* and walk about contented, cheerful, and merry? Have not I spirit? Ought I not to be a soldier? (*LJ*, p. 108)

2 *VERONICA A BREAKFAST CONVERSATION.*

'*Mr Johnson was pleased with my Daughter Veronica, then a Child of about four Months old. She had the appearance of listening to him. His motions seemed to her to be intended for her amusement, & when he stopped, she fluttered & made a little infantine noise, & a kind of signal for him to begin again. She would be held close to him, which was a proof, from simple nature, that his figure was not horrid. Her fondness for him endeared her still more to me, & I declared she should have Five Hundred Pounds of additional fortune.*' Vide Journal p. 17

3   *SCOTTIFYING THE PALATE.*
*'I bought some Speldings, fish salted and dried in a particular manner, being dipped in
the Sea & dried in the Sun, and eaten by the Scots by way of relish.—He had never seen
them though they are sold in London. I insisted on Scottifying his palate, but he was
very reluctant.—With difficulty I prevailed with him—He did not like it.'* Vide Journal
p. 50

One of the many paradoxes that surround Boswell was that such energy, vanity, and ambition should inform the conflicting elements of the personality. 'Ambition', he was to acknowledge, 'has ever raged in my veins like a fever' (*Letters*, p. 220). To Boswell's eyes, Burke enjoyed continual happiness because 'he has so much knowledge, so much animation, and the consciousness of so much fame' (*Letters*, p. 173). Boswell's considerable mental energies were channelled into the attempt at self-identification and the pursuit of fame; and in his view the achievement of the latter had much to contribute to the former.

Paradoxically, out of the recurrent problems of personality—problems that were to remain unresolved—there sprang writing of the highest order. Unable to shape actual experience to his satisfaction, Boswell was expert in the transmutation of experience into literature without loss of verisimilitude. Literature he could structure and give the appearance of life; the ordering of life was beyond him. The following exemplifies the extent to which Boswell was obsessed with self and self-images:

> I talked really well—the degree of distance due to a stranger restrained me from my effusions of ludicrous nonsense and intemperate mirth. I had a good opinion of myself, and could perceive my friend Temple much satisfied with me . . . I have these ideas strong and pride myself in thinking that my natural character is that of dignity. (*LJ*, pp. 25–8)

How did such a man become a master of biography? How did he succeed in restraining that preoccupation with self when he came to render the events of the lives of others? To begin to attempt to answer such questions involves examination of the man's personality and situation.

That James Boswell became the man and the writer that he did can be explained at least in part in terms of his Scottish upbringing and his family circumstances. Like many Scots, then and since, he was the product of an educational system which emphasised rote-learning and written exercise. He was to regret this later in the following terms:

> To confess the truth, I was badly brought up. I was taught the ancient languages, but I was not taught things. I had naturally an excellent memory, and that memory became still better through cultivation. But, alas! what was it that I remembered? It was a mass of phrases, of rules of grammar, and perhaps a few little stories. But I was not trained to think about what I was reading; on the contrary, I acquired a habit of skimming through a book without extracting any ideas from it.[3]

Here may be one source of the ensuing lack of direction.

Presbyterianism also left its mark. Boswell recalled his 'boyish days' when he 'used to walk down the Canongate and think of players with a mixture of narrow-minded horror and lively-minded pleasure' (*LJ*, p. 84). Herein is a subsequent dichotomy in embryo. Boswell deplored the Scottish practice of taking young children to church before they could possibly understand what the minister said.[4] The over-riding impact of Presbyterianism upon him was its joylessness, as this poem attests:

> Th' approach of Sunday still I can't but dread,
> For still old Edinburgh comes into my head,
> Where on that day a dreary gloom appears,
> And the kirk-bells ring doleful in your ears.
> Enthusiasts sad, how can you thus employ
> What your Redeemer made a day of joy?
> With thankful hearts to your Creator pray,
> From labour rest, be cheerful and be gay
> Let us not keep the Sabbath of the Jews;
> Let generous Christians Christian freedom use.[5]

A visit in London from Webster, son of one of the foremost of the strict party in the Church of Scotland, was recalled as follows:

> . . . he brought into my mind some dreary Tolbooth Kirk ideas, than which nothing has given me more gloomy feelings. I shall never forget the dismal hours of apprehension that I have endured in my youth from narrow notions of religion while my tender mind was lacerated with infernal horror. I am surprised how I have got rid of these notions entirely. (*LJ*, p. 102)

That last claim is a typical self-delusion. The conflict between hereditary religion and natural inclination was reflected in the fact that at the age of eighteen Boswell both became a Freemason and decided to become a Catholic. Of a Presbyterian service in London some years later he observed, 'The whole vulgar idea of the Presbyterian worship made me gloomy. I therefore hastened from this place to St. Paul's, where I heard the conclusion of the service, and had my mind set to right again' (*LJ*, p. 259).

Where such tensions exist decision-taking and unequivocal commitment become difficult procedures, and this was accentuated in Boswell's case by a Presbyterian fatalism. Of this, Boswell was fully cognisant and wrote,

> . . . I am rather passive than active in life. It is difficult to make my feeling clearly understood. I may say, I act passively. That is, not with my whole heart, and thinking this or that of real consequence, but because so and so things are established and I must submit. (*LJ*, p. 77)

The fatalist sense discouraged commitment but induced a compensatory rôle-playing. It also exacerbated an inherent tendency to melancholy. From his teens to his last years Boswell was to be a prey to recurrent bouts of deep melancholia. Even in his letters to Temple and his *London Journal* (written for John Johnston) he had to make a deliberate effort to emphasise his spirit and energy, to present a brave face to the world. He admitted, 'I have, together with my vivacity and good-humour, a great anxiety of temper which often renders me uneasy. My grandfather had it in a very strong degree' (*LJ*, p. 126).

In such intense form the union of swaggering bluster and inner dejection was characteristic of various Scottish writers of the eighteenth century; and the effect seems to have been heightened during participation in London society-life. Sir James Macdonald was puzzled by the fact that 'Boswell and Macpherson got into a coach together; both exclaimed they were miserable; and both burst out in loud peals of laughter'; to which Boswell responds thus: 'This was literally true. Indeed I have often found that when I vented my complaints of melancholy, it appeared somewhat ludicrous and I could not but laugh' (*LJ*, p. 258). Three days later he returns to the incident, noting that 'Sir James . . . wondered how I could complain of being miserable who had always such a flow of spirits', and conceding, 'Melancholy cannot be clearly proved to others, so it is better to be silent about it' (*LJ*, pp. 261–2). Boswell has fallen foul of his ability in rôle-playing: when the inner voice makes itself heard the risk is that it will be dismissed as simply another *persona*.

Possibly the earliest antecedent of Boswell's personality problems was his relationship with his father. Lord Auchinleck, with his reverence for classical literature and his broad, at times coarse, Scots tongue, was in himself an embodiment of contradictions. However he was true to certain beliefs. Those that most affected his son were his detestation of contemporary imaginative writers and his insistence on system in all things. His splendid new Adam mansion bore the emblem, translated from Horace, 'All you seek is here, here in the remoteness and quiet of Auchinleck—if you have fitted yourself with a good steady mind'. In his treatment of his son the limitations of his own 'good steady mind' became obvious. He seems to have failed to see that his restless and imaginative son would scarce be content with the life of an Edinburgh lawyer punctuated by sojourns in the rural retreat; nor does he seem to have realised that his persistent attempt to impose his will on his son was likely to be counter-productive. Boswell joins Scott, Stevenson, and, one suspects, Burns, in that band of Scottish writers whose personalities and writing have been influenced by the nature of the father–son relationship. There is much to suggest that in the Boswell family Stevenson found part of his inspiration for *Weir of Hermiston*. Certainly the effect of his father on Boswell was deep-rooted and enduring. While lodging with the generally amiable Mr Terrie in London, Boswell acknowledged,

> From having been so long and so lately under strict family discipline at home, whenever I have been a little too late abroad at night, I cannot help being apprehensive that Terrie my landlord will reprove me for it next morning. Such is the force of custom. (*LJ*, p. 221)

The considerable disparity between the man that Boswell was and the man his father wished him to be, and more particularly Boswell's recognition of the disparity, was a further pressure towards rôle-playing. Here Boswell presents the problem with a characteristic mixture of dejection and vanity:

> I write to him with warmth, with an honest pride, wishing that he should think

of me as I am; but my letters shock him, and every expression in them is interpreted unfavourably. To give you an instance, I send you a letter I had from him a few days ago. How galling it is to the friend of Paoli to be treated so! I have answered him in my own style: I will be myself. (*Letters*, p. 88)

After offering a highly idealised portrait of himself and his future he continues,

Temple, would you not like such a son? would you not feel a glow of parental joy? I know you would; and yet my worthy father writes to me in the manner you see, with that Scots strength of sarcasm which is peculiar to a North Briton. But he is offended with that fire which you and I cherish as the essence of our souls; and how can I make him happy? Am I bound to do so at the expense, not of this or the other agreeable wish, but at the expense of myself?

The following passage demonstrates even more emphatically the effect of the father on the fragmentation process and the subsequent rôle-playing:

. . . he has a method of treating me which makes me feel myself like a *timid boy*, which to *Boswell* (comprehending all that my character does in my own imagination and in that of a wonderful number of mankind) is intolerable. (*Letters*, p. 175)

Much of Boswell's adolescence and early manhood was marked by battles of will with his father. In the spring of 1760 he fled to London, partly for the purpose of secretly joining the Catholic church. To the joys of London life he was introduced by, first, Samuel Derrick, and then the Earl of Eglinton. He met the Duke of York and attended Newmarket races, both events being celebrated in an undistinguished poem, 'The Cub at Newmarket'. More importantly, he met Sterne, then a centre of attention by virtue of the appearance of the first two volumes of *Tristram Shandy*. In the example of Sterne, Boswell found endorsement of his existing tendency to minute self-examination. He wrote a pamphlet imitative of Sterne, and the Shandean mode was to recur throughout his later writing, as, for example, in the assertion, 'I should live no more than I can record, as one should not have more corn growing than one can get in'.[6]

The other important aspect of the first London visit was the decision to seek a commission in the Guards. Now there was nothing martial about Boswell's nature. In his *Letter to the People of Scotland* (1785) he confessed that he was 'not blest with high heroic blood, but rather I think troubled with a natural timidity of personal danger, which it costs me some philosophy to overcome',[7] while on one occasion he argued vigorously the case against war with John Home, the latter adducing the fine qualities which war brings into play.[8] The attraction of the army was that it offered entrée to London society, a convivial life-style, a uniform—in short, an identity. These aspirations were checked by the arrival of Lord Auchinleck who, by May 1760, had restored his son to Edinburgh. The parochialism of life there was felt keenly by Boswell, but he consoled himself with, on one level, the ladies of the town, and, on another, the friendship of Lord and Lady Kames. The next mentor was to be Thomas

Sheridan, whose obsession with propriety of speech and dignity of behaviour seems to have left its mark on one element of Boswell's personality.

In the summer of 1762 Boswell passed examinations in civil law and finally got his father's consent to go to London. On 15 November 1762 he bade a farewell to Edinburgh that was notable for both self-dramatising and sentimentality:

> I had a long conversation with my father and mother. They were very kind to me. I felt parental affection was very strong towards me; and I felt a very warm filial regard for them. The scene of being a son setting out from home for the wide world and the idea of being my own master, pleased me much . . . I made the chaise stop at the foot of the Canongate . . . walked to the Abbey of Holyroodhouse, went round the Piazzas, bowed thrice: once to the Palace itself, once to the crown of Scotland above the gate in front, and once to the venerable old Chapel. I next stood in the court before the Palace, and bowed thrice to Arthur Seat, that lofty romantic mountain on which I have so often strayed in my days of youth, indulged meditation and felt the raptures of a soul filled with ideas of the magnificence of GOD and his creation. (*LJ*, pp. 40–2)

In his relationship with Scotland and his own Scottishness is one of the most pronounced of Boswell's dichotomies. He was capable of both genuine and sentimental nationalism, but to each he brought the tincture of self-drama. He lamented the demise of the Scottish language and he planned a dictionary of Scottish terms, but he did so as one who has 'the fine patriotic soul of an old Scotsman' (*BH*, p. 161). Worthy of note is his response to Johnson's claim that 'the noblest prospect that a Scotsman ever sees is the road which leads him to England':

> . . . I could not help thinking that Mr. Johnson showed a want of taste in laughing at the wild grandeur of nature, which to a mind debauched by art conveys the most pleasing awful, sublime ideas. Have not I experienced the full force of this when gazing at thee, O Arthur Seat, thou venerable mountain! whether in the severity of winter thy brow has been covered with snow or wrapped in mist; or in the gentle mildness of summer the evening sun has shone upon thy verdant sides diversified with rugged moss-clad rocks and rendered religious by the ancient Chapel of St. Anthony. Beloved hill, the admiration of my youth! Thy noble image shall ever fill my mind! Let me travel over the whole earth, I shall still remember thee; and when I return to my native country, while I live I will visit thee with affection and reverence. (*LJ*, p. 294)

This is quintessential Boswell in that the initial, and thoroughly valid, defence of the sublime soon degenerates into striking of sentimental attitudes. Like many of his countrymen Boswell was a patriotic Scot when it suited him. Throughout the quest for identity reassurance could be found in self-reminders such as 'the blood of *Bruce* flows in my veins'.[9] Boswell was capable of reminding George III that he was his cousin and evincing a sentimental Jacobitism. An encounter with a veteran of the 'Forty-Five produced this complex of associations:

> As he narrated the particulars of that ill-advised, but brave attempt, I could not refrain from tears. There is a certain association of ideas in my mind upon that subject, by which I am strongly affected. The very Highland names, or the sound of a bagpipe, will stir my blood, and fill me with a mixture of melancholy and respect for courage; with pity for an unfortunate and superstitious regard for antiquity, and thoughtless inclination for war; in short, with a crowd of sensations with which sober rationality has nothing to do. (*JTH*, p. 122)

What is striking here is that Boswell can identify the mélange of his emotions and the predominant irrationality. At one and the same time he is both subject and observer.

The *London Journal* is replete with evidence of the ambivalence of Boswell's attitude to things Scottish. From London, with father at a distance, he could indulge in extolling to Lady Northumberland the 'romantic beauties' (*LJ*, p. 134) of Auchinleck. When his self-confidence wavered consolation could be found in the prospect of returning to be 'a man of consequence . . . in my own country' (*LJ*, p. 200). And in company with the family of his friend Andrew Erskine, younger son of the Earl of Mar and Kellie, he could indulge in closet Jacobitism.[10] But the predominant effect of meeting fellow-Scots was irritation and embarrassment. Here is his reaction to the arrival of the Kellie family:

> To tell the plain truth, I was vexed at their coming. For to see just the plain *hamely* Fife family hurt my grand ideas of London. Besides, I was now upon a plan of studying polite reserved behaviour, which is the only way to keep up dignity of character. (*LJ*, p. 61)

The intrusion of past reality upon present illusion was to be avoided; the identity required for participation in London society must be acquired and kept. The fault of the Kellie ladies was that they would not cease to be themselves:

> They grew hot and showed a strong example of the Edinburgh women's roughness of manners, which disgusted me. They have all a too-great violence in dispute, and are sometimes quite put out of humour by it. (*LJ*, p. 80)

Such qualities were betrayingly and embarrassingly Scottish for Boswell. At the time he was courting one Louisa in the manner of a young London gallant (or so he believed). Here he has to leave her only to go to take tea with the Edinburgh ladies:

> After the elegant scene of gallantry which I had just been solacing my romantic imagination with, and after the high-relished ideas with which my fancy had been heated, I could consider the common style of company and conversation but as low and insipid. But the Fife tongue and the Niddry's Wynd address were quite hideous. (*LJ*, p. 116)

Presently he was to tell the Kellie family, 'I like your company much. But then I want to be among English people and to acquire the language.' When their response was to laugh, Boswell's reaction was this:

> I declaimed on the felicity of London. But they were cold and could not understand me. They reasoned plainly like people in the common road of life, and I like a man of fancy and whim. Indeed, it will not bear reasoning. (*LJ*, p. 123)

The chameleon nature would defend whim to the last. Yet when the family returned north Boswell admitted, 'I felt a little regret at the ladies of Kellie being gone altogether. It was a very comfortable society for me' (*LJ*, p. 216). With their departure he increased the frequency of his visits to Lord Eglinton's, only to be discomfited by his 'housekeeper', Mrs Brown, whom he found 'such a gawky, and so much of a low censorious Scots lass that I am in a rage, or rather in a discontent, with her' (*LJ*, p. 258).[11]

Boswell sought to suppress his Scottishness because it was an obstacle to his desideratum—'dignity of behaviour'. He reports an occasion when he discussed this subject with Hugh Blair and James Macpherson:

> Macpherson cursed at it, and Blair said he did not like it. It was unnatural, and did not show the weakness of humanity. In my opinion, however, it is a noble quality. It is sure to beget respect and to keep impertinence at a distance. (*LJ*, p. 266)

Blair, doubtless, was sincere, and Macpherson had other parts to play. But to Boswell it was a matter of vital importance. Thus a morning spent with such luminaries as William Robertson and David Fordyce offended by virtue of its 'mixture of Edinburgh familiarity and raillery' (*LJ*, p. 288). Boswell seems to have been motivated by a curious blend of egotism and genuine realism about the inevitable implications of the Union for Scottish manners and values. For instance, he suggested that some of the Scottish public offices should be filled by Englishmen since 'such an interchange would make a beneficial mixture of manners, and render our union more complete' (*JTH*, p. 15). What he craved in personal terms was a union of disparate elements within himself under the control of the *persona* of a sophisticated London intellectual. Yet, try as he might, he is habitually betrayed by his candour and appears at times as a naïve and impressionable tourist. Of a visit to the House of Lords he enthuses, 'I here beheld the King of Great Britain on his Throne with his crown on his head addressing both the Lords and the Commons' (*LJ*, p. 49).

The *London Journal* affords abundant evidence of Boswell's division of ideal and actual, illusion and reality. At times the juxtaposition is so blatant as to suggest that Boswell was fully cognisant of the irony. The entry for Wednesday 13 July 1763 reads as follows:

> . . . I must find one fault with all the *Poker Club*, as they are called; that is to say, with all that set who associate with David Hume and Robertson. They are doing all that they can to destroy politeness. They would abolish all respect due to rank and external circumstances, and they would live like a kind of literary barbarians. For my own share, I own I would rather want their instructive conversation

than be hurt by their rudeness. However, they don't always show this. Therefore
I like their company best when it is qualified by the presence of a stranger. This
afternoon I had some low debauchery with girls who patrol the courts in the
Temple. (*LJ*, p. 300).

Boswell's intellectual aspirations were surpassed only by his physical
appetites, and he appears to have relished their juxtaposition. The most
revealing example of his consciousness of the mind-body duality is this, his
account of his conducting Hugh Blair around London:

> I was diverted at walking the streets of London with Dr. Blair. I marched him
> down Southampton Street in the Strand, from the whimsical idea of passing
> under the windows of my first London lady of the town with an Edinburgh
> minister whom I had so often heard preach in the New Church (*LJ*, p. 236).

Often reference to an evening's fornication is followed by a record of the
subsequent attendance at church.[12] Like Burns, Boswell divided his amorous
adventures into two distinct categories—the idealised courtship of society
ladies,[13] and energetic fornication with whores. In one journal entry he
remarks upon his 'present wonderful continence'; discusses amorous relationships in terms of rôle-playing; stresses the importance of retaining one's
dignity and superiority; and exclaims, 'These paradisal scenes of gallantry
have exalted my ideas and refined my taste, so that I cannot think of stooping'
(*LJ*, p. 84). So much for the illusion; the reality was that he took a pride in
the frequency and the prowess of his sexual encounters with girls from the
streets (including an experience upon Westminster Bridge of a kind scarce fit
for inclusion in Wordsworth's august celebration of that noted landmark (*LJ*,
p. 255)). In all his sexual adventures Boswell was preoccupied with status
and appearance. On one occasion he dressed as a blackguard and hit the
town, intent on infamous exploits. His account of the evening's debauchery
concludes, 'My vanity was somewhat gratified tonight that, notwithstanding
of my dress, I was always taken for a gentleman in disguise' (*LJ*, p. 273). His
vanity must have taken a knock when the next day found him paying court
to his *inamorata* of the moment, Miss Temple, with the following ludicrously
unfortunate result:

> She was in fine spirits; gave me strawberries and cream, and used every endearing
> amorous blandishment. But alas! my last night's rioting and this morning's
> indulgence, joined with my really being in love with her, had quite enervated
> me, and I had no tender inclinations. I made an apology very easily; and she was
> very good, and said it happened very commonly after drinking. However, I was
> much vexed. (*LJ*, p. 273)

In matters of love, as in so much else, Boswell lived in a fantasy world
and acted in the real world. In his fine introduction to the *London Journal*
Frederick A Pottle has shown clearly that Boswell was writing the account
with John Johnston in mind and that the superficial zest and confidence often
belie his actual mental state. As Pottle points out, the *persona* presented was

that of 'a brilliant, high-bred man of pleasure',[14] whereas the true self was that of 'a raw, loud, romping, over-eager boy: greedy, stingy, and with brutal tastes. And scared' (*LJ*, p. 15). Sometimes the one seems slightly bemused by the other. 'I really am surprised at the coolness and moderation with which I am proceeding', he writes on one occasion, 'God grant that I may continue to do well, which will make me happy and all my friends satisfied' (*LJ*, p. 65). A little later he was to remark, 'It is inconceivable with what attention and spirit I manage all my concerns' (*LJ*, p. 81). Occasionally, however, reality pricked the bubble of illusion. A visit to Oxford in which he anticipated his playing the part of 'the Spectator taking one of his rural excursions' (*LJ*, p. 244) proved a sad disappointment: the students 'were just young old men without vivacity' and, he laments, 'I could form no idea of happiness, and was vexed at having deprived myself of the venerable ideas I had of Oxford' (*LJ*, p. 246).

Some aspects of reality disturbed Boswell deeply. On a visit to Newgate he encountered one Paul Lewis, under sentence of death for robbery. Boswell spent a deeply troubled night but, acknowledging that he had 'a sort of horrid eagerness to be there', he secured a vantage-point close to the scaffold. The purpose, he informs us, was 'to see the last behaviour of Paul Lewis, the handsome fellow whom I had seen the day before' (*LJ*, p. 252). Such were the 'gloomy terrors' that came upon Boswell with the approach of night that he had to beg of Erskine that he might share his bed. This whole episode is typical of an element within Boswell which compelled him from time to time to confront the spectacle of reality in its blackest aspects. It had much to do with a need which he seems to have had to feel fear and deep melancholy. This was in no way diminished by the vicarious nature of the experience.

Boswell opens his *London Journal* with a recognition of the supreme import-ance of the maxim, 'Know Thyself' (*LJ*, p. 39). But the book is not merely a personal record of the writer's search for identity. As the journal was written with its recipient in mind there is the additional dimension of Boswell's observing and structuring for presentation his own self-drama. Incidents appear for the light in which they will render their principal subject—Boswell. There is the episode of his donating sixpence to a little boy, of which he comments, 'Such a little incident as this might be laughed at as trifling. But I cannot help thinking it amusing, and valuing it as a specimen of my own tenderness of disposition and willingness to relieve my fellow-creatures' (*LJ*, p. 100). He chats with the sentries outside Buckingham Palace, then affirms, 'I have great pleasure in conversing with the lower part of mankind, who have very curious ideas' (*LJ*, p. 100). He took pleasure in enumerating the celebrities whom he had met in the course of a day, one such list ending in the joyous exclamation, 'What variety!' (*Letters*, p. 156). Boswell reports that Temple, ever the sober counsellor, 'imagined that my journal did me harm, as it made me hunt about for adventures to adorn it with, whereas I should endeavour to be calm and studious and regular in my conduct, in order to attain by habit a proper consistency of conduct'. Boswell's answer is this:

No doubt consistency of conduct is of the utmost importance. But I cannot find fault with this my journal, which is far from wishing for extravagant adventures, and is as willing to receive my silent and serious meditations as my loud and boisterous rhodomontades. Indeed, I do think the keeping of a journal a very excellent scheme if judiciously executed. (*LJ*, p. 269)

In fact Boswell actively sought out both adventures and personalities. From the outset, where he presents himself as superstitious, religious, and poetical, the *London Journal* serves as an exercise in the projection of diverse self-images. Of his first sight of London he notes, 'I repeated Cato's soliloquy on the immortality of the soul, and my soul bounded forth to a certain prospect of happy futurity.' But another voice follows immediately:

> I sung all manner of songs, and began to make one about an amorous meeting with a pretty girl, the burthen of which was as follows:
>> She gave me *this*, I gave her *that*;
>> And tell me, had she not tit for tat?
> I gave three huzzas and we went briskly in. (*LJ*, pp. 43–4)

Boswell claims to respond to London as 'a person of imagination and feeling, such as the Spectator finely describes' (*LJ*, p. 68), and he observes that an ordinary person would view it quite differently. One of the recurrent models for Boswell's behaviour is the *Spectator* ('The Spectator mentions his being seen at Child's, which makes me have an affection for it. I think myself like him, and am serenely happy there' (*LJ*, p. 76)).[15] Friends, too, are required to take parts in the play: Temple, decides Boswell, 'will be just the clergyman in the *Spectator*' (*LJ*, p. 233).

In the quest for his own identity Boswell appropriated the characteristics of others. Within two weeks of his arrival in London he was recording,

> . . . I hoped by degrees to attain to some degree of propriety. Mr. Addison's character in sentiment, mixed with a little of the gaiety of Sir Richard Steele and the manners of Mr. Digges, were the ideas which I aimed to realize. (*LJ*, p. 62)

What he was attempting was the systematic creation of an identity. This is the memorandum for Friday 31 December (roughly six weeks into his sojourn):

> Dress; then breakfast and be denied. Then journal and Hume, busy till three. Then Louisa; be warm and press home, and talk gently and Digges-like. Acquire an easy dignity and black liveliness of behaviour like him. Learn, as Sheridan said, to speak slow and softly. See not Kellies today. At six, Sheridan's. Be like Sir Richard Steele. Think on Prologue, and of being in the Blues, and so pushing your fortune fine. Write to Somerville about Kirk. Study calm and deliberate. (*LJ*, p. 113 n. 5)

The aim of fixing an identity was doomed to failure, however, simply because Boswell's nature was incurably chameleon. Spending a night of bliss with Louisa at Hayward's, Boswell assumed the name of Digges, occupied his room, and slept in his bed. The pleasure with which Boswell recounts this indicates the importance to him of such surrogate identities. He attended the first night of Mallet's *Elvira* under the pseudonym of 'Johnston' (who happened to be the recipient of the journal) (*LJ*, p. 155).

Several of the great names with whom Boswell became familiar appear to have recognised the nature of his personality-problem and succeeded in pandering to his particular mixture of vanity and insecurity. Garrick, for one, played his part admirably in the masquerade that was of such seriousness to Boswell: he told Boswell that he would be a very great man. This was music to Boswell's ears:

> What he meant by my being a great man I can understand. For really, to speak seriously, I think there is a blossom about me of something more distinguished than the generality of mankind. (*LJ*, p. 161)

Most fruitful of all, both in terms of Boswell's psychological equilibrium and his literary work, was the timely encounter with Samuel Johnson. In place of the actual father with his devotion to system, here was the perfect sub-stitute-father, a man who 'said he would not advise a plan of study, for he had never pursued one two days' (*LJ*, p. 302). Paradoxically, such apparent licence had a beneficially restraining effect: the relationship with Johnson brought an engaging constant into Boswell's life. At the same time it rep-resented the ultimate accolade, the feast for the vanity. Boswell records, 'I said I was afraid of being troublesome. He said I was not; and he was very glad to see me. Can I help being vain of this?' (*LJ*, p. 279). In one quite remarkable entry, the journal seems almost to be made to assume the identity of one of Boswell's selves, which he then proceeds to address. Johnson had told Boswell to keep a journal, to which he replied that he had done so all along. Then follows this revealing exclamation: 'O my journal! art thou not highly dignified? Shalt thou not flourish tenfold?' (*LJ*, p. 305). For the parasite of identity the relationship with Johnson was to have a profound effect. Boswell could write of Johnson, 'I think better of myself when in his company than at any other time . . . (he has) assisted me to obtain peace of mind.'[16] Two weeks after meeting Johnson, Boswell felt he had finally assumed an English identity and enthused over having spent 'a day truly English and genteel' (*LJ*, p. 270). He commenced mimicking Johnson's prose style and continued long to do so.[17] And the fantasy of identification reached its peak in his proposing to himself that he would occupy Johnson's garret when the great man was no more.[18]

Johnson's most immediate service was to afford much fascinating con-versation which, from the first encounter, Boswell dutifully noted for future use. He saw as much as possible of Johnson in the weeks before his departure for Holland, and the great man paid him the tribute of accompanying him to Harwich. Unable to contain his pride, Boswell announced to Temple, 'I have been a great deal with Mr. Johnson of late, and (would you believe it?) his friendship to me is so great that he insists on seeing me sail, and has actually taken a place in the coach to accompany me to Harwich' (*Letters*, p. 38).

Boswell's experiences in Holland, and the absence of his new mentor, reactivated the identity problem. There was a proliferation of memoranda such as 'Mem. Johnson. Think. Maintain character gained at Utrecht, nor ever rave. Mem. Father. If you whore, all ideas change'.[19] The writing of the Holland period abounds in self-commentary and attempts at self-control. The following is representative:

> You did very well yesterday, only you transgressed a little in talking of yourself. Let your memorandum always give a just review of the past day, and that will assist you to regulate the future (*BH*, p. 49).

At this time too the awareness of the multiple nature of his personality seems to have increased. This is Boswell's account of his ability to be simultaneously the intellectual and the dandy:

> When I enter an assembly, I appear to be a young man of family on my travels, elegantly dressed in scarlet and gold. I am seen to chat pleasantly with the ladies of wit and beauty; I am seen to play a game of cards and to be as fashionable and as frivolous as the rest. No doubt, therefore, it would seem safe in talking to me to make fun of the author of a dictionary as being a heavy man; it might even be supposed that in talking thus one would be paying a compliment to a man of vivacity, and that he would be charmed to hear the most piquant witticisms directed against a man so different from himself. It might seem that in abusing the blockhead one would be praising the man of genius. But how taken in are they when they learn that the blockhead and the man of genius are one and the same! How surprised they are when they learn that I am writing a dictionary myself! (*BH*, p. 158)

Boswell was deluding himself in believing that he had acquired a rich but integrated personality. In fact the fluctuation amongst the various *personae* continued apace. It seems to have been the rock on which his relationship with his beloved Zélide (Belle de Zuylen) foundered. The accuracy of that lady's analysis of Boswell's personality can be gauged from this, part of her account of her reasons for rejecting his proposal:

> The fact is you do not love conclusions; you love problems which can never be solved. The debate you have been conducting for so long concerning our fate if we were married is proof of this taste of yours. I leave it to you to ponder, my dear Boswell. (*BH*, p. 357)

The irony is that life in Holland was altogether too systematised, too Presbyterian for Boswell. He kept encountering the mirror-image of the Scottish ways from which he was trying to escape, and he was forever meeting fellow-Scots.[20] While he was quite deliberately trying to suppress national characteristics within himself ('. . . pray be *retenu* to avoid Scotch sarcastic jocularity' (*BH*, p. 133), he reminds himself), all around were signs of Scotland (another entry includes, 'You was dreary and thought the journey just like a *Scots* journey' (*BH*, p. 226)). Though he might extol 'the excellent society at Edinburgh' (*BH*, p. 338) when presenting his case for marrying Zélide, in reality the last thing he wanted was to be reminded either of it or of those aspects of his Scottish personality which by that point, so he believed, he had succeeded in restraining.

The next landmark was the visit to Rousseau and the subsequent journey to Corsica. The attraction of Corsica for Boswell can be explained largely in terms of his being a Scot: identification with the cause of Corsican freedom was a means of vicarious expression of the nationalist spirit which the Union had checked. 'I defy Rome, Sparta, or Thebes to show me thirty years of such patriotism as Corsica can boast',[21] he asserted. As Byron was to do in relation to Greece, Boswell diverted frustrated patriotism and libertarianism into the grand gesture of supporting the cause of Corsican independence. Corsica appealed as a place where he should 'find what was to be seen no where else, a people actually fighting for liberty, and forming themselves from a poor inconsiderable oppressed nation, into a flourishing and independent state' (*JTC*, p. 49). It mattered little that the cause had been fought only sporadically since 1729; what was important was its potential for rôle-playing. Thus *The Journal of a Tour to Corsica* is both about Corsica and about Boswell. It is a first-rate travel-book which also offers acute insight into the personality of its author. In his preface Boswell proclaimed,

> No apology shall be made for presenting the world with An Account of Corsica. It has been for some time expected from me; and I own that the ardour of publick curiosity has both encouraged and intimidated me. (*JTC*, p. 41)

He omitted to mention that he had been largely responsible for exciting that curiosity.

Boswell's travels in Europe were an extension of his search for great men. Fragmentation of the self is conducive to the cult of personality. Before the Corsican visit Boswell had met, among others, Earl Marischal Keith, Rousseau, Voltaire, and Wilkes. The function of such meetings was to help create an identity which he might deem worthy of himself. Yet, paradoxically, his adventures were a tribute to his adaptability. At Leghorn he was warned of the dangers of proceeding to Corsica. Boswell had no such fears:

> I had now been in several foreign countries. I had found that I was able to accommodate myself to my fellow-creatures of different languages and sentiments. I did not fear that it would be a difficult task for me to make myself easy with the plain and generous Corsicans. (*JTC*, p. 53)

Boswell encouraged both the Italians and the Corsicans in their belief that he was a minister of his government. The rôle delighted him: 'When I stopped to refresh my mules at a little village, the inhabitants came crouding about me as an ambassadour going to their General' (*JTC*, p. 66).

In his preface Boswell went to some lengths to stress the complete authenticity of his account, and there is no reason whatever to challenge that claim. Thomas Gray was guilty of a serious misjudgement when he asserted,

'The pamphlet proves what I have always maintained, that any fool may write a most valuable book by chance, if he will only tell us what he heard and saw with veracity.'[22] The book is valuable because of the *way* in which Boswell tells what he saw and heard. His material is engrossing and is authentically portrayed. Equally authentic is the portrayal of the author. It is decidedly Boswell's account. Courtesy of Thomas Day's translations of Seneca's *Epigrams* and with the benefit of Monboddo's 'thorough acquaintance with ancient learning' (*JTC*, p. 45), Boswell intersperses classical allusions and extracts through his account. He describes his purpose in doing so as follows:

> Those by whom I wish to be judged, will, I hope, approve of my adding dignity to Corsica, by shewing its consideration among the ancients, and will not be displeased to find my page sometimes embellished with a seasonable quotation from the Classicks. (*JTC*, p. 46)

At first reading, the concatenation of Boswell's vivid report of a progress along a cliff-face path and an extract from Seneca's *De Consolatione* (admittedly on a similar theme) seems either incongruous or mere show. Yet by the end of the book one is left undeniably with the impression that Boswell has taken a great risk but has succeeded: he has managed to suggest the continuity and universality of human experience.

Nor is he Gray's 'any fool' in that he has an unerring eye for what is of interest (he has promised to present only what is 'most worthy of observation' (*JTC*, p. 59)). Innately absorbing events are enlivened further by his presence and by the nature of his report. Brief residence in a convent is recorded thus: 'It appeared a little odd at first. But I soon learnt to repair to my dormitory as naturally as if I had been a friar for seven years' (*JTC*, p. 59). Then, true to the Scottish tradition of ironic self-revelation,[23] he adds the observation, 'A little experience of the serenity and peace of mind to be found in convents, would be of use to temper the fire of men of the world' (*JTC*, pp. 59–60). The book abounds in instances of that distinctly Boswellian compound of insatiable curiosity and compulsive rôle-playing. He is fascinated by the fact that no Corsican would accept the post of public hangman. When the Chancellor sends for the seal of the kingdom, Boswell notes, 'I thought myself sitting in the house of a Cincinnatus' (*JTC*, p. 65).

Accompanied by native guides on his journey Boswell assumes temporarily the rôle of natural man ('It was just being for a little while one of the *"prisca gens mortalium*, the primitive race of men"*, who ran about the woods eating acorns and drinking water' (*JTC*, p. 66)). At Bastelica, Boswell chose to harangue the men 'with great fluency'. His prescription is a model of compromise:

> Their poverty, I told them, might be remedied by a proper cultivation of their island, and by engaging a little in commerce. But I bid them remember, that they were much happier in their present state than in a state of refinement and vice, and that therefore they should beware of luxury. (*JTC*, p. 67)

The book is notable for Boswell's candour, not least about himself. As the meeting with the great Paoli drew imminent Boswell was beset by fears and 'almost wished to go back without seeing him' (*JTC*, p. 68). Introduced to the famous leader, Boswell told him that he was 'much surprised to find him so amiable, accomplished, and polite' (Boswell expected 'an Attila, King of the Goths', he admits (*JTC*, p. 75)). Such disarming frankness extends beyond those whom he meets to include the reader also. Boswell makes no attempt to hide the psychological significance of the rôle-playing in which he was able to indulge in Corsica. The following typifies his delight in simultaneous participation and self-observation:

> One day when I rode out I was mounted on Paoli's own horse, with rich furniture of crimson velvet, with broad gold lace, and had my guards marching along with me. I allowed myself to indulge a momentary pride in this parade, as I was curious to experience what could really be the pleasure of state and distinction with which mankind are so strangely intoxicated. (*JTC*, p. 71)

Not least Mr James Boswell, one is tempted to add.

The rôles which Corsica offered happened to be of a most rewarding kind. 'My time passed here in the most agreeable manner', he acknowledges, 'I enjoyed a sort of luxury of noble sentiment' (*JTC*, p. 71). On projecting one of his favourite self-images he had the satisfaction of Paoli's identifying him as a melancholic. He was able to discourse to Paoli on the subject of his 'revered friend Mr. Samuel Johnson' (*JTC*, p. 96), thus acting as intermediary between the Sage and the Hero and appropriating their distinctions as his own. Like Scott and Stevenson, Boswell was obsessed with the Man of Action. (The recurrence of this in Scottish writers may be related to the fact that the restrained, largely urban and middle-class, world of Scottish letters since the Union offered little scope for great public deeds; hence compensatory hero-worship thrived). In the case of Boswell, behind the appearance of the impresario a deep psychological need was struggling to achieve fulfilment. What especially impressed Boswell about Paoli was the intensity of his belief and commitment, qualities which Boswell noted as unfashionable in what he deemed an age of incredulity. The effect of meeting Paoli was to 'set [him] free from a slavish timidity in the presence of great men' (*JTC*, p. 107). And the effect of recording his experiences was equally salutary. 'I am now seriously engaged in my account of Corsica', he informed Temple, 'it elevates my soul and makes me *spernere humum*' (*Letters*, p. 65).

By virtue of his Corsican adventures Boswell felt entitled to project himself as a person of distinction. 'I am really the *great man* now' (*Letters*, p. 121), he boasted to Temple. Having listed visitors that include Hume, Johnson, Franklin, and Garrick, he congratulated himself, 'This is enjoying the fruit of my labours, and appearing like the friend of Paoli' (*Letters*, p. 121).[24] This rôle was to suffice for some time. Boswell presented himself to the Prime Minister in full Corsican attire. In September 1769, months after Paoli had been put to flight by the French, Boswell appeared in his Corsican costume at the Shakespeare jubilee at Stratford. Mere fact was powerless before the grand illusion. When Paoli came to Auchinleck Boswell wrote of 'the joy of my worthy father and me at seeing the Corsican Hero in our romantick groves'.[25] To Lord Auchinleck, according to Scott's testimony, Paoli was 'a land-louping scoundrel of a Corsican'.[26]

Boswell had hoped to find an identity by means of his Corsican Journal. To Temple he wrote,

> I wish at last to be an uniform, pretty man . . . I am always for fixing some period for my perfection as far as possible. Let it be when my account of Corsica is published; I shall then have a character which I must support. (*Letters*, p. 98)

And his preface contains this frank acknowledgement of his urgent motive for writing:

> For my part, I should be proud to be known as an authour; and I have an ardent ambition for literary fame; for of all possessions I should imagine literary fame to be the most valuable. A man who has been able to furnish a book which has been approved by the world, has established himself as a respectable character in distant society, without any danger of having that character lessened by the observation of his weaknesses. (*JTC*, p. 47)

The pantomime of Boswell's behaviour on his return should not be allowed to obscure his considerable achievement in *The Journal of a Tour to Corsica*, and not least his mastery of prose technique, his control of narrative, and his modulation of fact and impression. The book thoroughly warrants the tribute Johnson paid it:

> You express images which operated strongly upon yourself, and you have impressed them with great force upon your readers. I know not whether I could name any narrative by which curiosity is better excited or better gratified.[27]

Given his nature, Boswell could not rest content with the identity he had won. It brought no significant unification or stabilisation of personality; rather, the internal divisions remained, the melancholy deepened, and the restlessness intensified. Characteristic of Boswell is the fact that he turned his concern with his own condition to significant literary effect. In the years 1777–83 he made seventy contributions to *The London Magazine* under the pseudonym, 'The Hypochondriack'. He was, of course, writing about himself and his self-images, as his definition of the hypochondriac shows: 'Nothing characterises a Hypochondriack more peculiarly than irresolution, or the want of powers over his own mind'.[28]

It is undeniable that Boswell did suffer from acute melancholy: a letter of 23 August 1789 reveals deep despair and an 'avidity for death' (*Letters*, p. 251). But it is equally true—as that same letter shows—that he could not dwell long on the subject of his melancholy (or on any other subject) without striking attitudes or projecting self-images. Thus *Boswell's Column* ('The Hypochondriack' essays collected) is informed by duality. As Margery Bailey has noted, 'the purpose of the essays was to defeat inertia and depression by a definite task' (*BC*, p. xii). With typical candour and self-concern Boswell presents and analyses his condition in a manner that anticipates the confessional literature of two centuries later. The subject-matter and treatment substantiate the claim which Boswell makes in his essay 'On Diaries'—'"The importance of a man to himself", simply considered, is not a subject of ridicule; for, in reality, a man is of more importance to himself than all other things or persons can be' (*BC*, p. 331). Yet it would be a mistake to assume that the predominant note is one of an overpowering egotism or that the work is primarily of interest as a case-history. In fact Boswell reveals himself as a master of the essay form. The capacity to discern the interesting is again evident, allied to an adeptness in the structuring and pacing of material. And, above all, Boswell simply has lots of valuable observations to make: having seen the Eskimoes whom Cartwright brought to England he refuses to agree with Rousseau or Monboddo on man's original nobility of nature; there are witty comments on the propensity of authors to self-importance; he speculates on how children would be treated if they were rare; and, in an essay entitled 'Past and Present', Boswell, unlike many of his countrymen, refuses to romanticise the past; and, in a superb self-irony, he begins his essay 'On Hypochondria' with the admission,

> I have for so long a time been free of the direful malady from which the title of this periodical paper is taken, that I almost begin to forget that I ever was afflicted with it; and as Philip of Macedon had one, who every morning when he awaked, put him in mind that he was a man, it may become necessary for me to be put in mind that I am an Hypochondriack. (*BC*, p. 318)

Over all these years, of course, Boswell had been observing Johnson and recording his behaviour and utterances. The considerable literary skills were being honed in preparation for the representation of what he rightly conceived would be his worthiest subject. When the long-projected tour to the Hebrides came to fruition Boswell commented, 'I considered that I was upon an expedition for which I had wished for years, and the recollection of which would be a treasure to me for life' (*JTH*, p. 109). The first and not inconsiderable aspect of Boswell's achievement was in getting Johnson to undertake the journey at all. Martin Martin's *Description* of the Hebrides, which Johnson had read when young, had, says Boswell, 'impressed us with a notion that we might there contemplate a system of life almost totally different from what we had been accustomed to see' (*JTH*, p. 1). For long, Johnson had encouraged Boswell to think that the visit might take place. When he again contemplated it in the spring of 1773 Boswell helped things along by privately securing invitations to him from the chiefs of the clans Macdonald and Macleod and enlisting the aid of Elibank, Robertson, and Beattie. This is yet another instance of Boswell's abilities as impresario.

In the account itself Boswell feigns self-effacement with a measure of success. 'I beg it to be understood', he writes, 'that I insert my own letters, as I relate my own sayings, rather as keys to what is valuable belonging to others, than for their own sake' (*JTH*, pp. 4–5). In fact he was extremely adept

at setting up the scenarios and creating the situations whereby Johnson
would be induced to participate and pronounce. Thus the reader is treated to
Johnson's judgements of such figures as Knox, Hume, and Beattie. Thanks
to Boswell's skilful management Johnson pronounces on emigration, tragic
acting, smoking and drinking, and bare-footed lairds. The tour elicited from
Johnson some of his most profound observations, including that prompted by
the visit to Iona (which Boswell, rightly, thinks fit to reproduce): 'Whatever
withdraws us from the power of our senses, whatever makes the past, the
distant, or the future, predominate over the present, advances us in the
dignity of thinking beings' (*JTH*, p. 325)

One of Boswell's greatest accomplishments in the *Journal* is that both he
and Johnson are vividly characterised. Boswell appears in the character of
the trustworthy reporter. In the dedication to Malone he stresses the importance of authenticity and he intervenes in the narrative to reiterate the point
('I must again and again apologize to fastidious readers, for recording such
minute particulars. They prove the scrupulous fidelity of my Journal. Dr.
Johnson said it was a very exact picture of a portion of his life' (*JTH*, p. 268)).
But the truth is that, despite such claims for naturalistic authenticity, Boswell
is a subtle manipulator of both subject and readers. There is an indication of
this in the appearance of Shandean asides, promises, and directions to the
reader ('. . . by-and-by, my readers will find this stick will bud, and produce
a good joke' (*JTH*, p. 8).

Boswell and Johnson are further characterised by their contrasting
responses to the same event or experience. Fort George induced cool delib-
eration in Johnson but stimulated Boswell's 'warm imagination' (*JTH*, p. 108).
En route to Forres, Johnson enjoyed himself enormously with adaptations of
speeches from *Macbeth*, while the visit to Macbeth's castle gave Boswell 'a
romantick satisfaction in seeing Dr. Johnson actually in it' (*JTH*, p. 110).
Boswell was acutely alert to the presence of Johnson and he accomplishes
masterly representation of some thoroughly memorable incidents (the 'ludicrous scene' (*JTH*, p. 124) of the Highland guide's attempt to divert Johnson's
attention, as one would with a child, during a steep descent; Johnson reciting
an ode of Horace during the stormy crossing to Raasay). Nonetheless, Boswell
is also a significant presence within the narrative in his own right (not least
when suffering from the famous hangover). When his daughter Veronica,
aged four months, showed a fondness for Johnson this endeared her still
further to her father who 'declared she should have five hundred pounds of
additional fortune' (*JTH*, p. 13). Witnessing the presence of Johnson in familiar
or cherished Scottish settings seemed to fulfil some sort of psychological need
in Boswell. The sight of Dr Johnson asleep in the Young Pretender's bed in
the house of Flora Macdonald struck Boswell 'with such a group of ideas as
it is not easy for words to describe, as they passed through the mind' (*JTH*, p.
168). 'Think', he exclaims later, 'what enthusiastick happiness I shall have
to see Mr. Samuel Johnson walking among the romantick rocks and woods
of my ancestors at Auchinleck!' (*JTH*, p. 339). It is as if by witnessing Johnson
in the context of such familiar landmarks Boswell is able to advance the
process of self-identification.

Paradoxically, what is instrumental to this process is Boswell's compulsion to think in terms of rôles. He notes the strong impression made on his imagination by seeing 'for the first time on horseback, jaunting about at his ease in quest of pleasure and novelty' (*JTH*, p. 113) the author of *London* and the *Rambler*. And he comments, 'To me it was highly comick, to see the grave philosopher,—The Rambler,—toying with a Highland beauty!' (*JTH*, p. 251). The explanation of Boswell's fascination with observing Johnson in diverse situations is that Johnson's is manifestly a rich but also integrated personality, the latter quality being precisely what Boswell lacked and sought. In one crucial passage Boswell states that he 'regretted that Dr. Johnson did not practise the art of accommodating himself to different sorts of people'. But then Boswell, characteristically, inverts this judgement completely:

> ... but I have often maintained, that it is better he should retain his own manner. Pliability of address I conceive to be inconsistent with that majestick power of mind which he possesses, and which produces such noble effects. A lofty oak will not bend like a supple willow. (*JTH*, pp. 277–8)

But this particular willow's suppleness could also prove a strength, albeit of a distinct kind. Boswell is the subtle creator and organiser of situations, the impresario. He was well aware of the psychological dimension of this function. Here he expresses the satisfaction he feels in having got Johnson to Skye:

> I was elated by the thought of having been able to entice such a man to this remote part of the world. A ludicrous, yet just image presented itself to my mind, which I expressed to the company. I compared myself to a dog who has got hold of a large piece of meat, and runs away with it to a corner, where he may devour it in peace, without any fear of others taking it from him. (*JTH*, p. 201)

Thereafter there is talk of his accompanying Johnson to Sweden and seeing the king. Johnson doubts whether he would speak to them, but Colonel McLeod asserts, 'I am sure Mr. Boswell would speak to *him*' (*JTH*, p. 201). Boswell rushes to defend to the reader that tendency of his as 'nothing more than an eagerness to share the society of men distinguished either by their rank or their talents, and a diligence to attain what I desire' (*JTH*, p. 202).

The record of the pursuit of what he desired gave rise to some of the finest prose of the eighteenth, or any other, century. For instance, the lead-up to the collision between Johnson and Boswell's father at Auchinleck is managed superbly. The modulation of pace and tone throughout this whole episode is quite brilliant. The entry for Saturday 6 November 1773 can stand comparison with the very best of Sterne as a model of benignly humorous prose observation. Such episodes exemplify the nature of Boswell's success: it is in the management of the situations and incidents contained in the *Journal* and the manner of their recording.

In its achievement the *Journal* anticipates that of *The Life of Samuel Johnson LL.D.* Indeed the *Journal* contains several advance-notices of the later work, commencing with Boswell's reporting Johnson's esteem for biography and

4   *THE DANCE ON DUN-CAN.*
*'Old Mr Malcolm McCleod, who had obligingly promised to accompany me was at my
Bed-side between five & Six. I sprang up immediately and he & I attended by two other
Gentlemen traversed the Country during the whole of this day. Though we had passed
over not less than four &-twenty Miles of very rugged Ground & had a Highland Dance
on the top of DUN-CAN, the Highest Mountain in the Island, We returned in the Evening
not at all fatigued & piqued ourselves at not being outdone at the Nightly ball, by our
less active friends who had remained at home.'* Vide Journal p. 192

5   *THE RECOVERY.*
'I awaked at noon with a severe headach. I was much vexed that I should have been guilty of such a riot and afraid of a reproof from Dr Johnson.—When I rose I went into Dr Johnson's room and taking up Mr M'Kinnon's Prayer-book I opened it at the twentieth Sunday after Trinity in the epistle for which I read And be not drunk with wine, wherein there is excess Some would have taken this as a divine interposition.' Vide Journal p. 318

including an acknowledgement that 'a vast treasure of [Johnson's] conversation' has already been collected. And, most importantly, it is the method of 'leading, as one does in examining a witness,—starting topics, and making him pursue them' (*JTH*, p. 255), already so effective in the *Journal*, that is refined to its subtlest form in the *Life* and is integral to that triumph. From first meeting, Johnson had warmed to Boswell's 'ingenuous open way' (*LJ*, p. 283). Boswell himself had recognised his 'particular art of nettling people without seeming to intend it' (*LJ*, p. 182). And Goldsmith had paid tribute to his social and conversational art, as the following indicates:

> [Goldsmith] said I had a method of making people speak. 'Sir', said I, 'that is next best to speaking myself'. 'Nay', said he, 'but you do both.' (*LJ*, p. 288)

Boswell took pride in those occasions when he 'gently assisted those little arts which serve to make people throw out their sentiments with ease and freedom' (*LJ*, p. 292).

The perfection of this talent is reflected in the *Life*. There the art of rendering dialogue, increasingly used in the earlier works, is brought to perfection. The *Life* certainly justifies its author's several claims on its behalf: that it is 'told with authenticity and in a lively manner' (*Letters*, p. 258); that 'it is a view of much of the literature, and many of the literary men, of Great Britain for more than half a century' (*Letters*, p. 265); and that his 'mode of biography, which gives not only a *History* of Johnson's *visible* progress through the world, and of his publications, but a *view* of his mind in his letters and conversations, is the most perfect that can be conceived, and will be more of a Life than any work that has ever yet appeared' (*Letters*, p. 218). That someone who was so much a prey to self-delusion in his life should have been capable of such accurate evaluation of his work is not the least of the many paradoxes that surround that most paradoxical of men. In the example of the *Life* is the clearest manifestation of the paradoxical relationship between the life and personality of its author and his biographical writings: plastic man has esemplastic power. 'I have *Johnsonized* the land'[29] was his justifiably triumphant boast.

That Boswell was a mass of paradoxes may well account for his relative neglect until our own time. In his very plasticity is one of the respects in which he anticipates the modern condition. The fragmentation of the personality meant that he had an identity for every company; he was truly, as Wilkes said, a citizen of the world.[30] Moreover he was able to identify fragmentation of personality and rôle-playing in others. A friend, Douglas, who was a doctor, was neatly dissected by Boswell in terms of 'Douglas as friend' and 'Douglas as surgeon' (*LJ*, pp. 157–8). He was capable too of penetrating the masquerade to see the reality of the *beau monde*. When Lady Northumberland failed yet again to further his interest as promised he exclaimed,

> O these Great People! They are a sad set of beings. This woman who seemed to

be so cordially my friend and promised me her good offices so strongly is, I fear, a fallacious hussy. (*LJ*, p. 238)

Boswell is poignantly relevant to our time in that he epitomises the restless pursuit of the unattainable and the constant dissatisfaction with whatever is attained. Here he shares his melancholy with Temple:

> What a state are we in! dissatisfied with the present, and longing for some other situation, and, when we reach *that*, very often experiencing more uneasiness, nay, imagining that what we wished to quit was better. Surely, my dear friend, there *must* be another world, in which such beings as we are will have our misery compensated. (*Letters*, p. 271)

And perhaps most significant of all is the way in which he heralds twentieth-century man's fixation with observation of his own self-drama. Boswell is the divided self—both actor and audience. There is a late letter to Temple in which Boswell writes of further disappointments in his attempts to secure a government post for Temple's son but promises to approach Dundas on his behalf. Then comes this:

> If you will allow me I will try him in my way, requesting he may do a kindness of much consequence to an old friend, unconnected with politics; *and let me have it to tell*. (*Letters*, p. 275)

Experience may have some importance in its own right, but it is doubly important in that it affords material for *telling*; and it is largely by that means (if indeed at all) that identity is attained. It is not what we experience that matters finally but how we observe ourselves as participants and how we present that experience—this is the significance of the example of Boswell, and in this he is a forerunner of the modern personality and the modern condition.

And throughout, with all his blemishes (perhaps because of them), he is endearingly human. On a visit to Eton to arrange his son's acceptance he found his egotism unexpectedly bolstered. Here is his typically candid version of events:

> I was there last week to prepare matters, and to my agreeable surprise found myself highly considered there, was asked by Dr. Davies the Head-master to dine at the Fellows' table, and made a creditable figure. *I certainly have the art of making the most of what I have*. (*Letters*, p. 255)

CHAPTER 6

The Limits of Sentiment: The Works of Henry Mackenzie

'The history of the authors is always in a great degree the history of the literature of a country' wrote Henry Mackenzie in *An Account of the Life and Writings of William Tytler, Esq.*[1] The example of Mackenzie himself substantiates the point. Mackenzie's early manhood coincided with the time when, according to Tate Wilkinson, Edinburgh made 'the most rapid strides in art, elegance, and luxury, of any place in the three kingdoms'.[2] In the course of his long life Mackenzie grew up during the eminence of the *literati*, played a leading part in the Ossian controversy, introduced Burns to literary Edinburgh, witnessed the rise of Scott, and lived through the great age of the Edinburgh periodicals. In his own day he enjoyed great personal fame. There is a certain irony in the fact that Mackenzie, by no means an imaginative writer of the first rank, should have gained pre-eminence by adopting and then projecting the *persona* of the man of feeling.

A man of conflicting elements of personality, Mackenzie writes in various voices (and not solely as the man of feeling or 'our Scottish Addison', as has been generally believed). His range of styles reflects the cultural dichotomy of the post-Union Scot. Like most of his contemporaries Mackenzie set out to vie with English writers in their modes and using their language (there is an ironic parallel in the fact that he went to London to learn Exchequer law, the only branch of Scots law governed by English practice). In his writing there are indications of an awareness of his identity as Scot, a national self-consciousness that seemed to accompany a national inferiority-complex. Commenting on the situation of the humorous writer, Mackenzie remarks wryly that 'a joke in writing is like a joke in conversation; much of its wit depends upon the rank of its author'. But it was not just lack of status that inhibited Scottish humorous writing: according to Mackenzie the art of laughter does not come easily to the Scot:

> In Scotland we can be very bitter in our Wrath, seldom jocose in our Satire; we can lash an Adversary but want the Art of laughing at him, which is frequently the severer Revenge of the two.[3]

It is typical of the compartmentalisation of the post-Union Scottish literary personality that Mackenzie expresses his considerable comic talents in his contributions to the *Mirror* and the *Lounger* and keeps a tight rein on the humorous possibilities inherent in some of the situations of his sentimental novels. For a Scot such as Mackenzie it would have been impossible to render the flux and the composite nature of emotions, embracing both laughter and feeling, in the way that Sterne does. It was in character for Mackenzie to chastise Sterne for wanting 'the dignity of wit'.[4]

Of prime interest in Mackenzie's work is his version of sentimentalism. A poem entitled 'Verses, written after recovering from the first anguish of a severe family-affliction' contains the stanza,

> Though deep the sigh, the sigh was dear,
> To joys long lost reflection gave;
> And sweet to me the conscious tear
> That drops upon affliction's grave!

The sweetness of the conscious tear serves as a useful index to Mackenzie's brand of sentimentalism. In *The Man of Feeling* one editor, Henry Morley, noted that there are forty-seven instances of tears being shed. On each occasion a major part of the author's concern is with the arousing of emotion in the reader. Brian Vickers contends that 'this concern with the consumer rather than the work of art is a sign of decadence'.[5] This may be, but it is essential to take account of the peculiarly Scottish element: in part it derives from the emphasis placed by the *literati* on rhetoric, on process and effect rather than substance. The most forceful statement of sentimentalist doctrine came from Rousseau who, in his *Discours sur les Sciences et les Arts* of 1750, propounded this central principle: that natural man was both virtuous and happy and that it is the processes of civilisation, in their artificiality and sophistication, that corrupt. Mackenzie was to adopt this, but he lent to it a distinctly Scottish colouring when, for instance, he wrote in October 1770, 'There is no Topic more favourable for eloquent Declamation than the Eulogy of unpolish'd Nature: yet after all, we owe our Rousseaus to Society, & their Eloisas to the Empire of the Woman.'[6] Identifiably Scottish features are the emphasis on declamation and the recognition of the importance of social factors.

In *The Man of Feeling* the Indian whom Edwards frees, thus allowing his benevolence to be demonstrated, may well be the earliest of Mackenzie's versions of the noble savage. The ravaging of the village and the closure of its school to meet the demands of the squire's vanity indicate, with more than a glance at 'The Deserted Village' and *The Vicar of Wakefield*, the deleterious effects of social refinement which Rousseau had claimed. Yet it is revealing that the heroine, Miss Walton, shows her kindly concern for the Edwards children by clothing them in expensive finery. Noteworthy, too, is Harley's treatment of nature:

> Harley had contrived to lead a little bubbling brook through a greenwalk in the middle of the ground, upon which he had created a mill in miniature for the diversion of Edwards's infant-grandson, and made shift in its construction to introduce a pliant bit of wood, that answered with its fairy clack to the murmuring of the rill that turned it. I have seen him stand, listening to these mingled sounds, with his eye fixed on the boy, and the smile of conscious satisfaction on his cheek;

while the old man, with a look half-turned to Harley, and half to Heaven, breathed
an ejaculation of gratitude and piety. (101–2)

The man of feeling has tamed and stylised nature in the interests of his
benevolism, the practice of which promotes his own 'conscious satisfaction'.
There is a further dimension, however, in that the contemplation of the
spectacle induces the narrator to exclaim,

Father of mercies! I also would thank thee! that not only hast thou assigned
eternal rewards to virtue, but that, even in this bad world, the lines of our duty,
and our happiness, are so frequently woven together. (102)

Such writing shows that Mackenzie sensed the extent and the intensity of the
vogue of sentimentalism that Rousseau's ideas had helped to stimulate, and
he capitalised upon it. In his version of sentimentalism he greatly increased
the declamatory element, emphasised the importance of benevolence to the
benefactor, and presented Rousseau's original 'nature' in a rather more effete
and hybrid form.

In part the spirit in which Mackenzie wrote was that of a conscious reaction
against scepticism and what he regarded as anti-romanticism. On 10 March
1771 he wrote to his cousin,

The romantic is now exploded in every Thing . . . Ridicule, the great Engine of
modern Philosophy has beaten us out of these Heights to a Climate less pleasant,
& it may be doubted if more salubrious.—He, who has Feelings to be awaken'd
may be often guilty of Follies; but we have Grounds of Reclamation which we
can urge with Satisfaction; the gross System which would bury these Emotions
is deaf to every Argument that a liberal Mind could bear to urge.[7]

Two weeks later he was counselling her as follows:

You distinguish with the utmost Propriety between the Good & Evil of the
romantic; but popular Systems have more Effect, I believe, than you imagine, on
all Hearts whatever. The same Turn of thinking that has free'd the present Times
for the Influence of Romance, has had many Consequences upon their general
Complexion. The Pride of that Knowledge they possess has grown in Proportion
as they discovered some little Deceits that were practis'd upon their Fathers,
Scepticism has followed this.[8]

To understand why Mackenzie wrote in this way it is necessary to consider
the nature of the Europe-wide movement of emphasis from reason to feeling
as an agent and index of moral response. Rousseau wrote of the 'sixth sense,
the moral sense'.[9] Such thinking was part of an attempt to regard human
nature predominantly in terms of feeling or spontaneous generous emotion.
The benevolent natural man, the friend of mankind, the man of feeling,
reached the centre of the European intellectual stage around the middle of
the century, and Scottish thinkers were partly responsible for that. Here is

David Fordyce writing in 1754 on the particular satisfactions of the natural benefactor:

> His Enjoyments are more numerous, or, if less numerous, yet more intense than those of bad Men; for he shares in the Joys of others by Rebound; and every Increase of *general* or *particular* Happiness is a real Addition to his own. It is true, his friendly *Sympathy* with others subjects him to some Pains which the hard-hearted Wretch does not feel; yet to give a loose to it is a kind of agreeable Discharge. It is such a Sorrow as he loves to indulge; a sort of pleasing Anguish, that sweetly melts the Mind, and terminates in a Self-approving Joy. Though the good Man may want Means to execute, or be disappointed in the Success of his benevolent Purposes, yet . . . he is still conscious of good Affections, and that Consciousness is an Enjoyment of a more delightful Savour than the greatest Triumphs of successful Vice.[10]

In a definitive essay R S Crane delineated the various aspects of the emphasis upon feeling. Virtue was regarded as universal benevolence, and benevolence was held to be inseparable from the capacity for, and manifestation of, feeling. To be effective, benevolence must spring from the 'tender emotions' such as compassion or pity, and man ought to show or express these emotions in that they identify the genuinely practical benefactor, as distinct from the merely righteous. The ideal was the tenderhearted benefactor who first pities, but is also moved to relieve suffering. Love of one's fellow-beings should include in its manifestation sympathetic identification, since this is beneficial to both sufferer and sympathiser. Here, as Crane noted, is a very early definition of sensibility as offered by the anonymous contributor to the *Prompter*, no. 63, 17 June 1735:

> Humanity, in its first and general Acceptation, is call'd by Holy Writers, *Good-will towards Men*; by Heathens, *Philanthropy*, or *Love* of our *Fellow Creatures*. It sometimes takes the Name of *Good-nature*, and *delights* in *Actions* that have an *obliging* Tendency in them: When strongly *impress'd* on the *Mind*, it assumes a *higher* and nobler Character, and is not satisfy'd with good-natured Actions alone, but *feels* the *Misery* of others with *inward Pain*. It is then deservedly named *Sensibility*, and is considerably increased in its intrinsick Worth.[11]

It came to be recognised that the therapeutic effect derived not merely from the benevolent action but also from sympathetic identification. Further, it was argued that benevolent feelings are natural to man. Rightly, Crane regards this as a reaction against both Puritanism and the political and moral beliefs of Hobbes. In the Scottish context it can be seen especially as a reaction against Presbyterianism and an assertion that man is not absolutely and irrevocably flawed. If the capacity to feel pity and tenderness is one of the features that identifies human nature, and if man ought to live according to his nature, then, as Crane notes, 'it follows that he does this most completely who not only practises an active benevolence towards all men but cultivates and makes manifest the "good Affections" of the heart'.[12]

Crane proved that the belief in the 'self-approving joy' of the benefactor was already current among such theologians and philosophers as Isaac Barrow, John Tillotson, Richard Kidder, and Samuel Parker towards the end of the seventeenth century. Barrow wrote of 'pleasing Anguish, that sweetly melts the Mind, and terminates in a Self-approving joy'.[13] This introduces a distinctly hedonistic and egotistical element to the relief of distress. Mackenzie's Harley is characteristic of the majority of the literary men of feeling in that on occasions he does engage in altruistic emotions and conduct for personal satisfaction. Invited to visit Bedlam, Harley at first declines on the grounds that it is inhuman to make a spectacle of human misery and especially trying for the humane since they can do nothing to alleviate the misery which they witness. Persuaded to visit, Harley encounters a succession of personal tragedies (which owes something to Smollett's *Ferdinand Count Fathom*), prompting him to make a comment that has an ironic relevance to his own situation—'the passions of men are temporary madnesses; and sometimes very fatal in their effects' (32). In this episode, as throughout the book, there is an alternation between spectacle and involvement, between man of feeling as observer and man of feeling as participant.

Harley's attention is attracted by a young lady 'whose appearance had something of superior dignity' and whose face 'showed a dejection of that decent kind, which moves our pity unmixed with horror' (32-3). Mackenzie, it should be said, is outside, and in control of, such ironies. It is noted, for instance, that 'though this story was told in very plain language, it had particularly attracted Harley's notice: he had given it the tribute of some tears'. The young lady, a descendant of both Ophelia and Sterne's 'poor Maria', speaks in poignantly precious terms of the loss of her Billy, with the result that 'there was a plaintive wildness in the air not to be withstood; and, except the keeper's, there was not an unmoistened eye around her'.

The episode concludes:

> She walked with a hurried step to a little apartment at some distance. Harley stood fixed in astonishment and pity! his friend gave money to the keeper.—Harley looked on his ring.—He put a couple of guineas into the man's hand: 'Be kind to that unfortunate'—He burst into tears, and left them. (35)

Now it is significant that Harley's tears follow his act of benevolence: the egotistical and self-conscious aspects of Harley's behaviour are evident, and Mackenzie is detached from his creation. To underline this point, he introduces in juxtaposition with Harley's conduct the views of the misanthrope, a close kinsman of Fielding's Man of the Hill, who offers this interpretation of the benevolent:

> With vanity your best virtues are grossly tainted: your benevolence, which ye deduce immediately from the natural impulse of the heart, squints to it for its reward. There are some, indeed, who tell us of the satisfaction which flows from a secret consciousness of good actions: this secret satisfaction is truly excellent—when we have some friend to whom we may discover its excellence. (42)

What Mackenzie is doing becomes clear: in offering the views of Harley and the misanthrope he is dramatising a debate between the sentimental moralist elements in the thinking of Hutcheson, Hume, and Smith and the diametrically opposed thinking of Hobbes. Mackenzie the author is distanced from both.

Scottish philosophers made a major contribution to the growth of the belief in 'moral sentiment', which held that feeling was an index to virtue (and in so doing formed the basis for Romantic ideas on the subject—one thinks most readily of Keats and 'the holiness of the heart's affections'). It is undeniable that Mackenzie was familiar with the work of Steele and what Harold W Thompson calls 'dramas of sensibility cast into the form of short narratives'[14] in *Tatler*, no. 33 and *Spectator*, no. 375; and he knew the novels of Richardson, Fielding, and Sterne. Identifying the sentimental in Shaftesbury, Richardson, and Sterne, Thompson follows Ernest Bernbaum in claiming not French but English leadership of the European sentimentalist movement. To do so is to undervalue the Scottish contribution. In *Concerning Moral Good and Evil* Francis Hutcheson stressed the importance of what 'may be called a Moral Sense',[15] and this is merely one of the traces of Hutcheson's thinking that Adam Smith was later to claim he found in the work of Rousseau.[16] Hutcheson emphasised the significance of the intuitive, as against the rational, and he upheld the validity of the immediate, and hence unproven or untested, responses of fellowship and sympathy (which the rationalist would wish first to have validated). Sense perception was enlarged by Hutcheson to encompass 'every determination of our minds to receive ideas independently of our will',[17] and David Hume asserted that 'the ultimate ends of human actions can never . . . be accounted for by reason, but recommend themselves entirely to the sentiments and affections of mankind'.[18]

Hutcheson's philosophy, emphasising the original and natural benevolence of man, had a two-fold effect: it stimulated the quest for the remnants of natural man (with the Red Indian, the Negro, and the Highlander being considered in these terms), and it prompted consideration of how sophisticated modern man could best set about recovering his original condition, or how he could practise benevolence. Now Hume's sceptical critique of reason made both of these quests the more urgent.

For Hume, 'the sentiments of humanity . . . brighten up the very face of sorrow and operate like the sun, which shining on a dusty cloud or falling rain paints on them the most glorious colours which are to be found in the whole circle of nature'.[19] Previously Hutcheson had expressed the desirability of showing benevolence towards rational and moral beings 'in the most distant planets'.[20] The man of feeling receives this endorsement from Hume:

> No qualities are more readily intituled to the general good-will and approbation of mankind than beneficence and humanity, friendship and gratitude, natural affection and public spirit . . . and a generous concern for our kind and species.[21]

In his *Theory of Moral Sentiments* (1759) Adam Smith introduced the important element of sympathy with his claim that the victims of circumstances, by relating their misfortunes . . . in some measure renew their grief. Their tears accordingly flow faster than before . . . They take pleasure, however, in all this, and it is evident are sensibly relieved by it, because the sweetness of the by-stander's sympathy more than compensates the bitterness of their sorrow.[22]

The debt of the literature of sentimentalism to the philosophers is, then, a considerable one. The following features are reflected in the sentimental novel: virtue is identified with acts of benevolence and feelings of universal good-will; good affections are regarded as part of natural man, before he has been tainted by habits of vice; there is endorsement of sympathy, and weeping is seen as honourable; and, frequently, anguish terminates in 'self-approving joy'.

Outwith his novels Mackenzie elaborated upon these principles. Using the *persona* of Eubulus, a correspondent to the *Lounger*, he argues for the existence of a close relationship between contemplation of nature and sympathy:

> It is certain, that we experience a high degree of pleasure in certain emotions, excited by the general contemplation of nature, when the attention does not dwell minutely upon any of the objects that surround us. Sympathy, the most powerful principle in the human composition, has a strong effect in constituting the pleasure here alluded to. The stillness of the country, and the tranquillity of its scenes, have a sensible effect in calming the disorder of the passions, and inducing a temporary serenity of mind. By the same sympathy, the milder passions are excited, while the turbulent are laid asleep. (V, 269–70)

For Mackenzie the springs of feeling should be responsive to even the most commonplace of events. Of the death of an acquaintance he wrote, 'I cannot express how much Pity his Family deserves. These Things are common; but I never envied that Philosophy which sets us above the Feelings they excite'.[23] Surroundings and familiar objects evoke particular feelings, and in this pass-age, similar to several in Sterne,[24] Mackenzie offers, through one of his *personae*, the sentimentalist formula wherein objects prompt the release of feelings which they have originally occasioned and with which they have come to be associated:

> There is a silent chronicle of past hours in the inanimate things amidst which they have been spent, that gives us back the affections, the regrets, the sentiments of our former days; that gives back their joys without tumult, their griefs without poignancy . . . many an evening, when I have shut the door of my little parlour, trimmed the fire, and swept the hearth, I sit down with the feelings of a friend for every chair and table in the room. (IV, 254)

Emotion is relived in tranquillity. Evocation of past experiences means that the emotions which they occasioned can be recaptured, but with the dis-concerting extremes of immediacy tempered. In a compromise that is charac-teristic of Mackenzie raw emotion has been civilised by the passage of time. The writer proceeds,

There is, perhaps, a degree of melancholy in all this; the French, who are a lively people, have, I think, no term that answers to our substantive *home*; but it is not the melancholy of a sour unsocial being; on the contrary, I believe, there will always be found a tone of benevolence in it both to ourselves and others:—I say ourselves, because I hold the sensation of peace and friendship with our own minds to be one of the best preparatives, as well as one of the best rewards, of virtue. Nor has Nature given us this propensity in vain. From this the principle of patriotism has its earliest source, and some of those ties are formed, which link the inhabitants of less favoured regions to the heaths and mountains of their native land. In cultivated society, this sentiment of home cherishes the useful virtues of domestic life. (IV, 256)

This is very revealing in two respects: the self-consciousness, introspection, even a certain fear of the schizoid, are significant in terms of the post-Union crisis of Scottish identity; and the inculcation of patriotism is typical of the increasingly sentimental nationalism among Scots.

In the *Mirror*, no. 72 (IV, 272ff) is an essay entitled 'On the moral effects of scenes of sorrow. Funeral of Maria' which clearly indicates the melancholic cast of Mackenzie's doctrine of sympathy and its moral dimension. After contrasting moralists' and voluptuaries' attitudes to death, Mackenzie remarks, 'There is a sympathetic enjoyment which often makes it not only better, but more delightful, to go to the house of mourning, than to the house of feasting.' Of his attendance at Maria's funeral he comments,

I think I would not have exchanged my feelings at the time, for all the mirth which gaiety could inspire, or all the pleasure which luxury could bestow . . . It is by such private and domestic distresses, that the softer emotions of the heart are most strongly excited . . . the death of Maria presents to us a little view of family affliction, which every eye can perceive, and every heart can feel.

However, a more realistic, commonsense side of Mackenzie has a habit of appearing and qualifying the stance which he is trying to project. Here he goes on to recognise that

There needs a certain pliancy of mind, which society alone can give, though its vices often destroy, to render us capable of that gentle melancholy which makes sorrow pleasant, and affliction useful.

It is not from a melancholy of this sort, that men are prompted to the cold unfruitful virtues of monkish solitude. These are often the effects rather of passion secluded than repressed, rather of temptation avoided than overcome . . . but amidst all the warmth of social affection, and of social sympathy, the heart will feel the weakness, and enjoy the duties, of humanity.

Social intercourse is essential to Mackenzie's man of feeling. It presents the material for sympathetic identification and the pleasures of melancholic contemplation; and, perhaps most importantly, it provides the arena in which he can play the part of benefactor. What has surfaced here is a manifestation of the realistic and social bias of Scottish Enlightenment thinking, and even when Mackenzie would wish to project the image of the self-satisfying sentimentalist he cannot fail to take cognisance of it.

When Mackenzie considers the significance and function of sympathy he stresses that contemplation of suffering and identification with the sufferer can be beneficial to the sympathiser. In one letter he replies to his cousin's question 'whether Misfortunes brought on us by ourselves or others are the hardest to support', and he speaks of sympathetic identification and rectitude together. Then follows this crucial passage:

> I will not however scruple to own, that in Minds open to the finer Affections, there are Links of Connection so tender and susceptible, that the Soul seems as deeply wounded as is possible from the Weaknesses and Wanderings of those Objects on whom it has fix'd it's [sic] Regard; but even amidst these Sensations of exquisite Distress the Voice of internal Satisfaction will sometimes be heard; and though the Heart may bleed even to Death, it will never experience a torture equal to the Rendings of Remorse.[25]

Once again, Mackenzie is realistic in recognising the limitations of sensibility. Complete empathy can never be achieved, just as pure and absolute altruism is beyond the accomplishment of human nature—'the Voice of internal Satisfaction will sometimes be heard'. Precisely this awareness informs his comment on the blind poet, Dr Thomas Blacklock:

> It was a sight highly gratifying to philanthropy, to see how much a mind endowed with knowledge, kindled by genius, and, above all, lighted up with innocence and piety like Dr. Blacklock's, could overcome the weight of its own calamity, and enjoy the content, the happiness, and the gaiety of others. (VII, 68–9)

Mackenzie seems to derive pleasure and strength from the spectacle of deep emotions, including suffering and grief. Once he made a detour via Birmingham to visit the widow of Sir Lister Holte because, he enthused, 'her letters . . . were no less beautiful than uncommon; breathing the most artless & eloquent Grief, that I ever remember to have seen'.[26] On the subject of the poet, Michael Bruce, who died aged twenty-one, Mackenzie wrote,

> There is something peculiarly pleasing to me in these Meditations of a Soul in Expectance of it's [sic] Dissolution, when, anticipating the State it is soon to put on, it assumes a Dignity superhuman.[27]

Bruce spoiled things, it seems, by proving himself human and fallible; for Mackenzie proceeds,

> But alas! the Movements of our Minds are little in the Pow'r of Philosophy. This very Man, who writes with such Composure on a Prospect, not very distant, of Death, was sunk to a very unmanly Degree when his last Hours arrived.

That Mackenzie should feel such disappointment on discovering the disparity between the mask (which he had created) and the man is telling indeed.

From an early age Mackenzie had aimed at cultivating his finer feelings and projecting an image of himself as a man of feeling. Aged twenty-three, he wrote to his cousin,

> There is something of an acquired as well as a natural Delicacy, & the soul as well as the Body has Nerves, which are only affected in a certain indescribable Manner, & gain by frequent Exertion a very superior Degree of Feeling.[28]

For Mackenzie a very superior degree of feeling has to be worked at; but, plainly, belief in the superior refinement of one's feelings takes one a long way. A few weeks later he was writing to her of the desirability of shunning 'common-Place Beings', and claiming, 'There is a Language of Nothingness, which of all Languages, dead or living, seems to me the most difficult to acquire'.[29] In a later letter he was to warn her,

> In the Midst of your own Sensations you must make Allowance for common Minds. The Self-Enjoyment of the Soul is not the Property of every one.[30]

(In this there is a marked resemblance to the note struck by Burns in his letters to Clarinda.)

Sensibility is a distinction, and its possessor can relish it, but it seems to be inseparable from a dangerously heightened and egotistical self-consciousness. In the main this element is confined to the letters, but *Lounger*, no. 48, contains a very revealing essay entitled 'The sentiment and the moral of Time'. After a fairly orthodox account of how sights and sounds can induce remembrance that brings with it tenderness and melancholy, Mackenzie declares that 'every man is virtuous in recollection; he rests with peculiar satisfaction on the remembrance of such actions as are most congenial to the better parts of his nature'. Mackenzie continues,

> Not only in those greater and more important concerns, which are what Shakespeare calls 'stuff o' the conscience', but in the lesser and more trivial offences of life, we should be more apt to conduct ourselves aright, did we think that we were one day to read the drama in which we now perform, and that of ourselves, and the other personages of the scene, we were to judge with a critical severity.

This view of today's conduct as tomorrow's drama, and the concomitant self-consciousness—both symptomatic of the Scottish crisis of identity—are at the opposite pole from the natural innocent benevolence of original natural man. That awe of judgement, too, bespeaks a distinctly Scottish characteristic.

Of the genesis of *The Man of Feeling* and the autobiographical elements in the book, Mackenzie commented,

> In London I not only conceived the plan of this novel, different from most others as containing little plot or incident but merely a sketch of some particulars of the life and sentiments of a man of more than usual sensibility; some of the incidents I had a certain degree of share in myself. I was often the martyr of that shyness which Harley is stated as being affected by in his intercourse with mankind, and

I had likewise the disgust at some parts of the legal profession to which I was destined.[31]

Harley is 'a man of more than usual sensibility'. 'A man of more than usual sensibility' is what Mackenzie consciously studied to become. Harley, then, is one of the various images of self which Mackenzie projected. The following note makes even clearer this relationship between autobiographical elements in *The Man of Feeling* and projection of images of self:

> *The Man of Feeling* a real picture of my London adventures.—Palpitation of heart walking along the pavement of Grosvenor Square to a man of high rank to whom I had a letter of introduction . . . My being urged to remain in London; probable success if I had; but shy and unambitious and fond of my family; but tho' I missed probably rank and wealth I found comfort and content; and I have said somewhere that the brother of the misanthrope in *The Man of Feeling* found he should never be rich but he might be very happy. That character and his disgust with his profession nearly my own case.[32]

And the prefatory note to the poem, 'Poetry and Business: A Moral Tale', includes the comment,

> There is a sort of naïveté, and some observation of manners (such as a lad who had seen little might observe) amidst the prosaic expression and trite morality which will readily be perceived in this specimen of them. In this one is feelingly mentioned that bashfulness under which I have so often suffered myself, and had so often seen merit suffer. (VIII, 24)

Harley's experiences are a fuller fictional reworking of these experiences. The poem contains this account of the sensitive naif, the *persona* with which Mackenzie wished his early manhood to be identified:

> For there are some whom Nature makes
> Scarce for their own or others sakes,
> But just to try if she can plan,
> The first great outlines of a man;
> And having penciled out the soul,
> Throws in her blush, and spoils the whole.

There is something very studied about all of this, as there is too about Mackenzie's explanation of his habitually quoting Harley in his letters:

> Forgive me for so often making Quotations from myself; it does not proceed altogether from vanity, but partly from my writing so much from the immediate Impulse of the Mind, that when the same Sentiments arise, much the same words present themselves to express them.—If my Performances have any Merit, they owe it to this.[33]

What this shows is that Mackenzie had learned his part. It accorded with the image which he wished to project to have his writing regarded as the expression of the impulse of the mind when directed by intense feeling.

As happened also in the case of Burns, Mackenzie found that he became stuck in the rôle which he himself had created. To Elizabeth Rose he wrote,

> . . . something also is due from my Vanity for your honouring me with the Name of Harley. Some of that Gentleman's Acquaintances here believ'd him to have been actually meant as a Representative of myself; while others, who had Sagacity enough to discover the Fallacy of that Opinion, pronounced decisively on another Character being designed for the Author's Portrait.[34]

In fact, to have his readers involved in such games is precisely what the egotistical side of Mackenzie wants.

Here too, for instance, is Mackenzie presenting to his cousin his authorised version of his literary virtues:

> A sollicitous Attention to Nature, something of those Feelings which her Children possess, with a Tincture of melancholy Enthusiasm which a disappointed Situation in Life is apt to nourish & increase; these, assisted by a Sort of Talent for Composition, acquired by an early Habit of attempting it,—make up the little Stock I am Master of.[35]

This comes from the pen of a young man of twenty-five who is already a lawyer and a writer of some, albeit limited, success, and it was written less than a month before the publication of *The Man of Feeling* on which he had been working at intervals during the preceding five years. When Mackenzie indulges in this sort of projection it may well be that he is inspired by the description of Shenstone which, as Thompson noted,[36] prefaces the 1764 edition of his poems. Certainly 'performance' is an apposite name for such attudinising.

The narrative method employed in *The Man of Feeling* was chosen deliberately by Mackenzie to highlight precisely these qualities—the attention to nature, the alleged purity and naïveté of feelings, and the melancholy enthusiasm. In various comments on his method Mackenzie argued that the fragmentary nature of the presentation is more effective than consecutive narrative, with its emphasis on order and consequentiality, for the portrayal and the evocation of feeling. On 8 July 1769 he wrote,

> You must know then that I have seldom been in Use to write any Prose, except what consisted of Observations (such as I could make) on Men & Manners. The way of introducing these by Narrative I had fallen into in some detach'd Essays, from the Notion of it's interesting both the Memory & the Affection deeper, than mere Argument, or moral Reasoning. In this way I was somehow led to think of introducing a Man of Sensibility into different Scenes where his Feelings might be seen in their Effects, & his Sentiments occasionally delivered without the Stiffness of regular Deduction.[37]

A year later, while stressing his didactic intention, he was sufficiently confident of his method to disclaim any resemblance to that of the novelist:

> It consists of some episodical adventure of a Man of Feeling where his sentiments
> are occasionally expressed and the features of his mind developed as the incidents
> draw them forth. It has, however deficient in other respects, I hope, something
> of Nature in it, and is uniformly subservient to the cause of virtue. You may
> perhaps, from the description, conclude it a novel; nevertheless it is perfectly
> different than that species of composition.[38]

As well as seeking economy and intensity of effect, Mackenzie wished to eschew those predictable or formulaic features by which the novel was already increasingly limited (and which Sterne had parodied to riotously comic effect in *Tristram Shandy*). Mackenzie cautioned Elizabeth Rose,

> You need not regret the want of the subsequent Chapters of the Man of Feeling.
> The winding up of a Story is one of the dullest Things in the world. You remember
> a Miss Walton; you have nothing to do but imagine him somehow or other
> wedded to her & made happy;—so must all Stories conclude you know; the Hero
> is as surely married as he was born; because marriage is a good Thing & made
> in Heaven.[39]

Mackenzie, rather, had devised a new formula, which he would exploit to the fullest effect. Its basis is the affecting episode, which can be read as exactly that and no more. Mackenzie regarded the 'want of Connection in the Parts' as 'one Reason why they bear better to be read at Intervals than some other Books would'.[40]

The other striking feature of Mackenzie's method in *The Man of Feeling* is the distance which he contrives to place between himself and his creation. Mackenzie invents a fictitious editor. He in turn encounters a curate who is using as wadding for his gun parts of an account of the life of Harley written by 'a grave, oddish kind of man', known while he stayed in the area as 'The Ghost' (4). If Sterne distanced himself from the material of *Tristram Shandy* by creating a substitute author upon whom the onus could be laid, Mackenzie redoubles the distancing effect by this elaborate contrivance. The first chapter (ch. XI) has the prefatory note, 'The Reader will remember, that the Editor is accountable only for scattered chapters, and fragments of chapters; the curate must answer for the rest' (7). In a letter Mackenzie dropped one stage of the subterfuge and stressed that he was not writing a novel:

> You will remember that I have made myself accountable only for Chapters &
> Fragments of Chapters; the Curate must answer for the rest: besides from the
> general Scope of the Performance, which that Gentleman informed you, might
> be as well called a Sermon as a History, you wou'd find the Hero's Story, even if
> it were finish'd & I were to send it to you entire, simple to Excess; for I would
> have it as different from the Entanglement of a Novel as can be.[41]

One of the reasons for Mackenzie's doing this readily becomes clear. The invention in each of his books of a substitute author or editor is attractive to Mackenzie because of the opportunity of creating further *personae*. In a letter he extols the virtues of reading books with, as he says, 'the Portrait of the Author before me', since it is 'a Method I have found so pleasing to myself, that I have endeavour'd, in my own Productions, with what Success I know not, to introduce them to their Readers by setting up a Person on whom they might look as the Writer'.[42]

From that person, as from Harley, Mackenzie is, in his view properly, distanced. While praising Henry Brooke's *The Fool of Quality* as being 'laudably subservient to the Cause of Virtue', Mackenzie was quick to voice this objection to the narrative method:

> The Dialogues betwixt the Author & his Friend have this manifest impropriety, that they destroy the Deception necessary in a work of that sort: 'tis just as if a Man should write a Play with Five or Six Prologues in the midst of it.[43]

Mackenzie is trying to have the best of every world: he is contriving—quite ingeniously—to avoid the traditional requirement of the novelist to present consecutive and consequential action; his chosen method and form make for intensity of feeling and the didactic possibilities thereof; and he still would wish to be seen to be abiding by neoclassical doctrines of propriety. By virtue of the distance which he maintains between himself and his material his books become, on one level, dramatised dialogues between aspects or elements within himself. As in the case of *Tristram Shandy* the degree of distancing allows for the possibility of making comment obliquely (i.e. the *nature* of Mackenzie's fiction is in a sense a comment on his part), but the important point of difference with Sterne is that Mackenzie does not exploit the ironic potential which such authorial distance generally offers. That potential is tantalisingly present, but Mackenzie *cannot* exploit it to any great extent because it would undermine his ostensible aim (or the aim of one of the selves he has projected), namely to endorse sensibility.

Integral to the realisation of that aim is the establishment and the sustaining of a distinct mood and tone. This is certainly accomplished in the editor's introduction: all the trappings of sentimentalism are there. The futile pursuit of the game-birds with which the book begins bespeaks one of the central themes of Mackenzie's fiction—expectation disappointed. The import does not escape the editor who offers a little sermon on the subject. He then turns to observe 'a venerable pile' about which hung 'an air of melancholy'. The 'languid stillness in the day' is broken by the croaking of 'a single crow'. The only signs of 'human art' are carving on the bark of trees and the lopping of some branches 'to give a view of the cascade, which was formed by a little rill at some distance'. This is an appropriately stylised landscape in which to introduce 'a young lady with a book in her hand', Miss Walton. Miss Walton is the archetypal sentimental heroine: for her, 'humanity was a feeling, not a principle'. Mention of her leads to the introduction of Harley and his history. In a reductive irony the fate of the history seems to parallel that of its subject. The editor's attitude to it seems to be ambivalent, or at least to fluctuate. Here he tries to demean its significance, only to have to concede to being moved by it:

> I found it a bundle of little episodes, put together without art, and of no importance on the whole, with something of nature, and little else in them. I was a good deal affected with some very trifling passages in it; and had the name of a Marmontel, or a Richardson, been on the title-page—'tis odds that I should have wept: But One is ashamed to be pleased with the works of one knows not whom. (5)

In the fragments that follow Mackenzie communicates with his readers in two main ways: through the opinions of his characters (e.g. on the sentimental education, the sufferings of the oppressed (in India, for instance)); and he presents affecting scenes or incidents (such as the prison scene in Italy in Sedley's account). The incidents are chosen carefully for the extent to which they can demonstrate the eliciting of the virtuous feelings and the moral sense, and hence the tears, of the hero, with the further intention that they should affect the reader similarly. Mackenzie aims for continuity of feeling. After admitting on one occasion that he writes a dull letter because he is surrounded by parchment records, he comments,

> It is lucky that I have my Friends Harley & Atkins to speak for me; it is lucky for them that they speak to those who can understand them. Yet I would not have them break in unseasonably on your Mirth; & as the inclosed Chapter (ch. 29) is also of the melancholy kind, let it not be read till you have a mind to indulge those Feelings which it endeavours to produce.[44]

The mood must be right for the emotional work-out which his sequence of affecting scenes induces. The mood must be the right one, and it must be single, and verbalisation of it by the writer must render it in its pure form. Here Mackenzie argues that the feelings and the rendering of them must be so close as to be identical:

> It is indeed to be much remark'd in general, that Poets, who write professedly from a certain State of Mind, are sometimes led from the Unity of these Feelings by the Exertion of expressing them; Monodies do not alwise breathe the unaffect-edness of Sorrow, nor Pastorals the Simplicity of Love.[45]

Hence Mackenzie opts for the episodic, fragmentary form where there is least danger of the exertion of discursive or consecutive narration complicating the single note.

In the accounts of Emily Atkins and Edwards, Mackenzie misses no opportunity for wringing pathos from events and scenes. Habitually the climax of action is the shedding of tears. The purpose of each account is to show tears, to elicit tears, or—ideally—to do both. This is Edwards's description of the eviction of the family:

> 'Had you seen us, Mr. Harley, when we were turned out of South-hill, I am sure you would have wept at the sight. You remember old Trusty, my shag house-

dog; I shall never forget it while I live; the poor creature was blind with age, and could scarce crawl after us to the door; he went however as far as the gooseberry-bush; that you may remember stood on the left side of the yard; he was wont to bask in the sun there: when he had reached the spot, he stopped; we went on: I called to him; he wagged his tail, but did not stir: I called again; he lay down: I whistled, and cried "Trusty"; he gave a short howl, and died! I could have laid down and died too; but God gave me strength to live for my children'.

The old man now paused a moment to take breath. He eyed Harley's face; it was bathed in tears: the story was grown familiar to himself; he dropped one tear and no more. (88–9).

Two features of this are striking—the way in which Edwards, as senti-mentalist, works upon his material in order to produce the desired effect (and checks to ensure that he has done so); and the extent to which the detailed observation that originates in the Scottish tradition of realism is redirected to the service of sentimentalism. To Elizabeth Rose, Mackenzie affirmed, 'If Nature is fairly copied her Friends the Passions will not fail to discover the Resemblance; & minute incidents, like that of Trusty, are those smaller Features, by which her Intimates recognize the Picture.'[46]

Inseparable from the sustained appeal to the emotions is the reduction of character. Of the scenes involving Atkins and his daughter, Mackenzie remarked,

These are scenes I delight to describe; but it is delicate to describe them with Propriety: the Feelings must appear; but not obtrusive; just so much as to call forth the Hearts of our Readers—And if we can put the Pencil into their own Hands, a few Outlines will serve for our Part of the Picture.[47]

Depict enough to evoke an emotion in the reader, Mackenzie seems to say, and the reader will do the rest. As Brian Vickers has noted, 'The main process is one of simplification of character and situation to easily grasped patterns in which emotion is the main interest' (xi).

This makes for limitation and uniformity in characterisation. Several of the characters (the beggar, the misanthropist) exists as foils to Harley, whose notions of the beautiful include the capacity for showing emotion, and of whom the narrator remarks, 'It was ever the privilege of misfortune to be revered by him.' The villains are tricksters (the elderly gentleman of benign look) or men on the make (the gauger) and these characters, appropriate to comedy or satire, allow the appearance-v.-reality theme to be exemplified. But there are also villains whose actions are more–potentially at least—tragic (Winbrooke and Respino) who abuse power and exploit the innocent. In deliberate contrast are the openly emotional and hence, on the sentimentalist thesis, virtuous characters: Ben Silton, Miss Walton, Miss Atkins, Atkins ('the swellings of whose Heart I have endeavour'd to describe',[48] wrote Mackenzie), Edwards (a 'particular Friend' of Mackenzie of whom, significantly, he felt the need to add, 'I found him in a simple Farm-house; yet, I flatter myself, he is not the less a Hero').[49] Noting his fondness for old characters, Mackenzie commented, 'I somehow affix to Age the united Ideas of Tenderness & Dignity;

& I naturally write what is easiest to me, that is what I am most pleas'd with; and hence my Propensity to the Pathetic.'[50] That propensity is typified in this description of the discovery of the father's grave by Edwards and the grandchildren:

> Edwards gazed upon it without uttering a word: the girl, who had only sighed before, now wept outright; her brother sobbed, but he stifled his sobbing. 'I have told sister', said he, 'that she should not take it so to heart; she can knit already, and I shall soon be able to dig: we shall not starve, sister, indeed we shall not, nor shall grandfather neither.'—The girl cried afresh; Harley kissed off her tears as they flowed, and wept between every kiss. (99)

Almost on cue, virtually every character permits of a demonstration of Harley's sensibility (Mackenzie wrote that one of the reasons for depicting Edwards was 'raising Harley higher in your Esteem').[51] Each has a feeling heart and they combine with Harley, the 'author' (who, especially latterly, is deeply moved by Harley's experiences), and, it is hoped, the reader, to form a composite man of feeling.[52]

Arguably, it is the quality of emotional response, rather than the figure of Harley, that is the unifying element in *The Man of Feeling*. Mackenzie is careful to point out, through Ben Silton, that emotional responsiveness can manifest itself as an embarrassing bashfulness. According to Silton,

> '. . . there are two distinct sorts of what we call bashfulness; this, the aukwardness of a booby, which a few steps into the world will convert into the pertness of a coxcomb; that, a consciousness, which the most delicate feelings produce, and the most extensive knowledge cannot always remove.' (9)

Alongside this should be set Mackenzie's recognition that 'there is a certain Expansion of the Heart that makes a Child of our Reason'.[53]

In *The Man of Feeling* it is made plain that Harley's values and behaviour, particularly under the stress of emotional excitement, can appear absurd to others. It is said of Harley that 'though he was a child in the drama of the world, yet was it not altogether owing to a want of knowledge on his part; on the contrary, the most delicate consciousness of propriety often kindled that blush which marred the performance of it'; (17) and Harley's love for Miss Walton prompts the comment,

> . . . it were sufficient to describe its effects; but they were sometimes so ludicrous, as might derogate from the dignity of the sensations which produced them to describe. They were treated indeed as such by most of Harley's sober friends, who often laughed very heartily at the aukward blunders of the real Harley, when the different faculties, which should have prevented them, were entirely occupied by the ideal. (17)

Rather it is Ben Silton who corresponds to Mackenzie's ideal of a man of feeling who can yet assess the ways of the world. What Mackenzie sets alongside Harley's feeling heart is a certain prudent sense. Without demeaning Harley's sensibility, Mackenzie would appear to wish to temper it with a measure of practical realism. Here, in the advice of the 'author', is Mackenzie's compromise of sensibility allied with practical realism:

> Indeed I have observed one ingredient, somewhat necessary in a man's composition towards happiness, which people of feeling would do well to acquire; a certain respect for the follies of mankind. (11)

This leads to the question of the extent of the conscious irony in Mackenzie's treatment of Harley. It has to be said that for a more realistic (or perhaps more cynical) age, an age suspicious of open emotionalism, the temptation is strong to regard *The Man of Feeling* as parody. There is, undeniably, an intermittent irony of both circumstance and observation. There is gently ironic comment at the expense of the aunt and the curate, and the occasional barb such as the comment prompted by the blissful marriage of the misanthropist's brother, to the effect that 'the sagacious world pitied him for finding happiness' (37); such things are Fielding or the Augustan essayists in a diluted form. But in that purportedly poignant irony at the outset, when Harley's history is found serving as wadding, is the first sign of the problems that await Mackenzie: irony, be it verbal or circumstantial, by its very nature posits two polarities—the actual and the feigned, or the real and the ideal— and it requires mastery of the mode to avoid ambivalence.

It is also true that the language in which both the writer and the characters express themselves is so stylised as to come perilously close to parody, and, to modern eyes at least, the emotional pitch of the characters' responses teeters on the verge of absurdity. Of Miss Walton's voice, it is noted that 'the effect it had upon Harley, himself used to paint ridiculously enough; and ascribed to it powers, which few believed, and nobody cared for' (16).

There are, too, occasions when Mackenzie seems to be undercutting Harley's response with an element of the mundane. At one point Harley sits 'delineating portraits in the fire'. His romantic reverie is halted when 'at last Peter bethought him, that the fire needed stirring; and, taking up the poker, demolished the turban'd-head of a Saracen, while his master was seeking out a body for it' (106). There is, too, a definite irony in the report of Harley's 'skill in physiognomy' (43), which, in a letter, Mackenzie acknowledged he had 'ridiculed'.[54]

Harley's naïveté and hypersensitivity incapacitate him at times for dealing with the real world, and Mackenzie is aware of the comic possibilities of this. Here Harley is confronted by the fainting prostitute, later identified as Miss Atkins:

> Harley started from his seat, and, catching her in his arms, supported her from falling to the ground, looking wildly at the door, as if he wanted to run for assistance, but durst not leave the miserable creature. It was not till some minutes after, that it occurred to him to ring the bell, which at last however he thought of, and rung with repeated violence even after the waiter appeared. Luckily the waiter had his senses somewhat more about him. (49)

Harley's capacity for sympathetic identification is such as to lead to a blurring of the distinction between actuality and what is being related. So vivid is Edward's account of the disruption of the family's game of blind-man's-buff by the press-gang, that Harley believes he is there and 'with a convulsive sort of motion . . . grasping Edwards's sword, drew it half out of the scabbard, with a look of the most frantic wildness' (91). There is so much of this sort of thing that it is reasonable to conclude that while Mackenzie approved of Harley's benevolence he also recognised that the manifestation of this response could mark him out as an unusual, if not at times comic, figure. The undeniable presence of a degree of irony indicates that Mackenzie is detached from Harley, and it suggests that Mackenzie is well aware of the extent to which conduct regulated by the feeling heart deviates from society's norm. The irony is double-edged, however, and the disparity between open emotionalism and 'normal' behaviour serves also as a censure of the latter.

Indeed the recognition that Mackenzie is distanced, sometimes ironically, from Harley does not diminish his endorsement of the open heart. While the extreme nature of Harley's dedication to feeling can be granted, this detracts nothing from the practical worth of his behaviour. Harley is significant as the first literary man of feeling who is a practical benefactor, and he may be contrasted with, for instance, Goethe's Werther, who lives largely in the world of his own melancholic sensibility. Harley's innocence is not unwitting; rather, his faith is a result of conscious choice—'though he was a child in the drama of the world, yet it was not altogether owing to a want of knowledge in his part' (17). And Harley does possess a measure of self-awareness. On his leaving home, his contemplation of the familiar landscape induces a romantic melancholy. When this is terminated abruptly by the need to remove a stone from his shoe he sees an approaching beggar and reflects,

> 'Our delicacies are fantastic; they are not in nature! that beggar walks over the sharpest of stones barefooted, while I have lost the most delightful dream in the world, from the smallest of them happening to get into my shoe.' (19–20)

Intermittently Harley does reveal a realistic awareness. Rural isolation is not, he feels, the best situation for imaginative writing since 'the mind may be there unbent from the cares of the world; but it will frequently, at the same time, be unnerved from any great exertion: it will feel imperfect ideas which it cannot express, and wander without effort over the regions of reflection' (80–1).

Despite the proximity to the absurd of some of Harley's behaviour there is a definite merit in his commitment to the romantic and the emotional. Latterly Mackenzie's 'author' goes out of his way to emphasise this point. Harley's pleasure on returning home prompts the comment,

> Fashion, Bon-ton, and Virtu, are the names of certain idols, to which we sacrifice the genuine pleasures of the soul: in this world of semblance, we are contented with personating happiness; to feel it, is an art beyond us. It was otherwise with Harley. (100)

The approval of the 'author' may well be an attempt on Mackenzie's part to show that Harley is not an isolated representative of feeling. To the 'author' 'Harley was one of the few friends whom the malevolence of fortune had yet left me' (127). In his last conversation with the 'author' Harley outlines his philosophy of life and they join in weeping together. After his death the 'author' pays tribute to 'that form, which, but a little before, was animated with a soul which did honour to humanity' (131); and a visit to the grave, he finds, 'is worth a thousand homilies! every nobler feeling rises within me! every beat of my heart awakens a virtue!' (133). By the end the fictitious author is himself a man of feeling.

The main claims of *The Man of Feeling* to originality are in the creation of a man of feeling who is an active benefactor, and in the fragmentary form and episodic narrative. Fiction had already shown itself to be more flexible than the old-established genres, but in his book Mackenzie made a major contribution to that movement in the second half of the eighteenth century away from adherence to rigid rules of form and towards the belief that form should derive largely from the relationship between the act of perception and the nature of the subject-matter. There is indeed a case for offering *The Man of Feeling* as, like *Tristram Shandy*, one of the first examples in English of spatial fiction.[55]

Beyond that, one of the most striking features of the book is the extent of Mackenzie's eclecticism. At pains to stress that his book was not a novel, Mackenzie was far from reluctant to borrow from earlier novels. Here the shrewd practical sense of Mackenzie was much in evidence. The Scot who had noted the paucity of Scottish novelists was prepared to raid the works of French and English novelists, and those of his compatriot, Smollett, for material. And, like Burns, Mackenzie had absorbed the works of Sterne. Take this, for instance:

> There is some rust about every man at the beginning; though in some nations (among the French, for instance) the ideas of the inhabitants from climate, or what other cause you will, are so vivacious, so eternally on the wing, that they must, even in small societies, have a frequent collision; the rust therefore will wear off sooner: but in Britain, it often goes with a man to his grave; nay, he dares not even pen a *hic jacet* to speak out for him after his death (7)

where *A Sentimental Journey* provides the initial stimulus, only to be overtaken by a most un-Sternean ponderousness. Distinctly Shandean is Harley's guardians' treatment of their ward. The beggar's 'I never kept a friend above a week, when I was able to joke' (22) is redolent of Yorick. One of Harley's companions advises him, 'as for faces—you may look into them to know, whether a man's nose be a long one or a short one' (53), which is unashamedly Sterne. And Harley's unnatural way of doing things recalls Walter Shandy (and also, perhaps, Parson Adams). There are, too, manifest debts to Fielding. The description of Miss Walton has some affinities with the introduction of Sophia in *Tom Jones*; the account of the characters in the stagecoach has echoes of *Joseph Andrews*; and Sedley's depiction of the prison scene in

Italy owes something to *Amelia*. Rightly, Thompson has claimed the influence of Richardson, seeing Miss Walton as a variant on Clarissa Harlowe. Defoe lurks too, most obviously in the fact that Winbrooke's treatment of Emily Atkins resembles the elder brother's treatment of Moll Flanders. The visit of the press-gang recalls similar in Smollett's *Sir Launcelot Greaves*; and Harley on the corruptive power of wealth sounds remarkably like Smollett's Matt Bramble on the same theme.

To consider *The Man of the World* in conjunction with *The Man of Feeling* is to be confronted by the tension of elements within Mackenzie's fiction. Calvinism's influence directed the Scottish writer towards concern with society rather than the individual, and this bias was strengthened by the practical bent of Scottish Enlightenment thought. Thus Harley is a practical benefactor. But it is also the case that the form of *The Man of Feeling*, geared towards concentration on emotion, focuses upon the individual as exemplar of feeling; and the pre-eminence of sensibility leads to the highly individualist emotional elements of the Gothic. Mackenzie's work reflects this tension, and *The Man of the World* is part of a tradition of Scottish high emotionalism, closely related to the Gothic, that links *Ferdinand Count Fathom* and Byron.

The Man of the World, which appeared in February 1773, approximates more closely to conventional consecutive narrative, and it is wider in scope in that it has several variant types of the man of feeling. However there is a comparable distancing mechanism in that Mackenzie again creates an author-substitute. He, visiting his native village, is moved by remembrance of past experiences, which serves to identify him at the outset as a romantic melancholic. An old acquaintance, Jack Ryland (of whom it is said that 'though he commonly looked but on the surface of things, yet Ryland had a heart to feel' (I, 253)) gives details of the fate of 'worthy old Annesly' who 'died of a broken heart'. The 'author's' interest leads Ryland to introduce him to one Mrs Wistanly who has a box of papers and letters relating to Annesly. These the 'author' tells us,

> were the basis of what I now offer to the public: had it been my intention to *make a book*, I might have published them entire . . . but I have chosen rather to throw them into a narrative, and contented myself with transcribing such reflections as naturally arise from the events, and such sentiments as the situations alone appear to have excited. (I, 257)

Here are problems which the method and form of *The Man of Feeling* did not present. The process whereby letters, papers, and additional information become a 'form of a narrative' must be directed by someone. Thus, enter Mackenzie's fictitious 'author', and he is conscious of his function. After he has presented, by means of a letter of Rawlinson, the dying words of Annesly, the 'author' begins the next chapter with this:

> I am not in a disposition to stop in the midst of this part of my recital, solicitous to embellish, or studious to arrange it. My readers shall receive it simple, as

becomes a tale of sorrow; and I flatter myself, they are at this moment readier to feel than to judge it. (II, 118)

An integral part of his function he sees as so to present things as to make the maximum impact on the emotions of the reader; to ensure, in fact, that the reader becomes a man of feeling. So, for instance, we find

The reader will pardon the digression I have made [to contrast Sindall's 'generosity' with that of Harley]; I would not, willingly, lead him out of his way, except into some path, where his feelings may be expanded, and his heart improved. (II, 187)

The principal means of working on the emotions of the reader is the presentation of a succession of men of feeling, with a fullness of account that is not attempted in *The Man of Feeling*. The first is Annesly who, left by the death of his wife to bring up a son and daughter, serves as a means of reviving the theme of the sentimental education, first mooted in the discussion between Harley and Silton. Annesly's son, Billy, has a warm temper, whereas the daughter, Harriet, 'would often weep all night from some tale which her maid had told of fictitious disaster' (I, 277). Their respective natures are demonstrated in the sentimental set-piece anecdote of the linnet. The father sees his purpose in educating them in these terms: 'to repress the warmth of temerity, without extinguishing the generous principles from which it arose, and to give firmness to sensibility where it bordered on weakness, without searing its feelings where they led to virtue, was the task he had marked out for his industry to accomplish' (I, 282). It was his maxim 'that the heart must feel, as well as the judgement be convinced, before the principles we mean to teach can be of habitual service' (I, 289). This would seem to be a fairly orthodox statement of the principles of the sentimental education.

When he has Annesly discourse at length under the title, 'Paternal Instructions' on such subjects as taste, sceptics, the movements of the soul, conscience, and the pursuit of knowledge (including this tilt at Hume—'It is a capital error in the pursuit of knowledge, to suppose that we are never to believe what we cannot account for' (I, 302)), it might be assumed that Mackenzie is employing Annesly as a mouthpiece for views of which he approves. Several points, however, suggest ironic distancing of author from character: Annesly's readiness to discourse at length and his fondness for aphorism betoken a certain complacency that originates in limited vision; the tone of the comment that follows Annesly's advice points plainly to irony ('It was thus that the good man instructed his children. But behold! the enemy came in the night and sowed tares!' (I, 313)); and the success of Sindall's scheme for leading the brother astray as a means of access to the sister suggests a certain naïveté and impracticality surrounds the sentimental education as practised by Annesly.

The achievement of pathos is Mackenzie's main purpose in depicting naïve sentiment beleaguered by a libertinism that operates by means of a calculating rationalism. The man of feeling and his children fall foul of the man of the world; natural goodness falls victim to worldly wisdom in its amorality. The result is a succession of what Mackenzie intends should be moving scenes. Tears fall first in abundance when news of Billy's misbehaviour reaches father and sister. Annesly sends to his son a letter blotted by a tear; Harriet does likewise. Annesly receives a letter 'in the most sympathizing terms' from Sindall, with the result that Annesly's 'unsuspecting heart overflowed with gratitude towards the friend of his son, and he now grew lavish of his confidence towards him' (I, 351). The point about the Man of the World is that he is an accomplished dissembler. In the pursuit of his will he is a master of disguises, including that of the man of feeling. (There is a certain irony here in that his creator, Mackenzie, is equally demonstrating his capacity to assume a range of voices). Like Smollett's Count Fathom, Sindall subtly employs 'the cloak of prudence' (I, 369) in the pursuit of extreme aims. The simple and unified personality of natural goodness is no match for his chameleon opportunism. There is something undeniably modern about him. Like Fathom, he can be counted among the harbingers of Romantic Satanism.

Increasingly, the moving scenes are informed by irony. In Newgate Billy Annesly is on the verge of suicide when he recalls the miniature of his father which the fond parent has pressed upon him at their parting. 'He flung himself on the ground, and burst into an agony of tears'; at which point, enter Sindall. Later, Harriet, abducted and raped by Sindall, is reunited with her father, but the reactions in the situation speak of sensibility misunderstood, indeed show the limitations of sensibility:

> [Harriet] shrank from the sight of a parent, of whose purity she now conceived herself unworthy, and fell blushing on his neck, which she bathed with a profusion of tears. This he imagined to proceed from her sensibility of those woes which her unhappy brother had suffered; and he forebore to take notice of her distress, any otherwise than by maintaining a degree of cheerfulness himself, much above what the feelings of his heart could warrant. (II, 76–7)

In the second half of the novel appear two men of feeling, each decidedly more practical and worldy-wise than Annesly. Rawlinson's 'genuine plainness of manners, and a warm benevolence of heart, neither the refinements of life, nor the subtleties of traffic, had been able to weaken'. The other, and more important, is Harry Bolton, 'possessed of a disposition instinctively benevolent, and an exquisite sensibility of heart' (II, 149). Bolton is contrasted with Sindall, with his own father (described as a 'projector'), and with Annesly (Bolton is equally the object of Sindall's machinations, but the practical dimension to his virtues is proof against them).

Bolton is quite the most complex of Mackenzie's men of feeling. In *The Man of the World* he is Mackenzie's principal means of demonstrating the pleasures of sorrow. When Bolton learns of his commission to the army and receives a consolatory letter from Lucy Sindall, the 'author' is moved to comment,

> Yet those tender regrets which the better part of our nature feels, have something in them to blunt the edge of that pain they inflict, and confer on the votaries of

sorrow a sensation that borders on pleasure. He visited the walks which his Lucy had trod, the trees under which he had sat, the prospects they had marked together, and he would not have exchanged his feelings for all that luxury could give, or festivity inspire. Nor did he part with the idea, after the object was removed; but, even on the road to London . . . 'twas but pulling out his letter again, humming over that little melancholy air which his Lucy had praised, and the scene was present at once. It drew indeed a sigh from his bosom, and an unmanly tear stood in his eye; yet the sigh and the tear were such, that it was impossible to wish it removed. (II, 189–90)

This establishes beyond doubt Bolton's sensibility, but he is more practical and extrovert than most men of feeling. Bolton 'had a disposition towards society, that did not allow him an indifference about anything of human form with which he could have an opportunity of intercourse. He was everyone's friend in his heart, till some positive demerit rendered a person unworthy his good-will' (II, 196). A measure of irony informs the intimation of Bolton's practical sense and worldly-wisdom. When Rawlinson (whom he has earlier rescued from a fire) bequeaths him his estate and fortune Bolton refers to him in a letter to Lucy as 'the friend of mankind as well as of your Harry' (II, 222). Addressing his new tenants and servants as squire, Bolton enjoins them, 'be industrious, be virtuous, be happy' (II, 225), and he writes, 'I am too selfish to be contented with money; I would increase the love of my people' (II, 229). Sentimentalism has encompassed both the dignity of labour and a certain egotism.

Smollett's *Ferdinand Count Fathom* revealed a remarkable union of embryonic Gothic elements and sentimentalism. Plainly influenced by Smollett's novel, Mackenzie achieves a comparable fusion in *The Man of the World*. In the manner of Smollett he identifies, as a development of the pleasures-of-pain theme, the sensuous attractions of the afflicted lady to the sympathiser. Now whereas the Gothic elements in *Ferdinand Count Fathom* are given free play, only to be subsumed ultimately within Smollett's rationalist vision by being reduced to farce, Mackenzie renders them, only to offset them with a fussily moralistic commentary. The sensuous description of Harriet as she appears to Sindall when visiting her brother in prison leads, as if by way of compensation, to a severe denunciation of Sindall. That, in turn, gives way to a sensuously indulgent account of the joys of the virtuous voluptuary (II, 9–11). Similarly, the account of the parting of Sindall and Billy Annesly, on the occasion of the latter's transportation, includes both a strong moralising strain and reference to 'the form of the weeping Harriet, lovely in her grief' (II, 44).

The other high Gothic episode occurs when, during lightning and storm, Bolton passes amongst graves and over bones and through 'a narrow Gothic door' (II, 281) into a ruined chapel. Sheltering there, he hears the adventures of a traveller (later identified as Billy Annesly) who has endured trials of fortitude among the Indians only to be accepted among them. Smollett had offered a splendid burlesque of such adventure-tales in his account of Lismahago's experiences among the Indians in *Humphry Clinker*. Mackenzie's version is not leavened by humour. Annesly's eulogy on the Indians identifies them in terms of original natural man, the noble savage. Contrasting sophisticated society with the primitive, he comments, 'My imagination drew, on this side, fraud, hypocrisy, and sordid baseness; while on that seemed to preside honesty, truth, and savage nobleness of soul.' Restored to 'civilization', he falls foul of fraudulent and hypocritical beings who are required, in a singularly unsubtle irony, to make frequent unfavourable reference to the values of the 'savage'. Their genuinely savage conduct is followed by that of Sindall, from whose clutches Bolton and Annesly manage to rescue Lucy.

Now while Mackenzie exploits such Gothic features, his own treatment is, ultimately, very much a civilised compromise. There are pointers to this through the book. After the terrible deeds and extreme emotions of Part I Mackenzie prepares the reader for his compromise by presenting Bolton as the man of feeling in love. And here is Mackenzie's natural world, a suitably stylised and civilised landscape:

> He had strayed in one of those excursions, about half a mile from the house, through a copse at the corner of the park, which opened into a little green amphitheatre, in the middle of which was a pool of water, formed by a rivulet that crept through the matted grass, till it fell into this bason by a gentle cascade.
>
> The sun was gleaming through the trees, which were pictured on the surface of the pool beneath; and the silence of the scene was only interrupted by the murmurs of the water-fall, sometimes accompanied by the querulous note of the wood-pigeons, who inhabited the neighbouring copse. (II, 162)

Characteristically, Bolton, having inspected the estate inherited from Rawlinson, writes,

> I have been employed in surveying the grounds adjoining to the house. Nature here reigns without controul; for Mr. Rawlinson did not attend very much to her improvement. (II, 229)

It can be left to Mackenzie's final version of the man of feeling, the practical one, to improve nature!

In a similar compromise the conclusion sees the repentance of the villain, Sindall of monstrous deeds. Again the reader has been fore-warned of this possibility when Sindall's visit to Billy Annesly in Newgate prompts the observation,

> At that instant [Sindall] was less a villain than he used to be. The state of horror to which he saw this man reduced was beyond the limits of his scheme; and he began to look upon the victim of his designs, with that pity which depravity can feel, and that remorse which it cannot overcome. (I, 400–1)

When, finally, Lucy is identified as Annesly's niece, Annesly, in marked contrast with his forbearance when tortured by the Indians, proves himself a true man of feeling by bursting into tears, and at the reconciliation 'even the languor of Sindall's face was crossed with a gleam of momentary pleasure'

(II, 343). After confessing his guilt, Sindall 'seemed to feel a sort of melancholy satisfaction in having the company of those he had injured under his roof' (II, 350). Before dying, he asks Annesly to 'spare the memory of him whose death shall then have expiated the wrongs he did you!' (II, 354). As the fictitious author's final identification of virtues and pleasures indicates, *The Man of the World* ends on a note of benign compromise.

Of *The Man of the World* Mackenzie commented,

> . . . this book, if I may judge from its Effects here, is of a sort not easily to be born by delicate Minds. I have always held an opinion similar to yours in Favour of Harley; there is a soothing Gentleness in his Sorrows, that can be press'd to the Heart even while they wound it.[56]

In *The Man of the World*, partly because of the succession of men of feeling, it is Sindall who is the dominant character, and about the sorrows which he inflicts there is rather less of such 'soothing gentleness'. Mackenzie recognised this, writing,

> I think I can easily discover the Reason why the Man of Feeling should be the more popular of the Two. In the one, the Characters of Harley, Miss Walton, Edwards, Mrs. Margery, & Peter, are Figures of that mellow Colouring, on which, if they are tolerably drawn, we can look repeatedly with Pleasure; &, even when Misfortune is among 'em, it shades the Picture only with that Moonlight Gloom that makes Affliction lovely; in the other, it is cover'd with the Darkness of a Storm from which we shrink with Horror. In the one there is nothing we wish removed; in the other the Portrait of the Villain is discoverable in every Group, & presses disagreeably upon us.[57]

In his next book, *Julia de Roubigné*, Mackenzie retained some of the Gothic elements but dispensed with the villain. The villain possessed in almost equal measure advantages and disadvantages for the writer of sentimental fiction. The enormity of his deeds increased the sympathy felt by the reader for his victims and magnified the pathos of their suffering, but if, on the sentimentalist thesis, man was naturally good, how could such villainy come to be? The answer had to be that civilisation had corrupted, but that the villain could revert to his original state of intrinsic goodness. This explains the apparent *volte-face* executed by Sindall (and by Fathom) in the final repentance. The disparity between atrociously evil practices and ultimate pious protestation is difficult for the modern reader to accept. It seems likely that the eminently reasonable side of Mackenzie, which predominated, also found it hard to accept; and the promptings of Lord Kames, as Scott notes, led Mackenzie to embark on a novel without a villain:

> A friend of the author, the celebrated Lord Kames, we believe, had represented to Mr. Mackenzie, in how many poems, plays, and novels, the distress of the piece is made to turn upon the designing villainy of some one of the *dramatis personae*. On considering his observations, the author undertook, as a task fit for his genius, the composition of a story, in which the characters should be all naturally

virtuous, and where the calamities of the catastrophe should arise, as frequently happens in actual life, not out of schemes of premeditated villainy, but from the excess and over-indulgence of passions and feelings, in themselves blameless, nay, praiseworthy, but which, encouraged to a morbid excess, and coming into fatal though fortuitous concourse with each other, lead to the most disastrous consequence.[58]

The broader reasons behind this become clear: Calvinism encouraged fatalism; the moral sense would not be offended by villainy; pathos would be increased; and Mackenzie's civilised compromise would be achieved more readily.

So in *Julia de Roubigné* fate is the villain. Julia, mimicking Tristram, laments, 'there is a fatality which everywhere attends the family of the unfortunate Roubigné' (III, 64). Of the day marked out for her wedding she writes to Maria, 'Set down *Tuesday* next for your Julia—but leave its property blank— Fate will fill it up one day!' (152). Towards the end of the book she begins to reflect that fate may not be entirely to blame; rather, the possession of a feeling heart seems to invite misfortune, as she notes,

> Is it unjust in Providence to make this so often the lot of hearts little able to struggle with misfortune? or is it indeed the possession of such hearts that creates their misfortunes? Had I not felt, as I have done, half the ills I complain of had been nothing, and at this moment I were happy. Yet to have wanted such a heart, ill-suited to the rude touch of sublunary things—I think I cannot wish so much. (305)

Julia de Roubigné is an ironic tragedy of fate involving a triangular relationship, each of the participants in which is, in his/her own way, a person of deep feelings. Julia, in love with Savillon, is informed, wrongly, of his having married abroad. Out of gratitude, not love, she agrees to marry Montauban, who has rescued her father from bankruptcy. After Savillon's return Montauban, suspecting Julia of an affair with him, poisons her, only to learn of his error and so take his own life. Each of the principals has a feeling heart, but there are important differences amongst them.

'My story', proclaims Julia early in the book, 'is the story of sentiment' (79). Julia has the essential attributes of the sentimental heroine. To Maria she announces, 'I will speak to you on paper when my heart is full, and you will answer me from the sympathy of yours' (16). Her passion for Savillon has sprung, she realises, from her virtue in observing his worth. Such intensity of feeling as she experiences is, to her, proof of her superior sensibility. She is involved in a succession of affecting episodes, and either present suffering or the recollection of past suffering or joy moves her. Such movements of feeling can be initiated by scenes or objects. Here she relates how she visits regularly the corner of the garden where Savillon had planted carnation seeds:

> . . . not long after he was gone, the flowers began to appear. You cannot easily imagine the effect this trifling circumstance had upon me. I used to visit the spot by stealth, for a certain conscious feeling prevented me going openly thither, and watched the growth of those carnations with the care of a parent for a darling

child; and when they began to droop, (I blush, Maria, to tell it) I have often watered them with my tears. (81–2)

The function of her correspondent is regarded by Julia in two ways: she provides the *raison d'être* for the therapeutic activity of formulating Julia's own feelings on paper; and she affords Julia the pleasing prospect of her sharing in the emotions which Julia has communicated. So Julia can write, 'when the soul is torn by contrary emotions, it is then that we wish for a friend to reconcile us to ourselves: such a friend am I blessed with in you' (86), and (of the sorrows of her mother's death), 'We have indulged them to the full: their first turbulence is subsided, and the still quiet grief that now presses on my bosom, is such as my friend may participate' (113). To help ensure that she does, Julia reproduces in full her dying mother's final speech to her.

In her letters Julia attempts to identify her often-complex feelings. Relating how her father has told of Montauban's renouncing his claims upon her and offering to pay off the family debt, Julia describes her feelings just prior to her agreeing to marry Montauban as 'a sort of enthusiastic madness' (140). While aware of the cathartic nature of her writing Julia is equally conscious of the discrepancy between feeling and the verbal formulation thereof. 'Writing to you', she tells Maria, 'is only another sort of thinking' (151). Just previously she had written, 'My very thoughts are not accurate expressions of what I feel: there is something busy about my heart, which I cannot reduce into thinking' (142). After marriage she writes, 'There is an intricacy in my feelings on this change of situation, which, freely as I write to you, I cannot manage on paper' (158). In this Mackenzie has achieved a measure of psychological realism. In describing the discussions between her father and Montauban that follow her agreeing to the marriage, Julia refers to herself as 'the silent victim of the scene'; scores out the word 'victim'; wonders why she has done so; and then acknowledges it is a 'bad word' (143).

Montauban is, undeniably, a man of feeling, but in him feeling combines with pride and is tempered by a degree of scepticism. With greater flamboyance and slightly more brooding he might be termed Byronic. Society, argues Montauban, is not essential to men's happiness, and he upholds the merits of both pride and solitude. He expresses orthodox benevolist views at times ('I find much less pleasure in being the master of acres, than the friend of men' (45); 'We increase the sense of virtue in ourselves, by the consciousness of virtue in others' (47)), but he is sceptical as to the significance of human achievements (his own included) and shows signs of a high idealism beginning to founder ('I begin to entertain doubts of my own dignity, and to think that man is not altogether formed for the sublime place I used to allot him' (62)).

Savillon manifests both the practical goodness of Harley and an egotism beyond that of any of Mackenzie's earlier men of feeling. To Beauvaris he writes, 'you have been the friend, the brother of my soul, and with yours it mingles as with a part of itself' (182). Revealingly, he writes of his relationship with Julia that 'the misfortune of her family first showed me how I loved . . .

I was a spectator of the scene', and he has been a witness to Julia's excellencies, including 'all that sublimity of mind, which bore adversity unmoved' (185–7). He longs to be of more practical use, partly because of his pleasure in contemplating such a role: he writes, 'the luxury of the idea still rushes on my mind;—to heal the fortunes of my father's friend; to justify the ways of heaven to his saint-like wife; to wipe the tears from the eyes of his angel daughter' (185–6). In his description of his departure from Belville he follows, in the manner of Sterne, the sentimentalist formula whereby the contemplation of scene evokes intense emotion:

> As I passed that hall, the door was open; I entered to take one last look, and bid it adieu! I had sat in it with Julia the night before; the chairs we had occupied were still in their places; you know not, my friend, what I felt at the sight; there was something in the silent attitude of those very chairs, that wrung my heart beyond the power of language. (191–2)

The two sides of Savillon's sensibility—the practical benevolism and the rather egotistical indulgence of feeling—are reflected in both his attitude to slavery and his relations with his correspondents, Beauvaris and Herbert. Appalled by the severity of the treatment of the slaves in Martinique, Savillon sets about improving their conditions and freeing them. One, named Yambu, attracts Savillon's attention by virtue of his natural nobility and reveals the essential capacity to manifest feeling. Here is the scene when Savillon frees one slave:

> The negro fell at my feet and kissed them; Yambu stood silent and I saw a tear on his cheek.—'This man has been a prince in Africa!' said I to myself. (211)

Savillon justifies his freeing of the slaves in a way that is very revealing: he talks, as he acknowledges, first as a merchant and second as a man (in which context he uses quasi-religious language), and notes with satisfaction that 'they work with the willingness of freedom, yet are mine with more than the obligation of slavery'.

His correspondence with Beauvaris and Herbert reveals a comparable degree of self-interest and shows him savouring the joys of empathising with the unfortunate. Mrs Herbert's letters, which Savillon has memorised and reproduces for Beauvaris's benefit, prompt the comment,

> Such was the wife whom Herbert lost; you will not wonder at his grief; yet, sometimes when the whole scene is before me, I know not how, I almost envy him in tears . . .
>   . . . 'Tis perhaps a selfish movement in our nature, to conceive an attachment to such a character; one that throws itself on our pity by feeling its distresses, is ever more beloved than that which rises above them. (230–1)

Savillon's benevolism is motivated largely by the possibilities for experiencing 'self-approving joy'. He is interested in people if relationship with them offers the likelihood of his playing the rôle he so cherishes. Of Herbert he writes,

His sorrows gave him a sacredness in my regard, that made every endeavour to serve or oblige him, like the performance of a religious duty: there was a quiet satisfaction in it, which calmed the rufflings of a sometimes troubled spirit, and restored me to peace with myself. (234)

When there seems a possibility of his correspondents' meeting one another in Paris he displays the cloyingly egotistical aspect of his sensibility, exclaiming, 'Could I be with you!—What a thought is there!—but I shall not be forgotten at the interview' (235). The occasion of the death of Beauvaris transports Savillon into an ecstasy of melancholic sentiment in which he can proclaim his grief to the living friend while extolling the virtuous sensibility of the dead one, and all the while evincing his own feeling heart.

While there is a range of men of feeling in *Julia de Roubigné* (Beauvaris, as described by Savillon, seems to outdo Harley in bashfulness and social unease; Rouillé, possessed of a 'winning liveliness' (250) seems Bolton with added wit and social ease), Savillon is the foremost representative in the book. It may be that his combination of practical benevolence and egotistical indulgence reflects, in extreme form, aspects of Mackenzie's own personality (certainly the awareness of the alleged superiority which the manifestation of feeling bestows, upon which Savillon harps, was something upon which Mackenzie capitalised in his relationship with his contemporary readership). Despite the customary distancing mechanism of the fictitious 'author' (here he gets the papers from a Frenchman whose father got them from a boy who had just failed to sell them as wrapping to a grocer), and despite the range of men of feeling presented, it may be that Mackenzie realised that aspects of his own personality had come uncomfortably close to surfacing. Thus the flamboyant gesture of the 'author's' valediction to his readers may be a tacit acknowledgement by the actual author that he had gone as far as he could with the genre.

Technical and formal considerations would strengthen this view. The 'author' acknowledges, 'I found it a difficult task to reduce [the papers] into narrative, because they are made up of sentiment, which narrative would destroy' (7). Certainly the epistolary mode does help maintain the emphasis on sentiment, but at the cost of some reduction in the credibility of the characters. Despite that, there are occasions when Mackenzie does achieve a measure of psychological realism (e.g. the letter in which Montauban considers his and Rouillé's respective suitability as husband for Julia (258–9); Julia's urgent request for confirmation of Savillon's reported presence in Paris (262); her account of the walk in the countryside that, as she says, 'gave me back myself' (281–2); and various vivid renderings of Montauban's jealousy). One of the justifications of the epistolary mode is that it makes it quite feasible for the sentimentalist to write expressing his wish to share his emotion with the recipient; and Mackenzie exploits this to the full. Yet another is that it enables Mackenzie to engage in ironic juxtaposing of attitudes. For instance, Julia ends one letter enjoining Maria, 'Assist me, counsel me, guide me—but say not that I should listen to Montauban', while in the next letter Montauban confesses his 'passion for that loveliest of women' (69–71).

In a tragedy of fate or circumstances the use of letters emphasises the isolation of the individual within the self and underlines the poignancy of the misunderstandings. Montauban, for instance, finds Julia's reluctance 'more winning than all the flush of consent would have made her' (147). It is highly ironic that the writers habitually communicate far more to their correspondents than they do to those with whom they are actually involved. Montauban observes that he could not ask Julia why she spilled the soup at his mentioning Savillon's name; contemplates burning the letter in which he has just written this; but thinks it would be insincere not to trust Segarva 'with the very thought of the moment'; then remarks, 'Julia is better, and has been singing to me the old Spanish ballad, which you sent us lately' (267) (the reader, unlike Montauban, knows the reason for this recovery). And the final tragic misunderstanding is compounded by the irony wherein Julia was about to tell Montauban of her '*former* attachment' (303) to Savillon but was discouraged by his sternness, which is occasioned by his certainty of that attachment's active continuation.

Against these various features of the epistolary mode which Mackenzie uses to advantage have to be set the more obvious weaknesses of his method. It is undeniable that the one-sidedness of the correspondence creates a certain artificiality, and at times the recipient would seem to be superfluous. Here Montauban tells Segarva how he will reply: 'I am confident how much reason is on my side, and will now hear Segarva with patience. He will tell me of that fascinating power which women possess . . . I have canvassed all your objections, and, I think, I have answered them all' (72–4). Another problem is the way in which the characters write. As in the earlier books, Mackenzie's characters cannot resist the apothegm (Julia writes, 'To feel distress is painful; but to dissemble it, is torture' (88)), and too readily they become Mackenzie the essayist (for Julia, 'comedies and romances, you know, always end with a marriage, because, after that, there is nothing to be said' (246)). The requirement to respond feelingly at every turn can produce studied effects. When Savillon is in Martinique Julia can exclaim, 'that this little heart should have its interests extended so far!' (84); or, of her parents' mutual comforting on the occasion of the bankruptcy, she writes, 'Methought, as I looked on them, I was above the fears of humanity' (97).

Revealingly, Mackenzie was to defend bombast in German writers in these terms:

> It has been generally held as a maxim in dramatic dialogue, that the pathetic should be expressed in the simplest language . . . yet I think it will be found in nature, that a certain elevated diction will often be that in which the mind will pour its most genuine and deepest sorows. There is a pride and dignity in sorrow which renders it eloquent.[59]

Here Mackenzie promotes bombast to a level synonymous with eloquence, to which, simply, it is not entitled. Too often what his characters achieve is the former. This is especially the case as the action moves towards its highly melodramatic climax. Once again Mackenzie borrows the Gothic elements of

Ferdinand Count Fathom. Smollett's novel inspired the account of the tantalising power of music, the description of Julia playing the organ, and the highly sensuous depiction of Julia taking the poison. Towards the conclusion the debt to *Othello* becomes increasingly apparent, and this leads to the characters engaging in sub-Shakespearian dialogue (e.g. Montauban's 'it is Montauban's to see his disgrace, and, seeing, to revenge it' (293); his 'Killing is poor—canst thou not invent me some luxurious vengeance!' (302); Julia's 'methinks I could, at this time, beyond any other, die contented' (328), and 'methought I saw the guardian spirits around me, listening with a rapture like mine' (330)). With justification Thompson claims that 'one has the impression that Mackenzie is trying to present a drama in the form of the novel, and writing well only when he fails in this attempt and frankly drops back into the method of the short tale of which he really is a master'.[60] In fact the book is similar to Home's *Douglas* in the extent to which the artificiality of form and diction exacerbates the melodramatic effect as the action moves towards its climax. Here the epistolary mode, far from containing the drama as might be expected, is a springboard to melodrama and the letters of Julia and Montauban record events up to the point of death. Thus when Montauban administers the poison he can write to Segarva, 'It is done' (331). Involving the correspondents in this way is the most extreme expression of the sentimentalist's relishing of vicarious experience. Beyond such limits of sentimentalism it would be hard to go.

To turn from Mackenzie's imaginative writing to his literary criticism is to become acutely aware of the various, quite distinct, voices of the man. Given his own style, there is a certain irony in his claiming, in a note entitled 'Modern Composition', that 'we of the old school complain of a diffuseness, an ultra exuberance of language, disproportioned to the ideas in modern composition, often destructive of the clearness of narrative, and of impression on the mind of the reader',[61] and he observes that fluency in speech leads to excessive length. On the subject of ancient and modern poetry he wrote that the former has 'a certain manly & unaffected Simplicity' while 'we are often obliged to resort to Expression for that Energy which they found in Idea'.[62] William Richardson's 'Epithalamium' prompted him to complain, 'That Sort of Poetry . . . of all others offends me the most, which presents the Ear with elaborate Words and smooth Verses, without conveying one Sentiment to the Heart, one Image to the Fancy, or one Lesson to the Understanding.'[63]

The most significant critique of his own literary practices is to be found in two essays, 'On Novel-writing' and 'An Examination of the Moral Effects of Tragedy'. In a quite startling way these contradict almost every tenet of Mackenzie's practice as imaginative writer. Noting that the novel 'represents domestic scenes and situations in private life' (V, 177), and that it has an exemplary function, he pleads that reason should be seen to temper sentiment and notes the rival claims of virtues and duties. Here there is a clear sense of the dangers of sentiment and an indictment of the improper inculcation of it:

> In the enthusiasm of sentiment there is much the same danger as in the enthusiasm of religion, of substituting certain impulses and feelings of what may be

called a visionary kind, in the place of real practical duties, which in morals, as in theology, we might not improperly denominate good works. (V, 182–3)

And he warns of the existence of

> refined sentimentalists, who are contented with talking of virtues which they never practise . . . This separation of conscience from feeling is a depravity of the most pernicious sort; it eludes the strongest obligation to rectitude, it blunts the strongest incitement to virtue; when the ties of the first bind the sentiment and not the will, and the rewards of the latter crown not the heart but the imagination. (183)

Such vigorously didactic championing of restraint comes strangely from the pen that created the outlandish Gothic effects of his second and third sentimentalist fictions and deliberately set about arousing the passions of the reader (and not always to a clear and unambiguous moral purpose). The following seems incongruous as the judgement of one who, both in his own voice and through his characters, made much of the distinction which sensibility bestows:

> That creation of refined and subtle feeling . . . has an ill effect, not only on our ideas of virtue, but also on our estimate of happiness . . . It inspires a certain childish pride of our own superior delicacy, and an unfortunate contempt of the plain worth, the ordinary but useful occupations and ideas of those around us. (184)

From the creator of Sindall comes the claim that what he finds objectionable is the depiction of 'that character of mingled virtue and vice . . . where the hero of the performance has violated, in one page, the most sacred laws of society, to whom, by the mere turning of the leaf, we are reconciled . . . It is dangerous thus to bring us into the society of vice, though introduced or accompanied by virtue' (185). With a didactic zeal that recalls Richardson, Mackenzie urges,

> Of youth it is essential to preserve the imagination sound as well as pure, and not to allow them to forget, amidst the intricacies of sentiment, or the dreams of sensibility, the truths of reason, or the laws of principle. (186–7)

What is the explanation of such statements from the creator of three of the foremost sentimentalist fictions of the century? It would be tempting to suggest that, after the event, the canny Mackenzie realised what monsters he had created and tried to retract. Rather, the truth is that the various, and at times contradictory, voices of Mackenzie reflect the general fragmentation of the Scottish personality in that period. In much of his literary criticism is heard the voice of a rather narrow didacticism, in part inspired by some of the English novelists and essayists of almost half a century earlier, in part the product of an alliance of Presbyterianism and Scottish Enlightenment practicality.

The same voice resounds through 'An Examination of the Moral Effects of Tragedy'. Having claimed that 'the engines which tragedy professes to use for moral instruction are the passions' (V, 223), Mackenzie observes that the clear-cut moral distinctions of ancient tragedy have become blurred in modern drama. He argues that

> Reason condemns every sort of weakness, but passion, enthusiasm and sickly sensibility, have dignified certain weaknesses with the name of amiable, and the young, of whom some are susceptible, and others affect susceptibility, think it often an honour to be the subject to their control. (230)

Here, as in the essay on the novel, he professes a concern about the misuse of imaginative literature and a belief that tragedy, like the novel, has fallen into inferior hands. With, one suspects, the underlying assumption that the category includes himself he pronounces that 'wisdom and virtue, simple, uniform, and unchanging, only superior artists can draw, and superior spectators enjoy' (231). With fine control of irony Fielding could put such views into the mouth of the narrator of *Tom Jones*. Here no such irony is present.

In the 'Continuation of the remarks upon Tragedy' Mackenzie examines the effects of what he regards as the irresponsible arousal of emotions by tragic writers. 'Real calamity', he states, 'offends with its coarseness, and therefore is not produced on the stage, which exhibits in its stead the fantastic griefs of a delicate and high-wrought sensibility' (233). As a consequence,

> The real evils which the dignity of the scene hides from our view, are those which we ought to pity in our neighbours; the fantastic and imaginary distresses which it exhibits, are those which we are apt to indulge in ourselves. Here then tragedy adds to the list of our calamities, without increasing the catalogue of our virtues . . . (Tragedy) exalts (virtue) to a point beyond our imitation, and ennobles (vice) to a degree above our abhorrence. (235–6)

By way of substantiation he then cites the example of *Macbeth*.

In what could be seen as an indictment of much of the imaginative literature of the time (his own included) Mackenzie avers that

> In what relates to passive excellence, prudence to avoid evils, or fortitude to bear them, are not the virtues of tragedy, conversant as it is with misfortune; it is proud to indulge in sorrow, to pour its tears without the controul of reason, to die of disappointments which wisdom would have overcome. There is an aera in the life of most young people, and those too the most amiable, where all this is their creed of excellence, generosity, and heroism, and that creed is drawn from romance and tragedy. (242–3)

Before the end of the essay he dallies for a moment with sentimental literature and grants this merit to the creations of the imagination: 'The region of exalted virtue, of dignified sentiment, into which they transport us, may have a considerable effect in changing the cold and unfeeling temperament of worldly minds; the indifferent and the selfish may be warmed by the fiction of distress, and the eloquence of feeling' (244). The cautionary note which predominated previously is reasserted in his conclusion, however, when he warns 'there is a certain sort of mind, common in youth, and that too of the most amiable kind, tender, warm, and visionary, to which the walks of fancy and enthusiasm, of romantic love, of exaggerated sorrow, of trembling sensibility, are very unsafe' (245). Rousseau, one suspects, would have disowned him; and it is a wonder that this Mackenzie did not burn the other Mackenzie's books. In this multiple personality, however, prudence reigned.

These two distinct voices of Mackenzie meet in his *Account of the German Theatre*, which he read to the Royal Society of Edinburgh on 21 April 1788. There Mackenzie shows himself responsive to the proto-Romantic resonances in German literature. As Thompson says, 'He is most interesting when he applies the philosophical sentimentalism of Scotland to the products of Germany's *Geniezeit* and *Sturm und Drang.*'[64] Now there is an undeniable connection between the experience of high Romanticism and the process whereby nationalism comes to fruition: each represents a genuine idealism being translated into action. No clearer pointer is there as to why Scotland remained fast in the mire of an increasingly stagnant sentimentalism than this, Mackenzie's response to the vigour of early German Romanticism:

> Besides the delicacy of decorum, and propriety in the manners and language of a play, there is a sort of delicacy in its very passions and distress, which highly polished theatres require, the neglect of which is disagreeable to the feelings and the taste of a very refined people. The sorrow that melts, not the anguish that tears; the fear that agitates, not the terror that overwhelms the soul, are the passions which such an audience relishes in a tragedy. The German theatre does not allow for this delicacy of feeling. Its horrors and its distress assault the imagination and the heart of the reader with unsparing force . . . This strong painting will sometimes disgust the delicacy of him who has been used to the finer tints of the modern school; but it gives room for that boldness and sublimity of picture, which is so often ill exchanged for the flat insipid representation of restrained passions and chastened manners.[65]

Despite the *volte-face* of that last sentence (which suggests how perilously Mackenzie's aesthetic values balanced on a knife-edge) it was the Augustan virtues of refinement, restraint, and delicacy that Mackenzie and the rest of literary Edinburgh resolved to reproduce; and this long after their heyday in London, and despite Mackenzie's conscious acknowledgement of the vigorous growth of European Romanticism.

Scots such as Mackenzie were among the first to identify the properties of Romanticism (with justification, Thompson sees Mackenzie's essay on *Hamlet* as 'the first romantic criticism of Shakespeare, a prelude to Coleridge and Hazlitt'),[66] but without a natural and an integrated cultural identity, and without the possibilities for the expression of an active and genuine nationalism, they were powerless to feel and express it. Hence the relapse into a rather prissy preaching about refinement and delicacy, with the by-then-outmoded tenets of neoclassical didacticism ready to hand. So Goethe's *Stella* is 'strongly marked with that enthusiastic sentiment and refined sensibility which, in *The*

Sorrows of Werter, he has so warmly indulged; and in point of immoral effect, the drama is equally reprehensible with the novel'.[67] While Schiller's *The Robbers* is a 'wonderful drama', it has, for Mackenzie, this major fault: 'It covers the natural deformity of criminal actions with the veil of high sentiment and virtuous feeling, and thus separates (if I may be pardoned the expression) the *moral sense* from that morality which it ought to produce.'[68] There is more than a measure of irony in Mackenzie's pronouncing upon a dichotomy in Schiller.

Given all these factors, it is not surprising that Mackenzie found his métier as an essayist. In the *Mirror* and the *Lounger* he could give vent to his dramatic talent in the creation of a range of correspondents that includes Colonel Caustic (his own favourite) and Barbara Heartless. In the advertisement to the *Mirror* he presents the assumption of voices other than one's own as one of the duties incumbent on the editor of a periodical. He must, he writes, 'sometimes assume a gaiety of subject, and a vivacity of stile, foreign to his immediate situation, or to the actual state of his mind' (IV, 1). In no. 2 of the *Mirror* he writes,

> I must fairly acknowledge, that my mind is naturally much more various than my situation. The disposition of the author will not always correspond with the temper of the man: in the first character I may sometimes indulge a sportiveness to which I am a stranger in the latter, and escape from a train of very different thoughts, into the occasional gaiety of the MIRROR. (IV, 11)

The debt to Addison's *Spectator* essays is considerable. In a letter Mackenzie had admitted that he noted impressive parts in books and added his own comments, seeing this as a way to achieving 'freedom of thinking on all subjects'.[69] Pre-empting such charges, he had a 'correspondent' to the *Mirror* accuse him of 'Plagiarisms' (IV, 368–70) of such writers as Addison, Fielding, and Johnson. The affinity with Addison is evident from the statement of aims of the periodicals. The final number of the *Lounger* describes it and the *Mirror* as 'works that endeavoured to list amusement on the side of taste, and to win the manners to decency and to taste' (VII, 43), and the concluding number of the *Mirror* adds the important quality of purity of sentiment in the authors' wish that 'if they have failed in wit, they have been faultless in sentiment; and that, if they shall not be allowed the praise of genius, they have, at least, not forfeited the commendation of virtue' (V, 89).

Foremost in the substantiation of this were the exemplary tales, such as those of La Roche (with the character of the philosopher owing much to Hume), of Louisa Venoni, and of Father Nicholas, which both demonstrate, and aim to arouse, virtuous feelings. Mackenzie also uses the essays as a platform for presenting the orthodox sentimentalist views of rural life as being closer to man's natural condition, and contemplation of the countryside conducing to virtuous feelings. However he does introduce an element of the forum in that on one occasion he carefully juxtaposes in *Lounger* 87 and 89 (IV, 274ff, 288ff) and essay on 'Effects of rural objects on the mind' which, after a highly stylised account of rural life, expounds upon the 'sort of moral use' of the countryside, and an essay which offers the diametrically opposed view of 'rural sentiment' in a description of a fashionable house-party. Likewise, while many essays vindicate the feeling heart there are several which clearly delineate the limitations of sensibility. This correspondent offers, albeit in slightly muted form, the views expressed by Mackenzie in his essays on the novel and tragedy, and warns against pushing sentiment and sensibility too far, 'for the rules of our conduct should be founded on a basis more solid, if they are to guide us through the various situations of life; but the young enthusiast of sentiment and feeling is apt to despise those lessons of vulgar virtue and prudence, which would confine the movements of a soul formed to regulate itself by finer impulses' (V, 3–4).[70]

One of the functions of the *Mirror* and the *Lounger* was, like the *Spectator*, to guide the emergent middle-class on matters of taste. It has been shown that Scots of the time were concerned much more than their English counterparts with the guidance that such journals could give, which is perhaps another indication of a Scottish sense of insecurity or inferiority within the Union.[71] In one essay, however, Mackenzie fulminates over the visible demise of the 'purity of conduct and delicacy of manners' of the ladies of Scotland and attributes it to 'our frequent communication with the metropolis of our sister kingdom' (IV, 120–1).

Now Mackenzie, undeniably, dons the mask of urbane social commentator out of a real desire to offer advice on taste and manners to his fellow-Scots. But his rôle as essayist fulfilled another, and personal, function. Writing on the geniture of the *Mirror* (V, 83–5), Mackenzie noted the disadvantages of living in one's place of publication in terms that convey very clearly the claustrophobic nature of Edinburgh literary society. To be able to assume the *personae* of the 'correspondents' fulfilled a pleasingly liberating function. It had, too, an important psychological rôle, as Mackenzie acknowledged (in terms that anticipate the more drastically fragmented self of Burns):

> A Lounger of the sort I could wish to be thought, is one who, even amidst a certain intercourse with mankind, preserves a constant intimacy with himself; it is not therefore to be wondered at, if he should sometimes, if I may be allowed the expression, *correspond with himself*, and write down, if he can write at all, what he wishes this favourite companion more particularly to remark . . . These little papers formed a new kind of society, which I could command at any time, without stirring from my fire-side. (V, 102–3)

This sense of literature as self-dialogue, this retreat into the self-created 'selves' that masks the longing for psychological reintegration, is very typical of the Scottish reaction at a time when many other European literatures were beginning to reflect the wholeness associated with Romantic idealism. It identifies Mackenzie with a whole line of Scottish writers that encompasses Burns, Scott, Hogg, and Stevenson.

Mackenzie had a keen sense of the division of the self. This section of a letter to Elizabeth Rose shows an awareness of the dichotomy of private and public selves:

I have often quarrell'd, as you do, with the equivocating Politeness of the World; but I endeavour to make the best of it; & since it gives us two Persons, to dispose of that one which I most value to those who are most deserving of it; leaving the other (like a false Purse to a Highwayman) with those to whom I dare not refuse it.[72]

The two sides of Mackenzie appear and reappear throughout his writing—that which proclaims the merits of sentimentalism, and a realistic sense of the limits, and at times the questionable virtues, of sensibility. They correspond to a sentimental idealism and a practical realism.

Repeatedly a strong rationalist sense surfaces and qualifies the view of the feeling heart. Of the mind of a female relative he writes, 'We suspect that it is strongly tinctured with Enthusiasm; there is something not unpleasant in this while it is confined to the Heart; but there is a certain Pitch at which the Head is often weaken'd by its Influence.'[73] Of the education of the female he observed, 'There is a bewitching Sensibility we are apt to encourage in them, which I begin to fear is often a very unsafe Guide thro' Life, & I am sometimes at Repentance myself, for having done even the little that was in my Power towards it's Encouragement.'[74] A practical sense informs many of his judgements. To Elizabeth Rose he observed, 'I cannot easily allow your Idea of Fatality in Family . . . It is even dangerous to repress Effort by indulging Despair; Fatality is in ourselves, & even Predestinarians can only say that we are determined by Fate to *do* &, of Consequence, to suffer' (here Mackenzie, in the rationalist spirit of the Scottish Enlightenment, challenges the drift of Presbyterianism).[75]

Later, in his *Anecdotes and Egotisms*, the creator of the man of feeling sounded this cautionary note about the funding of overseas missions:

(Sending of missionaries) is well meant, and proceeds generally, I believe, from an extensive philanthropy; but of late it has gone much too far, I think, when we consider the distresses of people at home and that the large contributions in aid of the missions trenches on the fund of charity to our own people.[76]

In real life, it would seem, benevolence is subject to a scale of priorities. As Thompson pointed out,[77] Mackenzie, in his *Review of the Principal Proceedings of the Parliament of 1784*, presented a view of the slave trade diametrically opposed to the humanitarian sentiments voiced on the subject in *Julia de Roubigné*. Such examples lend substance to the remark of his wife, prompted by his enthusing over a cockfight he had witnessed—'Oh, Harry, Harry, your feeling is all on paper.'[78] To read only Mackenzie's imaginative literature is to confirm Scott's judgement that 'no man is less well known from his writings'.[79] Lockhart's portrait of Mackenzie in *Peter's Letters to his Kinsfolk* reinforces the sense of dichotomy, suggesting clearly the division of shrewd legal mind and an eternal adolescence that found expression in flights of fancy.[80]

In the case of Mackenzie such division is probably most blatant when he is writing on things Scottish. Like many staunch Unionists he was capable of a sentimental Jacobitism, as befits a man whose grandfather received both Prince Charles Edward and Cumberland. Mackenzie chided John Home for his whitewash of events, for fear of offending George III, in his *History of the Rebellion*, and recognised the cruelty of General Hawley and the unjustly severe treatment of Cameron of Lochiel and his brother.[81] His view of Mary Queen of Scots was well to the romantic side of those of Hume and Robertson. Hume's attitude, highly critical of Mary, prompted Mackenzie to comment, 'from my respect for his memory, I am rather inclined to wish that it had not been written' (VII, 153). Regarding Mary, rather, as victim of 'an evil destiny' (VII, 157), Mackenzie notes that 'even in the pages of Robertson . . . the dramatic effect of the story is uniformly, compassion for the princess, and resentment against her enemies' (VII, 158).

Where Mackenzie gave vent to Jacobite sympathies the mode of expression was at odds with the subject, suggesting a distancing, indeed a cultural dislocation. In his poem 'The Exile', expanded from a window-poem in the Highlands and printed in the *Mirror*, the standard poetic diction and the degree of stylisation intrinsic in the elegiac mode obliterate anything identifiable with the 'Forty-Five. Instead Mackenzie deals in terms such as 'gallant vassals', 'desert plain', 'the heath', and the 'ancient mansion' (IV, 330–1)— terms quite foreign to the normal Scottish usage. Similarly, the tale of Albert Bane, published in the *Lounger*, of which Burns wrote, '[it] has cost me more honest tears than anything I have read for a long time',[82] includes Bane's master's account of his hiding-place (from the Government troops) 'when he could recollect it in its sublimity, without its horror', and a record of the brutality of the troops enacted in a setting that is rendered in romantic terms (VI, 88). However, it is only fair to set against such sentimentalising the expression of Mackenzie's practical sense in his considerable contribution to the work of the Highland Society of Scotland.

Perhaps the clearest indication of the divided nature of Mackenzie's values is in his response to Burns. Despite immediately obvious dissimilarities, Mackenzie and Burns had much in common. Both experienced problems of identity. At times, as when he writes, 'I have a Degree of unbending Pride about me that cannot easily sollicit either Patronage or Introduction'[83] Mackenzie can sound remarkably like Burns; and Burns was to don the mask of the man of feeling with relish. In an essay in the *Mirror*, no. 91, 'On the demeanour of the great', Mackenzie remarks that it is strange that the great 'should prefer being feared to being loved' (IV, 331) and offers views on condescension very similar to those of Burns. Despite such points of similarity, Mackenzie regarded Burns in the light of rigidly-held preconceptions. Macpherson's Ossian poems and the poems of Michael Bruce had popularised the notion of the natural man as poet. Here then, in Burns 'the Ayrshire plowman', (VI, 378) he was.

This, the opening paragraph of Mackenzie's account of Burns, says more about Mackenzie than its ostensible subject:

> To the feeling and the susceptible there is something wonderfully pleasing in the
> contemplation of genius, of that supereminent reach of mind by which some men

are distinguished. In the view of highly superior talents, as in that of great and stupendous natural objects, there is a sublimity which fills the soul with wonder and delight, which expands it, as it were, beyond its usual bounds, and which, investing our nature with extraordinary powers and extraordinary honours, interests our curiosity, and flatters our pride. (VI, 378)

Mackenzie regards himself as the arbiter of taste and the custodian of such properties as the sublime. There is a strong sense of Burns's being welcomed because he meets the need of a Scotland within the Union to have a national poet. Mackenzie wishes 'to place [Burns] in a higher point of view, to call for a verdict of his country on the merit of his works, and to claim for him those honours which their excellence appears to deserve'. Natural man as poet is to be rescued from the oblivion of Mauchline. There are problems, however: lowness of birth and lack of education have led to a certain coarseness; and his recourse to the vernacular limits his readership. Mackenzie affirms,

> One bar, indeed, his birth and education have opposed to his fame—the language in which most of his poems are written. Even in Scotland, the provincial dialect which Ramsay and he have used is now read with a difficulty which greatly damps the pleasure of the reader: in England he cannot be read at all, without such a constant reference to a glossary, as nearly to destroy that pleasure. (381–2).

As a consequence Mackenzie quotes 'To a Mountain Daisy' and glosses, for instance, 'wee' as 'little'. His main criteria, formality of diction and refinement of feeling, govern his choice of poems for praise, as when he writes,

> Of strains like the above, solemn and sublime, with that rapt and inspired melancholy in which the poet lifts his eye 'above this visible diurnal sphere', the poems entitled Despondency, The Lament, Winter, a Dirge, and the Invocation to Ruin, afford no less striking examples. Of the tender and the moral, specimens equally advantageous might be drawn from the elegiac verses, intitled, Man was made to Mourn, from The Cottar's Saturday Night, the stanzas To a Mouse, or those To a Mountain Daisy. (385)

Of the 'lighter and more humorous poems' he cites 'his Dialogue of the Dogs, his Dedication to G-- H--, Esq., his Epistles to a Young Friend, and to W S--n' as demonstrating 'with what uncommon penetration and sagacity this heaven-taught ploughman, from his humble and unlettered situation, has looked upon men and manners' (388). In fairness to Mackenzie it should be said that Burns seems to have been quite willing to play his part (indeed he helped create it) in the charade in deadly earnest which was his reception by literary Edinburgh.

Mackenzie came to hear that 'grief and misfortune' might drive Burns to the West Indies, and his decision to try to raise funds to make this unnecessary enabled him to proclaim,

> To repair the wrongs of suffering or neglected merit; to call forth genius from the

> obscurity in which it had pined indignant, and place it where it may profit or
> delight the world; these are exertions which give to wealth an enviable superi-
> ority, to greatness and to patronage a laudable pride. (391)

It would be tempting to say that in the meeting of Mackenzie and Burns there met also two sides of Scottish life, two literary traditions—the new and refined tradition of literary Edinburgh, and the remnants of the popular tradition; but it would also be simplistic and inaccurate. Each man, and what he represents, is more complex than that. And each man was playing a rôle. One wonders just how much either of them realised this.

Years later, in his *Anecdotes*, Mackenzie wrote a short account, 'Three Native Poets'. Of Ramsay he wrote, 'Having by his good conduct and liveliness got into very respectable society, he lived happily and died leaving a family well enough provided for.' Fergusson, 'dissipated and drunken, died in early life, after having produced poems faithfully and humourously describing scenes of Edinburgh of festivity and somewhat of blackguardism'. Noteworthy in Burns were his pride ('his Contempt of rank was a little affected'), his 'sarcastic humour', and his falling foul of 'the patronage of dissipated men of high rank, and the Companionship of clever and witty, but dissipated, men of lower rank'. For Mackenzie, when Burns 'allowed his mind its proper play, he produced poetry of a very high cast, full of tenderness and sublimity'.[84]

As this shows, there lurks always behind Mackenzie the sentimentalist a rather staid and fussy moralist. To that Mackenzie, compromise is irresistible. One of the most revealing things Mackenzie ever wrote was this response to Samuel Rogers's 'Human Life':

> 'You have pitched, methinks, human life too high, and have not descended to
> the somewhat lower situations, the middle walks, in which it is passed, with
> enjoyments . . . perhaps of a less elevated, but not of a less poetical kind. Not that
> I admire so much as many, I should say most readers do, that squalid sort of
> Nature which disgusts while it distresses, which a man of great genius (Crabbe)
> delights to paint. He traces nature amidst the filth of its back lanes and blind
> allies, where I think the Muse, if she does not forget her rank, soils her petticoats
> and begrimes her face; and I cannot, while I read, believe,—I should hate to
> believe—that it is Man he is painting except in circumstances of uncommon
> depravity and uncommon wretchedness.[85]

Be realistic, but only about the 'middle walks'; avoid the 'back lanes' and 'blind allies'.

Mackenzie projected his various voices with considerable success. Fame was his, and there are no signs, as there are in Burns, of inner psychological stress. Yet one senses a note of longing, of envy even, in this, his admiring judgement on a Scot of single, integrated, consistent voice and personality, William Tytler of Woodhouslee:

> On all Mr. Tytler's compositions, the character of the Man is strongly impressed,
> which never, as in some other instances, is in the smallest degree contradicted
> by, or at variance with, the character of the author. (VII, 168)

Mackenzie, rather, was one of those 'other instances'.

CHAPTER 7

The Many Voices: The Poetry of Burns

The range of voices in Burns's poems and the fluctuations of voice within individual poems can be explained at least in part in terms of the 'Caledonian antisyzygy' theory, first expounded by G Gregory Smith and developed in terms of the Scottish dissociation of sensibility by Edwin Muir and Hugh MacDiarmid. But they derive also from the personality of the poet and, as Thomas Crawford has shown, from the relationship—often one of conflict— between the poet's personality and his environment. Introducing the 1978 edition of *Burns: A Study of the Poems and Songs*, Crawford wrote,

> I began from one blindingly simple premiss—that in investigating any phenom- enon whatsoever you look first for the 'principal contradiction', the main oppo- sition around which all the other conflicts can be grouped. That contradiction, I soon saw, was not linguistic and cultural—a tension between reason and emotion manifested in a tension between Scots (feeling) and English (thought), as the followers of both MacDiarmid and Edwin Muir appeared to think, but something much more concrete: the conflict and inter-penetration of the poet's innate gifts and temperament on the one hand with his total environment on the other— nature, the family, the local, national and international communities. Each of the entities which oppose and mould him, and which he seeks so desperately to master and bend to his creative purposes, is in itself contradictory; and it is this which makes Burns criticism at once so fascinating and so complex.[1]

Crawford is right to highlight the conflict of temperament and environment, but this does not mean that the dissociation-of-sensibility theory should be rejected. The contradictions in Burns encompass both Crawford's interpret- ation and the theory of Muir and MacDiarmid. In the many and contradictory voices of Burns's poems are to be found the interpenetration of the conflict of personality and environment and the conflict of native and English cultures. In Burns can be seen the interfusion of personal pressures and cultural and linguistic pressures.

Burns offers a particular, and acute, example of the multiplicity of voice and the rootlessness which Scots experienced in the eighteenth century. Ramsay of Ochtertyre remarked of Burns, 'That poor man's principles were abundantly motley—he being a Jacobite, an Arminian, and a Socinian'.[2] His attitude to the Union was ambivalent, as this extract from a letter to Pitt in his most formal English shows:

> . . . turn your eyes, Sir, to the tragic scenes of our fate.—An ancient nation that

for many ages had gallantly maintained the unequal struggle for independance with her much more powerful neighbour, at last agrees to a union which should ever after make them one people.[3]

The Union brought to Scotland both an uncertainty as to identity and a need to compete with the English. As Scots directed their energies into becoming commercially adaptable, so their writers assumed a wide range of voices. The adoption of alternative voices was facilitated in Burns's case by an innate dramatic talent. However it would be a mistake to regard his assumption of voices purely in terms of dramatic art. Burns offers a diversity of voices because he is a talented dramatic poet; because he is an eighteenth-century Scot trying to find his identity; and because he is the distinct individual that was Robert Burns.

Writing of the epistles, Crawford made this penetrating observation:

> The self-dramatisations of the epistles express a mind in motion, giving itself over at different times to conflicting principles and feelings; they mirror that mind as it grappled with a complex world. In order to body it forth, Burns had to be, in himself, and not simply in play, both Calvinist and anti-Calvinist, both fornicator and champion of chastity, both Jacobite and Jacobin, both local and national, both British and European, both anarchist and sober calculator, both philistine and anti-philistine.[4]

The price that had to be paid for this chameleon quality was, if not the extinction of the self, the dispersal of the self amongst the many rôles which it could play. What may have originated at least in part in playful wit became a matter of extreme seriousness for the poet himself.

The first signs of this process are to be seen in a progressive distancing of the poet from his own community. Burns's roots were in a specific rural community. He was both very much a part of that community and increasingly set apart within it. It is undeniable that his detailed and first-hand experience of the life of his community was to be invaluable to him as a poet. In such a poem as 'The Mauchline Wedding' (163–4)[5] meticulous particularization bred of familiarity serves to sustain general statement: it is a poem about two Mauchline people marrying and about universal human emotions. It succeeds as such because it is rooted in the particular. But the point is that this very capacity to observe and then render particular as general, and general once more as particular, is a distinction that sets the poet apart from his fellows. In similar vein, is 'Epithalamium' (Barke, 232):

> O a' ye hymeneal powers
> That rule the essence-mixing hours!
> Whether in eastern monarch's bow'rs
>   Or Greenland caves,
> A nuptial scene in Machlin tow'rs
>   Your presence craves.
>
> Threescore-fyfteen, a blooming bride,
> This night with seventy-four is ty'd;

> O mak the bed baith saft an' wide
>   Wi' canie toil,
> An' lay them gently side by side,
>   At least a while.

Ranging widely before focusing in this way; juxtaposing a stanza of formal diction with a stanza that includes vernacular; carefully modulating tone—such are talents which both attract an audience and set the poet apart within the company. Burns was quick to recognise this and fashioned his behaviour accordingly; hence the cutting of a figure, hence the actions appropriate to someone whose gifts made him a local 'personality'. His fellow-poet, David Sillar, commented,

> Mr. Robert Burns was sometime in the parish of Tarbolton prior to my acquaintance with him. His social disposition easily procured him acquaintance; but a certain satirical seasoning, with which he and all poetical geniuses are in some degree influenced, while it set the rustic circle in a roar, was not unaccompanied by its kindred attendant—suspicious fear. I recollect hearing his neighbours observe he had a great deal to say for himself, and that they suspected his *principles*. He wore the only tied hair in the parish; and in the church, his plaid, which was of a particular colour, I think *fillemot*, he wrapped in a particular manner around his shoulders . . .[6]

In Burns's early manhood in Tarbolton–Mauchline society are the first signs of the man becoming the rôles. Swagger and bluster—in both behaviour and language—are the early reflection of the self-consciousness that was to terminate in multiple personality. The 'satirical seasoning' functioned as both self-assertion and self-defence. In personal terms the wide range of Burns's poetic voices may be seen as in part the result of the distinguishing—even alienating—effect of poetic talent, combined with the inherent dramatic ability. For Burns, as one of 'the harum-scarum Sons of Imagination and Whim',[7] one of the rights, indeed one of the joys, of the poet was the freedom of the imagination.

This point has to be stressed much more when writing of Burns than when dealing with most other poets. There is a tendency for Burns devotees to assume that the poetic voice is always that of the poet himself. Now it is true that some of the poems are close to the poet himself and originate in his own immediate experience. Some were written to meet the demands of the moment and some have a personally therapeutic function. For instance, for some time Burns had contemplated writing on the Earl of Galloway. The ruining of a pair of fine new boots provided the stimulus to put pen to paper, and the savagely denunciatory 'Epigrams on the Earl of Galloway' (696–7) were the result. Similarly treated was another enemy, Mrs Oswald of Auchincruive (of whom Burns wrote, 'I spent my early years in her neighbourhood, and among her servants and tenants I know that she was detested with the most heartfelt cordiality').[8] Convivially ensconced on one occasion in the inn at Sanquhar, Burns found his evening's pleasure disrupted by the arrival of 'the funeral pageantry of the late great Mrs. Oswald'.[9] After riding twelve miles to the next inn, Burns vented his annoyance in the composition of the 'Ode, Sacred to the Memory of Mrs. Oswald of Auchincruive' (446–7). Of Burns, Maria Riddell commented,

> The keenness of satire was, I am almost at a loss whether to say his forte or his foible; for though nature had endowed him with a portion of the most pointed excellence in that dangerous talent, he suffered it too often to be the vehicle of personal, and sometimes unfounded, animosities. It was not always that sportiveness of humour, that 'unwary pleasantry', which Sterne has depictured with touches so conciliatory, but the darts of ridicule were frequently directed as the caprice of the instant suggested, or as the alterations of parties and of persons happened to kindle the restlessness of his spirit into interest or aversion. This however, was not invariably the case; his wit (which is no unusual matter indeed) had always the start of his judgment, and would lead him to the indulgence of raillery uniformly acute, but often unaccompanied with the least desire to wound . . . ''Twas no extravagant arithmetic' to say of him, as was said of Yorick, 'that for every ten jokes he got an hundred enemies'.[10]

She also deemed Burns 'a good hater', but added that 'the warmth of his passions was fortunately corrected by their versatility'.

Burns was acutely responsive to insult, injustice, or oppression. On the immediate level language was to him the readiest weapon in personal or public battles. When the minister and progressive (New Licht) thinker, Dr McGill, became the target of Auld Licht censure, Burns affirmed,

> . . . if the prosecution which I hear the Erebean Fanatics are projecting against my learned and truly worthy friend, Dr. McGill, goes on, I shall keep no measure with the savages, but fly at them with the faulcons of Ridicule, or run them down with the bloodhounds of Satire, as lawful game, wherever I start them.[11]

To Patrick Heron he promised, 'I swear by the lyre of Thalia to muster on your side all the votaries of honest laughter, and fair, candid ridicule!'[12] 'To the Rev. John McMath' (124–6) includes

> O Pope, had I thy satire's darts
> To gie the rascals their deserts,
> I'd rip their rotten, hollow hearts,
>   An' tell aloud
> Their jugglin' hocus pocus arts
>   To cheat the crowd.

The sustained and bitter irony of 'Address of Beelzebub' (254–5) shows that Burns could direct considerable expressive and satiric energies to the service of a particular cause. There was also a strongly cathartic element to such writing. To Dr Moore Burns admitted, 'My Passions when once they were lighted up, raged like so many devils, till they got vent in rhyme; and then conning over my verses, like a spell, soothed all into quiet.'[13]

Now because certain of the poems originate in the poet's own moods and experiences many devotees assume this of virtually all the poems and read them literally. A poem such as 'Scotch Drink' (173–6) has a bravado and bluster which suggests that a large part of the poet's intention was to parody just such rattling jingoism. However one effect of the Burns cult is to close minds to awareness of any self-irony in Burns's poems and to respond, not to a *persona*, but to the 'true' voice of the poet. In fact, far from being records of actual experience, many of Burns's poems render experiences which are the creations of the imagination. In Burns, those energies which might have led to the writing of plays were channelled instead into his poems, his conversation, and his behaviour.

Many of the poems are obviously dramatic. 'The Twa Dogs' (137–45) is a dialogue between Caesar, the benign aristocratic dog, and Luath, the honest and sociable working dog. Caesar is both identifiable dog and Burns's ideal aristocrat who is at home among ordinary people, while Luath is both dog and sociable peasant. As with the best of allegories, the foundation of Burns's is realism of observation and expression. From such a basis Burns can then employ the dogs to articulate such views as Luath's to the effect that honest and hard-working peasants are being driven out at the whim of landlords who are ambitious parliamentarians, and Caesar's attack on the *beau monde* and the grand tour. There is a measure of psychological insight in that Burns shows each dialogist deliberately working upon the response of the other. Caesar's speech beginning, 'But then, to see how ye're negleket,/How huff'd, an' cuff'd, an' disrespeket!' is pitched quite deliberately to elicit a proud defence of the poor from Luath.

Not only is Burns capable of ironic stratagem, but he invests some of his *personae* with that capacity also. 'The Brigs of Ayr' (280–9) has the old brig and the new giving voice to the debate between the generations in harangues of deliberate overstatement that are the direct descendants of the *flyting*. In 'The Death and Dying Words of Poor Mailie' (32–4) Burns, with that fusion of comic and serious which is distinctly his, has his pet 'yowe' offer a version of the thoughts of Rousseau on the natural rearing of the young which includes

> 'Tell him, if e'er again he keep
> As muckle gear as buy a sheep,
> O, bid him never tye them mair,
> Wi' wicked strings o' hemp or hair!
> But ca' them out to park or hill,
> An' let them wander at their will:
> So, may his flock increase an' grow
> To scores o' lambs, an' packs o' woo'!'

Mailie, the protective and genteel mother, has been reading not just Rousseau, it would seem, but Adam Smith as well. Equally subtle is 'Poor Maile's Elegy' (34–6) where Burns, taking care to distinguish between the speaker and 'Our Bardie', presents a comic treatment of sentimentalism in that 'Our Bardie's' behaviour is an extreme version of that of the man of feeling. 'The Auld Farmer's New-Year-Morning Salutation to his Auld Mare, Maggie' (165–8) is a masterly rendering of a particular viewpoint. Through his monologue the farmer is characterised with great effectiveness. Terming this poem 'photography, not painting . . . documentary, not art', Thomas Crawford remarks that 'one feels that the farmer does not want to understand *why* his life has been such a hard one; all he can do is to endure',[14] and he implies that such reluctance is distinctly Scottish. It may well be that by depicting such a man, untouched by Enlightenment curiosity or aspirations, Burns is making the comment—uncharacteristically obliquely perhaps, but no less effectively for that—that the Enlightenment does not reach such people.

Of the dramatic poems probably the most vivid is 'Death and Doctor Hornbook' (79–84) in which the speaker encounters Death, who complains that he is close to being redundant since the advent of the gruesomely incompetent doctor. Typical of Burns is the way in which his spokesman addresses Death as a familiar in the vernacular:

> It spak right howe—'My name is Death,
> But be na' fley'd.'—Quoth I, 'Guid faith,
> Ye're maybe come to stap my breath;
>   But tent me, billie;
> I red ye weel, tak care o' skaith,
>   See, there's a gully!'

And Death's facility in the vernacular reduces him to the level of the human—

> 'Ye ken Jock Hornbook i' the Clachan,
> Deil mak his king's-hood in a spleuchan!
> He's grown sae weel acquaint wi' *Buchan*,
>   And ither chaps,
> The weans haud out their fingers laughin,
>   And pouk my hips.
>
> See, here's a scythe, and there's a dart,
> They hae pierc'd mony a gallant heart;
> But Doctor Hornbook, wi' his art
>   And cursed skill,
> Has made them baith no worth a fart,
>   Damn'd haet they'll kill!'

—while the effect of what he is saying is to inflate the status of Hornbook, only to reveal that his claim to recognition rests in his ghoulish incompetence; so much so that Death appeals for sympathy and tells of his secret plot to 'nail the self-conceited sot'. Skilfully Burns personifies and reduces Death to serve as his agent in the inflation and deflation of Hornbook. Central to his technique in this poem are the establishing of clear *personae* for his narrator and Death, and the subsequent subtle modulation of tone.

A development of the technique of inflation and reduction is to be found particularly in the 'Addresses'. There Burns excels in reductive juxtaposition of two levels of language, or of subject and manner of tone. This, the opening of 'To a Haggis' (310–12), epitomises the technique:

> Fair fa' your honest, sonsie face,
> Great Chieftan o' the Puddin-race!
> Aboon them a' ye tak your place,
> > Painch, tripe, or thairm;
> Weel are ye wordy of a grace
> > As lang's my arm.

In such—considerations of language apart—there is a certain similarity to Fielding's use of the comic-epic, but more striking still is the resemblance to Smollett's caricatures in respect of the central function fulfilled by the manifest disparity between the considerable expressive energy of the poet and the 'normal' significance of his apparent subject-matter. In stanza four of 'Address to the Unco Guid' (52–4), for instance, exalted address is neatly undermined by the sudden introduction of truth:

> Ye high, exalted, virtuous Dames,
> > Ty'd up in godly laces,
> Before ye gie poor Frailty names,
> > Suppose a change o' cases;
> A dear-lov'd lad, convenience snug,
> > A treacherous inclination—
> But, let me whisper i' your lug,
> > Ye're aiblins nae temptation.

Irresistible to Burns are the use of *persona*, the ironic use of voice, rhetorical bluster, and the witty union of dissimilars. Here, for instance, in 'To a Haggis', the speaker demeans and then pities the devotees of foreign cooking:

> Is there that owre his French *ragout*,
> Or *olio* that wad staw a sow,
> Or *fricasee* wad mak her spew
> > Wi' perfect sconner,
> Looks down wi' sneering, scornfu' view
> > On sic a dinner?
>
> Poor devil! see him owre his trash,
> As feckless as a wither'd rash,
> His spindle shank a guid whip-lash,
> > His nieve a nit;
> Thro' bluidy flood or field to dash,
> > O how unfit!

As this suggests, Burns is often at his most expressive when he has something against which to argue, and this is frequently achieved in the contrast of vernacular and standard English or in the employment of rhetorical formulae in the service of deflating their object. Here, for instance, the louse is addressed:

> Ha! whare ye gaun, ye crowlan ferlie!
> Your impudence protects you sairly:
> I canna say but ye strunt rarely,

> Owre gawze and lace;
> Tho' faith, I fear ye dine but sparely,
>   On sic a place.
>
> Ye ugly, creepan, blastet wonner,
> Detested, shunn'd, by saunt an' sinner,
> How daur ye set your fit upon her—
>   Sae fine a Lady!
> Gae somewhere else and seek your dinner
>   On some poor body.
>
> Swith, in some beggar's hauffet squattle;
> There ye may creep, and sprawl, and sprattle,
> Wi' ither kindred, jumpin cattle,
>   In shoals and nations;
> Whare horn nor bane ne'er daur unsettle,
>   Your thick plantations.
>   (193)

Such writing is a *tour de force* of expressive energy comparable to that in some of the harangues which Smollett's characters are made to deliver. Probably the function was comparably therapeutic in the case of Burns. Such habitual release of expressive energy seems to bespeak an imaginative and expressive talent of considerable stature which cannot find an entirely worthy object. The expressive energy of the older Scottish tradition survived in Burns, but frequently it was directed to the service of reduction.

There are important implications in this in respect of the subject–object relationships that are so integral to Burns's poems, and to the Addresses in particular. Undeniably the speaker who habitually declaims, or appears to declaim, on minor subjects, or who addresses insignificant creatures in a grand manner, becomes himself comic. The regular exponent of irony or sarcasm becomes comic himself and runs the danger of self-caricature. Burns must have recognised this. Hence it is conceivable that in such a poem as 'To a Louse' Burns has created a *persona*. It is at the *persona*, not Burns, that we laugh for addressing the creature in a manner whose expressiveness seems ludicrously in excess of what the object warrants. It is the *persona* and the vain lady, not the louse, that elicit our amused censure: each exemplifies human pretension.

Two riders have to be added to any such thesis which sees Burns regularly inventing a *persona*. The first is that it cannot be applied across the board. It would be tempting, for instance, to regard 'To a Mountain Daisy' (228–9) as a poem in which Burns establishes a *persona*, only to show him engaging in maudlin sentimentality and empty pontification. Yet even if one could concede here that Burns is subtly distanced (though this does not seem to me to be so) it does not alter the fact that he wrote in this case a decidedly inferior poem. The second point that has to be recognised is that the invention of *personae* is further evidence of the distancing of the poet from his material.

This aspect is especially important with regard to those poems in which Burns writes on religious matters. The legacy of the religious wrangling of the previous century, as reflected in the 'Auld Licht' *v.* 'New Licht' controversies, was a considerable one and, particularly in rural areas, it seems to have created closed and obsessive minds of the kind typified in 'Holy Willie's Prayer' (74–8). Such had long been anathema to Burns. In 'The Twa Herds: Or, The Holy Tulzie' (70–3), for instance, he adopts the stratagem of feigning adherence to the beliefs of those to whom he was opposed, a tactic which was to serve him well. He does likewise in 'The Ordination' (213–17), and there the paradox which informs Burns's ironic use of *persona* becomes especially evident: to mimic the voice of bigotry to ironic ends requires familiarity, while its successful execution inevitably distances the poet. In 'Holy Willie's Prayer' the poet, in sublime detachment, witnesses his creation unwittingly reveal his limitations. There are two dangers, however. One is that the ironic self-revelation may well be so merciless that the reader may come to sympathize with its victim. The other danger is that in such sublime detachment the poet may be unable to modulate distance and will so remain remote from the converse view, that to which he would adhere.

This, in fact, is exactly what happens in 'The Ordination'. Crawford has made the point in observing that

> The Burns of this poem is the man described by W. P. Ker as being not of the people but far above them, for the world of 'The Ordination' is put at such a distance that even the New Licht adherents are observed from the outside, and seen to be as limited—and almost as laughable—as their diehard enemies.[15]

One danger of the ironic mimicking of the blinkered vision is that it may have, in itself, a blinkering effect. The alternative risk is that, while preferable to obsessive vision or slavish adherence to system, as it undeniably is, ironic use of voice may lead its exponent down the road to scepticism. Burns's facility in the mode was double-edged, and he may well have been aware of this. Temperamentally opposed as he was to systems of thought, he may well have seen himself becoming trapped within the system which this particular talent created and falling foul of its distancing mechanism.

There may be several reasons for Burns's habitual dismissal of systematic thought. The simplest explanation would be that he was intellectually incapable of it. Yet this is hard to equate with the abundant signs of clear-sightedness. Burns's judgements on public events were often sound and sometimes highly perceptive. A letter to Mrs Dunlop includes an astute account of how politicians manipulate the masses, while various letters attest to the fact that he saw clearly the import of what was happening in both North America and France.[16] Why, then, did Burns write thus in 'Letter to James Tennant, Glenconner' (225–7):

> I've sent you here by Johnie Simson,
> Twa sage Philosophers to glimpse on!
> Smith, wi' his sympathetic feeling,
> An' Reid, to common sense appealing.
> Philosophers have fought an' wrangled,

An' meikle Greek an' Latin mangled,
Till with their Logic-jargon tir'd,
An' in the depth of science mir'd,
To common sense they now appeal,
What wives an' wabsters see an' feel;?

Crawford's suggestion that this poem shows Burns 'reacting against the disguises of the Edinburgh interlude'[17] is valid as part of the explanation. When Burns blusters about philosophy it is an indication of his unease. Perhaps an element of parochialism which he never shed completely induced an over-readiness to be dismissive of philosophic thought. Given the ample proof of his intellect, it seems odd that Burns, when writing of himself in relation to philosophy, should have been so determined to confirm himself in the rôle of peasant-poet. Of his attitude to philosophy he wrote, 'I likewise . . . ventured in "the daring path Spinoza trod"; but experience of the weakness, not the strength, of human powers, made me glad to grasp at revealed religion.'[18] David Hume's exhaustive study of man had led him to a reluctant recognition of man's weakness, but he refused to 'grasp at revealed religion'. Such comments as Burns's make one appreciate the exceptional nature of Hume's rigorous examination of man's condition, and also lament the evasion of such tough intellectual activity by the majority of his descendants.

One reason for such evasion—and a further reason for Burns's anti-intellectualism—lies in the fact that the Scottish propensity to image-building and rôle-playing, intensified by the loss of nationhood, was inimical to serious thought. It is easier, and more entertaining, to play a rôle than to think out a solution. One of the rôles which the Scot created for himself—and Burns played a major part in this—was that of the egalitarian. Now it is undeniable that the acrimonious class-divisions that have beset its neighbour have been less pronounced in Scotland, but Scottish life is only relatively more egalitarian than English. In fact it is the self-image of the Scot as sentimental egalitarian that, more than anything else, has obstructed progress towards the achievement and practice of a genuine egalitarianism in Scottish life. It is a striking paradox: the whole thrust of the Scottish Enlightenment was towards progress, while social and cultural conditions encouraged Scottish writers in the direction of rôle-playing, which impeded that very progress.

Burns was unable to resist such cultural pressures; indeed, given his personality, he may almost have welcomed them. In pledging his loyalty to superstition, instinct, and simplicity, and inveighing against rationalism and prudence, Burns was projecting an image. It was an image that he personally found attractive; it was an image that, with a shrewd eye for the market, he must have seen would be rewarding; and it was an image that met the needs of the *literati*, who had been deceived by Macpherson and disappointed by the early death of Michael Bruce. Here is stanza four of 'On Willie Chalmers' (264–5):

I doubt na Fortune may you shore
Some mim-mou'd pouthered priestie,

> Fu' lifted up wi' Hebrew lore,
>   And band upon his breastie;
> But oh! what signifies to you
>   His lexicons and grammars;
> The feeling heart's the royal blue,
>   And that's wi' Willie Chalmers.

Though they were often its targets, Edinburgh intellectuals never seem to have wearied of this strain in Burns, and it was a strain he was happy to play almost as a formula.

What the *literati* wanted, and what they largely got, was an ersatz version of the peasant tradition. Hugh Blair succeeded in having 'Love and Liberty' omitted from the Edinburgh edition of 1787. The critical shortcomings of the Scottish 'cult of critical sensibility' have been identified as follows by David Daiches:

> When serious critics put the preposterous and trivial poems of Dr. Blacklock beside the work of Pope—or John Home's *Douglas* above Shakespeare, or the impossible *Epigoniad* of Dr. Wilkie beside the *Iliad*; when the *literati* of Edinburgh advised Burns to give up writing in Scots and model himself on Shenstone or Homer; when the same *literati* some years earlier wholly ignored the remarkable and to this day underestimated Scots poems of Fergusson—obviously something was very wrong with critical practice, however brilliant Scottish critical theory might be at this time.[19]

Burns himself seems to have been troubled by some of the critical direction he received. From Edinburgh on 8 March 1787 he wrote,

> My two Songs, on Miss W. Alexander and Miss P. Kennedy were likewise tried yesterday by a jury of Literati, and found defamatory libels against the fastidious Powers of Poesy and Taste; and the Author forbid to print them under pain of forfeiture of character.—I cannot help almost shedding a tear to the memory of two Songs that had cost me some pains, and that I valued a good deal, but I must submit . . . My poor unfortunate Songs come again across my memory—Damn the pedant, frigid soul of Criticism for ever and ever![20]

Plainly Burns recognised the widening gap between the creative impulse (especially towards song) and the legislative nature of Scottish criticism.

Against this background the attractions of the poetic epistle for Burns become apparent. The epistle demanded little by way of formality and offered little temptation to indulge in rhetorical formulae. More importantly, it afforded the opportunity to render the flux of the feelings of 'one of the harum-scarum sons of Imagination and Whim'. That control of tone which he exercised in, for instance, 'Address to the Deil' (168–72), where the speaker could be in turn respectful, abusive, pitying, and almost affectionate towards the devil, could now be brought to bear on the expression of personal experience. A crucial part of Burns's experience was the projection of various images of the self, a task for which the verse-epistle became a ready vehicle. In 'To

Mr. John Kennedy' (220–1) Burns offers three of his recurrent refrains: he seeks enough liquor to make him 'shine'; he hopes he is not one of those 'wha rate the wearer by the cloak'; and he drinks to Kennedy since, as he says, 'Ye hate as ill's the vera de'il/The flinty heart that canna feel.' In the 'Epistle to Dr. Blacklock' (490–1) Burns projects an image of himself as family man who will 'sned boosoms and thraw saugh-woodies/Before they want'. To his question, 'But why should ae man better fare/And a' Men brithers!', he responds with a vague and rather abstract homily beginning 'Come, Firm Resolve take thou the van,/Thou stalk o' carl-hemp in man', with the uneasy mixture of standard English and vernacular mirroring his own uncertainty. Towards the end of the poem Burns reverts to projecting this sentimental view of domestic life:

> To make a happy fireside clime,
>   To weans and wife,
> That's the true Pathos and Sublime
>   Of Human life.—

That telling conjunction of 'pathos and sublime' suggests that Burns had at least one eye on the needs of polite Edinburgh society.

In such epistles Burns exploits the potential of the epistolary mode for flexibility of attitude and range of material. Recently G Scott Wilson offered this astute comment on Burns's use of the verse-epistle:

> One convention of epistolary verse, the conscious adoption of different *personae* or roles, often within the same poem, allowed Burns to be different men without insincerity or contradiction. The very freedom of the epistolary form gave ample room for expression to Burns's wish to form an image of himself suited to differing correspondents. The different, occasionally conflicting, elements of his personality could co-exist happily within the ill-defined bounds of such verse.[21]

Wilson substantiates these claims by reference to the 'Second Epistle to Lapraik' (89–93), but they apply in varying degrees to each of the epistles. In the first 'Epistle to Lapraik' (85–9), for instance, Burns engages in one of his favourite tactics—feigned self-demeaning—when he claims that he is 'nae Poet, in a sense,/But just a Rhymer like by chance'.[22] This is a deliberate device to enable him to mount the ensuing attack on academic learning:

> What's a' your jargon o' your Schools,
> Your Latin names for horns an' stools;
> If honest Nature made you fools,
>   What sairs your Grammars?
> Ye'd better taen up spades and shools,
>   Or knappin-hammers.
>
> A set o' dull, conceited Hashes
> Confuse their brains in Colledge-classes!
> They gang in Stirks, and come out Asses,
>   Plain truth to speak;

> An' syne they think to climb Parnassus
> By dint o' Greek!

> Gie me ae spark o' Nature's fire,
> That's a' the learning I desire;
> Then tho' I drudge thro' dub an' mire
> At pleugh or cart,
> My Muse, tho' hamely in attire,
> May touch the heart.

Thereafter the informality and the flexibility of the epistle enable him to range through a number of themes, including the scarcity of real friends and his 'wee faut' in liking the lasses, and an expressive attack on the pursuit of wealth ('Catch-the-Plack').

As noted earlier, Burns seems to need something against which to argue. This may be merely a rhetorical device, but it is likely that a deeper, psychological dimension underlies it. 'Epistle to Dr. John Mackenzie' (Barke, 263–5) begins with Burns projecting his familiar ploughman-poet image and disclaiming any religious or academic learning in such deliberate contrasting as

> Sma skill in holy war I boast,
> My wee bit spunk o' Latin's lost,
> An *Logic* gies me ay the hoast
> An' cuts my win,
> So I maun tak the rear-guard post
> Far, far behind.

> I see the poopet ance a week,
> An' carefu' every sentence cleek;
> Or if frae—a smirking keek
> Spoil my devotion,
> My carnal een I instant steek
> Wi' double caution.

> Still, tho' nae staunch polemic head
> O lang-win'd Athanasian breed,
> I hae a wee-bit cantie *creed*
> Just ae my ain,
> An tho' uncouthly it may read,
> It's unco plain.

Defiant mock-humility of this kind becomes tedious. The opposition to Scottish Presbyterianism, the championing of individual rights, and the strident anti-intellectualism degenerate at times into an alliance of the Kailyard and 'Wha's like us!' Such a note in Burns is difficult to equate with any sense of his being a child of the Enlightenment. It is, rather, a sign of the way in which Presbyterianism and the Scottish character could combine to channel, or interpret, or thwart, Enlightenment thinking.

In this context 'To Smith' (178–83) is the most revealing of the epistles.

Much of the poem is given over to striking of attitudes. Here Burns projects
the image of the happy-amateur poet:

> Some rhyme a neebor's name to lash;
> Some rhyme, (vain thought!) for needfu' cash;
> Some rhyme to court the countra clash,
> > An' raise a din;
> For me, an aim I never fash;
> > I rhyme for fun.

He sees himself as 'blest . . . with a random-shot/O' countra wit', and then
strikes an attitude in bidding this farewell to fame and fortune:

> Henceforth, I'll rove where busy ploughs
> > Are whistling thrang,
> An' teach the lanely heights an' howes
> > My rustic sang.

There follow Burns's version of the *carpe diem* theme; a valediction to 'dear
deluding Woman,/The joy of joys!'; the claim, 'But give me real, sterling
wit/And I'm content'; and the view of himself as joking 'beneath Misfortune's
blows'. Towards the end, however, mood and tone change significantly. Here
are stanzas 26–8:

> O ye, douse folk, that live by rule,
> Grave, tideless-blooded, calm and cool,
> Compar'd wi' you—O fool! fool! fool!
> > How much unlike!
> Your hearts are just a standing pool,
> > Your lives, a dyke!
>
> Nae hare-brain'd, sentimental traces,
> In your unletter'd, nameless faces!
> In *arioso* trills and graces
> > Ye never stray,
> But *gravissimo*, solemn basses
> > Ye hum away.
>
> Ye are sae grave, nae doubt ye're wise;
> Nae ferly tho' ye do despise
> The hairum-scairum, ram-stam boys,
> > The rattling squad:
> I see ye upward cast your eyes—
> > —Ye ken the road—

This is defiant, and also moving. Interestingly, the poem develops latterly a
real momentum and energy after Burns has expended the earlier striking of
attitudes. Here the self-projection is set aside and pressure of feeling surfaces.

Such is the range of Burns's voices, however, and such are the fluctuations
of voice within individual poems, that it becomes virtually impossible to

identify and categorise any voice as the original or authentic voice of the man himself. Out of a desire to see in Burns the perpetuation of an older, native folk-tradition, it would be tempting to claim that Burns's 'true' voice is that which is heard when his imagination works upon and renders rural experience. So James Kinsley claims,

> The literary world that mattered to Burns—the poetic world that truly made him, and was to be transformed by him—was the native Scotch tradition of balladry, love-lyric, and manners-poetry. The human world that mattered to him was the rural society in which that tradition flourished.[23]

It is certainly true that Burns participated in the life of the rural community and retained an acute capacity for detailed observation of it. Here he writes of a visit to a corn market:

> I sold my crop on this day se'ennight past, & sold it very well: a guinea an acre, on an average, above value.—But such a scene of drunkenness was hardly ever seen in this country.—After the roup was over, about thirty people engaged in a battle, every man his own hand, & fought it out for three hours.—Nor was the scene much better in the house.—No fighting, indeed, but folks lieing drunk on the floor, & decanting, untill both my dogs got so drunk by attending them, that they could not stand.—You will easily guess how I enjoyed the scene as I was no farther over than you used to see me.[24]

Quite rightly, Kinsley identified in Burns 'the capacity to see the rustic society about him with the sympathy and critical clarity of a Brueghel'.[25]

Two features particularly distinguished the life of that society—the integration of man and nature, and the collective nature of experience. In 'Epistle to J. Lapraik' (85–9) it is awareness of the energies of the natural world that induces Burns to recall the social energies of man:

> While briers an' woodbines budding green,
> An' Paitricks scraichan loud at e'en,
> And morning Poossie whiddan seen,
>   Inspire my Muse,
> This freedom, in an unknown frien',
>   I pray excuse.
>
> On Fasteneen we had a rockin,
> To ca' the crack and weave our stockin;
> And there was muckle fun and jokin,
>   Ye need na doubt;
> At length we had a hearty yokin,
>   At sang about.

There is a movingly simple effectiveness in the use of nature in the poem, 'On the Birth of a Posthumous Child' (554–5). In 'Tam Samson's Elegy' (273–6) there is the summoning, at once amused and compassionate, of man and nature to pay tribute to the deceased.

For Burns in such poems, the community is the total community of man and nature. In other poems, however, the poet, as well as being participant in the life of the community, is also a rather self-conscious observer. The opening verses of 'The Vision' (103–13) typify this note:

> The sun had clos'd the winter day,
> The Curlers quat their roarin play,
> And hunger'd Maukin taen her way
>   To kail-yards green,
> While faithless snaws ilk step betray
>   Whare she has been.
>
> The Thresher's weary flingin-tree,
> The lee-lang day had tir'd me;
> And when the Day had clos'd his e'e,
>   Far i' the West,
> Ben i' the Spence, right pensivelie,
>   I gaed to rest.

There, 'lanely, by the ingle-cheek', the poet 'backward mused on wasted time'. Such self-consciousness is not rare in Burns.

In a manner that unites him with the older Scottish tradition, however, Burns is adept at rendering the drama of communal life, as, for instance, here in 'The Holy Fair' (128–37):

> Here, farmers gash, in ridin graith,
>   Gaed hoddan by their cotters;
> There, swankies young, in braw braid-claith,
>   Are springan owre the gutters.
> The lasses, skelpan barefit, thrang,
>   In silks an' scarlets glitter;
> Wi' sweet-milk cheese, in mony a whang,
>   An' farls, bak'd wi' butter,
>   Fu' crump that day.

In 1828 John Gibson Lockhart wrote that 'it was acknowledged . . . that the Muse of *Christ's Kirk on the Green* had awakened, after the slumber of ages . . . in "the auld clay biggin" of Mossgiel'.[26] More recently 'The Holy Fair' has been related to the medieval genre of the peasant-brawl. James Kinsley has identified a sequence of Scottish poems—from 'Chrystis Kirk of the Grene' (probably by James I, died 1437, and accessible to Burns in Ramsay's version of 1718) to Fergusson's 'Leith Races'—characterised by 'not merely the theme of rustic revelry and licence, or the convention of hilarious and often sardonic observation, but also the old 'Chrystis Kirk' stanza: a persistent association, over three centuries, of theme and form.' The characteristic of this stanza is its suggestion of carefully patterned fluctuation. As Kinsley notes, 'the convoluted, progressive build-up of the stanza, its medial break, and its witty twist away at the end seem to have enthralled the Scotch mind at a primitive level'.[27]

Such a stanza-form is instrumental in conveying Burns's complexity of attitude to his subject-matter. The effect is that one is left with the impression of the patterned expression of ambivalence. Burns is both sympathetic to the peasants who are his subject and humorously distanced from them, and it is impossible to identify one or other as his final—or even his predominant— attitude. For Kinsley, '"The Holy Fair" is built out of the basic irony of worship, drunkenness, hypocrisy, and sensuality; and Burns's elaboration of this irony transforms the brawl convention'.[28] Given the evidence of some of Burns's letters,[29] it would be tempting to see him as being not significantly distanced from the accounts of sensuality (e.g. that in stanza 9). With the description that follows, however, there are clear signs of comic distancing:

> Here, some are thinkan on their sins,
>   An' some upo' their claes;
> Ane curses feet that fyl'd his shins,
>   Anither sighs an' prays:
> On this hand sits a Chosen swatch,
>   Wi' screw'd-up, grace-proud faces;
> On that, a set o' chaps, at watch,
>   Thrang winkan on the lasses
>   To chairs that day.

In stanza 11 the poet exclaims, with apparent sincerity, upon the happiness of the man who is joined by his 'ain dear lass, that he like best' and is able, by degrees, to get his 'loof upon her bosom,/Unkend that day'. This serves as splendidly ironic prelude to the hell-fire sermon of the preacher, Moodie. Here Burns's expressive energy and masterly sense of detail succeed in realising the grotesque vitality of the man when preaching on human weaknesses:

> Hear how he clears the points o' Faith
>   Wi' rattlin an' thumpin!
> Now meekly calm, now wild in wrath,
>   He's stampan, an' he's jumpan!
> His lengthen'd chin, his turn'd up snout,
>   His eldritch squeel an' gestures,
> O how they fire the heart devout,
>   Like cantharidian plaisters
>   On sic a day!

The irony here is well managed: the preacher is the embodiment of animal features and physical grotesquerie (there is a marked affinity with the use of animal imagery in older Scottish poetry and in the caricatures of Smollett), and it is the already 'devout' heart that is affected by his sermon, the windy rhetoric of which is neatly conveyed in the ironic juxtaposition of 'cantharidian plaisters'. A similar reductive effect is achieved in the description of the sermon of 'Black Russell'. The point is that the poet who masters such reductive irony is considerably distanced from those beings who are its subject, whereas at several points earlier in the poem Burns had seemed rather closer to at least some of the participants.

As its title suggests, 'The Holy Fair' is concerned with the disparate natures of religion and the physical life in Scotland. Towards the end of the poem Burns appears to celebrate life and to say that, despite the threats of damnation, life-energies endure. Here, in the penultimate stanza, is the first explicit mention of 'love', and there is a softening of the sharp edge of Burns's terms:

> Now Clinkumbell, wi' rattlan tow,
>   Begins to joy an' croon;
> Some swagger hame, the best they dow,
>   Some wait the afternoon.
> At slaps the billies halt a blink,
>   Till lasses strip their shoon:
> Wi' faith an hope, an' love an' drink,
>   They're a' in famous tune
>   For crack that day.

Rightly, Crawford speaks of the appearance of a 'spirit of tolerance and love'[30] here. In the final stanza Burns makes it plain that it is not religion but day, the renewal of light and life, that converts the 'hearts o' stane'. The poem ends with the triumph of 'Houghmagandie'; Burns celebrates the primacy of sexual energy over religious dictates. If Burns relishes this triumph, at the same time the comic dimension to the expressive energy with which he proclaims it (the reductive contrast of 'fou o' love divine' and 'fou o' brandy'; the rhyming of 'brandy' and 'Houghmagandie'; and the very sound of 'Hough-magandie', implying that it is not something to be taken entirely seriously) necessarily indicates a degree of self-distancing on the part of the poet. Craw-ford remarks of 'The Holy Fair' that 'if he is aloof, as befits the "makar", the creator of it all, Burns is also delighted with what he beholds'.[31] If he is delighted by the sexual energies exemplified by his creations, he is equally amused by the manifestation of their limitations.

The co-existence of contrary attitudes is a feature of many of Burns's poems. For Kinsley, their interaction accounts for the success of some of Burns's finest achievements, and he claims,

> A man may laugh at the community in which he lives, without ceasing to laugh with it and feel with it. Ridicule and affection are complementary aspects of one kind of Scotch mind ... and they interact at the level of genius in 'Tam o' Shanter' and 'Love and Liberty'.[32]

The somewhat restrictive nature of the predominantly rural Scottish community may account for the ambivalence of attitude. Whether Burns continued to feel emotionally integrated within such a community seems to me to be questionable, to say the least. And while the interaction of ridicule and affection may well account in part for the success of 'Tam o' Shanter' and 'Love and Liberty', their co-existence elicits a necessarily complex response from the reader.

Central to the meaning of 'Tam o' Shanter' (557–64) is the nature and function of the narrative voice. Burns takes care to personalise his narrator as someone who knows Tam well enough to drink with him but who can yet distance himself sufficiently from Tam to see the wider significance of his experiences and responses. With the narrative voice thus established, the alternation between incident and commentary—which so contributes to the effect and the success of the poem—becomes entirely plausible. In the precise characterisation of Burns's narrator lies the basis of the poem's remarkable union of realistic observation and fantasy elements. The narrator is drinking crony of Tam (as Daiches noted),[33] possessor of a more sophisticated intelligence than Tam (as the ironic observations attest), and master of the tale of suspense. He cares for Tam, but, equally, he is amused by him.

To say this is not to imply that the narrator is self-consciously superior to Tam. Burns avoids any such danger by presenting the narrator himself as a partly-comic character. The narrator introduces us early to his 'sulky, sullen dame' who awaits the return of her carousing husband with well-nursed wrath. When Tam has met the aged hags who are the witches the narrator vows that, had they only been young and attractive,

> Thir breeks o' mine, my only pair,
> That ance were plush, o' gude blue hair,
> I wad hae gi'en them off my hurdies,
> For ae blink o' the bonie burdies!

One of the witches is winsome, however, and the shortness of her sark prompts the narrator into this comic apostrophe:

> Ah! little kend thy reverend grannie,
> That sark she coft for her wee Nannie,
> Wi' twa pund Scots ('twas a' her riches),
> Wad ever grac'd a dance of witches!

And there follows this mock-apology: 'But here my Muse her wing maun cour;/Sic flights are far beyond her pow'r.' The narrator possesses, as well as the capacity for ironic observation of others, an endearing self-irony. This informs the exclamations and generalisations to which he is prone ('Ah, gentle dames! it gars me greet . . .'; 'Care, mad to see a man sae happy . . .').

The self-irony is only one of several indications of the multi-faceted nature of the speaker's personality. He is able to vary his language-level to suit his mood and purpose. 'Tam had got planted unco right' renders Tam's condition exactly. In the following the progression from standard English to the vernacular conveys very well the narrator's amusement at his own situation, human nature, and Tam's condition:

> Inspiring bold John Barleycorn!
> What dangers thou canst make us scorn!
> Wi' tippeny, we fear nae evil;
> Wi' usquabae we'll face the devil!

> The swats sae ream'd in Tammie's noddle,
> Fair play, he car'd na deils a boddle.
> But Maggie stood right sair astonish'd,
> Till, by the heel and hand admonish'd,
> She ventured forward on the light;
> And, vow! Tam saw an unco sight!

The poem is marked by just such fluctuations in the tone and the mood of the narrative voice. For instance, a catalogue of horrors gives way to a lively account of the witches' dance. The account of Tam's pleasantly drunk state, culminating in the lines, 'Kings may be blest, but Tam was glorious,/O'er a' the ills o' life victorious!', is followed by these lines of generalised commentary:

> But pleasures are like poppies spread,
> You seize the flower, its bloom is shed;
> Or like the snow falls in the river,
> A moment white—then melts for ever;
> Or like the borealis race,
> That flit ere you can point their place;
> Or like the rainbow's lovely form
> Evanishing amid the storm.—

These lines were adduced by Muir in support of his thesis of the Scottish dissociation of sensibility (the Scottish writer feels in Scots and thinks in English). Quite rightly, however, Daiches has commented,

> Burns is seeking a form of expression which will set the sternness of objective fact against the warm, cosy, and self-deluding view of the half-intoxicated Tam, and he wants to do this with just a touch of irony. What more effective device than to employ a deliberate neoclassic English poetic diction in these lines?[34]

It is true that in some other poems the alternation between vernacular and standard English is more difficult to justify, but in 'Tam o' Shanter' the orchestration of language-levels is extremely deftly managed (the one exception being the line, 'There, at them thou thy tale may toss', which is surely the most awkward line that Burns wrote).

Burns's narrator pitches brilliantly the note of exaggeration which recurs through the poem. The effect achieved by such catalogues of horrors as

> Coffins stood round, like open presses,
> That shaw'd the dead in their last dresses;
> And by some devilish cantraip slight
> Each in its cauld hand held a light.—
> By which heroic Tam was able
> To note upon the haly table,
> A murderer's banes in gibbet airns;
> Two span-lang, wee, unchristen'd bairns;
> A thief, new-cutted frae a rape,
> Wi' his last gasp his gab did gape;

Five tomahawks, wi' blude red-rusted;
Five scymitars, wi' murder crusted;
A garter, which a babe had strangled;
A knife, a father's throat had mangled,
Whom his ain son o' life bereft,
The grey hairs yet stack to the heft;
Wi' mair o' horrible and awefu',
Which even to name wad be unlawfu'.
Three Lawyers' tongues, turned inside out,
Wi' lies seamed like a beggar's clout;
Three Priests' hearts, rotten, black as muck,
Lay stinking, vile, in every neuk.
(Barke, 205–6)

is to make plain that, despite the superstitions of Tam and those like him, the speaker does not take this—or indeed himself—very seriously. Yet while there is a clear suggestion of comic mockery, this note, as Daiches observes, 'does not lessen the suspense'.[35] Moreover, by subtle gradation of the items within the catalogue, culminating in the epitome of evil in the 'Lawyers' tongues' and 'Priests' hearts' (these four lines, dropped by Burns from the Edinburgh edition on the advice of Alexander Fraser Tytler, are omitted by Kinsley but included by Barke and others), Burns makes very well the point that, while man may be fascinated to contemplate the supernatural, before the workings of actual human evil he is powerless.

Just as the narrator appears as a complex figure, so too does Tam. Tam is comic, but he also has heroic stature. Superstitious he may be, yet—admittedly fortified by whisky—he will brave the storm. And, confronted by the witches and warlocks, 'heroic Tam' did not flee but 'glowr'd, amaz'd, and curious'. Tam comes to be the representative of the ordinary man, and this process is aided by the speaker's habit of interrupting his narrative to offer commentary. Almost as vivid as the account of Tam's ride is the presence of the narrator as intermediary. We are strongly aware of the mind that is regulating the relationship between action and picture (Crawford writes astutely that 'the whole landscape is like the *décor* of a fantastic ballet'),[36] between reality and fantasy, and between drama and commentary. (There is a similarity with *Tristram Shandy*: admittedly less pronounced, the effect on the reader is comparable to that achieved by Sterne when, for instance, he has Tristram intersperse commentary within the account of the expected collision between Dr Slop and Obadiah.)[37]

Paradoxically, the obvious presence of the speaker as commentator and conscious stylist fosters a mythopoeic effect. Tam prompts both amusement and concern. The result of his being the hero of a poem whose style is frequently mock-heroic is not unequivocally reductive. When Burns employs mock-heroic apostrophe or engages in comic-epic simile, such as—

As bees bizz out wi' angry fyke,
When plundering herds assail their byke;
As open pussie's mortal foes,

> When, pop! she starts before their nose;
> As eager runs the market-crowd,
> When 'Catch the thief!' resounds aloud;
> So Maggie runs, the witches follow,
> Wi' mony an eldritch skreech and hollow.

—one feels that the target of any reductive element in the humour is not Tam and the other participants but, rather, the heroic mode. As with that splendid exercise in the mock-heroic, Fielding's description of the battle in the grave-yard in *Tom Jones*,[38] the effect is both to elevate and deflate: the heroic mode and its exponents are reduced, while the manifestly ordinary human participants acquire archetypal status. The graveyard battle in *Tom Jones* becomes *the* village set-to, while Tam's journey becomes *the* wild ride. Burns, just as much as Fielding, is alive to the mythopoeic tendency of such writing, where ordinary beings can, at one and the same time, be found to be amusing and be aggrandised.

In 'Love and Liberty' (or 'The Jolly Beggars') (195–209) Burns's attitude to his subject is altogether more difficult to define with any degree of consistency. The poem abounds in mock-heroic effects and in comic juxtaposition such as

> Wi' hand on hainch, and upward e'e,
> He croon'd his gamut, one, two, three,
> Then in an *arioso* key,
>   The wee Apollo
> Set off wi' *allegretto* glee
>   His *giga solo*.

Burns describes his low-life characters in a highly expressive and carefully controlled mixture of the vernacular and the clichés of polite romantic literature. The following is typical:

> The Caird prevail'd—th' unblushing fair
>   In his embraces sunk;
> Partly wi' Love o'ercome sae sair,
>   An' partly she was drunk.

The poet's song includes the verse,

> I never drank the Muses' stank,
>   Castalia's burn an' a' that,
> But there it streams an' richly reams,
>   My Helicon I ca' that.

Of this Daiches has noted,

> The internal rhyme helps to suggest the proud snapping of the fingers at conventional society, while the use of the Scots word 'stank' in connection with the

> Muses produces in us exactly the kind of shock that is most effective at this point—the shock of recognising that a beggar can also be a poet.

And of the lines, 'Great love I bear to a' the fair,/Their humble slave an' a' that', wherein he finds implicit dismissal of 'the entire Petrarchan tradition of love poetry', Daiches observes that the phrase, 'an' a' that' 'at first seems merely the regular repetition of what by this stage in the song is an expected refrain, but it is no sooner read (or sung) that it is recognized as a sneer at those poets who are mere slaves of literary convention'.[39]

Despite differing on points of emphasis, Crawford and Daiches see as the targets of Burns's satiric juxtaposition in this poem the conventions of behaviour—both literary and social—of the middle and upper classes. Kinsley will have none of this, claiming instead,

> There is indeed much linguistic variety and paradox in 'Love and Liberty', and it is vastly amusing—a concomitant of the mock-heroic posturing of the beggars; but I do not read it as deliberate social criticism . . .
> . . . the victims of (Burns's) irony, indeed, are not his moral readers, but the beggars themselves.[40]

How are we to account for such diametrically opposed views? The concluding song serves as a useful focus for such divergence of reading. There the problem centres upon the sustained employment of a formal standard English which seems at variance with both the nature of its users and their use of the vernacular in the earlier songs. For Daiches, 'The occasional generalizations in standard English diction add a fitting note of solemnity, as though this is a profession of faith, which the song needs if it is to bring the cantata fittingly to a close.'[41] Crawford is broadly in agreement, though he deems 'faith' 'altogether too solemn a word for this poem' and finds that 'the underlying pattern of humour persists to the very end, despite the absence of Scots in the final stanzas', being present in the 'pompous' terms, 'variorum' and 'decorum', and in 'the vigorous plebeian abandon of the sixth and final stanza'.[42] In marked contrast, Kinsley regards the final chorus as ironic, and argues that

> It celebrates, in finely simple rhetoric, ideals which are in themselves dubious and are anyhow not practised by the beggars. Logically considered, the chorus is nonsense; and even if it is taken merely as a mindless cheer for liberty, what liberty do its singers enjoy? . .
> . . . there is no more love in the cantata than there is liberty; there is only libertinism masquerading as both.[43]

That the beggars' final statement of their faith should take the form of standard English is plainly problematic. Kinsley's response in regarding this as a deliberate ironic stratagem on the part of Burns is understandable. Yet this seems to me to be just as sophisticated and 'modern' a reading as that which he has rejected as 'heady criticism which reads "Love and Liberty" as a dramatic statement of Burns's social faith, with the choric climax as its hymn'.[44]

Rather, I believe Crawford to be closer to the truth when he writes that the cantata mirrors 'a general European squalor and a general European energy of which Rousseau and Blake, each in his own way, were also aware'.[45] The language of the final chorus—blatantly dissonant with the behaviour of the beggars and with the sentiments of the last stanza in particular—can be explained as one of several instances of Burns's feeling the need to resort to standard English for the dignified statement of general truths.[46]

The language duality can serve as a useful index to Burns's multi-faceted personality and to his problems of self-integration. An immediate sense of Burns's facility in different modes and language-levels can be acquired merely by comparing 'Tam o' Shanter' with Burns's account of the subject in standard English in his letter to Francis Grose:

> Among the many Witch Stories I have heard relating to Aloway Kirk, I distinctly remember only two or three.
>
> Upon a stormy night, amid whirling squalls of wind and bitter blasts of hail, in short, on such a night as the devil would chuse to take the air in, a farmer or farmer's servant was plodding and plashing homeward with his plough-irons on his shoulder, having been getting some repairs on them at a neighbouring smithy. His way lay by the Kirk of Aloway, and being rather on the anxious look-out in approaching a place so well known to be a favourite haunt of the devil and the devil's friends and emissaries, he was struck aghast by discovering through the horrors of the storm and stormy night, a light, which on his nearer approach, plainly shewed itself to proceed from the haunted edifice. Whether he had been fortified from above on his devout supplication, as is customary with people when they suspect the immediate presence of Satan; or whether, according to another custom, he had got courageously drunk at the smithy, I will not pretend to determine; but so it was that he ventured to go up to, nay into the very Kirk.— As good luck would have it, his temerity came off unpunished. The members of the infernal junto were all out on some midnight business or other, and he saw nothing but a kind of kettle or caldron, depending from the roof, over the fire, simmering some heads of unchristened children, limbs of executed malefactors, &c. for the business of the night. It was, in for a penny, in for a pound, with the honest ploughman; so without ceremony he unhooked the caldron from off the fire, and poring out the damnable ingredients, inverted it on his head, and carried it fairly home, where it remained long in the family a living evidence of the truth of the story.[47]

Here there are signs of a certain unease in the use of formal standard English and a straining after effect ('struck aghast'; 'the haunted edifice'; 'fortified from above on his devout supplication'; 'his temerity came off unpunished'; 'the members of the infernal junto'; 'the damnable ingredients'). To compare 'rather on the anxious look-out' with 'glow'ring round wi' prudent cares', or 'he had got courageously drunk' with 'Tam had got planted unco right', is to be made aware of the expressive deficiencies of the formal manner.

Likewise, to encounter the stock diction of the opening lines of 'On scaring some Water-fowl in Loch Turit' (364–5)—

Why, ye tenants of the lake,

For me your watry haunt forsake?
Tell me, fellow-creatures, why
At my presence thus you fly?
Why disturb your social joys,
Parent, filial, kindred ties?

—is to become rapidly aware of, and regret, the loss of expressive energy of vernacular addresses such as 'To a Mouse' (127–8). Plainly when so much of his reading was of the English poets it was natural that Burns should wish to write poems in standard English and in English poetic forms; and no less than other Scottish writers of the time he felt the need to compete with the English on their terms. Thus, despite his belief that 'Elegy is so exhausted a subject that any new idea on the business is not to be expected',[48] Burns was a competent exponent of that form and of other orthodox forms such as the ode, the sonnet, and the poetic allegory. Of the poems exclusively in English, 'The Lament' (230–2), 'To Ruin' (219–20), 'Stanzas Written in Prospect of Death' (21–2), 'From Esopus to Maria' (769–71), 'Address to the Shade of Thomson' (577–8) are merely competent exercises in conventional modes. But there are some significant achievements. 'Man was Made to Mourn' (116–19) has echoes of Shenstone, Gray, and Johnson, admittedly, but its opening stanza anticipates Wordsworth, and the sentiments of the poem, which has at its heart the account of the peasant's plea for work, point forward (as Crawford has noted)[49] to Tressell's *The Ragged-Trousered Philanthropists*. Here, with an impressive command of standard English, Burns has succeeded in universalising what may have been inspired by his own particular experience. 'Winter: A Dirge' (16–17) is much more than a stock expression of melancholy. The poet's vision encompasses the totality of nature, and the poem, for Crawford, reveals Burns as 'not merely a typical Scot, but a typical man of the Enlightenment'.[50]

It has to be conceded, however, that—almost inevitably, given Burns's personality and cultural situation—his reading of English poetry provided Burns with a range of *personae* to adopt and attitudes to strike. For instance, 'To Mr. Graham of Fintry, On being appointed to my Excise Division' (475) ends thus: 'I lay my hand upon my swelling breast,/And grateful would— but cannot speak the rest.' Such striking of attitude may well have originated in a desire to try out various poetic modes and *personae*. Another *persona* which attracted Burns was that of the spectator of man. Of varied and lively personal commitment himself, Burns could present himself as an Olympian observer of life. Aged twenty-three, he wrote to Murdoch, 'I seem to be one sent into the world, to see, and observe . . . the joy of my heart is to "study men, their manners, and their ways".'[51] In later years this voice could be adopted as required. To Bishop Geddes of Dunkeld he affirmed, 'I am determined to study man and Nature, in that view, incessantly.'[52]

Alongside the Popean influence has to be set that—of a quite different kind—of Shenstone. In several English poets, but pre-eminently in Shenstone, Burns found an image of the poet to which he was especially drawn by temperament—that of the man of sensibility. This image of himself as poet further isolated Burns from the rural community but served him well in his dealings with Edinburgh society ladies who were eager to play along with such attitudinising; hence such poems as 'Sylvander to Clarinda' (or 'Answer to the foregoing—Extempore') (372–4) and 'To Chloris, written on the blank leaf of a copy of the last edition of my poems . . .' (798–9). Burns was deliberately projecting an image of himself upon an eager audience. In his *First Commonplace Book* he wrote, 'It may be some entertainment to a curious observer of human-nature to see how a ploughman thinks, and feels, under the pressure of love.'[53] The Edinburgh experiences further encouraged the preoccupation with rôle-playing, and the poems of sensibility of this period reflect a certain self-consciousness and unease. For instance, it would be gratifying to believe that Burns was fully in control of the reductive detail and bathos in these lines from 'To Clarinda' (410):

> Fair Empress of the Poet's soul,
> And Queen of Poetesses;
> Clarinda, take this little boon,
> This humble pair of Glasses.

Burns liked to project the image of the poet as a man at once distinguished and entitled to greater licence by virtue of his heightened sensibility. In a letter to Wilhelmina Alexander he prefaces a highly stylised pastoral description with the claim that 'Poets are outré Beings, so much the children of wayward Fancy and capricious Whim, that I believe the world generally allows them a larger latitude in the rules of Propriety, than the sober Sons of Judgement & Prudence'.[54] Similarly, his view of himself as a discerning tourist endowed with sensibility could lead to such comments as 'My journey through the Highlands was perfectly inspiring; and I hope I have laid in a good stock of new poetical ideas from it'.[55]

The language duality induced self-consciousness on Burns's part and, in particular, an almost-obsessive awareness of his situation as poet and the rôles which he could adopt. While he himself did much to popularise the image of himself as ploughman-poet he could write of himself to educated acquaintances in the most refined and formal of language. To Moore he wrote, 'meeting with Fergusson's Scotch Poems, I strung anew my wildly-sounding, rustic lyre with emulating vigour'.[56] He delighted in projecting himself in the rôle of the national bard. This effusion was to Lord Eglinton: 'There is scarcely any thing to which I am so feelingly alive as the honor and welfare of old Scotia; and, as a Poet, I have no higher enjoyment than singing her Sons & Daughters.'[57] Burns could strike precisely the note of nostalgia and sentimental nationalism which accorded with the mood of many of his contemporaries. 'To William Simpson of Ochiltree' (93–8) includes

> At Wallace' name, what Scottish blood,
> But boils up in a spring-tide flood!
> Oft have our fearless fathers strode
> By Wallace' side,

> Still pressing onward, red-wat-shod,
> Or glorious dy'd!

It was, as Crawford has noted,[58] particularly in the Edinburgh years that Burns sought to appear as the national bard. The results were sometimes far from happy. 'To the Guidwife of Wauchope House' (325–7) is self-consciously autobiographical and rings false. Having claimed that he wishes to write 'for poor auld Scotland's sake', the poet proceeds,

> The rough bur-thistle spreading wide
>   Amang the bearded bear,
> I turn'd my weeding heuk aside,
>   An' spar'd the symbol dear.
>   No nation, no station
>   My envy e'er could raise:
>   A Scot still, but blot still,
>   I knew no higher praise.

Here the inappropriateness of the metrical form makes the sentimental nationalism ring the more suspect. Revealingly, Burns immediately turns to projecting the image of himself as inspired rustic, child of feeling, and lover of the lasses.

This voice was capable of embracing a sentimental Jacobitism, as such poems as 'A Birthday Ode. December 31st 1787' (375) and 'On Seeing the Royal Palace at Stirling in Ruins' (348) show. Paradoxically, Burns was given to voicing such feelings in standard, even highly formal, English. The effects were sometimes incongruous, as this verse from 'To William Tytler of Wood-houslee' (332) suggests:

> Tho' something like moisture conglobes in my eye—
>   Let no man misdeem me disloyal;
> A poor, friendless wand'rer may well claim a sigh,
>   Still more, if that Wand'rer were royal.

And 'On the Death of Sir J. Hunter Blair' (340) opens with an Ossianic scene, described in the stock formal terms of eighteenth-century English landscape poetry, as setting for the solitary poet's nostalgic lamentation over the loss of Scotland's nationhood:

> The lamp of day, with ill-presaging glare,
>   Dim, cloudy, sunk beneath the western wave:
> Th' inconstant blast howl'd thro' the darkening air,
>   And hollow whistled in the rocky cave.
>
> Lone as I wander'd by each cliff and dell,
>   Once the lov'd haunts of Scotia's royal train;
> Or mus'd where limpid streams, once hallow'd, well;
>   Or mould'ring ruins mark the sacred Fane.

Such writing lends substance to Crawford's claim that Burns 'desperately tried to be the *wrong* sort of national bard'.[59]

Those nationalist feelings which elsewhere in the eighteenth century (and also in the nineteenth) accompanied the movement towards independence and democracy had in Scotland, as the example of Burns attests, to be diverted into sentimental and retrospective nationalism and an identification with the libertarian movement outwith Scotland. Events in France and Jacobin stirrings in Scotland prompted the endorsement of egalitarianism which finds expression in 'The Tree of Liberty' (910–13). Such pleas for enlightenment and freedom indicate what Burns might have accomplished had the Scottish situation permitted the spirits of libertarianism and nationalism to catalyse a Romantic idealism.

The poetic expression of Romantic idealism is generally characterised by the sustaining of a single voice in the articulation of an ideal that has some possibility of fulfilment. Like the majority of Scots of his day (and since, one might add), Burns had no such ideal with which to engage. Successful adaptation to the competitive ethos which the Union had fostered might bring prosperity, but it had little to attract the romantic side of the Scottish personality; whereas dreams of 'Caledonia' offered much. Double-vision—fantasy and distortion on the one hand, and a pragmatic realism on the other—became the condition of the Scot.

Here, then, is the source of those problems which surround Burns's use of irony, and in particular the difficulty in locating a consistent object of the irony and attempting to identify a sustained attitude on the part of the poet. If critics can differ so widely about 'Love and Liberty' the explanation lies in the conflicting elements within Burns—the reductive or realist, and the romantic or fantastic—which the poem comes to reflect. Conscious as he was that these conflicting elements would inevitably surface if given the opportunity, Burns sought a single poetic voice that he could maintain at a level of ironic consistency. Burns wrote so many poems attacking hypocrisy, pomposity, and formality not solely because these were anathema to him (and he was at times as capable of them as anyone) but for the further reason that this was one voice, from among the many and conflicting voices within him, which he could sustain with some facility.

Often the reductive effect is accomplished by establishing standard English as an apparent norm and allowing the vernacular to undermine it. In 'Elegy on the Year 1788' (454–5), for instance, there is a prolonged interplay of formal diction and vernacular:

> For Lords or kings I dinna mourn,
> E'en let them die—for that they're born!
> But oh! prodigious to reflect,
> A Towmont, sirs, is gane to wreck!
> O Eighty-Eight, in thy sma' space
> What dire events ha'e taken place!
> Of what enjoyments thou hast reft us!
> In what a pickle thou hast left us!

> The Spanish empire's tint a head,
> An' my auld teethless Bawtie's dead;
> The toolzie's teugh 'tween Pitt and Fox,
> An' our gudewife's wee birdy cocks:
> The tane is game, a bluidy devil,
> But to the hen-birds unco civil;
> The tither's dour, has nae sic breedin',
> But better stuff ne'er claw'd a midden!

The effect is striking. By linguistic polarisation Burns succeeds in levelling the human subjects: the great are reduced and the lowly are elevated. And in 'On the Late Captain Grose's Peregrinations thro' Scotland' (494–6) the formality of the title and the expressive vernacular that comprises much of the poem are so juxtaposed as to form the basis of a satire that is both affectionate and highly witty.

Elsewhere (e.g. 'Epistle to Davie, A Brother Poet', stanza 5 (67)), however, the stridency, prolongation, and repetition of the formula whereby the poet defines by a series of negatives, or sets up a premise only to renounce it in a variety of contexts, give rise to the suspicion that for Burns such rhetoric served as psychic therapy. One letter of the Edinburgh period gives an account of Miss ——[60] which approximates closely to a Smollett caricature and seems to serve as a means whereby Burns can give vent to his hostility to the society people whom he had just previously encountered. Likewise, a letter to Hill contains a graphic account of the two Edinburghs and an energetic attack in comic–epic mode on wealth, both intended to fulfil a cathartic function.[61] The irony of Burns's employing modes learned from the early English novel for therapeutic purposes should not go unremarked (the more so since it was the cultural duality which exacerbated the dislocation of his personality). There is further evidence in the letters to suggest that his eclectic capacity and talent for mimicry were deliberately directed to the service of psychic therapy. To 'Clarinda' he wrote,

> I like to have quotations ready for every occasion.—They give one's ideas so pat, and save one the trouble of finding expression adequate to one's feelings.—I think it is one of the greatest pleasures attending a Poetic genius, that we can give our woes, cares, joys, loves &c. an embodied form in verse, which, to me, is ever immediate ease.[62]

It may also be the case that it was an awareness of the lack of a single absolutely authentic voice amongst the wide range of voices that he adopted which produced such irritation with his imitators as, 'My success has encouraged such a shoal of ill-spawned monsters to crawl into public notice under the title of Scots Poets, that the very term, Scots Poetry, borders on the burlesque.'[63]

Certainly there are many poems characterised by fluctuations of voice and a concomitant linguistic medley. Here are the concluding stanzas of 'Epistle to Davie, a Brother Poet' (69):

All hail! ye tender feelings dear!
The smile of love, the friendly tear,
    The sympathetic glow!
Long since, this world's thorny ways
Had number'd out my weary days,
    Had it not been for you!
Fate still has blest me with a friend
    In ev'ry care and ill;
And oft a more endearing band,
    A tye more tender still.
        It lightens, it brightens
            The tenebrific scene,
        To meet with, and greet with,
            My Davie or my Jean!

O, how that Name inspires my style!
The words come skelpan, rank and file,
    Amaist before I ken!
The ready measure rins as fine,
As Phoebus and the famous Nine
    Were glowran owre my pen.
My spavet Pegasus will limp,
    Till ance he's fairly het;
And then he'll hilch, and stilt, and jimp,
    And rin an unco fit:
        But least then, the beast then,
            Should rue this hasty ride,
        I'll light now, and dight now,
            His sweaty, wizen'd hide.

Presumably endorsement of the 'sympathetic glow' was Burns's genuine intention, but the combined effect of the language (especially such terms as 'tenebrific scene') and the form towards the end of the stanza comes close to undermining that intention. Crawford has commented,

> Was it because Burns knew in his heart of hearts that these 'positives' are not in themselves enough to offset the real ills of life that the poem remained an interesting but imperfect experiment clogged by abstract monstrosities of diction like 'sympathetic glow' and 'tenebrific scene'? Perhaps Burns flew to pompous-sounding English words because he did not really believe what he was saying.[64]

There is substance in this, though there are abundant examples of highly effective use of the vernacular where Burns does not really believe what he is saying. But the suggestion that Burns's turning to English for general observation or 'message' leads to doubts about his sincerity is often borne out.

There is evidence, too, to indicate that Burns sometimes could not long endure the particular voice that he had felt obliged to assume. For example, 'Extempore Epistle to Mr. McAdam of Craigen-Gillan' (329–30) is a curious mélange of gratitude and defiance, with the latter making the former seem suspect. In the second stanza the poet claims, or affects to claim (either way, it does him little credit) that, having secured the praise of Craigen-Gillan, he will ignore 'the senseless, gawky million'. Here the defiant assertion of his independence gives way to something perilously close to bathos:

> Tho', by his banes wha in a tub
>   Match'd Macedonian Sandy!
> On my ain legs thro' dirt and dub
>   I independent stand ay.—
>
> And when those legs to gude, warm kail
>   Wi' welcome canna bear me;
> A lee dyke-side, a sybow-tail,
>   And barley-scone shall chear me.—

Thereafter he reverts to compliment. The flux of tone and feeling in this short poem says much about the ambivalence of Burns's attitude to authority and patronage: it implies that benevolence from someone socially his superior could rarely elicit an unequivocal response from him.

Happily there are poems where Burns establishes and sustains a single authentic voice, where what Crawford calls 'the harmony that once existed between the Scots and English sides of Burns's consciousness'[65] is miraculously recovered. Such a poem is the admirable 'Elegy on Captain Matthew Henderson' (438–42), from the year 1788, where the invocation of the various creatures, elements, and powers of Nature proceeds expressively, naturally, and without dissonance of mood or tone from vernacular to standard English. Here, writing in the ancient tradition of the elegy, Burns points forward to the Romantics. There are several poems, too, which betoken a proto-Romantic awareness of the spiritual dimension inherent in responsiveness to the natural world. This, stanza four of 'Elegy on the late Miss Burnet of Monboddo' (569–70), finds the poet sensing a communion of landscape and soul (albeit in a rather self-conscious manner):

> Ye healthy wastes immix'd with reedy fens,
>   Ye mossy streams with sedge and rushes stor'd,
> Ye rugged cliffs o'erhanging dreary glens,
>   To you I fly, ye with my soul accord.—

Similarly, in 'Castle Gordon' (359), after renouncing the Gothic landscape in favour of the familiar Scottish stream, the poet presents himself as a pensive solitary responding feelingly to Nature. In 'Written with a Pencil over the Chimney-Piece, in the Parlour of the Inn at Kenmore, Taymouth' (351–2) Burns overcomes the self-consciousness which afflicts most of his writing in this vein to produce this description which, poetic diction ('unbosomed', 'meand'ring sweet', 'verdant side') and rhythmical monotony apart, does seem to anticipate Wordsworth in so far as there is some recognition of the importance of the relationship between perceiver and perceived:

> The meeting cliffs each deep-sunk glen divides,
> The woods, wild-scattered, clothe their ample sides;
> Th' outstretching lake, imbosomed 'mong the hills,
> The eye with wonder and amazement fills;
> The Tay meandering sweet in infant pride,
> The palace rising on his verdant side;
> The lawns wood-fringed in Nature's native taste;
> The hillocks dropt in Nature's careless haste;
> The arches striding o'er the new-born stream;
> The village glittering in the noontide beam.[66]

The description which Burns offered of his method of song-composition presents him as an aspirant to something close to the 'Wordsworthian or egotistical sublime':

> My way is: I consider the poetic Sentiment, correspondent to my idea of the musical expression; then chuse my theme; begin one Stanza; when that is composed, which is generally the most difficult part of the business, I walk out, sit down now & then, look out for objects in Nature around me that are in unison or harmony with the cogitations of my fancy & workings of my bosom; humming every now & then the air with the verses I have framed: when I feel my Muse beginning to jade, I retire to the solitary fireside of my study, & there commit my effusions to paper; swinging, at intervals, on the hind-legs of my elbow-chair, by way of calling forth my own critical strictures, as my pen goes on.—Seriously, this, at home, is almost invariably my way. What damn'd Egotism![67]

But even here there are signs of the self-consciousness and self-projection which prevented his reaching the true 'egotistical sublime'. Such an ascent was obstructed by a combination of personal, psychological, and national characteristics. In a letter to George Thomson in which he had been mentioning the song, 'Craigieburnwood', Burns offers a eulogy on the lady who inspired it, culminating, 'The lightning of her eye is the godhead of Parnassus, & the witchery of her smile the divinity of Helicon!'[68] And immediately follows the comment, 'To descend to the business with which I began.' That is, Burns has been conscious throughout of the fact that he has been projecting a voice, and, inevitably, another voice intervenes to undermine it.

It is noticeable that many of the most imaginative and inventive of Burns's poems end feebly. That masterly allegory, 'The Twa Dogs' (137–45), peters out thus:

> When up they gat, an' shook their lugs,
> Rejoic'd they were na *men*, but *dogs*;
> A'n each took off his several way,
> Resolv'd to meet some ither day.

Likewise, 'Death and Dr. Hornbook' (79–84) is a superb imaginative creation, but Burns does not know how to end it and has to resort to this:

> But just as he began to tell,

> The auld kirk-hammer strak the bell
> Some wee, short hour ayont the twal,
>   Which rais'd us baith:
> I took the way that pleas'd mysel,
>   And sae did Death.

Other poems that end tamely include 'Scotch Drink', 'The Cotter's Saturday Night', and 'Epistle to J. Lapraik'.

Why was it that Burns's manifestly considerable powers of invention so often failed to lead to any significant conclusion? How was it that that fertile imagination could create vivid situations but was unable to bring them to a culmination? The answer was not, surely, lack of intellect; nor was it any expressive deficiency. Rather, these qualities, which Burns possessed in abundance, could not find a purpose or a goal. He who by compulsion—of either nature or situation—would habitually observe can never be a natural and unselfconscious participant. There were, I believe, two dimensions to this in the case of Burns: increasingly he became alienated from the community in which he had his roots (the very talent of poet having initiated the process); and the Scottish cultural situation militated against wholehearted responsiveness to the voice of embryonic Romantic idealism.

One of the most revealing poems that Burns wrote was his 'Address to Edinburgh' (308–10). There the poet pays tribute to Edinburgh as the scene of so much of importance in Scottish history and as the centre of the Scottish Enlightenment. What is so telling is the fact that he projects an image of himself wherein he praises Edinburgh from a position of rural isolation, or even exclusion. The poem begins and ends with this stanza:

> Edina! Scotia's darling seat!
>   All hail thy palaces and tow'rs,
> Where once beneath a Monarch's feet
>   Sat Legislation's sov'reign pow'rs!
>   From marking wildly-scatt'red flow'rs,
> As on the banks of Ayr I stray'd,
>   And singing, lone, the ling'ring hours,
> I shelter in thy honor'd shade.

Behind the projection of the image of the solitary rustic poet lies a very real sense of alienation. In that classic study, 'Towards Defining an Age of Sensibility', Northrop Frye points out that 'the qualities that make a man an oracular poet are often the qualities that work against, and sometimes destroy, his social personality'. Of this, Burns is a prime example.[69] Burns was isolated, and in this he both anticipated the voice of the Romantic solitary and suffered considerably in terms of his own personality. Burns was alienated, in which he anticipated twentieth-century man whose world seems increasingly to suggest that Romantic idealism was an impossible dream.

Burns the outsider created a whole range of voices—from the morose Ossian-figure and the sentimental lover to the wittily satirical observer. When, as it were, on the inside, participating, he did so almost in the manner of the devil with whom he was half in love, busily undermining and wreaking havoc. It is no accident that he shares with Byron a fascination with the devil, a need alternately to reduce and inflate the devil, and a habitual Romantic self-mockery. These are manifestations of the divided nature of the Scottish self. As William Montgomerie noted, Auld Nick 'is part of the human personality suppressed by Calvinism'.[70] The many voices of Burns's poems enact the tragi-comedy of the fragmentation of the Scottish personality. It is noteworthy that here, in 'Epistle to a Young Friend' (248–51), the poet commends a stance that is close to that of the Unco Guid or Holy Willie and is the epitome of petty diabolism:

> Conceal yoursel as weel's ye can
>   Frae critical dissection;
> But keek thro' ev'ry other man,
>   Wi' sharpen'd, sly inspection.

CHAPTER 8

The Shandean Voice: Sterne and Burns's Letters

In the opinion of J De Lancey Ferguson, 'The biographers of few modern authors are so completely dependent upon their subject's letters for knowledge of the details of his life as are those of Burns.'[1] Not only is it the case that, as Thomas Crawford has stated, Burns 'was brought up on the epistolary dogma that one should suit one's style to the needs and personality of one's correspondents,'[2] but it is equally true that in many of his letters Burns, to meet the needs of his own personality, assumed distinctive voices. Catherine Carswell's claim that 'to a unique extent the man and his work are one'[3] acquires a certain poignant irony, given the complexity of the man's personality and the nature of his circumstances: the diversity of voices which Burns's letters reveal is a direct reflection of the fragmentation of the self.

It was in the work of Laurence Sterne that Burns found a voice that was to recur throughout his own letters. To Dr John Moore Burns wrote,

> My life flowed on much in the same tenor till my twenty-third year.—Vive l'amour et vive la bagatelle, were my sole principles of action.—The addition of two more Authors to my library gave me great pleasure; Sterne and McKenzie.— Tristram Shandy and the Man of Feeling were my bosom favorites. (I, 141)[4]

To such a personality as that of Burns access to the *persona* of the sentimentalist at this stage of his life was to have great significance. Despite his acute eye for the comic, it was with the pathetic rather than the risible elements of sentimentalism that Burns was to find a strong affinity. Moreover this letter suggests that Burns shared the view of Cowper and Jefferson[5] that *Tristram Shandy* was a force for good:

> If Miss Georgina Mckay is still at Dunlop, I beg you will make her my Compliments, and request her in my name to sing you a song at the close of every page, by way of dissipating Ennui; as David . . . playing on his harp chased the Evil Spirit out of Saul.—This Evil Spirit, I take it, was just, long-spun Sermons, & many-pag'd Epistles, & Birthday Poetry, & patience-vexing Memorials, Remonstrances, Dedications, Revolution-Addresses, &c. &c. &c. while David's harp, I suppose was, mystically speaking, Tristram Shandy, Laugh & be fat, Cauld kail in Aberdeen, Green grow the rashes, & the rest of that inspired and inspiring family. (I, 343)

As often with Burns, comic reduction cloaks a serious point: good is on the side of the individual man, but the whole man; it is life in its private, personal, witty, bawdy dimensions. The phrase, 'mystically speaking' is significant: that

Tristram Shandy held for Burns this mystique—essentially celebratory of life in its fullness—perhaps explains his omission of Sterne from his projected comparative evaluation of the novelists, Moore, Fielding, Richardson, and Smollett (II, 37).

The earliest sustained echoes of Sterne occur in the letter to John Arnot, written late in 1785, in which Burns offers an account of how he 'lost a Wife' (Jean Armour). In a manner distinctly Shandean the tone vacillates between genuine, if at times maudlin, self-pity and jocular self-dramatisation. The prefatory 'story of the letter' includes an attack, which might have been written by Sterne, on Prudence. In the letter a formal preamble gives way to an increasingly ironic tone, and then, in the following, the voice becomes unmistakably that of Tristram:

> You have doubtless, Sir, heard my story, heard it with all its exaggerations; but as my actions, & my motives for action, are peculiarly like myself, & that is peculiarly like nobody else, I shall just beg a leisure-moment & a spare-tear of you, untill I tell my own story my own way.[6]
>
> I have been all my life, Sir, one of the rueful-looking, long-visaged sons of Disappointment.—A damned Star has always kept my zenith, & shed its baleful influence, in that emphatic curse of the Prophet—'And behold, whatsoever he doth, it shall not prosper!'—I rarely hit where I aim; & if I want anything, I am almost sure never to find it where I seek it. (I, 34–5)

The direct address; the appeals for sympathy and licence to relate in one's own way; the belief in a personally hostile providence; and the awareness of one's failure to match intention and realisation: all of these clearly echo Sterne's 'small HERO'.[7]

The letter proceeds to what is, in effect, a brilliantly contrived debate between instinct and conventional morality. In terms closely imitative of Sterne at his most sensual, Burns relates that his 'mouth watered deliciously' to visualise the consummation of a marriage. Then he launches, with unconcealed relish, into a lengthy piece of bawdry which, in terms of linguistic energy and sustained metaphorical invention, matches anything in Sterne ('I was well aware . . . more total defeat' (I, 35–6)). The use of military metaphor for the expression of sexual activity owes much to the example of Sterne (e.g. Widow Wadman's courtship of Uncle Toby, and the account of how Tristram came to be circumcised by the window, in *Tristram Shandy*).[8] Burns's innate sensuality has found expression in a highly skilled use of a derivative literary manner—the comic-epic. Burns gives an account of the rise and the frustration of his passion in a remarkable passage where the verbal dynamism and the correlation of formal and referential aspects of the prose may again stand comparison with Sterne (See 'How I bore this . . . another wife'). After this account of what he calls 'this fatal era of my life', Burns asserts that he will evade 'the holy beagles, the houghmagandie pack' that are already on to him; and the letter ends in this characteristically Shandean manner:

> I am so struck, on a review, with the impertinent length of this letter, that I shall

not increase it with one single word of apology; but abruptly conclude it with assuring you that I am, Sir, Your, & Misery's most humble serv^t. (I, 37)

The Sternean features of this relatively early letter recur across the whole range of the letters. For instance, the defiant proclamation of the writer's entitlement to be whimsically himself is a favourite strategy of Burns. Echoing Tristram's preoccupation with the way in which experience will not readily submit to the systematic ordering of chronology, Burns asserts, 'I have no idea of corresponding as a clock strikes; I only write when the spirit moves me' (I, 160). Above all else the validity of individual experience is to be upheld, and it includes the writer's freedom to wander off 'in this rhapsodical tangent' (I, 365). (Compare Tristram's description of his book as 'this rhapsodical work' (*Tristram Shandy*, I, ch. 13).) The right to be oneself, indeed the inevitability of being oneself, come to be expressed in terms of Sterne's 'hobby-horse'. 'Ballad-making', Burns wrote to Thomson, 'is now as compleatly my hobby-horse, as ever Fortification was Uncle Toby's; so I'll e'en canter it away till I come to the limit of my race' (II, 204).[9] Here the very phrase 'I'll e'en canter it away' mimics Sterne's manner.

But Burns, like Tristram, falls foul of the difficulty of achieving freedom of expression by means of an artificial medium; hence the writer's heightened awareness of both his role as writer and the limitations of his medium. For both Burns and Sterne letter-writing is an art-form and the writer is a self-conscious artist who can exploit the artificiality of his medium for comic purposes. For instance, Sterne begins a letter to Mary Macartney thus:

> An urn of cold water in the driest stage of the driest Desert in Arabia, pour'd out by an angel's hand to a thirsty Pilgrim, could not have been more gratefully received than Miss Macartney's Letter—pray is that Simile too warm? or conceived too orientally? if it is; I could easily mend it, by saying with the dull phlegm of an unfeeling John Trot, (*suivant les ordinances*) *That Yrs of the 8th Inst came safe to hand.* (*Letters*, 117)

To Cunningham Burns wrote,

> It is not that I *can* not write you: should you doubt it, take the following fragment which was intended for you some time ago, and be convinced that I can *antithesize* Sentiment & *circumvolute* Periods, as well as any Coiner of phrase in the regions of Philology (II, 15),

and he proceeds to write in the most formal and inflated of modes. Burns is capable too of a Shandean blank space: 'I should return my thanks for your hospitality' (I leave a blank for the epithet, as I know none can do it justice) (I, 248); and a letter in the mock-sublime to Wilhelmina Alexander has, by way of postscript, a dialogue between writer and reader that begins, 'Well, Mr. Burns, & *did* the Lady give you the desired 'Permission'?—No! She was too fine a Lady *to notice* so plain a compliment' (I, 64).

Burns's stylistic dynamism has clear affinities with that of Sterne. The vigorous account of the horse-race with the Highlander alongside Loch

Lomond owes something to Tristram's description of Dr Slop's fall (*Tristram Shandy*, II, ch. 9). And the same letter includes this statement which has, as well as a reference to *Tristram Shandy*, a distinctly Shandean cadence: 'But I am an old hawk at the sport; & wrote her such a cool, deliberate, prudent reply, as brought my bird from her aerial towerings, pop, down at my foot, like Corporal Trim's hat' (I, 126). To Mrs Dunlop Burns was to describe Francis Grose not only in terms of Dr Slop but in prose whose rhythms and cadences reproduce thus those of their original: 'if you discover a chearful-looking grig of an old, fat fellow, the precise figure of Dr Slop, wheeling about your avenue in his own carriage with a pencil & paper in his hand, you may conclude, "Thou art the man!"' (I, 423).[10] The following owes much to Tristram's comic correlation of physical and mental states:

> Well, Divines may say what they please, but I maintain that a hearty blast of execration is to the mind, what breathing a vein is to the body: the overloaded sluices of both are wonderfully relieved by their respective evacuations.—I feel myself vastly easier then [*sic*] when I began my letter, and can now go on to business. (II, 66)

There are, too, a few letters where Burns writes blatantly and at length as Tristram (e.g. to Provost Maxwell of Lochmaben (I, 461–2)).[11]

The love of pattern, which Kurt Wittig noted as a characteristic of the poems,[12] is a feature of the conscious artistry which informs the letters. The interplay of formal manner and comically commonplace detail is carefully managed. Burns writes, for instance, to Maria Riddell, 'On the conditions & capitulations you so obligingly make, I shall certainly make my plain, weather-beaten, rustic phiz a part of your box furniture on Tuesday' (II, 260).[13] The repeated use of ironic juxtaposition, comic-heroic, and mock-sublime may give rise to the suspicion that the formulaic use of literary modes is being made to serve the purpose of diverting, restraining, or sublimating within a process of style, something which is intensely and emotionally personal. It is as if by fixing the stylistic extremes of the sublime and the banal Burns hopes, or perhaps *needs* in terms of his own psychic health, to shed or conceal somewhere between them the serious concern—personal, emotional, or political—which has stimulated him to write.

That granted, it can be recognised that there is a further area of affinity with Sterne. In the habitual use of the reductive mode the grand generalisation often gives way to, and is undermined by, the bizarrely particular. This exemplifies Sterne's and Burns's shared cry for freedom, the defence of the individual's right to be—both personally and stylistically (and with each writer Buffon's 'le style c'est l'homme' holds good)—splendidly, riotously himself. Thus the flux of language mirrors the flux of the writer's thought.

Yet in a letter of advice to his brother William, Burns questioned the adequacy of language as a vehicle for the expression of mental activity, and he proceeded to advocate proof by individual experience, in terms of which any orthodox empiricist might be proud:

There is an excellent Scots Saying, that 'A man's mind is his kingdom'—It is certainly so; but how few can govern that kingdom with propriety.—The serious mischiefs in Business which this Flux of language occasion, do not come immediately to your situation . . .

. . . Whatever you read, whatever you hear, concerning the ways and works of that strange creature, MAN, look into the living world about you, look into Yourself, for the evidences of the fact, or the application of the doctrine. (I, 384–5)

Later, in a letter to Mrs Dunlop, he stated,

The most cordial believers in a Future State have ever been the Unfortunate.— This of itself; if God is Good, which is I think the most intuitive truth in Nature; this very propensity to, and supreme happiness of, depending on a Life beyond Death & the Grave, is a very strong proof of the reality of its existence.—Though I have no objection to what the Christian system tells us of Another world; yet I own I am partial to those proofs & ideas of it which we have wrought out of our own heads and hearts.—The first has the demonstration of an authenticated story, the last has the conviction of an intuitive truth. (II, 34)

Here the term, 'intuitive truth', is plainly significant. Seeing its origin in the Common Sense School of thought, perhaps as communicated to Burns by Dugald Stewart, Fairchild claims that 'its usefulness in rationalizing the cult of feeling is obvious'.[14] Perhaps this is to assume a degree of success which Burns never realised: what can be said is that on occasion he *attempted* to rationalise the cult of feeling.

Burns's use of the term represents, like much else in his thought, an uneasy compromise. If he felt at times the need to attempt to rationalise experience into truth, equally he exemplified, and upheld the importance of, the flux of the mind. It is no accident that Locke is mentioned in his letters on several occasions (e.g. I, 138, 212), or that Burns refers to the association of ideas (I, 225; II, 347). 'We know nothing or next to nothing of the substance or structure of our Souls, so cannot account for those seeming caprices in them' (I, 348), Burns wrote to Mrs Dunlop. In similar vein, and in terms even more reminiscent of Sterne, he informed William Dunbar,

In vain do we talk of reason, my dear Sir; we are the offspring of Caprice, & the nurslings of Habitude.—The most pleasurable part of our existence, the strings that tie heart to heart, are the manufacture of some hitherto undescribed and unknown power within us. (I, 368)

To the offspring of Caprice and nursling of Habitude the temptations of Wit are irresistible. Thus to Mrs Dunlop he admitted, 'Politics is dangerous ground for me to tread on, & yet I cannot for the soul of me resist an impulse of any thing like Wit' (I, 392). That Burns had clearly before him as foremost example of the impulse of wit the work of Laurence Sterne is substantiated by this letter to Ainslie where the Shandean legacy is blatant:

I rec^d your last, & was much entertained with it; but I will not at this time, nor at any other time, answer it.—Answer a letter? I never could answer a letter in my life!—I have written many a letter in return for letters I have received; but then—they were original matter—spurt—away! zig, here; zag, there; as if the Devil that, my grannie (an old woman *indeed*) often told me, rode on Will-o'-wisp, or, in her more classic phrase, SPUNKIE, were looking over my elbow.—A happy thought that idea has ingendered in my head! SPUNKIE—thou shalt henceforth be my Symbol, Signature, & Tutelary Genius! Like thee, hap-step-&-loup, here-awa-there-awa, higglety-pigglety, pell-mell, hither-&-yon, ram-stam, happy-go-lucky, up-tails-a'-by-the-light-o'-the moon, has been, is & shall be, my progress through the mosses & moors of this vile, bleak, barren wilderness of a life of ours . . .

        . . . I feel myself vastly better.—I give you friendly joy of Robie Waters' brother.—'Twas a happy thought his begetting him against a *Book press*.—No doubt, as you with equal sagacity & science remark, it will have an astonishing effect on the young BOOK-WORM'S head-piece. (II, 212)[15]

Wit becomes a welcome refuge in a world where experience is complex, response is ambivalent, and both resist language's attempts to render them. To Mrs Dunlop Burns acknowledged,

        . . . the word, 'Love', owing to the intermingledoms of the good & the bad, the pure & impure, in this world, being rather an equivocal term for expressing one's sentiments & sensations, I must do justice to the sacred purity of my attachment. (II, 143)

Time and again in reading Burns's letters one encounters his keen sense of the disparity between man's version of experience and experience itself. This was to Graham of Fintry:

        I have heard and read a good deal of Philanthropy, Generosity and Greatness of soul, and when rounded with the flourish of declamatory periods, or poured in the mellifluence of Parnassian measure, they have a tolerable effect on a musical ear; but when these high sounding professions are compared with the very act and deed as they are usually performed, I do not think there is any thing in or belonging to Human Nature, so baldly disproportionate. (I, 425)

At its widest the gulf for Burns exists between the ideal and the actual. 'Like any other fine sayings,' he remarked of some lines from Thomson's *Alfred*, 'it has, I fear, more of Philosophy than Human-nature in it' (II, 34). For Burns, as for Sterne, the system which man erects out of experience, in an attempt to comprehend that experience, simply takes him ever further from it. 'Good God, why this disparity between our wishes and our powers?' (II, 202), he exclaimed, echoing both Sterne and Goethe;[16] and elsewhere (II, 46–7) he was to lament as additional constraints the poet's strength of imagination and delicacy of sensibility, the terms once more being redolent of Sterne.

    If this is man's situation, thus severely circumscribed, what is more natural than that he should regard himself as ill-fated, the plaything of a whimsical and at times malign Providence? Burns is very close to Tristram when he writes of 'that evil Planet, which has almost all my life shed its baleful rays on my devoted head' (I, 203); and he sees himself as 'a poor hairum-scairum Poet whom Fortune had kept for her particular use to wreak her temper on, whenever she was in ill-humour' (I, 217). And the following owe something to the plaints of Tristram: 'A damned Star has almost all my life usurped my zenith, and squinted out the cursed rays of its malign influences' (I, 408); 'I have not yet forgiven Fortune for her mischievous game of Cross Purposes that deprived me of the pleasure of seeing you again when you were here' (I, 460); 'However, Providence, to keep up the proper proportion of evil with the good, which it seems is necessary in this sublunary state, thought proper to check my exultation by a very serious misfortune' (II, 85). At various points in his life Burns was abused by 'Fate, or Providence, or whatever is the true Appellation for the Power who presides over & directs the affairs of this our world' (II, 61). Equally incontrovertible, however, is the facility with which he adopted the *persona* of the victim, the model for which he found in Tristram.

In both Sterne and Burns the awareness of man's limitation leads to a defiant and compensatory assertion of individuality (in Sterne's terms, the hobby-horse is ridden all the harder). It leads, too, to fierce attacks on the artificial restraints which man imposes upon himself. While Blake lamented 'the mind-forg'd manacles', Sterne demonstrated, especially through the figure of Walter Shandy, the absurdity of slavish adherence to rationalism. Burns's innate anti-rationalism, which could occasion his writing that 'with all reverence to the cold theorems of Reason, a few honest Prejudices & benevolent Prepossessions, are of the utmost consequence' (I, 419), found endorsement in Sterne. Burns attacked rationalism's Presbyterian manifestation as Prudence.

It was because of the deep division within Burns that he persisted in pleading for instinct and intuition in an almost plaintive manner. To Mrs McLehose he wrote, 'some yet unnamed feelings; things, not principles, but better than whims, carry me farther than boasted reason ever did a Philosopher' (I, 182). And these terms are distinctly Shandean:

> I have always found an honest passion, or native instinct, the trustiest auxiliary in the warfare of this world.—Reason almost always comes to me, like an unlucky wife to a poor devil of a husband—just in time enough to add her reproaches to his other grievances. (I, 257)

The following extract from a letter written on the same day as the above shows Burns grasping at revealed religion:

> . . . a man, conscious of having acted an honest part among his fellow creatures; even granting that he may have been the sport, at times, of passions and instincts; he goes to a great unknown Being who could have no other end in giving him existence but to make him happy; who gave him those passions and instincts, and well knows their force. (I, 258)

This is worthy of Tristram's Uncle Toby himself. But Burns's hold on revealed religion was altogether more precarious. Two years later he was to write to Mrs Dunlop:

> Still the damned dogmas of reasoning Philosophy throw in their doubts; but upon the whole, I believe, or rather I have a kind of conviction, though not absolute certainty, of the world beyond the grave. (II, 144)

The result of such doubts was, in addition to a defiant assertion of self, a spirited attack on 'that cardinal virtue' (I, 390), Prudence, and its practitioners. For Burns (with unmistakable echoes of Rousseauism),

> We come into the world with a heart and disposition to do good for it, untill by dashing a large mixture of base alloy called Prudence alias Selfishness, the too precious Metal of the Soul is brought down to the blackguard Sterling of ordinary currency. (I, 303)

In much of this, as in most of Burns's letters, there is an element of attitudinising along with more than a grain of truth. When he struck attitudes he was aware of it. A letter to Mrs McLehose ends,

> If you send me a page baptised in the font of sanctimonious Prudence—By Heaven, Earth & Hell, I will tear it into atoms!— . . .
>   . . . I need scarcely remark that the foregoing was the fustian rant of enthusiastic youth. (II, 190)

Burns shares with Sterne a benevolent emotionalism and offers the heart as source of positive good (or as much good as can be man's, given his condition). 'Almost all my religious tenets originate from my heart' (II, 73), he proclaims, with a certain degree of scarce-concealed satisfaction; and since his heart is that of a poet it has a 'bedlam warmth' (I, 155). Again sounding like Uncle Toby, he claims, for the benefit of Clarinda, that his is 'the Religion of the bosom' (I, 204). Quoting *Tristram Shandy* (III, ch. 10), he tells Maria Riddell, 'If it is true, that "Offences come only from the heart";—before you, I am guiltless' (II, 275). To Mrs Dunlop he affirms, 'The heart of the Man and the fancy of the Poet are the two grand considerations for which I live' (I, 341); and to the same lady he was to extol 'a heart glowing with the noble enthusiasm of Generosity, Benevolence and Greatness of Soul' (I, 420). The primacy of feeling bears upon his rare excursions into literary criticism: amongst his 'few strictures on Miss Williams Poem on the Slave Trade' is, 'Verse 46th I am afraid is rather unworthy of the rest: "to dare to feel", is an idea that I do not altogether like' (I, 428–9).

For Burns and Sterne the heart is life; it is the source of good; and in it originates any consolation that may be man's for his victimisation by Providence, to which limitation he adds by creating the constraints of rationalist systems. To set Burns on the subject of man (e.g. II, 283) alongside Sterne is to be made aware of distinct similarities. Yet one is left after a reading of *Tristram Shandy* (though not, admittedly, Sterne's letters) with a strong sense of Sterne's genuine compassion for man, whereas too often with Burns the predominant response is one of sentimentality. In a profound essay on Sterne, Edwin Muir wrote that in his work 'the mind was free to consider every object in it . . . this ubiquity of interest is at the root of Sterne's humour'.[17] Was Burns's mind free in this sense? Did he possess this ubiquity of interest? Regrettably, the answers have to be that his mind lacked the imaginative range and freedom of Sterne's, being constrained both by personal needs and the cultural disorientation of his country. Moreover, Sterne's sentimentalising is invariably part of an emotional flux or totality; too often Burns merely sentimentalises, or sentimentalises in isolation.

Hitherto I have been contending that the linguistic energy endemic in the Scots literary tradition is further strengthened in the instance of Burns by virtue of the poet's distinctive personality and his situation; that the post-Union cultural disorientation of the Scottish writer induced a compensatory emphasis on style; and that this is reflected in Burns's letters, which are the result of conscious artistry. They also reflect a considerable dramatic capacity in Burns. As early as December 1789 Burns wrote, 'I have some thoughts of the Drama' (I, 464); and three months later he was requesting copies of English and French dramatists from Hill, the bookseller (II, 20), (principally those of the major neo-classicists).[18] That the dramatic capacity found expression through the *personae* of the poems and the letters, rather than in a play, may be attributed in part at least to the cultural and religious bias against drama.

Before further consideration of the letters in terms of self-dramatisation, and Sterne as a particular source of *personae*, it is worth anticipating one of several contradictions yet to be identified in Burns. Noting the 'dancing irresponsibility and the lashing whip of Burns's language', Kurt Wittig wrote of Burns's attack on Presbyterianism, 'Burns's attack . . . does not take the form of mere rational satire; it is in itself a liberating outburst of zest and vitality.'[19] Wittig is writing of the poetic satires, but the comment applies equally to the letters. The point is, however, that in the letters an antithetical process is in operation: the linguistic and satiric energy is temporarily liberating (as with Smollett), but the manifold self-dramatisation is limiting and, ultimately, self-destroying. Byron, after reading certain of Burns's letters, exclaimed, 'What an antithetical mind!'[20] Perhaps the Burns of the letters was divided between the self, which was complex in itself, and the many alternative selves that it projected. In time the self in effect *became* the various and fragmented substitute selves.

In his letters Burns manifests a heightened self-consciousness and a strong inclination to self-dramatisation. In one letter he exclaims,

> God have mercy on me! a poor d-mned, incautious, duped, unfortunate fool! The sport, the miserable victim, of rebellious pride; hypochondriac imagination, agonizing sensibility, and bedlam passions! (I, 216)

In another he comments, 'I am, just as usual, a rhyming, mason-making, raking, aimless, idle fellow' (I, 126). Probably the clearest indication that, at least earlier in his career, he was aware of the distinction between self and rôle occurs in the letter to Alexander Cunningham in which he relates thus the news of his marriage:

> I am, too, a married man.—This was a step of which I had no idea, when you & I were together.—On my return to Ayrshire, I found a much-lov'd Female's positive happiness, or absolute Misery among my hands; and I could not trifle with such a sacred Deposite.—I am, since, doubly pleased with my conduct.—I have the consciousness of acting up to that generosity of principle I would be thought to possess; & I am really more & more pleased with my Choice. (I, 298–9)

In his edition of the letters of Sterne, Curtis observes of the reader's attitude to the writer that 'it is in the eighteenth century that we watch the transition of the public's attitude from one of decorous respect to one of prying curiosity', and he remarks of Sterne's letters that they 'were intended to be shown about' (*Letters*, xxiv, xxviii). Burns exemplifies the writer's responsiveness to this shift in public attitude, and he begins to dramatise, and offer versions of, himself. But some versions were for a strictly limited circle.

That Burns had the capacity to adopt many varied *personae* is undeniable. Maria Riddell commented,

> Many others perhaps may have ascended to prouder heights in the region of Parnassus, but none certainly ever outshone Burns in the charms—the sorcery, I would almost call it, of fascinating conversation, the spontaneous eloquence of social argument, or the unstudied poignancy of brilliant repartee.[21]

Burns devotees who take his every word literally would do well to ponder that 'sorcery'. Recent criticism, most notably that of John C Weston, has recognised both the skill and the extent of Burns's use of ironic voice. Weston has noted,

> Nine of the eleven satires use, in several degrees of emphasis, the voice of the opponent. The other two . . . employ an irony which results from the poet's speaking in some degree other than what he means but not, as in the more typical, saying, more or less, the opposite of what he means.[22]

The ironic use of dramatic voice, the initial possibilities of which, as Weston suggests, Burns saw in Ramsay, bulks large in the letters. In some the 'opponent' is one of the poet's alternative selves, so that the letters as a whole may be regarded as a dramatisation of the conflicts within Burns's own personality. Wittig points out that 'in Scots literature, it is often the feelings of others that are expressed, from inside their minds'.[23] In Burns's letters the 'others' are projections, or versions, of himself.

It is erroneous to see in Burns's Edinburgh period the origins of his internal divisions and self-fragmentation. Range and versatility of voice are evident from the earliest letters. At the age of twenty-one he wrote in formal Augustan prose to William Niven, a friend since early schooldays, and even this early he was intent on presenting an image, or a version, of himself. To Niven he wrote, 'For my own part, I now see it improbable that I shall ever acquire riches, and am therefore endeavouring to gather a philosophical contempt of enjoyments so hard to be gained and so easily lost' (I, 5). The image of the self that he projected varied to suit the recipient. Accordingly he sent, as dutiful son, a letter from Irvine to his father in which he combines striking of noble attitudes with maudlin self-pity of this kind:

> Sometimes, indeed, when for an hour or two, as is sometimes the case, my spirits are lightened, I glimmer a little into futurity; but my principal, and indeed my only pleasurable employment is looking backwards & forwards in a moral & religious way—I am quite transported at the thought that ere long, perhaps very soon, I shall bid an eternal adieu to all the pains, & uneasiness & disquietudes of this weary life; for I assure you I am heartily tired of it, and, if I do not very much deceive myself I could contentedly & gladly resign it. (I, 7)

The question of how a young man of twenty-two could come to write in this way is answered by the post-script: having concluded 'I am, Honored Sir, your dutiful son, Robt. Burns', he adds, 'My meal is nearly out but I am going to borrow till I get more.'

In one of his earliest love-letters (probably to Alison Begbie) Burns proclaims,

> There is one rule which I have hitherto practised, and which I shall invariably keep with you, and that is, honestly to tell you the plain truth. There is something so mean and unmanly in the arts of dissimulation and falsehood, that I am surprised they can be acted by any one in so noble, so generous a passion as virtuous love. (I, 12)

Professing virtuous love and acting for all he was worth, Burns could voice similar sentiments to Clarinda seven years later, asserting, 'The dignified and dignifying consciousness of an honest man, and the well-grounded trust in approving Heaven, are two most substantial [foundations] of happiness' (I, 253). Where the occasion demanded, Burns could readily proclaim the importance of sincerity (I, 187), or the validity of orthodox morality and religion (I, 230).

It is certainly not the purpose of this study to argue that Burns was a hypocrite. The rôle-playing in which he engaged seems to have been typical of Scottish writers of the time. T S Eliot wrote of Byron, in terms that apply equally to Burns, 'Hypocrite . . . except in the original sense of the word, is hardly the term for Byron. He was an actor who devoted immense trouble to *becoming* a role that he adopted.'[24]

Burns's letters may be seen as part of an enduring tradition in Scottish literature, that strain which C M Grieve described as 'tremendously idiosyncratic, full of a wild humour which blends the actual and the apocalyptic in an incalculable fashion'.[25] Viewed in this light the extravagances and contradictions of the multiple voices of Burns's letters are more readily understood and less readily reprehended. Burns possessed in large measure the rhetorical capacity and the tendency to fantasise which are characteristic of the innate Scottish response. Both of these qualities are epitomised in the flyting. Kurt Wittig's description of the flyting as an integral part of the Scottish tradition has acute relevance to the linguistic force of Burns's letters and its origin:

> True flyting . . . has little in common with satire and social criticism. It is essentially an act of revolt, primitive and unashamed, against all socially-imposed restraint; it revels in the sensuous as such; and in seeking to assert its own stubborn individualism it is quite prepared to let everything else 'gang tapsalteerie', or to the Devil if need be.[26]

Some of Burns's behaviour, both personal and literary, is explicable in terms of revolt against socially imposed restraint. His writing, including his letters (perhaps *especially* his letters where the restraining influence of form is less effective), serves as a medium at times for the expression, through diverse voices, of his frustration. The essence of the flyting may be observed in Burns's letters, but it has been set to the services of the individual psychological needs of the writer. Wittig also notes that the flyting and extravaganza are a strong feature of the literature of the Celtic fringe. Thus the extravagant and dynamic elements in Burns and Sterne are part of the one tradition. And Burns was, as Curtis said of Sterne, 'preoccupied with the absorbing drama of his own existence' (*Letters*, xxxii).

Of the fashionable *personae* available to Burns the one which had the greatest appeal for one of his temperament was that of the man of feeling. By Burns's day Europe had been pervaded by the belief in man's natural benevolism, a belief for which Rousseau was the most eloquent and earnest spokesman. But by that time Rousseauism had bred various distorted forms: the sentimental comedies of Diderot who had claimed, 'If Nature ever made a sensitive soul, that soul, and you know it, is mine';[27] Goethe's *The Sorrows of Young Werther*, in which can be discerned a distinct distancing—sometimes ironic—of author from his hero; and Mackenzie's *The Man of Feeling*, where this is also a feature. It is true that Burns was most attracted to the pathetic and sentimental aspects of the work of Mackenzie, 'the Man of Feeling, that first of men' (I, 239). But the duality in his values is reflected in the fact that, while extolling Harley's sentiments, he could yet warn of the impracticality of his behaviour in these comments to Mrs Dunlop:

> From what book, moral or even Pious, will the susceptible young mind receive impressions more congenial to Humanity and Kindness, Generosity and Benevolence, in short, more of all that ennobles the Soul to herself, or endears her to others, than from the simple affecting tale of poor Harley? Still, with all my admiration of McKenzie's writings I do not know if they are the fittest reading for a young Man who is about to set out, as the phrase is, to make his way into life. (II, 25)

Similarly, in another letter, he declared, 'Sir, he is, without the least alloy, a universal Philanthropist; and his much beloved name is—A BOTTLE OF GOOD OLD PORT!' (I, 148).

Such qualification of the voice of feeling is rare, however. Burns and Sterne on the virtues of the honest heart sound remarkably similar. In one of his earliest letters Burns wrote to Niven,

> I shall be happy to hear from you how you go on in the ways of life; I do not mean so much how trade prospers, or if you have the prospect of riches, or the dread of poverty; as how you go on in the cultivation of the finer feelings of the heart. (I, 5)

The phrase is revealing: aged twenty-one, Burns was aware that the finer feelings of the heart required 'cultivation'. Benevolence he took care to project as one of his redeeming features. To James Smith he presented himself thus: 'For me, I am witless wild, and wicked; and have scarcely any vestige of the image of God left me, except a pretty large portion of honour and an enthusiastic, incoherent Benevolence' (I, 45).

In the letters the best exemplification of the way in which Burns capitalises on the doctrine of the feeling heart is in the sequence of accounts of his encountering the wounded hare. The first mention of this includes an element of ironic awareness (and self-awareness). For Burns the sight of the hare

> set my humanity in tears and my indignation in arms.—The following was the result, which please read to the young ladies—I believe you may include the Major, too; as whatever I have said of shooting hares, I have not spoken one irreverend word against coursing them. (I, 397–8)

Within a fortnight he produced the following, much more formal and moralistic, version of the same incident:

> . . . I heard the burst of a shot from a neighbouring Plantation, & presently a poor little wounded hared came crippling by me.—You will guess my indignation at the inhuman fellow, who could shoot a hare at this season when they all of them have young ones; & it gave me no little gloomy satisfaction to see the poor injured creature escape him.—Indeed there is something in all that multiform business of destroying for our sport individuals in the animal creation that do not injure us materially, that I could never reconcile to my ideas of native Virtue & eternal Right. (I, 404–5)

After a further six weeks the incident inspired this highly sentimental account:

> . . . I heard the report of a gun from a neighbouring wood, and presently a poor little hare, dragging its wounded limbs, limped piteously by me.—I have always had an abhorrence at this way of assasinating God's creatures without first allowing them those means of defence with which he has variously endowed them; but at this season when the object of our treacherous murder is most probably a Parent, perhaps the mother, and of consequence to leave two little helpless nurslings to perish with hunger amid the pitiless wilds, such an action is not only a sin against the letter of the law, but likewise a deep crime against the *morality of the heart*. (I, 417–18)

Nothing demonstrates more tellingly the way in which Burns worked at playing upon the feelings of his readers. Fairchild's comment that those of Burns's poems that are concerned with the 'sympathetic glow' reveal 'a mixture of genuine and fabricated feeling which suggests a lack of spiritual integration'[28] applies equally readily to the letters; and the lack of integration encompasses personal and psychological dimensions.

Burns enacts the various rôles which by his day were inseparable from the vogue of feeling. The following extract from an early letter suggests that the *persona* of the melancholic came easily to him:

> I have here, likewise, inclosed a small piece, the very latest of my productions. I am a good deal pleased with some sentiments myself; as they are just the native, querulous feelings of a heart, which, as the elegantly melting Gray says, 'Melancholy has marked for her own'. (I, 32)

Recalling the 'voluptuous enjoyment' of a blind grand-uncle in weeping while his mother sang 'The Life and Age of Man', Burns comments, 'It is this way of thinking, it is these melancholly truths, that make Religion so precious to the poor miserable Children of men' (I, 307). Habitually, then, Burns, as Sterne had done, offers melancholy as a component of an emotional compound. Awareness of the ambivalence, or the complexity, of feeling recurs. The birth of twins to Jean Armour led him to write, 'A very fine boy and girl have awakened a thousand (tender [deleted]) feelings that thrill, some with tender pleasure, and some with foreboding anguish, thro' my soul' (I, 51–2). One may compare Sterne's 'dined alone again today; and begin to find a pleasure in this kind of resigned Misery arising from this Situation, of heart unsupported by aught but its own tenderness'; and 'my Sentimental Journey will, I dare say, convince you that my feelings are from the heart, and that that heart is not of the worst of molds—praised be God for my sensibility! Though it has often made me wretched, yet I would not exchange it for all the pleasures the grossest sensualist ever felt' (*Letters*, 324; 395–6).

Burns shares with Sterne also the stylized and sentimental conception of the rural idyll. Burns made this request of Peter Miller: '. . . fix me in any sequester'd romantic spot, and let me have such a Lease as by care and industry I might live in humble decency, and have a spare hour now and then to write out an idle rhyme . . .' (I, 87). Sterne writes of 'a little sun-gilt cottage on the side of a romantic hill', and claims 'the loneliest Cottage that Love and Humility ever dwelt in' is preferable to the 'glittering Court' (*Letters*, 16; 333). In Burns there is again a duality in that he appears to relish both the romanticised domestic setting and the wild grandeur of the Highland landscapes (and its culture). Very much the tourist of sensibility, he enthuses, 'I have done nothing else but visited cascades, prospects, ruins, and Druidical temples, learned Highland tunes and pickt up Scotch songs, Jacobite anecdotes, &c. these two months' (I, 166). The dichotomy in Burns can be seen almost in geographical terms as he exclaims, 'warm as I was from Ossian's country where I had seen his very grave, what cared I for fisher-towns and fertile Carses?' (I, 157). The following union of wild untutored nature and man's creative fancy is even more revealing:

> My ready fancy, with colours more mellow than life itself, painted the beautiful wild scenery of Kilravock—the venerable grandeur of the castle—the spreading woods—the winding river, gladly leaving his unsightly heathy source, and lingering with apparent delight as he passes the fairy walk at the bottom of the garden. (I, 238)

This is almost Freudian, with the river representing Burns himself. His exemplification of sensibility reflects the uneasy union of wild scenery and fairy walk; and his attitude to the culture of the north is similarly ambivalent.

After the example of Sterne in his letters to Mrs Draper, Burns, in his correspondence with Mrs McLehose, plays the sentimental lover. Of Sterne's sentimentalism Curtis comments, 'His scene, to be sure, must contain the cherished room and tea-kettle and cat. But in addition to these it must contain a sweet and sympathetic woman to succour him' (*Letters*, xxxii). For Burns, by the winter of 1787 the sentimental relationship with 'Clarinda' fulfilled this function, while the prospect of domesticity became rapidly and inevitably inseparable from the figure of Jean Armour.

Such is the extent of the similarity that it seems almost certain that Burns must have read the *Letters of the late Rev. Mr. Laurence Sterne*, published in London in 1775 by his daughter, Lydia de Medalle. Burns made specific reference to Sterne's letters to Eliza. To Thomson he wrote of the song, 'Craigie-burnwood',

> The Lady on whom it was made, is one of the finest women in Scotland; and in fact (entre nous) is in a manner to me what Sterne's Eliza was to him—a Mistress, or Friend, or what you will, in the guileless simplicity of Platonic love. (II, 315)

Points of similarity abound: the worth of the honest heart; the pleasurable pain of love; the cruel providence which parts the lovers; the merits of solitude; and the stylisation of Nature and love. Burns presents himself to Clarinda as the sentimental lover in the Sternean mould. 'Cannot you guess, my Clarinda', he wrote, 'what thoughts, what cares, what anxious fore-bodings, hopes and fears, must crowd the breast of the man of keen sensibility?' (I, 254). In the Clarinda letters, according to Fairchild, Burns was 'trying his hardest not to be his real self'.[29] This is less than true. Part of Burns's 'real self' was precisely the projection of *persona* in which he indulged in this correspondence.

In one of the earliest letters to Mrs McLehose Burns wrote, 'I determined to cultivate your friendship with the enthusiasm of Religion' (I, 182). Soon a clear division within his attitude became apparent. Within one letter he proclaimed both, 'I like the idea of Arcadian names in commerce of this kind', and, almost immediately after, 'I wish you to see me as I am.' Thereafter he embarks on the self-romanticising that recurs throughout the Clarinda letters: 'I am, as most people of my trade are, a strange will o' wisp being; the victim too frequently of much imprudence and many follies.—My great constituent elements are Pride and Passion' (I, 189–90). For all the strong element of rôle-playing, Burns could yet assure Clarinda, 'You see I am either above, or incapable of Dissimulation' (I, 190), and, 'You are right . . . a friendly correspondence goes for nothing, except one write their undisguised sentiments' (I, 195).

Central to the relationship is the degree of emotional communion that is achieved, and especially the sharing of suffering or melancholy. But here the grandly emotional declamation sometimes descends into bathos or is undermined by reductively banal detail. It is difficult to believe that Burns was not conscious of the disruptive, even comic, effect of the intrusion of the particular in this:

> Did you, Madam, know what I feel when you talk of your sorrows! Good God! that one who has so much worth in the sight of Heaven, and is so amiable to her fellow-creatures should be so unhappy! I can't venture out for cold. My limb is vastly better; but I have not any use of it without my crutches. (I, 194)

Sterne's letters to Eliza contain a comparable fusion of elevated thoughts and sometimes bizarrely particular details (e.g. *Letters*, 314–16, where, on her departure for India, he warns her to beware of her shipmates and is deeply concerned that 'the fresh painting [of her cabin] will be enough to destroy every nerve about [her]').

From Mackenzie's Harley and from the example of Sterne's letters Burns adopts the formulaic use of weeping as proof of the feeling heart's empathic capacity. With Burns's 'You talk of weeping, Clarinda; some involuntary drops wet your lines as I read them' (I, 205) may be compared the following utterances of Sterne: 'I can never see or talk to this incomparable woman without bursting into tears' (*Letters*, 308); 'I wept my plate full, Eliza! and now I have begun, could shed tears till supper again' (*Letters*, 336); and he states (*Letters*, 325) that he cannot talk of Eliza without bursting into tears, which occasions outpourings of sympathy from his companion, Mrs James. No more telling instance of Sterne's exploitation for effect of the processes of emotion can be found than the following: '. . . upon taking up my pen, my poor pulse quickened—my pale face glowed—and tears (ran [deleted] stood ready in my eyes to fall upon the paper, as I traced the word Eliza' (*Letters*, 331–2). That substitution of 'stood' for 'ran' epitomises the habitual striving after pathetic effect on the part of the self-projected man of feeling.

Sterne is the source too of self-dramatising appeals for pity, as when Burns, describing his life as a ruined temple, exclaims, 'What strength, what proportion in some parts! what unsightly gaps, what prostrate ruins in others!' (I, 210). In Burns's 'I see you laughing at my fairy fancies, and calling me a voluptuous Mahometan' (I, 214) are clear echoes of Sterne's writing to Eliza as her 'Bramin' (*Letters*, 299). Common to each set of letters also is the sense of the torture of love. Burns writes, 'O Love and Sensibility, ye have conspired against My Peace! I love to madness, and I feel to torture' (I, 219); and Sterne, as well as writing in like vein, makes plain that his love for Eliza renders work, or anything else, impossible (*Letters*, 350, 351, 377). In each correspondence sensibility is a source of woe. Burns writes,

> Nature has been too kind to you for your happiness.—Your Delicacy, your Sensibility.—O why should such glorious qualifications be the fruitful source of woe! You have 'murder'd sleep' to me last night.—I went to bed, impress'd with an idea that you were unhappy; and every start I closed my eyes, busy Fancy painted you in such scenes of romantic misery that I would almost be persuaded you are not well this morning. (I, 222)

With this may be compared Sterne's 'Remember how I Love—remember what I suffer' (*Letters*, 346) and a lengthy passage (*Letters*, 334) which is the quintessence of the suffering of the sentimental lover.

When Burns declares to Clarinda,

> You are the first, the only unexceptionable individual of the beauteous Sex that I ever met with; and never woman more intirely possessed my soul.—I know myself, and how far I can depend on passions, well. It has been my peculiar study (I, 227),

he is both playing a rôle and, in so doing, being himself. In this he is very much the modern—obsessively self-conscious, pre-occupied with watching himself being himself in the variety of rôles that comprise him, one of which is that of watcher.

The episode as sentimental lover revealed much about his personality. Once back at Ellisland he delivered in a letter to Mrs Dunlop one of the most vituperative of his many attacks on the great and fashionable world (I, 381–2). The rush and expense of verbal energy was plainly therapeutic, venting, perhaps, his rage and dismay at finding himself playing such divergent rôles ('To a man who has a Home, however humble or remote; if that Home is like mine, the scene of Domestic comfort; the bustle of Edinburgh will soon be a business of sickening disgust'). Noting that Burns resorts to satire to relieve the pressure of anger, John Weston observed that Burns 'always was a man of negative feelings, never a man of sweetness or compliance'.[30] In his lengthy autobiographical letter to Moore Burns wrote, 'My Passions when once they were lighted up, raged like so many devils, till they got vent in rhyme; and then conning over my verses, like a spell, soothed all into quiet' (I, 141). The vehement attack on 'the iron pride of unfeeling greatness' (Mrs Oswald) (I, 363) fulfilled the same function. Such eruption of passionate feeling, frequently negative or hostile, into vigorous expression characterises the work of several major Scottish writers of the period (Smollett, Burns, Byron, Hogg); so much so that one wonders if it amounts to an unconscious expression of the disorientation which the loss of nationhood occasioned.

Possibly this is one of the factors that contribute to a feature of Burns's letters which Burns devotees prefer to overlook: the recurrent assertions of his superiority may well be rooted in a deep personal (reflecting a national) insecurity. This is a characteristic of Burns which cannot be attributed to the

Edinburgh sojourn since it appears in some of the earlier letters. On 17 November 1782 Burns wrote thus:

> I love to see a man who has a mind superior to the world and the world's men— a man who, conscious of his own integrity, and at peace with himself, despises the censures and opinions of the unthinking rabble of mankind. The distinction of a poor man and a rich man is something indeed, but it is nothing to the difference between either a wise man and a fool, or a man of honour and a knave. (I, 15)

Burns as poet and man of feeling, for all the sympathetic glow, sees himself as a man apart, and certainly elevated above the rabble. 'Remember this', he enjoins Niven, 'never blow my Songs among the Million, as I would abhor to hear every Prentice mouthing my poor performances in the streets' (I, 49). After his triumph he regretted, even resented, what he saw as slavish imitation by the inferior many, and complained, 'My success has encouraged such a shoal of ill-spawned monsters to crawl into public notice, under the title of Scots Poets, that the very term, Scots Poetry, borders on the burlesque' (I, 382).

Fairchild has claimed that the prime appeal of masonry to Burns was 'the combination of very hearty conviviality with a benevolism which hovered on the borderline between New Light religion and sentimental deism', while he also liked 'the democracy which enabled common folk to rub elbows with the gentry'. One suspects that, rather than the democracy, it was the union of brotherhood with exclusiveness which appealed. It is precisely the tension between these which issues out in the letters quoted above. Noting the ironies wherein Burns's 'artificially cultivated literary benevolism interfered with the true benevolism of his heart', Fairchild points out that he 'had spurned the antinomianism of the Evangelicals for antinomianism of a more attractive sort—the glorious freedom of the children of sensibility'.[31] In the fullest manifestation of that 'glorious freedom'—the Clarinda relationship—Burns evinces exactly the same paradox: such sentimental benevolism is inevitably contradictory since, aware of it, the sentimental lover recognises his distinction from the majority. So to Clarinda Burns wrote,

> Coarse minds are not aware how much they injure the keenly feeling tie of bosom-friendship, when in their foolish officiousness they mention what nobody cares for recollecting.—People of nice sensibility and generous minds have a certain intrinsic dignity, that fires at being trifled with, or towered, or even too nearly approached. (I, 197)

Four days later the white-heat of such fire was beginning to take its toll of him, and he ended a letter to her: 'John Milton, I wish thy soul better rest than I expect on my pillow to-night! O for a little of the cart-horse part of human nature!' (I, 202–3). This is the less predominant note, however. On another, more typical, occasion, after enthusing on the luxury of his bliss and noting how she has both stolen and refined his soul, he exclaims, 'What trifling silliness is the childish fondness of the every day children of the world!' (I, 211).

Precisely this sense of the distinction that is inseparable from extreme sensibility also characterises the letters of Sterne. To Eliza, Sterne writes that only 'men of nice sensibility' can be touched by her 'bewitching sort of nameless excellence' (*Letters*, 313). He hopes she will read his letters 'when weary of fools and uninteresting discourse' (*Letters*, 316). 'Time and distance, or change of every thing wch. might allarm [*sic*] the little hearts of little men, create now uneasy suspence in mine' (*Letters*, 332), he avows. With echoes of Donne he exclaims, 'the Room will not be too little for us—but We shall be *too* big for the Room' (*Letters*, 367). The tone and style of the Clarinda letters owe much to such passages in Sterne's letters as

> What a stupid, selfish, unsentimental set of Beings are the bulk of our Sex! By Heaven! not one man out of 50, informed with feelings—or endowed either with heads or hearts able to possess & fill the mind of such a Being as thee, with one Vibration like its own. (*Letters*, 364–5)

The essential point of difference is that, unlike Sterne, Burns took with him far beyond the confines of sentimental romance the conviction of the superiority with which sensibility endowed one. To Alexander Cunningham he declared,

> Love is the Alpha and the Omega of human enjoyment . . . It is the emanation of Divinity that preserves the Sons and Daughters of rustic labour from degenerating into the brutes with which they daily hold converse. (I, 365)

Similarly, to William Dunbar he wrote, 'We are not shapen out of the common, heavy, methodical Clod, the elemental Stuff of the plodding, selfish Race, the Sons of Arithmetick and Prudence . . . in the name of random Sensibility then, let never the moon change on our silence any more' (II, 3–4).

Increasingly, however, there appears a realisation that extreme sensibility is a questionable gift. The following typifies this sense:

> There is a species of the Human genus that I call, the Gin-horse Class: what enviable dogs they are!—Round, and round, and round they go—Mundell's ox that drives his cotton-mill, their exact prototype—without an idea or wish beyond their circle; fat sleek, stupid, patient, quiet and contented:—while here I sit, altogether Novemberish, a damn'd melange of Fretfulness and melancholy; not enough of the one to rouse me to passion, nor of the other to repose me in torpor; my soul flouncing and fluttering round her tenement, like a wild Finch caught amid the horrors of winter and newly thrust into a cage. (II, 265)

This is no mere attudinising: here is the agonised, resentful awareness of the man who knows he is caught in a cage which he has helped to make. The thought of his soul 'in her wanderings through the weary, thorny wilderness of this world' induces the exclamation,

> God knows I am ill-fitted for the struggle: I glory in being a Poet, and I want to be thought a wise man—I would fondly be generous, and I wish to be rich. After all, I am afraid I am a lost subject. (I, 174)

And to the Earl of Buchan he dramatised the conflict in terms of Prudence v. Pride and Instinct, and situation v. aspirations (I, 91). Reason and instinct coexisted in uneasy compromise in Burns. That he was aware of their contention within him is evident from this account of his father's death to his cousin James Burness:

> On the 13th. Currt. I lost the best of fathers. Though to be sure we have had long warning of the impending stroke still the tender feelings of Nature claim their part and I cannot recollect the tender endearments and parental lessons of the best of friends and the ablest of instructors without feeling, what perhaps, the calmer dictates of reason would partly condemn. (I, 21)

Too readily reason and emotion became, respectively, a somewhat underhand practicality and sentimental gesturing. Two adjacent letters in Ferguson's edition make a telling juxtaposition: in one Burns confides to Thomas Orr, 'I am at present so cursedly taken in with an affair of gallantry that I am very glad Peggy is off my hand as I am at present embarrassed enough without her', while the next contains a highly stylised account of the heightened sensibility of the poet (I, 24). One is reminded of Fairchild's comment that 'the poetry of Burns is curiously divided between Fergusson and Mackenzie'.[32]

For Goethe's Werther, 'A man is a man, and the little bit of sense he may have plays little or no part at all when passion rages in him, and the limitations of humankind oppress him.'[33] Burns had more than a little bit of sense, but it was powerless in the face of passion, not least his passion for rôle-playing; and whilst the limitations of humankind may be said to have oppressed him, there is a sense in which he was oppressed most of all by himself. The divisions within himself oppressed him, and he was well aware of them and powerless to resolve them. On the most obvious level this led to the threat which his allegedly republican sentiments posed to his position in the Excise. The problems arising from his alleged political radicalism he explained to Erskine of Mar as his falling 'under the temptation of being witty [rather] than disaffected' (II, 207).

Increasing pressures sundered even further the various conflicting elements within Burns. Adding a poignancy to his situation in his capacity for self-analysis, which is evident in the following, albeit that there is the almost-inevitable exploitation of the point for the fullest effect:

> My worst enemy is *Moimême*. I lie so miserably open to the inroads and incursions of a mischievous, light-armed, well-mounted banditti, under the banners of imagination, whim, caprice, and passion, and the heavy-armed veteran regulars of wisdom, prudence, and forethought, move so very, very slow, that I am almost in a state of perpetual warfare, and alas! frequent defeat.
>
> There are just two creatures I would envy, a horse in his native state traversing

the forests of Asia, or an oyster on some of the desart shores of Europe. The one has not a wish without enjoyment, the other has neither wish nor fear. (I, 185)

Such a comment is difficult to reconcile with Ferguson's claim that 'Burns was conscious of no schizophrenia in himself, though he was well aware that a legend surrounded him'.[34] In Burns are clear indications of the conflict between Calvinist predeterminism and sentimentalism. Of man's condition Burns wrote to Ainslie, 'Whether he shall rise in the manly consciousness of a self-approving mind, or sink beneath a galling load of Regret and Remorse— these are alternatives of the last moment' (I, 291).

The dichotomies within Burns are further reflected in the various levels and styles of language which he uses in his letters. Increasingly there are signs that, in fact, Burns became trapped within the formal mode of writing. A letter to Alexander Cunningham, one of his closest friends, includes this tale of 'Charlie Caldwell, a drunken Carrier in Ayr':

> Charles had a Cara Sposa after his own heart, who used to take 'caup-out' with him till neither could see the other.—When those honest Genii of old Scotch Social Life—'REAMING SWATS'—used to transport the tender Pair beyond the bounds of sober joy, to the region of rapture; the ardent Lover would grapple the yielding Fair to his bosom—'MARGET! YE'RE A GLORY TO GOD, & THE DELIGHT O' MY SOUL!!'
>   As I cannot in conscience tax you with the postage of a packet, I must keep this bizarre melange of an epistle untill I find the chance of a private conveyance. (II, 285)

Why did Burns employ a mode akin to the comic-epic, with its highly reductive connotations, when one side of him would almost certainly echo the carrier's sentiments? The answer must be that the *persona* which this mode expressed had become compulsive. On Burns more than any major Scottish writer since the Union did the cultural and linguistic dichotomy take its toll. The mask of the stylist in formal English prose would occasionally drop to reveal the depth of regret at the passing of a culture, some of the remnants of which he had permanised in song. 'These English Songs gravel me to death', he wrote, 'I have not that command of the language that I have of my native tongue.— In fact I think that my ideas are more barren in English than in Scottish' (II, 318).

In the letters of the later years of Burns's life the divisions within his personality become more blatant, and the self-dramatisation and self-distancing verge on the schizoid. He wrote to Gilbert from Ellisland early in 1790, 'My nerves are in a damnable State.—I feel that horrid hypochondria pervading every atom of both body & soul.—This farm has undone my enjoyment of myself' (II, 3). That phrase, 'my enjoyment of myself', exemplifies the extent to which his life had become meaningful in terms of self-drama: Burns was both cast and audience. Drink and bawdry offered some relief, but by late in 1791 he was lamenting to Ainslie, 'When I tell you even [bawdry] has lost its power to please, you will guess something of my hell within, and all around me' (II, 121). At times despair mingled with something close to paranoia. A late letter to Mrs Dunlop includes, 'I know not how to be the object of Pity.—My enemies may dislike (for they dare not despise me) & I can repay them in kind; but the Pity of a Friend is quite distressing' (II, 321).

The self-distancing and subterfuge became increasingly pronounced. In April 1793 a letter to Erskine of Mar contains this request:

> When you have honored this letter with a perusal, please commit it to the flames.—BURNS, in whose behalf you have so generously interested yourself, I have here, in his native colours, drawn *as he is*; but should any of the people in whose hands is the very bread he eats, get the least knowledge of the picture, it would ruin the poor Bard forever. (II, 210)

This epitomises his condition: Burns *as he is* is presented in a verbal *picture*, but the self by which he is known is that of the 'poor Bard'—illusion and reality, rôles and selves, have become interchangeable.[35] Burns might well be the forerunner of those whom Morse Peckham terms the Stylists—those who seek an answer to the dilemma of Romanticism in style. Stylism, as Peckham notes, 'degenerated into mannerism . . . Swinburne and Debussy ended up playing the roles of "Swinburne" and "Debussy" which they had invented and Hemingway ended up playing the role of "Hemingway".' Burns ended up playing the rôle of 'Burns', and as Hemingway *had* to commit suicide (as Peckham notes) so Burns *had* to die the rustic bard.

Peckham observes, in terms acutely relevant to Burns (though he is writing of the nineteenth century), that Stylism offered no solution to 'the great Romantic problem of re-entry, of commitment, of solving the paradox of entering into social action without betraying one's selfhood or the selfhood of others'. 'Stylism', he points out, 'could symbolize the self. But how was one to be the self? It had separated itself from all but one aspect of human life, but to the Romantic, sooner or later, history must be encountered, for history is reality.'[36] Burns's *personae* laid accretions of fantasy upon precisely that core of reality.

In this light one can more readily understand the increasing cultivation of solitude. When Burns begins a letter to Mrs Dunlop thus: 'Here, in a solitary inn, in a solitary village, I am set by myself, to amuse my brooding fancy as I may' (II, 297), he is not merely playing the part of the extreme sentimentalist whose acute sensibility isolates himself (cf. Sterne, *Letters*, 18, 331, 342, 345, 365): in himself he felt a growing isolation—again the self *became* the rôle. Concomitant with solitude came a heightened awareness of mortality which again, as the following indicates, evokes Sterne:

> What a transient business is life!—Very lately I was a boy; but t'other day I was a young man; and I already begin to feel the rigid fibre and stiffening joints of Old Age coming fast o'er my frame. (II, 333)

Latterly the cumulative effect of simultaneously acting and spectating wore him down. The following, from a letter written less than a month before his death, exemplifies this:

> Alas, Clarke, I begin to fear the worst! As to my individual Self, I am tranquil;—
> I would despise myself if I were not: but Burns's poor widow! & half a dozen of
> his dear little ones, helpless orphans, there I am weak as a woman's tear.—
> Enough of this! 'tis half my disease! (II, 383).

As this shows, Burns is very far from tranquil; he knows it, and indeed despises himself; but the disguise must be worn to the last.

For all the humour and wit, the overwhelming note of the letters is a black one. Burns was only twenty-eight when he wrote, 'The great misfortune of my life was, never to have AN AIM' (I, 139). (Here there are distinct echoes of Tristram, who has an aim but appears to fail quite spectacularly in his attempts to realise it.) A year later Burns wrote of 'gloomy conjectures in the dark vista of Futurity—consciousness of my own inability for the struggle of the world' (I, 305). In February 1789 he admitted to Mrs Dunlop, 'I am here more unhappy than I ever experienced before in Edinr.' (I, 378). To the same lady he wrote in October 1792, 'Alas, Madam! who would wish for many years? What is it but to drag existence until our joys gradually expire, and leave us in a night of misery' (II, 155). Early in the following year he was conceding to Thomson, 'It is impossible, at least I feel it in my stinted powers, to be always original, entertaining & witty' (II, 186). In respect of the sense of a loss of creative powers, as with regard to a despair of communing and a general feeling of alienation, there are in fact striking similarities between the utterances of Burns and those of Goethe's Werther. For instance, Werther writes, 'Suffice it to say that the source of all misery is within me just as I formerly bore within myself the source of all bliss . . . I suffer much, for I have lost what was my singular joy in life—the sacred, invigorating power with which I could create worlds around me', and, 'Thus I mock my pain. Were I really to let myself go, a whole litany of antitheses would be the result.'[37]

For the purpose of identifying the similarities and differences between Burns and Sterne, Edwin Muir's essay on Sterne is invaluable. Muir wrote of Sterne,

> By appearing only as his imaginative portrait in Tristram Shandy, he renounces
> the luxury of being himself; he never claims the reader's sympathies in the
> touching role of a human being. He is never a man, a gentleman, a husband, a
> father, a citizen, a clergymen. He is continuously encased in motley, and painted
> and wigged; every gesture and intonation is stylised; and Laurence Sterne is
> resolved into an imaginative sublimation of himself.

Such resolution of self into imaginative sublimation of self is what Burns in part attempted in his letters. Did he succeed, and with what results? The experience of Sterne helps towards providing an answer. In Sterne's case, says Muir,

> It not only enables us to do things which, with our own features presented to
> the world, we would not permit ourselves to do, or dare not do; it not only gives

us licence to be irresponsible, undignified, outspoken: it sets free in us a new personality with a suppleness and daring of movement which seems to belong to a dream world.[38]

With Sterne this is enlivening and liberating, and it involves the comic held in balance with the tragic. In Burns that balance is disturbed, and the dream becomes nightmare; not simply because his reality has its nightmarish aspects, but because of the inability ever to shed the masks. It is hard to decide whether it is the case with Burns that actuality and rôles fuse inseparably, or that actuality and version of actuality diverge irrecoverably. Either way, the result was anything but liberating.

Perhaps it was inevitable that the compulsive use of voice—so effective in the poems—with its concomitant emphasis on reductive vision, should come, in the letters, to reflect the overall limiting effect on the mind of the writer. The total effect of the habitual use of reductive *personae* must be to reduce— unless an alternative vision is offered. Burns could offer no such alternative. And perhaps the reason is not just in his own personality and circumstances but in the resistance of Scottish values to Romantic (as distinct from sentimental) vision and ideals. Calvinism, which was arraigned, by virtue of its discouragement of drama, for diverting Burns's dramatic energies into self-dramatisation, is now doubly villain. By stressing man's flawed nature and the predetermination of human behaviour, Calvinism positively encourages a quasi-diabolism.

Against this background may be viewed such comments of Burns as this:

> By the by, there is nothing in the whole frame of man which seems to me so unaccountable as that thing called conscience. Had the troublesome yelping cur powers efficient to prevent a mischief, he might be of use; but, at the beginning of the business, his feeble efforts are to the workings of passion as the infant frosts of an autumnal morning to the unclouded fervour of the rising sun: and no sooner are the tumultuous doings of the wicked deed over, than, amidst the bitter native consequences of folly, in the very vortex of our horrors, up starts conscience and harrows us with the feelings of the damned. (I, 393)

And to Clarinda he exclaimed, 'How wretched is the condition of one who is haunted with conscious guilt, and trembling under the idea of dreaded Vengeance!' (I, 225).

In this light too may be seen the origins of his fascination with Satan. To Mrs Dunlop he stated his resolve 'to study the sentiments of a very respectable Personage, Milton's Satan—"Hail horrors! hail, infernal world"!' (I, 108). Revealingly, he cites the same to convey his response to the behaviour of the Armour family (I, 121). Soon he was informing Nicol,

> I have bought a pocket Milton which I carry perpetually about with me, in order to study the sentiments—the dauntless magnanimity; the intrepid unyielding independance; the desperate daring, and noble defiance of hardship, in that great Personage, Satan. (I, 123)

He proceeds to give an account of his own situation in a way that suggests a need to identify with Satan. A little later he was to tell Mrs McLehose, 'My favorite feature in Milton's Satan is, his manly fortitude in supporting what cannot be remedied—in short, the wild broken fragments of a noble, exalted mind in ruins' (I, 198).

The basis of the attraction begins to become evident: Satan conforms to one of Burns's sentimental images of himself. Thus, on one occasion, he wrote to Mrs Riddell 'from the regions of Hell, amid the horrors of the damned' (II, 271); and later to the same lady:

> No! if I must write, let it be Sedition, or Blasphemy, or something else that begins with a B, so that I may grin with the grin of iniquity, and rejoice with the rejoicing of an apostate Angel.
>
> > —'All good to me is lost;
> > Evil, be thou my good!' (II, 382)

To Alexander Cunningham he described his life thus: 'The resemblance that hits my fancy best is, that poor, blackguard Miscreant, Satan, who, as Holy Writ tells us, roams about like a roaring lion, seeking, *searching*, whom he may devour' (II, 44). Burns sought, and devoured, alternative selves. In this there is a marked similarity with Byron. The comments of T S Eliot are acutely relevant to Burns. Having noted both that Byron's 'peculiar diabolism, his delight in posing as a damned creature' is related to his 'Scottish antecedence', Eliot continues,

> The romantic conception of Milton's Satan is semi-Promethean, and also contemplates Pride as a *virtue*. It would be difficult to say whether Byron was a proud man, or a man who liked to pose as a proud man . . . His sense of damnation was also mitigated by a touch of unreality: to a man so occupied with himself and with the figure he was cutting nothing outside could be altogether real.[39]

'Nothing outside could be altogether real'—why this should be so true of Scottish men of letters in that period is difficult to determine. *Something* disrupted the balance of Scottish values in the course of the eighteenth century. Something distorted the Scottish ego. Something greatly exacerbated inherent tendencies to fantasy and self-drama. Probably it was a composite, but the extent to which, respectively, Calvinism, the after-effects of the Union, and the transient pre-eminence of Scotland as purveyor of the needs of European sentimental primitivism, contributed to this is impossible to determine with certainty. Undeniably, Burns was a prominent exemplar of its effects.

If Burns admires the Devil as both hero and comedian, it is precisely because this is how he sees himself. In this may lie the reason for much of Burns's contemporary appeal beyond his own country. Scotland by-passed Romantic idealism and the traumas resultant from its disintegration, and in the later eighteenth century headed directly, though unwittingly, for that condition of alienation which now so characterises the literature of Western man. There is, undeniably, much to admire in this, Burns's account of his aspirations:

> It [is] ever my opinion that the great, unhappy mistakes and blunders, both in a rational and religious point of view, of which we see thousands daily guilty, are owing to their ignorance, or mistaken notions of themselves.—To know myself had been all along my constant study.—I weighed myself alone; I balanced myself with others; I watched every means of information how much ground I occupied both as a Man and as a Poet: I studied assiduously Nature's DESIGN where she seem'd to have intended the various LIGHTS and SHADES in my character. (i, 144)

Self-knowledge, however, seemed invariably accompanied by incapacity to act upon it, unless through *persona*, to the point that one wonders if the claims to self-knowledge were not in themselves the utterances of a *persona*.

The use of *persona* ultimately enslaved Burns. The ironic mask became so compulsive that he ceased—irony of ironies, given the claims for self-knowledge—to recognise it as such. Such irony may well have been endemic within Scottish values, but it also helps account for Burns's contemporary appeal. Part of Burns's appeal to the twentieth century   masks, and ironic use of voice—originates in what was to help to reduce him to a multi-faceted, even schizoid, personality. It is in precisely this respect that Burns was to encounter what Muir, writing of Sterne, calls 'the inevitability of a maze'.[40] This is the inevitability of the multiple surrogate selves of modern man.

Muir writes feelingly that 'for a Scotsman to see Burns simply as a poet is almost impossible . . . He is more a personage to us than a poet, more a figurehead than a personage, and more a myth than a figurehead.' Around Burns's diffusion of self into rôles there is a singular irony, given that he has come to have this significance for Scotland. Personally chameleon, he has become, nationally, static, a figurehead. Muir continues,

> He is a myth evolved by the popular imagination, a communal poetic creation, a Protean figure; we can all shape him to our own likeness, for a myth is endlessly adaptable; so that to the respectable this secondary Burns is a decent man; to the Rabelaisian, bawdy . . . He has the power of making any Scotsman, whether generous or canny, sentimental or prosaic, religious or profane, more wholeheartedly himself than he could have been without assistance; and in that way perhaps more human.[41]

Can it be that Burns, either unwittingly or else responsive to that popular imagination and its needs, assisted in the creation of the figure that is so Protean? Is it the case that this secondary Burns (in fact, these secondary Burnses) came into contention with, and finally overcame, the primary one? If so, it is poignantly ironic that, in having the power to make 'any Scotsman more wholeheartedly himself', Burns paid the price of surrendering that very capacity in himself.

Catherine Carswell wrote of Burns that 'there was in his fate a mingling of the tragic and the typical', and Muir saw him as 'a man indeed more really, more universally ordinary than any mere ordinary man could ever hope to be'.[42] Perhaps the corollary is that this is what is now the universally ordinary (which is also tragic)—the sacrifice of the self to rôles or images. For Muir, Burns is 'an object-lesson in what poetic popularity means'.[43] Auden has noted in the twentieth century an ever-widening gap between poet and readership.[44] Perhaps this is inevitable, unless the poet projects selves instead of self. Here, then, is the explanation for Catherine Carswell's observing that

> Had the still-earlier poetry of the *makars* . . . which was European as well as Scottish, continued its line down to Burns's day, Burns might have been, in a sense in which he is not now, a European poet. The extraordinary thing is that, as things are, he ranks as a world poet.[45]

'As things are', in a relativistic world, the emphatic bluff on the most fragile of bases is the best that man can achieve; hence the appeal of the *persona*. 'To lack sympathy with Burns', then, as Mrs Carswell said, 'is to lack sympathy with mankind.' For Burns, as for Sterne, the impulse of wit is, given man's condition, the last remaining assertion of self, but it takes Burns away from self into rôles and leaves him, irrecoverably, there.

Conclusion

The older, native Scottish literary tradition was characterised by its expression of what Edwin Muir termed a 'simple vision of life'. In 'A Note on the Ballads' Muir claimed,

> What distinguishes the Scottish peasantry is not only its cradling in the dialect, but a whole view of life, a view of life intensely simple on certain great, human things, but naturalistic, perhaps in a certain sense materialistic. This simple vision of life, of life as a thing of sin and pleasure, passing, but passing with an intense vividness as of a flame, before something eternal, is the greatest thing which Scotland has given to the literature of the world. Everything which obscures the clearness of this vision, making it less simple than itself when it is most simple, is antagonistic to the Scottish genius.[1]

Something of that 'simple vision of life' is there at times in Smollett and in Fergusson, and an element of it survives in such of Burns's poems as 'The Holy Fair' and 'Love and Liberty'. But by the time of Burns rôle-playing and projection of self-images had clouded that clarity of vision. Muir notes that 'even in Burns's songs for men the voice was not often Burns's; it was generally that of the ideal Scots peasant who is one of his chief creations'.[2] What characterises Scottish writing from the mid eighteenth century is the inability to feel whole and the compensatory need to project alternative selves. In fact, it is a feature of Scottish cultural life in general. While surveying in the Cairngorms, Robert Robinson, the eminent architect and landscape-gardener, dressed up in Ossianic costume. At Kinrara the Duchess of Gordon played at being a Highland Marie Antoinette.[3] The recent biography of Thomas Muir of Huntershill suggests that underlying the behaviour of the leading Scottish libertarian and democrat was an amalgam of radical idealism and a compulsion to rôle-playing and the grand gesture.[4]

It is precisely the 'legend-creating power' of the Scottish mind that has, according to Muir, much to do with 'the problem of Scotland'. He observes, 'Scotland's past is a romantic legend, its present a sordid reality. Between these two things there is no organic relation: the one is fiction, the other is real life.'[5] To a large extent this can be explained in terms of the fact that the post-Union crisis of identity seemed to have been solved, at least temporarily, by Scotland's meeting the requirements of the vogue of primitivist feeling. The assumption of the voice of allegedly naïve and natural feeling by Scottish writers in response to European primitivism accelerated the process of frag-mentation of the Scottish personality. This was well under way before the effects of Romantic idealism could begin to make themselves felt. As a result, the redemptive or healing power of Romanticism was powerless to effect any reintegration of the Scottish personality. Furthermore, the assumption by Scottish writers of the voice of feeling was a positive inducement to sentimentality.

To the period of Macpherson's success we owe our subsequent distorted narcissism. Scotland failed to progress beyond the vogue of sentiment to the realm of Romantic feeling in its fullest development. Tom Nairn noted that

> Elsewhere, the revelation of the romantic past and the soul of the people informed some real future—in the Scottish limbo, they *were* the nation's reality. Romanticism provided—as the Enlightenment could not, for all its brilliance—a surrogate identity.[6]

In Scotland the progress to high Romanticism was checked; it remained at the stage of the sentimental, and informed thereafter the expression of the Scottish identity.

The reasons for this are several. Most obvious, perhaps, are that complacency which is engendered by unexpected and widespread success, and the linguistic duality and 'dissociation of sensibility' on which commentators have placed much of the onus for Scotland's stunted literary growth. However there are other, major, reasons which may be related to a tension at the heart of the eighteenth-century Scottish experience. This is the tension between, on the one hand, the energy of the Scottish Enlightenment and the pace of its developments, and, on the other, the persistence of deep-rooted, traditional Scottish values, largely Calvinist in origin.

One of the most significant differences between the Scottish situation and that of the rest of Europe lay in the nature and the speed of the shift of emphasis away from rationalism and towards sentiment. In Europe this was a cumulative process through the century, whereas in Scotland the reorientation was extremely rapid. Perhaps, indeed, it was not change at all: arguably the European movement of values elicited a co-existence, a tension, of rationalism and sentiment which was innate within the Scottish value-system. Paradoxically, this process of catalysis served to drive these elements to extremes and precipitate their almost separate expression: the rationalist spirit fostered philosophical, social, economic and historical investigation, while the sentimental found refuge in imaginative literature where it had to learn to live with existing lyric and reductive strains. Then, and thenceforth, Scotland experienced division of self. Ironically, the general Enlightenment concern with the situation of man in society was confronted by a critical test-case in the problem—hitherto unsolved—of Scottish identity, a problem which the Enlightenment itself had done much to exacerbate.

One of the obstacles to the progress of Romanticism in Scotland was the fact that the Scottish tradition of community evoked an instant and instinctive suspicion of what appeared to be the Romantic emphasis on the individual (and a failure to appreciate that in Romantic thought knowledge of self was the pre-requisite to knowledge of world). Noting the moral primacy of community in Scottish fiction, Francis Russell Hart comments,

> It is implied that true community nurtures genuine individuality . . . a denial of community is a threat to personal integrity. Idolatrous self-hood destroys community.[7]

The point is that 'idolatrous self-hood' is precisely what Scotland, though no longer a nation, practised on a national level. This militated against genuine individuality. Fear of Romantic individualism—a fear unfounded but understandable, given the cultural and religious background—made Scotland resist both the Rousseauistic concern with the self and, later, what Keats designated the 'Wordsworthian or egotistical sublime'.[8] A precondition of the existence of the latter is that self, however complex, is at one with itself. This has never been the Scottish experience. The promptings of Calvinism in its Scottish form ensured the prolonged existence of an almost medieval sense of community within the Scottish value-system. In the second half of the eighteenth century the Scottish writer was caught between the Scylla of the reductivist and anti-individualist strains in the Presbyterian tradition and the Charybdis of the false individualism which the élitist notions of taste and sensibility promoted. In Burns one sees the strain between individualism and the enduring corporate sense. Again it has to be stressed that the rôle of Calvinism is ambivalent: from it derives the bias of Scottish Enlightenment activity towards the moral problems of man in society; but, equally, its influence made for immense difficulties for the creative imagination. In the Scottish situation what scope could there be for (as George Steiner remarks of Rousseau and the Romantics) 'placing the ego at the centre of the intelligible world'?[9] Could any Scot have written as Schiller did to von Humboldt: 'After all, we are both idealists, and should be ashamed to have it said that the material world formed us, instead of being formed by us'?

Scotland remained largely impervious to the central Romantic tenet which laid down both that knowledge of self as a total, complex, but ultimately integrated entity was a pre-requisite to relating beyond self to society, and that that second stage—the relating of self to world—must follow. Noting that one of the most remarkable features of the early Romantics is the homogeneous tone of both poetry and prose, John Bayley has offered the view that the real beneficiaries of Romanticism were the nineteenth-century novelists in that they proceeded to deal with the most important question raised by the Romantic movement—'the relationship between the individual imagination and the complications of society'.[10] It is in exactly this area that Scottish literature is most deficient. (A case might be made for Galt and, possibly, Stevenson's *Weir of Hermiston*, but against these have to be set the sentimentalising of the kailyard.)

Romanticism encountered another major obstacle in Scotland. For Morse Peckham, Romanticism represents 'a sharp break with the rationalising *and* sentimentalising Enlightenment, expressed in a number of works dramatising spiritual death and rebirth' (my italics).[11] Scotland did not experience that break. And, for all the influence of religion on Scottish values, where are our dramatisations of spiritual death and birth? Here is probably the greatest obstacle to the progress of Romanticism in Scotland: the Calvinist emphasis on man's flawed nature and the predetermination of human life is inimical to Romantic idealism, and in particular to its belief that man is redeemable and perfectible in terms of his individual creative labour (as against adherence to a code of prescribed, functional conduct). Calvinism prevented any Scottish writer from sharing in the Romantic vision of the redemptive function of the artist.

The nature of the Scottish Calvinist view of man's condition suggests a strong affinity with 'tragedy of fate', as exemplified in the ancient Greek tragedies. Of the Romantic redemptive mythology that can be found in Coleridge, Goethe, Hugo, and Wagner, George Steiner observes,

> (it) may have social and psychological merit, freeing the spirit from the black forebodings of Calvinism. But one thing is clear: such a view of the human condition is radically optimistic. It cannot engender any natural form of tragic drama. The romantic vision of life is non-tragic.[12]

Scotland resisted the genuinely Romantic vision; Scotland's values would seem to offer a sound bedrock for what Steiner opposes to Romanticism, namely 'a tragic sense of life'. Yet Scotland failed to develop any tradition of tragedy. Thus one of Scotland's main functions in the whole movement towards feeling was as a source of inspiration to the English and German Romantics. (Most readily one thinks of Schiller's *Maria Stuart*, which, for George Steiner, 'is, with *Boris Godunov*, the one instance in which romanticism rose fully to the occasion of tragedy'.)[13]

The reasons for Scotland's failure to produce great tragedy are not hard to find. If the egotistical sublime was beyond the reach of the divided self, so too was 'negative capability' which, in terms of drama, Keats found exemplified in Shakespeare's 'innate universality'.[14] Furthermore, for all the liberalising which Hutcheson and the circle of Hume initiated, the effects of centuries of religious hostility to drama could not be shaken off readily. When, eventually, conditions were right for nurturing Scottish drama Scotland felt deeply the lack of any basis or guidance in a native dramatic tradition; hence the fixedly retrospective vision of the *literati* when they sought criteria for the production of imaginative literature which would prove to Europe that their achievements were not confined to philosophy and the embryo social sciences.

Romanticism was identified by Jacques Barzun as part of 'the great revolution which drew the intellect of Europe . . . from the expectation and desire of fixity into the desire and expectation of change'.[15] One of the most poignant ironies of Scottish cultural history is that, at precisely the time when Scotland had much to offer Romanticism and even more to gain from it, her cultural arbiters had, by reason of the national crisis of identity and the language duality, to have recourse to the apparent stability and authority of the moribund neo-classical example. Thus Scotland gave to Romanticism much more than her nature and her situation allowed her to take. The sublimity of the

Highland landscapes; the finer feelings exemplified in the Ossian poems; the example of the life and work of Burns—all of these helped inspire the English and European Romantics. But the Scottish version of Romanticism is rarely free from self-consciousness or fragmentation. Beattie's *The Minstrel; or The Progress of Genius*, for instance, anticipates Wordsworth in respect of its concern with the growth of poetic genius; the importance of solitude; the responsiveness to the sublime; an awareness of the existence of a supreme energy in nature; and a suggestion of the transcendent effect of nature upon the soul. However such intimations are interrupted by rather trite pastoral descriptions, and the harping upon melancholy and striking of the note of pity recur to an extent far beyond anything in Wordsworth.

Partly of her own doing and partly as a result of a virtually inevitable combination of circumstances, Scotland failed to experience Romanticism in its fullest and purest forms. Such are the paradoxes that inform the situation of the eighteenth-century Scottish writer that it is tempting to suggest that the Scot of that century (and since) has been somehow programmed for, at best, an occasionally-creative tension of opposites, or, more regularly, a conflict or limiting deadlock of such elements. Denied the fruits of Romantic idealism, the Scot became the fore-runner of modern alienated man. Mac-Diarmid wrote that 'the whole impression of Scottish politics is like that of a man dominated by a sort of nightmare he cannot shake off. He would fain get back to his true self—but he cannot move'.[16] The relevance of this extends beyond politics to culture. Like the literature of alienation of the twentieth century, that of Scotland has been characterised by multiple voices, voices juxtaposed and often contradictory but originating from the one source. Burns epitomises this mingling of contraries or, in his terms, 'intermingledoms'.[17]

From Scott to James Kennaway the way of Scottish literature is strewn with split or multiple personalities. The prime example is Scott, with his evasion of the present or the immediate past; his dualities—orthodox Augustan and lover of the medieval world of the ballads, loyal Unionist and sentimental Jacobite; and his expressions of the divisions within himself in terms of his characters. For example, the hero of *Rob Roy* is the bland Francis Osbaldistone; the real focus of interest for Scott was Rob Roy himself, as this exclamation by Scott in his introduction shows: 'a character like his, blending the wild virtues, the subtle policy, and the unrestrained licence of an American Indian, was flourishing in Scotland during the Augustan life of Queen Anne and George I'.[18] Yet the Robin Hood who was active within forty miles of Glasgow has to come to terms with the nature of the future: he sees no possibility of his sons following his example in their own country. It is Glasgow's son, the Lowland opportunist, Bailie Nicol Jarvie, with his quaint speech and ways habitually a figure of fun, who exploits the present and inherits the future. For David Daiches this is the significant point of *Rob Roy*—'the necessity of sacrificing heroism to prudence, even though heroism is so much more attractive'.[19] Within Scott himself these qualities were to cohabit uneasily. Muir put the point more strongly when he claimed of Scott, 'It might be said that one side of him grew by a sort of blackmail on the other.'[20] This might serve to describe a whole host of Scottish writers. Stevenson, with his self-dedication to style and his eschewing of realism in favour of romance, adventure, and fantasy for so much of his career, springs most readily to mind. It is no accident that it was he who created the definitive version of the split personality and in so doing introduced into the language the term that is now synonymous with that condition—'Jekyll and Hyde'.

Irony, juxtaposition, multiple voices, habitual counterpointing—these are characteristic of Scottish culture over the past two centuries to an extent that distinguishes the Scottish among the cultures of Europe; and they derive from, and express, the ongoing crisis of identity. In the 1920s MacDiarmid visualised the turning of the 'Caledonian Antisyzygy' to good account in the development in Scottish music of 'a new technique, at once completely modern yet intimately related to the whole history of Scots psychology'.[21] That promise was not fulfilled. That psychology is unlikely to change. The best that literature can hope to do is to present it as it is.

That psychology was sufficient to resist Romanticism, or, where it received it, to subject it to distortion. It can hardly be accidental that, of the major Romantics, it was Byron, half-Scottish, who exemplified the crisis of Romanticism. In Byron is to be seen the outcome of Romantic idealism's recoiling from itself—Romantic irony leading to self-mockery and self-negation. And here again the Scottish propensity to projection is a major factor. Rightly I believe, Muir has claimed that Byron 'was not nearly so bad as he made himself out . . . (he) preferred to paint this weak good-nature as something like villainy, and considered it better to be thought wicked than feeble-willed'.[22]

For David Daiches the diverse and considerable achievements of the Scottish Enlightenment 'do not add up to the manifestation of a national culture'.[23] This is to presuppose as norm an ideal of an integrated and unified national culture. Need a culture, to be national, be thus unified? May not the Scottish Enlightenment be the manifestation of a dividing or divided culture? Is it perhaps the case that the division that was inherent within the Scottish personality and its literature was aggravated by the events of the eighteenth century and became predominant? There is, regrettably, more than a grain of truth in Muir's observation, 'Surveying English literature, one would say that the English are a people to whom the things which united them are of more importance than the things which divide them; and surveying Scottish literature, one would come to the exactly opposite conclusion.'[24]

In the eighteenth century Scottish culture experienced what was later to be the fate of several other national cultures—absorption within a larger cultural entity (at present, for instance, one wonders if the Greek alphabet will survive in use in its home-land into the twenty-first century). In such situations are sentimentality, nostalgia, and fantasy the standard responses? It is tempting to suggest that as the crisis of identity in eighteenth-century Scotland prompted sentimental nationalism and the creation of an alternative past so the contemporary vogue of science-fiction and space fantasy are our reaction to the prospect of the holocaust.

If, as Lionel Trilling has claimed,[25] uncertainty about the reality of self is one of the hallmarks of modern man, then from the eighteenth century the

Scot has been decidedly modern. Uncertainty about self induces a retreat into the mind, and from there one rebuilds the reality 'out there'. There are similarities between Scottish writers of the eighteenth century and the protean men of recent literature such as Bellow's Herzog and Augie March. And one of the great novels of our century, Malcolm Lowry's *Under the Volcano*, exemplifies the thesis which Lowry found expressed in Jose Ortega y Gasset's *Towards a History of Philosophy*—'man is a sort of novelist of himself'.[26] This line of thought can be traced back to David Hume. For Hume, "Tis certain there is no question in philosophy more abstruse than that concerning identity, and the nature of the uniting principle, which constitutes a person.'[27]

He sees the mind as

> a kind of theatre, where several perceptions successively make their appearance; pass, re-pass, glide away, and mingle in an infinite variety of postures and situations. There is properly no *simplicity* in it at one time, nor *identity* in different; whatever natural propension we may have to imagine that simplicity and identity. The comparison of the theatre must not mislead us. They are the successive perceptions only, that constitute the mind.[28]

Noting the despairing words on the subject of identity with which Hume ends the first book of his *Treatise of Human Nature* (1739–40), Ian Ross has pointed out that the fictional parallels are not in the novels of the time such as *Moll Flanders, Tom Jones,* and *Tristram Shandy,* where 'the theme of consciousness is worked out in richly satisfying ways',[29] but rather in Dostoevsky's 'underground man' or Sartre's Roquentin. Yet Ross recognises the fact that 'the mind has a positive rôle in "making" a "single person" of fleeting perceptions is a central doctrine in Hume',[30] and he shows that Hume avoids 'the nausea of the Sartrean hero or the silence of the Beckettian'. But his conclusion, in which he discerns the implications for fiction of Hume's view of identity, reveals clearly the extent to which eighteenth-century Scottish philosophy envisaged the contemporary condition:

> It would seem in the last analysis, that all of us are crypto-philosophers and novelists in our daily lives, forging in our imaginations fables of the self, and endlessly seeking associative links of cause and effect in our relations with other persons and the external world of objects. By the same token, novelists are those among us who can most sensitively distinguish between the fictitious and the factitious in organising fables of the self, and can express with most eloquence the self's negotiations with the world.[31]

'The self's negotiations with the world' have become the problem area for modern man. Sadly, the reality is that many of us, alone in McLuhan's global village, live in the 'real' world which is that of the mind, and there, like the eighteenth-century Scot, we create our legends.

The gulf that separates illusion from reality, ideal from actual, and the terrible disillusionment of the shortfall of experience—all now regarded as aspects of the 'modern' condition—were felt keenly by eighteenth-century

Scots. For instance, Iona was to elicit quite different responses from Johnson and Boswell, as the latter acknowledged:

> But I must own that Icolmkill did not answer my expectations; for they were high, from what I have read of it, and still more from what I had heard and thought of it, from my earliest years. Dr. Johnson said, it came up to his expectations, because he had taken his impression from an account of it subjoined to Sacheverel's History of the Isle of Man, where it is said, there is not much to be seen here.[32]

Likewise, Oxford was for Boswell a bitter disappointment and he wrote, 'I could form no idea of happiness and was vexed at having deprived myself of the venerable ideas which I had of Oxford.'[33] And James Macpherson, Boswell recorded, 'said that to retain our high ideas of anything, we should not see it'.[34] Reality, as Scots have found all too often, has a habit of unsettling illusions.

Notes

INTRODUCTION pp. 1 to 13

1   Robert Burns's *Commonplace Book 1783–1785*, Reproduced in facsimile from the poet's manuscript with transcript and the original introduction and notes of James Cameron Ewing and Davidson Cook. This edition introduced by David Daiches (London: Centaur Press, 1965), p.1.

2   *The Journal of a Tour to the Hebrides with Samuel Johnson LL.D.*, by James Boswell Esq., Everyman edition (London and New York, 1909), p.61.

3   Ibid., pp.93–4.

4   Paul Hazard, *European Thought in the Eighteenth Century* (Harmondsworth, 1965), p.254.

5   Malcolm Chapman has challenged, with some justification, the notion that Scottish culture before the Union was homogeneous (*The Gaelic Vision in Scottish Culture* (London and Montreal, 1979), p.31). Conversely, in *Society and the Lyric: a study of the Song Culture of eighteenth-century Scotland* (Edinburgh, 1979) Thomas Crawford has argued that critical orthodoxy has exaggerated the extent of the division between polite and popular song in the eighteenth century. Recent work by William Donaldson, notably his *Popular Literature in Victorian Scotland* and his edition of William Alexander's *The Laird of Drammochdyle*, represents an interesting counter to the view that the popular tradition withered after the Union of 1707.

6   John Speirs, *The Scots Literary Tradition* (London, 1962), p.64.

7   *Boswell in Holland 1763–1764*, ed Frederick A Pottle (London, 1952), p.53.

8   See *Boswell's London Journal 1762–1763*, First published from the original manuscript prepared for the press, with introduction and notes by Frederick A Pottle (London, 1950), p.77; *The Letters of Robert Burns*, ed J De Lancey Ferguson; second edition ed G Ross Roy (Oxford, 1985), II, pp.268, 378.

9   George Elder Davie, 'Hume, Reid, and the Passion for Ideas', *Edinburgh in the Age of Reason*, ed Douglas Young (Edinburgh, 1967), p.25.

10   *Boswell in Holland*, p.161.

11   David Daiches, *The Paradox of Scottish Culture: the Eighteenth-Century Experience* (London, 1964).

12   *Journal of Tour to Hebrides*, p.34.

13   'Was there a Scottish Literature?', *The Anthenaeum*, 1 August 1919, p.681.

14   *Letters of James Boswell to the Rev W J Temple*, with an introduction by Thomas Seccombe (London, 1908), p.200.

15   *The Works of William Robertson, D.D.*, 12 volumes (London, 1817), III, 197 (*History of Scotland*, Bk. VIII).

16   *The Anecdotes and Egotisms of Henry Mackenzie*, edited with an introduction by Harold W Thompson (London, 1927), p.15.

17   Ibid., p.145.
18   *Mirror*, no. 83; cited Harold W Thompson, *A Scottish Man of Feeling* (London and New York, 1931), p.191.
19   *Poems by Allan Ramsay and Robert Fergusson*, eds Alexander Manson Kinghorn and Alexander Law (Edinburgh and London, 1974), p.xvi.
20   Ibid., p.xiii.
21   See Carol McGuirk, 'Augustan Influences on Allan Ramsay', *Studies in Scottish Literature*, 16, 97–109; John Butt, 'The Revival of Scottish Vernacular Poetry in the Eighteenth Century', *From Sensibility to Romanticism: Essays Presented to Frederick A. Pottle*, eds F W Hilles and Harold Bloom (New York, 1965), pp.219–37.
22   'Summer', *The Seasons*, ed James Sambrook (Oxford, 1981), p.126.
23   M J W Scott, 'Scottish Language in the Poetry of James Thomson', *Neuphilologische Mitteilungen*, 82 (4), 370–85.
24   *The Complete Poetical Works of James Thomson*, edited, with notes, by J Logie Robertson (London, 1908), p.252.
25   *Journal of Tour to Hebrides*, p.212.
26   G S Rousseau, *Tobias Smollett: Essays of Two Decades* (Edinburgh, 1982), pp.4, 7, 8.
27   *Boswell in Holland*, pp.159–60.
28   *The Letters of David Hume*, ed J Y T Grieg (Oxford, 1969), II, 154.
29   Ibid., I, 470.
30   Ibid., II, 258. Hume was in London in the 1760s when anti-Scots feeling, especially as a reaction to the Bute ministry, was at its height (See *Letters*, I, 378, 382–3, 415, 417, 429, 436, 491–2, 497–8, 517, 521; II, 16, 208).
31   *London Journal*, p.63.
32   Ibid., p.145.
33   *Letters to Temple*, pp.159–60.
34   Ibid., p.247.
35   *Letters*, I, 378.
36   Prefatory Note to the Abridgement of the First Common-place Book, *Letters*, II, 126.
37   *Letters*, II, 246.
38   *European Thought in the Eighteenth Century*, p.472.
39   C M Grieve, *Albyn, or Scotland and the Future* (London, 1927), p.49.
40   Jacques Barzun, *Classic, Romantic, and Modern* (New York, 1961), p.91.
41   *The Paradox of Scottish Culture*, p.35.
42   *Letters*, II, 230.
43   Francis Russell Hart, *The Scottish Novel: A Critical Survey* (London, 1978), p.406.
44   *European Thought in the Eighteenth Century*, p.305.
45   *Letters*, I, 195.
46   *Journal of Tour to Hebrides*, p.383.
47   *The Gaelic Vision in Scottish Culture*, p.13.
48   G Gregory Smith, *Scottish Literature: Character and Influence* (London, 1919), p.169.
49   *London Journal*, p.182.
50   'Alternative Poetry: An Oxford Inaugural Lecture', *Encounter* (June, 1974), p.30. For an account of Macpherson's European reception and influence, see J S Smart, *James Macpherson: An Episode in Literature* (London, 1905), pp.11–16.
51   *James Macpherson: An Episode in Literature*, p.86.
52   *Journal of Tour to Hebrides*, p.391.
53   *Letters to Temple*, pp.162–3.

54   David Hume, *Four Dissertations* (New York: Garland, 1970), Facsimile of edition printed for A Millar, London, 1757, II: 'Of the Passions', p.123.
55   Adam Smith, *The Theory of Moral Sentiments*, eds D D Raphael and A L Macfie (Oxford, 1976), pp.48–9.
56   Ibid., p.113.

CHAPTER 1, pp. 14 to 40

1   *The Letters of John Keats*, ed Maurice Buxton Forman (London, 1947), pp.76–7.
2   Here the following observations of Edwin Muir are invaluable: 'There were not many genteel Scottish writers before Scott; there have not been many ungenteel ones since. His gentility can be seen in his *Border Minstrelsy* which he loved and yet could not but Bowdlerize. But the difference he introduced into Scottish poetry can be seen most clearly by comparing his own poems in the ballad form with the old ballads themselves. It is pretty nearly the difference between

> I lighted down my sword to draw
> I hacked him in pieces sma',

and

> "Charge, Chester, charge! On, Stanley, on!"
> Were the last words of Marmion,

the difference between a writer fully conscious that he is dealing with dreadful things and one who must make even carnage pleasing and picturesque' ('Scott and Tradition', *The Modern Scot*, ed J H Whyte [London, 1935], p.120.
3   *The Lives of the Novelists* (London and New York, 1910), p.112.
4   'On Humour', Lectures (1818), *Complete Works of Coleridge*, ed W G T Shedd (New York, 1853), IV, 277. V S Pritchett made almost the same point with reference to Smollett himself, claiming, 'Something is arrested in the growth of his robust mind; as a novelist he remains the portrayer of the outside, rarely able to get away from physical externals or to develop from that starting-point into anything but physical caricature' (*The Living Novel* [London, 1966], pp.20–1.
5   *The Adventures of Peregrine Pickle*, edited with an introduction by James L Clifford (London, 1964), pp.541–2. Editions used are those of the Oxford University Press, i.e. the above and *The Adventures of Roderick Random*, edited with an introduction by Paul-Gabriel Boucé (Oxford, 1979); *The Adventures of Ferdinand Count Fathom*, edited with an introduction by Damian Grant (London, 1971); *The Life and Adventures of Sir Launcelot Greaves*, edited with an introduction by David Evans (London, 1973); *The Expedition of Humphry Clinker*, edited with an introduction by Lewis M Knapp (London, 1966).
6   *A Literary History of Scotland* (London, 1903), p.561.
7   *Lives*, p.110.
8   *The Scots Literary Tradition* (London, 1962), p.68.
9   Martin Foss, *Symbol and Metaphor in Human Experience*, p.143; cited George Kahrl, 'Smollett as Caricaturist', *Tobias Smollett: Bicentennial Essays presented to Lewis M. Knapp*, ed G S Rousseau and P-G Boucé (New York, 1971), p.200.
10   Review of *To Circumjack Cencrastus, Criterion*, X (April, 1931), 518.
11   Compare Burns, whose scathing epigrams on the Earl of Galloway served a therapeutic end.
12   *The Letters of Tobias Smollett*, ed Lewis M Knapp (Oxford, 1970), p.69.

13 *Letters*, ed Knapp, p.140.
14 *Scottish Literature: Character and Influence* (London, 1919), p.15.
15 Cited Gregory Smith, *Scottish Literature*, p.18.
16 *Art and Illusion: A Study in the Psychology of Pictorial Representation* (London, 1959), pp.286, 296.
17 *Table Talk* (London, 1819), pp.448–9.
18 'Smollett's Achievement as a Novelist', *Tobias Smollett*, ed Rousseau and Boucé, p.11.
19 *Scottish Literature*, p.35.
20 *The Scots Literary Tradition*, p.47.
21 *The Living Novel*, p.19.
22 See further Gombrich, *Art and Illusion*, p. 290, for the origins of this practice in the work of the brothers Carracci. This is not to diminish the significance of animal imagery in earlier Scottish literature and the likely influence on Smollett.
23 'On Laughter and Ludicrous Composition', *Essays* (London, 1779), pp.431–2.
24 As John Butt noted, 'in Micklewhimmen he has drawn the first of a type of Scotch lawyer in whom Scott was later to specialize' (*Tobias Smollett*, ed Rousseau and Boucé, p.20). In the dancing-master and his pupil in *HC* may be the inspiration for Galt's MacSkipnish in *Annals of the Parish*.
25 Amongst a gallery of characters with affinities with those of Smollett one thinks of Mr Turveydrop and Prince in relation to the same dancing-master; and the *ménage* of Wemmick and the aged parent in *Great Expectations* may owe something to Trunnion.
26 *Art and Illusion*, pp.295, 301.
27 *Reason and Romanticism* (London, 1926), p.191.
28 *Scottish Literature*, p.20.
29 The following comment of Hugh MacDiarmid is apposite: 'I have always agreed with him [John Davidson] too, that if one has a healthy mind it is wholesome to go from extreme to extreme, just as a hardy Russian plunges out of a boiling bath into the snow' ('John Davidson: Influences and Influence', *Selected Essays* (London, 1969), p.202).
30 See also Matt Bramble's admiration of *chiaro oscuro* (*HC*, p.76).
31 Wittig writes of Dunbar, 'The beautiful and the grotesque dwell side by side in his breast. Both form part of the same undivided world' (*The Scottish Tradition in Literature*, p.73, Edinburgh, 1958).
32 *The Scottish Tradition*, pp.73, 121.
33 Compare the use of similar imagery to scurrilous effect with reference to the future William IV in Burns's 'A Dream', stanza 13.
34 See Galt, *Annals of the Parish*, ed James Kinsley (London, 1967), pp.1, 13, 15 and 21; Burns, 'Elegy on the Departed Year 1788'.
35 *FF*, ed Grant, p.263, n.3.
36 *Letters*, ed Knapp, p.98.
37 Cited Paul Hazard, *European Thought in the Eighteenth Century* (Harmondsworth, 1965), p.319.
38 *The Living Novel*, p.20.
39 *The Scottish Novel: A Critical Survey* (London, 1978), p.15.
40 Similarly, a lengthy attack on London life subsides into 'my letter would swell into a treatise, were I to particularize every cause of offence that fills up the measure of my aversion to this, and every other crowded city' (*HC*, p.123).
41 *Essays*, p.354.
42 *The Scottish Tradition*, p.74.
43 *Lives*, p.99; and see also Lord Woodhouselee, cited Scott, p.85. For examples see letters by Jery (p.8) and Lydia (p.27).

44   *The Triumph of Romanticism* (Columbia, S. Carolina, 1970), p.27.
45   *The Scottish Tradition*, p.121.
46   *Lives*, p.109.
47   *Letters*, ed Knapp, p.124.
48   *FF*, ed Grant, p.xviii.
49   *FF*, ed Grant, p.xiv.
50   *Lives*, p.84.
51   C M Grieve, *Albyn, or Scotland and the Future* (London, 1927), p.22.
52   *Scottish Literature*, pp.36–7.
53   *Lives*, p.110.
54   See, for instance, Thomas Crawford, *Burns* (Edinburgh and London, 1960), p.41.
55   *A Sentimental Journey through France and Italy*, ed Graham Petrie with an intro-
     duction by A Alvarez (Harmondsworth, 1967), p.112.

CHAPTER 2, pp. 41 to 69

1   Larry L Stewart, 'Ossian, Burke, and the "Joy of Grief",' *ELN*, vol. 15 (1977–8),
     no. 1 (Sept. 1977), p.30.
2   Northrop Frye, 'Towards Defining an Age of Sensibility', *ELH*, vol. 23 (1956),
     p.150.
3   References are to *Poems of Ossian*, with an introduction by John MacQueen
     (Edinburgh, 1971). This is a reprint of *The Poems of Ossian, containing the Poetical
     Works of James Macpherson*, with notes and illustrations by Malcolm Laing, in
     two volumes (Edinburgh, 1805).
4   J S Smart, *James Macpherson: An Episode in Literature* (London, 1905), p.30.
5   John MacQueen, *The Enlightenment and Scottish Literature*, vol. I: 'Progress and
     Poetry' (Edinburgh, 1982), p. 93.
6   Cited Smart, pp.7–8.
7   Malcolm Chapman, *The Gaelic Vision in Scottish Culture* (London and Montreal,
     1978), p.29.
8   Adam Smith, *The Theory of Moral Sentiments*, eds D D Raphael and A L Macfie
     (Oxford, 1976), introduction, p.3.
9   Op. cit., p.68.
10   Op. cit., p.11.
11   Op. cit., p.67.
12   *The Works of Allan Ramsay*, eds A M Kinghorn and A Law (Edinburgh and London,
     1970), IV, p.236.
13   David Daiches, *The Paradox of Scottish Culture: The Eighteenth-Century Experience*
     (Oxford, 1964), p.34.
14   Op. cit., p.13.
15   Adam Ferguson, *An Essay on the History of Civil Society* (London and Edinburgh,
     1767), p.280.
16   See Bailey Saunders, *The Life and Letters of James Macpherson* (London and New
     York, 1894), pp.37–9.
17   Jacques Barzun, *Classic, Romantic, and Modern* (New York, 1961), p.39.
18   David Daiches, *Charles Edward Stuart* (London, 1973), p.132.
19   Op. cit., p.23.
20   David Hume, *Essay on the Authenticity of Ossian's Poems*, in *Life and Correspondence
     of David Hume*, ed J Hill Burton (Edinburgh, 1846), p.464; cited Chapman, p.46.

21   Thomas Blackwell, *An Enquiry into the Life and Writings of Homer* (2nd edition) (London, 1736), p.24; cited Chapman, p.33.

22   Hugh Blair, *Critical Dissertation on the Poems of Ossian, Son of Fingal* (2nd edition) (London, 1765); cited Smart, p.87.

23   Op. cit., p.90.

24   Ibid., p.74.

25   Op. cit., p.75.

26   Ibid., p.73.

27   Ibid., p.56.

28   Cited Smart, p.105, n.1.

29   Cited Smart, p.179.

30   Op. cit., p.86.

31   See I, p.60, n.7; p.73, n.28; p.156, n.6.

32   See also I, p.75, nn.30, 31; p.77, nn.34, 35.

33   Matthew Arnold, *The Study of Celtic Literature* (London, 1891), p.128.

34   D M Stuart, ' "Ossian" Macpherson Revisited', *English*, VII (37) (1948), p.17; cited Chapman, p.49.

35   Op. cit., p.91.

36   Even Laing, acknowledged Macpherson's considerable poetic ability, commenting,

>   With a genius for poetry far superior to either (Wilkie or Glover), or perhaps to any contemporary poet, Gray excepted, Macpherson was released even from the rules of versification; and if we may judge from the subjects he had provided, the pretended translator might have produced, each year, an epic poem like an annual novel, had the Temora been equally successful with Fingal. (II, 264)

37   Op. cit., p.85.

38   George Steiner, *The Death of Tragedy* (London, 1961), p.201.

39   Op. cit., p.3.

40   Henry Mackenzie, *Letters to Elizabeth Rose of Kilravock*, ed Horst W Drescher (Edinburgh and London, 1967), p.150. See also *The Anecdotes and Egotisms of Henry Mackenzie 1745–1831*, edited with an introduction by Harold W Thompson (London, 1927), p.246.

41   *Letters*, I, 17.

42   See Saunders, pp.182–7.

43   Op. cit., p.xxi.

44   Op. cit., pp.124–5.

45   'Answer to Some Elegant Verses, Sent by A Friend to the Author, complaining that one of his descriptions was rather too warmly drawn', *Hours of Idleness* (1806), Lord Byron's *Complete Poetical Works*, ed Jerome J McGann (Oxford, 1980), I, 180.

CHAPTER 3, pp. 70 to 96

1   Cited Andrew Hook, *Scotland and America: A Study of Cultural Relations 1750–1835* (Glasgow and London, 1975), p.175.

2   Adam Smith, *Lectures on Rhetoric and Belles Lettres*, edited with an introduction and notes by John M Lothian (London, 1963), p.37.

3   Adam Smith, *The Theory of Moral Sentiments*, eds D D Raphael and A L Macfie (Oxford, 1976), p.124.

4   David Hume, *The History of England from the Invasion of Julius Caesar to the Revolution in 1688* (London, 1824), p.777.
5   William Robertson, *History of Scotland* (1759); *Works* (London, 1825), II, pp.245–6.
6   David Hume, *Essays Literary, Moral, and Political* (London and New York: Routledge, n.d.), p.68.
7   Ibid., pp.160–1.
8   Smith, *LRBL*, p.131.
9   Ibid., p.132.
10   T C Smout, *A History of the Scottish People 1560–1830* (New York, 1969), p.95.
11   Hume, *Essays*, p.119.
12   See Davis D McElroy, *Scotland's Age of Improvement: A Survey of Eighteenth-Century Literary Clubs and Societies* (Pullman, Washington, 1969). Roger L Emerson, 'The Social Composition of Enlightened Scotland: The Select Society of Edinburgh, 1754–1764', *Studies on Voltaire*, vol. 114 (1973).
13   Hume, *Essays*, p.122.
14   Loc. cit.
15   Loc. cit.
16   Hume, *Essays*, p. 79.
17   Loc. cit.
18   Ibid., p.68.
19   Ibid., p.164.
20   *The Correspondence of Adam Smith*, eds Ernest Campbell Mossner and Ian Simpson Ross (Oxford, 1977), p.313.
21   *The Letters of David Hume*, ed J Y T Grieg (Oxford, 1969), II, 214–15. See also *Letters* I, 415, 436; II, 208, 216, 218, 226, 261; and *New Letters of David Hume*, eds Raymond Klibansky and Ernest C Mossner (Oxford, 1969), pp.186, 189, 190, 196, 199.
22   *Letters*, I, 417. See also *Letters*, I, 415, 436.
23   Alexander Carlyle, *Anecdotes and Characters of the Times*, ed James Kinsley (London, 1973), p.265.
24   Cited *LRBL*, ed Lothian, p.xxiv.
25   Ernest C Mossner, *The Life of David Hume* (London, 1954), p.371.
26   Hume, *Essays*, p.79.
27   Smith, *LRBL*, p.1.
28   *Letters*, I, 255. Grieg attests that 'authorities agree that Hume spoke English with a broad Scots accent. He seems to have spoken French with the same accent' (*Letters*, I, 205, n.4).
29   *Letters*, I, 205. Hume's sojourn in France may have compounded the problem. Boswell reports that 'Mr. Johnson said that the structure of David Hume's sentences was quite French' (*Boswell's London Journal 1762–1763*, edited with introduction and notes by Frederick A Pottle (London, 1950), p.313).
30   David Hume, *Four Dissertations* (New York: Garland, 1970) (Facsimile of edition printed for A Millar, London, 1757), p.143.
31   Smith, *LRBL*, p.2.
32   Ibid., p.14.
33   Ibid., p.38.
34   Ibid., pp.16–17.
35   *The Scots Magazine*, XVII (March 1755), 126.
36   'Regulations' published by the Select Society for promoting the reading and speaking of the English language in Scotland; cited Mossner, *Life of Hume*, p.372.
37   Cited *LRBL*, ed Lothian, p.xxxv. Subsequently Sheridan voiced misgivings about

the extent to which the *literati* shared his belief that in propriety of speech lay the nucleus of social improvement. Boswell records,

> He inveighed much against the directors of his English scheme at Edinburgh, as if they thought from the beginning of knocking it on the head, and so had lost an opportunity of improvement and honour to their country (*Boswell's London Journal 1762–63*, with introduction and notes by Frederick A Pottle (London, 1950), p.58).

38 Thomas Crawford, *Society and the Lyric: a study of the Song Culture of eighteenth-century Scotland* (Edinburgh, 1979).
39 Francis Hutcheson, *An Inquiry into the Origins of our Ideas of Beauty and Virtue* (1725), Facsimile editions prepared by Bernhard Fabian (Hildesheim: Georg Olms, 1971), I, p.viii.
40 Ibid., p.66.
41 Smith, *TMS*, p.25.
42 Hume, *Essays*, pp. 10–11.
43 Ibid., p.11.
44 C and M Cowden Clarke, *Recollections of Writers* (London, 1878), p. 156.
45 Hume, *FD*, p.208.
46 Ibid., p.214.
47 Ibid., p.229.
48 Ibid., p.231.
49 Ibid., p.234.
50 Ibid., pp.236–7.
51 Ibid., p.180.
52 Ibid., p.231.
53 Smith, *LRBL*, p.192.
54 Hume, *Essays*, p.61.
55 Aged sixteen, Hume wrote of being 'mightily delighted' with Longinus (*Letters*, I, 11); and to Smith on 12 April 1759 he commended Burke's 'very pretty treatise on the Sublime' (*Letters*, I, 303).
56 Hugh Blair, *Lectures on Rhetoric and Belles Lettres*, with an introductory essay by the Rev. Thomas Dale (London, 1879), p.29.
57 Ibid., p.32; pp.38–9.
58 Cited Mossner, *Life of Hume*, p.366.
59 J H Millar, 'Literary Revival in Scotland after the Union', *The Union of 1707: A Survey of Events*, by various writers (Glasgow, 1907), p.144.
60 Henry Mackenzie, *An Account of the Life and Writings of John Home, Esq.* (Edinburgh, 1822), p.12.
61 Smith, *LRBL*, p.23.
62 Ibid., p.59.
63 Ibid., p.51.
64 This commonsense strain endured in Scottish aesthetics. Kames concludes thus his twenty-fifth chapter, 'Standard of Taste', of *Elements of Criticism*:

> If . . . the standard of taste be thought not yet sufficiently ascertained, there is still one resource in which I put great confidence—the principles that constitute the sensitive part of our nature . . .
> . . . the uniformity of taste here accounted for, is the very thing that in other words is termed the common sense of mankind (Henry Home, Lord Kames, *Elements of Criticism* (1762) with an introduction by Robert Voitle (Hildesheim and New York: Georg Olms Verlag, 1970), III, 373).

In 1763 Thomas Reid proclaimed,

> Taste and Judgment joined together are above all rules whatever. A man will be more profited and succeed better by endeavouring to copy exactly the most eminent and noble examples, than by paying the strictest attention to any rules (cited *LRBL*, ed. Lothian, p.xxx).

And for Hugh Blair, 'true criticism is a liberal and humane art. It is the offspring of good sense and refined taste' (*Lectures*, p.5). Despite this, rules are useful, and Blair lists a considerable number (*Lectures*, p.224).

65 Smith, *LRBL*, p.62.
66 Ibid., p.67.
67 Ibid., p.66.
68 Hume, *History*, pp.592–3.
69 Hume, *FD*, p.206.
70 Hume, *Essays*, p.75.
71 Hume, *Letters*, I, 121.
72 Hume, *Letters*, II, 269.
73 Smith, *TMS*, p.196.
74 Kames, *Elements*, III, 236.
75 G Gregory Smith, *Scottish Literature: Character and Influence* (London, 1919), p.149.
76 See *Letters*, I, 252, 262, 266, 268, 304, 308. Smollett's *Critical Review* (June 1757) and Goldsmith in the *Monthly Review* (July 1757) were strongly critical. On 3 September 1757 Hume wrote, 'Nothing surprizes me more than the Ill Usage which the *Epigoniad* has receiv'd' (*Letters*, I, 266). Blaming its failure on the dependence of critics on booksellers, he was to remark by the end of that month, 'Was ever so much fine versification bestowed on so indifferent a story?' (*Letters*, I, 268). But he continued doggedly to promote the poem, while conceding privately to Smith that it was 'somewhat up-hill work' (*Letters*, I, 304). One of Hume's comments reveals the extent to which literary evaluation was affected by considerations of both class and nationality. Noting that Lord Chesterfield had pronounced Wilkie a great poet, Hume added, 'Wilkie will be very much elevated by praise from an English earl . . . I observe that the greatest rustics are commonly most affected with such circumstances' (*Letters*, I, 308).
77 William Wilkie, *The Epigoniad*, second edition (London: A Millar, 1759).
78 Hume, Letter to the *Critical Review*, April 1759; cited Mossner, *Life of Hume*, p.385.
79 Hume, *Letters*, I, 184.
80 Loc. cit.
81 Hume, *Letters*, I, 195.
82 Ibid., I, 200.
83 Ibid., I, 201.
84 Loc. cit.
85 *Poems by Allan Ramsay and Robert Fergusson*, eds Alexander Manson Kinghorn and Alexander Law (Edinburgh and London, 1974), pp.xxv–xxvi.
86 John Butt, 'The Revival of Vernacular Scottish Poetry in the Eighteenth Century', *From Sensibility to Romanticism: Essays presented to Frederick A. Pottle*, eds F W Hilles and H Bloom (New York, 1965), p.231.
87 *The Poems of Robert Fergusson* (Scottish Text Society), ed Matthew P McDiarmid (Edinburgh, 1956), II, 269.

CHAPTER 4, pp. 97 to 116

1   Ernest C Mossner, *The Life of David Hume* (London, 1954), p.357.
2   Smith, *LRBL*, p.80.
3   Ibid., p.85.
4   Smith, *TMS*, p.12.
5   Ibid., p.21.
6   Ibid., pp.21–2.
7   Smith, *LRBL*, p.118.
8   Ibid., p.107.
9   Hume, *FD*, pp.185–6.
10 Ibid., p.188.
11 Ibid., p.189.
12 Ibid., p.199.
13 Alexander Pope, 'Preface', *Shakespeare: The Critical Heritage*, II (1693–1733), ed Brian Vickers (London and Boston, 1974), p.406.
14 Samuel Johnson, *The Rambler*, eds W J Bate and Albrecht B Strauss (New Haven and London, 1969), *The Yale Edition of the Works of Samuel Johnson*, V, 70.
15 Ibid., pp.66–9.
16 *Johnson on Shakespeare*, ed Arthur Sherbo (New Haven and London, 1968), p.75.
17 Ibid., p.78.
18 Ibid., p.84.
19 William Angus Knight, *Lord Monboddo and Some of his Contemporaries* (London, 1900), p.63.
20 Hume, *History*, p.593.
21 Smith, *LRBL*, p.119.
22 Kames, *Elements*, III, 276.
23 *The Plays of John Home*, edited with an introduction by James S Malek (New York and London, 1980), *Agis*, p.2.
24 Andrew Hook, *Scotland and America 1750–1835* (Glasgow and London, 1975), p.126.
25 Mackenzie, *Life of Home*, p.91.
26 Daiches, *The Paradox of Scottish Culture*, p.83; Alexander Carlyle, *Anecdotes and Characters of the Times*, ed James Kinsley (London, 1973), p.144. See also Kurt Wittig, *The Scottish Tradition in Literature* (Edinburgh and London, 1958), pp.159–60.
27 *The Death of Tragedy*, p.47. Steiner comments (p.49): 'The French language and the French style of life . . . include a range of pomp and grandiloquence which other cultures do not share. French solemnity becomes English pompousness and German rant.'
28 Ibid., p.96.
29 Hume, *Letters*, I, 204.
30 Hume, *Letters*, I, 261.
31 Ibid., I, p.269.
32 John Home, *Douglas*, ed Gerald D Parker (Edinburgh, 1972).
33 For Thomas Gray, Home had 'retrieved the true language of the Stage, which had been lost for these hundred years' (*Correspondence of Thomas Gray*, edited by Paget Toynbee and Leonard Whibley (Oxford, 1935), II, p.515); Mackenzie admired the diction (*Life of Home*, p.95); and Hazlitt noted that 'the style of the poetry is indeed one great charm of this play; it is at once familiar and figurative, neither affectedly old nor ostentatiously new' (*The Complete Works of William Hazlitt* edited by P P Howe (London and Toronto, 1935, IX, 94)).

34   *Johnson on Shakespeare*, p.84.

35   Sir Walter Scott, 'Essay on the Drama', *Miscellaneous Prose Works* (Edinburgh, 1847), I, 610–11, 615–16; George Steiner, *The Death of Tragedy* (London, 1961), p.164.

36   Mackenzie, *Life of Home*, p.96; Hume, *Letters*, I, 215–16.

37   *Life of Home*, p.95.

38   *Douglas*, ed Parker, p.i. This was precisely what the audience of the late eighteenth century wanted. Burns's response is representative: 'The first tragedy I ever saw performed, was Douglas; & Mrs. Henri eternally puts me in mind of the horrors I felt for Lady Randolph's distress' (*Letters*, II, 64). Mackenzie recorded: 'I have a perfect recollection of the strong sensation which Douglas excited . . . I was present at the representation; the applause was enthusiastic; but a better criterion of its merits was the tears of the audience, which the tender part of the drama drew forth unsparingly' (*Life of Home*, p.38).

39   *Life of Home*, p.91.

40   Hugh Blair, *Lectures on Rhetoric and Belles Lettres*, ed Thomas Dale (London, 1879), p.555.

41   The conflict of emotions in Lady Randolph is again evident in the exchange with her son, just prior to the fatal dispute, which offers a fuller version of the honour-versus-life debate (see especially V, 178–88).

42   *Life of Home*, p.116.

43   *Scotland and America 1750–1835*, p.118.

44   It is significant that the chief advocate of the heroic code is Lord Randolph (I, 105–9, 115–20, 140–4; II, 130–4; IV, 125–36); yet his reaction to the final catastrophe is, conspicuously, one of self-concern (V, 258–66, 275–7, 279–80, 297–9).

45   Against the nationalism of the Edinburgh prologue has to be set the pro-Union sentiment expressed in a speech of Lady Randolp (I, 121–39). Such tensions prefigure those in Scott, and *Waverley* in particular.

46   Francis Russell Hart, *The Scottish Novel: A Critical Survey* (London, 1978), p.8.

47   *Life of Home*, pp.5–6. Smollett attests to Home's 'sensibility' (see *The Letters of Tobias Smollett*, ed Lewis M Knapp (Oxford, 1970), p.38).

48   John Home, *The History of the Rebellion in the year 1745* (London, 1802), pp.54–5. For an account of Home's participation in the events of 1745, see Carlyle, *Anecdotes and Characters*, especially pp.58–76.

49   John Ramsay of Ochertyre, *Scotland and Scotsmen in the Eighteenth Century*, ed Alexander Allardyce (Edinburgh and London, 1888), II, 555. See also Mackenzie, *Life of Home*, pp.26, 66–7, 181; *Letters of Hume*, ed Grieg, I, 517–18, II, 307–8.

50   Mackenzie, *Life of Home*, pp.68–9.

51   *Life of Home*, p.63.

52   R George Thomas, 'Lord Bute, John Home and Ossian: Two Letters', *MLR*, 51 (1956), 74–5.

53   Page references are to *The Plays of John Home*, ed Malek.

54   Ibid., pp.xxxiv–xxxv.

55   Robertson Davies, *The Revels History of Drama in English*, VI (1750–1880), (London, 1975), p.154.

CHAPTER 5, pp. 117 to 143

1   *Boswell's London Journal 1762–1763*, with introduction and notes by Frederick A Pottle (London, 1950), p.47. (Hereafter referred to as *LJ*.)

2 *Letters of James Boswell to the Rev W J Temple*, with an introduction by Thomas Seccombe (London, 1908), p.59. (Hereafter *Letters.*)

3 *Boswell in Holland 1763–1764*, ed Frederick A Pottle (London, 1952), p.125. (Hereafter *BH.*)

4 *BH*, p.125.

5 Ibid., p.49.

6 See *BH*, p.175, where Boswell records that he was reading Sterne's letters, 13 March 1764.

7 Cited *Letters*, p.10.

8 *LJ*, p.244.

9 *The Journal of a Tour to the Hebrides with Samuel Johnson LL.D.* by James Boswell, Everyman edition (London and New York, 1909), p.13, n.1. (Hereafter *JTH.*)

10 See, for instance, *LJ*, p.146.

11 For other instances of Boswell's concern with manifest Scottishness, see *LJ*, pp.215, 221, 321–2.

12 See *LJ*, pp.54, 68, 231, 237, 280.

13 See *LJ*, p.94.

14 See also *LJ*, p.181, for the characterisation of himself that he wished his grand-children might read.

15 See *LJ*, pp.130, 240, 270.

16 *Letters of James Boswell*, collected and edited by Chauncey Brewster Tinker (Oxford, 1924), pp.24, 29, 30.

17 See *Letters*, p.198, where Temple is addressed in Johnsonian manner.

18 See *LJ*, p.311.

19 *BH*, p.226.

20 See *BH*, pp.175, 255, 279.

21 *The Journal of a Tour to Corsica; and Memoirs of Pascal Paoli* by James Boswell, Esq., edited with an introduction by Morchard Bishop (London, 1951), p.81. (Hereafter *JTC.*)

22 *Letter of Boswell*, ed Tinker, p.129n.

23 For another instance, see *LJ*, p.140, 'We awaked . . . eighteen shillings.'

24 See also *Letters*, pp.161–2.

25 *Letters of Boswell*, ed Tinker, p.184.

26 Compare his comment on the tour to the Hebrides to the effect that Boswell was 'going over Scotland with a brute' (*Letters*, p.167).

27 *The Life of Samuel Johnson LL.D.*, ed Mowbray Morris, Globe edition (London, 1914), p.197.

28 *Boswell's Column*, Being his Seventy Contributions to 'The London Magazine' under the pseudonym 'The Hypochondriack' from 1777 to 1783 here first printed in Book Form in England, Introduction and Notes by Margery Bailey (London, 1951), p.47. (Hereafter *BC.*)

29 Advertisement to the second edition, 1 July 1793.

30 Cited *BC*, p.xvii.

CHAPTER 6, pp. 144 to 184

1 *The Works of Henry Mackenzie*, in eight volumes (Edinburgh, 1808), VII, 140. References (hereafter following the extract) are to this edition, with the exception of *The Man of Feeling* where the edition used is the Oxford paperback, ed Brian Vickers (London, 1970).

2   Cited Henry Mackenzie, *Letters to Elizabeth Rose of Kilravock*, ed Horst W Drescher (Edinburgh and London, 1967), p.xiv.
3   Ibid., p.210.
4   *The Anecdotes and Egotisms of Henry Mackenzie 1745–1831*, edited with an introduction by Harold W Thomson (London, 1927), p.182.
5   Op. cit., p.x.
6   *Letters*, p.59.
7   Ibid., p.74.
8   Ibid., pp.77–8.
9   Jean-Jacques Rousseau, *Confessions* (Paris, 1826), III, 102; cited A R Humphreys, ' "The Friend of Mankind" ' (1700–60)—An Aspect of Eighteenth-Century Sensibility', *RES*, XXIV, 1948 (no. 95, July), 204.
10 Cited R S Crane, 'Suggestions toward a Genealogy of the "Man of Feeling" ', *ELH*, I, iii (December, 1934), 205.
11 Ibid., pp.219–20.
12 Ibid., p.227.
13 *Theological Works* (1830), II, 205.
14 Op. cit., p.95.
15 Francis Hutcheson, *Concerning Moral Good and Evil* (5th edn 1753), p.113; cited Humphreys, p.211.
16 Cited Harold W Thompson, *A Scottish Man of Feeling* (London and New York, 1931), p.43.
17 Hutcheson, *System of Moral Philosophy* (1755), I, 38; cited Humphreys, p.212.
18 David Hume, *Enquiries concerning the Human Understanding and concerning the Principles of Morals*, ed Selby-Bigge (Oxford, 1902), p.293.
19 Hume, *Essays Moral, Political, and Literary*, eds Green and Grose (London, 1875), Essay XVI, 'The Stoic', i, 208; cited Humphreys, p.214.
20 *Concerning Moral Good and Evil*, p.165.
21 *Enquiries*, p.178.
22 Adam Smith, *The Theory of Moral Sentiments*, eds D D Raphael and A L Macfie (Oxford, 1976), p.15.
23 *Letters*, p.32.
24 See *Letters of Laurence Sterne*, ed Lewis P Curtis (Oxford, 1935), pp.10, 16, 323.
25 *Letters*, p.104.
26 Ibid., p.160.
27 Ibid., pp.83–4.
28 Ibid., p.14. For further examples of Mackenzie projecting a Harley-like self see *Letters*, pp.60, 76.
29 Ibid., pp.18–19.
30 Ibid., p.139.
31 *Anecdotes*, p.186.
32 Ibid., p.190.
33 *Letters*, p.77.
34 Ibid., p.95.
35 *Letters*, p.77.
36 'Tenderness, indeed, in every sense of the word, was his peculiar characteristic; his friends, his domestics, his poor neighbours, all daily experienced his benevolent turn of mind. Indeed, this virtue in him was often carried to such an excess, that it sometimes bordered upon weakness . . .' (Thompson, p.121).
37 *Letters*, p.16.
38 Cited Thompson, p.112.
39 *Letters*, p.41.

40   Ibid., p.27.
41   Ibid., p.18.
42   Ibid., pp.142–3.
43   Ibid., p.54.
44   Ibid., p.29.
45   Ibid., p.39.
46   Ibid., p.37.
47   Ibid., p.29.
48   Ibid., p.28.
49   Ibid., p.37.
50   Ibid., p.36.
51   Loc. cit.
52   Contemporary reviews suggest that Mackenzie had succeeded in that aim. The
     Critical Review, XXX (1771), 482 vouchsafed the opinion that 'by those who
     have feeling hearts, and a true relish for simplicity in writing, many pages of
     this miscellaneous volume will be read with satisfaction'. Mackenzie wrote to
     Elizabeth Rose, 'among your Sex have been many of its's (*sic*) warmest Advocates;
     & I am indebted to them for many a Tear on Behalf of my Friends Harley,
     Edwards, &c.' (*Letters*, p.90).
53   *Letters*, p.60.
54   Ibid., p.25.
55   Joseph Frank writes as follows of Lessing's *Laocoon* (1766):

> For Lessing . . . aesthetic form is not an external arrangement provided by
> a set of traditional rules. Rather, it is the relation between the sensuous
> nature of the art medium and the conditions of human perception. The
> 'natural man' of the eighteenth century was not to be bound by traditional
> political forms but was to create them in accordance with his own nature.
> Similarly, art was to create its own forms out of itself rather than accept
> them ready-made from the practice of the past; and criticism, instead of
> prescribing rules for art, was to explore the necessary laws by which art
> governs itself. No longer was aesthetic form confused with mere externals
> of technique or felt as a strait jacket into which the artist, willy-nilly, had
> to force his creative ideas. Form issued spontaneously from the organization
> of the art work as it presented itself to perception. (*The Widening Gyre: Crisis
> and Mastery in Modern Literature* (New Brunswick, New Jersey, 1963), p.8.)

Mackenzie's experiment with form in *The Man of Feeling* can be seen as part of
this whole Europe-wide movement.
56   *Letters*, p.130.
57   Ibid., pp.141–2.
58   Scott, *Lives of the Novelists*; cited Thompson, p.148.
59   *Account of the German Theatre* (1788); cited Thompson, p.289.
60   Op. cit., p.150.
61   *Anecdotes*, p.183.
62   *Letters*, p.196.
63   Ibid., p.179.
64   Op. cit., p.287.
65   Ibid., p.289.
66   Ibid., p.207.
67   Ibid., p.290.
68   Loc. cit.
69   *Letters*, p.15.

70 Compare Burns's judgment of Mackenzie:

> Still, with all my admiration of McKenzie's writings I do not know if they are the fittest reading for a young Man who is about to set out, as the phrase is, to make his way into life. Do you not think, Madam, that among the few favored of Heaven in the structure of their minds (for such there certainly are) there may be a purity, a tenderness, a dignity, an elegance of Soul, which are of no use, nay, in some degrees absolutely disqualifying for the truly important business of making a man's way into life? (*Letters*, II, p.25).

71 Nicholas Phillipson, 'Hume as Moralist: a Social Historian's Perspective', *Philosophers of the Enlightenment*, ed S C Brown (Brighton, and Atlantic Highlands, N.J., 1979), pp.141–2.
72 *Letters*, p.27.
73 Ibid., p.89.
74 Ibid., p.199.
75 Ibid., p.163.
76 *Anecdotes*, p.102.
77 Op. cit., p.261.
78 Ibid., p.181.
79 Ibid., p.317.
80 John Gibson Lockhart, *Peter's Letters to his Kinsfolk*, ed William Ruddick (Edinburgh, 1977), pp.24 9.
81 *Anecdotes*, pp.23–7.
82 Cited Thompson, p.235.
83 *Letters*, p.41.
84 *Anecdotes*, pp.150–1.
85 Cited Thompson, p.333.

CHAPTER 7, pp. 185 to 218

1 Thomas Crawford, *Burns: A Study of the Poems and Songs* (Edinburgh, 1978), introduction, i.
2 Cited James Kinsley, 'Burns and the Peasantry', *PBA*, LX (1974), p.136.
3 *Letters*, I, p.373.
4 Op. cit., p.104.
5 References are to *The Poems and Songs of Robert Burns*, edited by James Kinsley, 3 vols. (Oxford, 1968). In the case of material deemed dubious or excluded by Kinsley the source is *Poems and Songs of Robert Burns* edited and introduced by James Barke (London and Glasgow, 1955).
6 *The Life and Works of Robert Burns*, ed Robert Chambers, revised by William Wallace, 4 vols. (Edinburgh and London, 1896), I, pp.68–9.
7 *Letters*, I, p.109.
8 *Letters*, I, p.386.
9 Loc. cit.
10 'Character Sketch' in *Dumfries Journal* by 'Candidior' (Maria Riddell), *Robert Burns: The Critical Heritage*, ed Donald A Low (London and Boston, 1974), pp.103–4.
11 *Letters*, I, p.175.
12 *Letters*, II, p.345.
13 *Letters*, I, p.141.
14 Op. cit., p.117.

15 Ibid., p.64.
16 *Letters*, II, pp.23–4; I, pp.334–5, 337; II, pp.165–6, 172, 173–4.
17 Op. cit., p.207.
18 *Letters*, I, p.99.
19 David Daiches, *Robert Burns* (Edinburgh, 1966), p.36.
20 *Letters*, I, p.98.
21 G Scott Wilson, 'Robert Burns: The Image and the Verse-epistles', *The Art of Robert Burns*, ed R D S Jack and Andrew Noble (London and Totowa, New Jersey, 1982), p.139.
22 See also 'Second Epistle to Lapraik', stanza 7: '. . . I shall scribble down some blether/Just clean aff-loof'; and in the third epistle, 'To J. Lapraik' he claims, 'But browster wives an' whisky stills—They are the Muses!'
23 Kinsley, p.136.
24 *Letters*, II, p.104.
25 Op. cit., p.138.
26 Cited Kinsley, p.141.
27 Op. cit., pp.141–2.
28 Op. cit., pp.142–3.
29 E.g. *Letters*, I, pp.24, 35–6, 251.
30 Op. cit., p.73.
31 Ibid., p.70.
32 Op. cit., p.147.
33 Op. cit., p.252.
34 Ibid., p.255.
35 Ibid., p.257.
36 Op. cit., p.228.
37 *Tristram Shandy*, vol. II, ch. 9.
38 *Tom Jones*, bk. 4, ch. 8.
39 Op. cit., p.205.
40 Op. cit., p.150.
41 Op. cit., p.207.
42 Op. cit., p.144.
43 Op. cit., p.152.
44 Ibid., p.150.
45 Op. cit., p.146.
46 The foremost example is 'The Cotter's Saturday Night'. Of it Crawford writes, 'The alternation between Scots and Scots-English is essential to the inner movement of the work: the English lines and diction of the earlier sections look forward to the later heightening and ennobling of reality, while the complete change-over to Scots-English in the fourteenth stanza is the outward and visible sign of a leap from the lowly to the "human sublime"' (*Burns: A Study of the Poems and Songs*, p.181).
    Crawford's is a valiant effort to justify the language duality. However, the view to which he is led—that the linguistic juxtaposition betokens a partially ironic attitude to those who are subsequently the subject and heart of the poem—is not entirely satisfactory.
47 *Letters*, II, pp.29–30.
48 *Letters*, II, p.70. Andrew Hook has examined the contents of six early American anthologies of the work of Scottish poets and has found that 'they all show a marked distrust of poems in the Scottish vernacular'. Burns's 'Man Was Made to Mourn' seems to have been a particular favourite (*Scotland and America: A Study of Cultural Relations 1750–1830* (Glasgow and London, 1975), p.172, n.127).

49   Op. cit., p.23.
50   Ibid., p.13.
51   *Letters*, I, p.17.
52   *Letters*, I, p.367.
53   *Robert Burns's Commonplace Book 1783–1785*, introduced by David Daiches (London, 1965), p.1.
54   *Letters*, I, p.63.
55   *Letters*, I, p.158.
56   *Letters*, I, p.143.
57   *Letters*, I, p.97.
58   Op. cit., p.206.
59   Ibid., p.199.
60   *Letters*, I, p.119.
61   *Letters*, I, pp.389–91.
62   *Letters*, I, p.207.
63   *Letters*, I, p.382.
64   Op. cit., p.88.
65   Ibid., p.199.
66   At home in Ayrshire, Burns had daily before him the truly sublime prospect of the mountains of Arran. Of these he never wrote, choosing instead to find 'charming, wild, romantic scenery' (*Letters*, I, p.370) on the banks of the Afton and finding ruggedness in the Highlands. Visiting Alloway, Keats found this worthy of comment (see *The Letters of John Keats*, ed H B Forman (London, 1895), p.166).
67   *Letters*, II, p.242.
68   *Letters*, II, p.316.
69   Northrop Frye, 'Towards Defining an Age of Sensibility', *ELH* XXIII (1956), p.151.
70   William Montgomerie, *New Judgments: Robert Burns* (Glasgow, 1947), p.79.

CHAPTER 8, pp. 219 to 245

1   J De Lancey Ferguson, 'Some Aspects of the Burns Legend', *Philological Quarterly*, XI, no. 3, July 1932, 264.
2   Thomas Crawford, *Burns: A Study of the Poems and Songs* (Edinburgh and London, 1960), p.xiv.
3   Catherine Carswell, 'Robert Burns (1759–1796)', *From Anne to Victoria: Essays by Various Hands*, ed Bonamy Dobree (London, 1937), p.416.
4   See Crawford, *Burns*, p.91, n.31, for David Sillar's account of Burns's absorption in *Tristram Shandy* during a meal.
5   Cited in *The Letters of Laurence Sterne*, ed Lewis Perry Curtis (Oxford, 1935), p.92, n.9.
6   Compare *Tristram Shandy*, I, ch. 6: '. . . bear with me,—and let me go on, and tell my story my own way.'
7   *T.S.*, I, ch. 5, where Tristram writes: 'I have been the continual sport of what the world calls fortune.' See also *T.S.*, I, ch. 10: 'There is a fatality attends the actions of some men'; III, ch. 8: 'Sport of small accidents, Tristram Shandy! that thou art, and ever will be!'
8   See *T.S.*, V, ch. 19; II, chs. 2–3; II, ch. 6.
9   For further references to hobby-horses, see Burns, *Letters*, I, 345; II, 237; II, 327.

10 Compare *T.S.*, II, ch. 9: 'a little, squat, uncourtly figure of a Dr. Slop.' Burns
    writes of 'one of our members, a little, wise-looking, squat, upright, jabbering
    body of a Taylor' (*Letters*, II, 213). That *Tristram Shandy* was set firmly in Burns's
    mind is confirmed by the appearance in his letters of specific phrases from the
    novel: 'the Chapter of Accidents' (II, 186); 'the Chapter of Chances & Changes'
    (II, 280); 'there is a fatality attends Miss [Peacock's] correspondence and mine'
    (II, 189).
11 Burns writes, 'Now that my first sentence is concluded, I have nothing to do but
    to pray Heaven to help me to another' (I, 462). Tristram claims: 'I begin with
    writing the first sentence—and trusting to Almighty God for the second' (*T.S.*,
    VIII, ch. 2).
12 Kurt Wittig, *The Scottish Tradition in Literature* (Edinburgh, 1958), p.219.
13 For further instances of the comic-epic or mock-sublime, see II, 125, 141–2,
    183–4, 316.
14 Hoxie N Fairchild, *Religious Trends in English Poetry* (New York and London,
    1949), III, p.58.
15 Compare Walter Shandy's concern with the risk of damage to his 'child's head-
    piece' at birth (*T.S.*, III, ch. 16).
16 'Inconsistent soul that man is!—languishing under wounds which he has the
    power to heal!—his whole life a contradiction to his knowledge!—his reason,
    that precious gift of God to him—(instead of pouring in oil), serving but to
    sharpen his sensibilities,—to multiply his pains and render him more melancholy
    and uneasy under them!' (*T.S.*, III, ch. 21). 'What is man, this exalted demigod?
    Doesn't he lack power just when he needs it most? (Goethe, *The Sorrows of Young
    Werther*, translated by Catherine Hutter (New York, 1962), p.99).
17 Edwin Muir, 'Laurence Sterne', *Essays on Literature and Society* (London, 1965),
    p.54.
18 Compare Sterne, *Letters*, p.87: 'Half a word of Encouragement would be enough
    to make me conceive, and bring forth something for the Stage (how good, or
    how bad, is another story).'
19 Op. cit., pp.208, 212.
20 *Works of Lord Byron* (London, 1898), IX, 376–7; cited Ferguson, 'Some Aspects
    of the Burns Legend', p.263.
21 'Character Sketch' in *Dumfries Journal* by 'Candidior' (Maria Riddell), *Robert
    Burns: The Critical Heritage*, ed Donald A Low (London and Boston, 1974), p.102.
22 John C Weston, 'Robert Burns's Satire', *Scottish Literary Journal*, I, no. 2,
    December 1974, p.22.
23 Op. cit., p.215.
24 T S Eliot, 'Byron', *On Poetry and Poets* (London, 1957), p.205.
25 C M Grieve, *Albyn, or Scotland and the Future* (London, 1927), p.22.
26 Op. cit., p.210.
27 Cited Paul Hazard, *European Thought in the Eighteenth Century* (London, 1965),
    p.409.
28 Op. cit., p.49.
29 Ibid., p.53.
30 Op. cit., p.16.
31 Op. cit., pp.42–3.
32 Op. cit., p.50.
33 Op. cit., p.61.
34 Op. cit., p.264.
35 See also *Letters*, II, 220, 224, 264.
36 Morse Peckham, *The Triumph of Romanticism* (Columbia, S. Carolina, 1970),
    pp.54–5.

37   Op. cit., p.95.
38   Op. cit., pp.52–3.
39   Op. cit., pp.194–5.
40   Op. cit., p.56.
41   Edwin Muir, 'Burns and Popular Poetry', *Essays on Literature and Society*, p.58.
42   Op. cit., p.416; op. cit., p. 59.
43   Ibid., p.62.
44   W H Auden, 'The Poet and the City', *Modern Poets on Modern Poetry*, ed James Scully (London, 1966), pp.180–3.
45   Op. cit., p.409.

CONCLUSION pp. 246 to 253

1   Edwin Muir, 'A Note on the Ballads', *Edwin Muir: Uncollected Scottish Criticism*, edited with an introduction by Andrew Noble (London and Totowa, N.J., 1982), p.157).
2   'Robert Burns', *Uncollected Scottish Criticism*, p.185.
3   A A Tait, *The Landscape Garden in Scotland 1735–1835* (Edinburgh, 1980), pp.71, 122.
4   Christina Bewley, *Muir of Huntershill* (Oxford, 1981).
5   'The Problem of Scotland', *Uncollected Scottish Criticism*, p.111.
6   Tom Nairn, 'The Three Dreams of Scottish Nationalism', *Memoirs of a Modern Scotland*, ed Karl Miller (London, 1970), p.39.
7   *The Scottish Novel*, p.401. T C Smout, *A History of the Scottish People 1560–1830* (London, 1969), p.95 stresses the strength of the group-ethic in Scotland as manifested in the kirk-session and the tradition of guild and burgh.
8   *The Letters of John Keats*, ed M B Forman (London, 1947), p.227.
9   George Steiner, *The Death of Tragedy* (London, 1961), p.136.
10   John Bayley, *The Romantic Survival: A Study in Poetic Evolution* (London, 1957), p.15.
11   Morse Peckham, *The Triumph of Romanticism* (Columbia, South Carolina, 1970), p.27.
12   *The Death of Tragedy*, pp.127–8.
13   Ibid., p.181.
14   *Letters*, ed Forman, p.72; C and M Cowden Clarke, *Recollections of Writers* (London, 1878), p.156.
15   Jacques Barzun, 'Romanticism: Definition of a Period', *Magazine of Art*, XLII (Nov. 1949), p.243.
16   *Albyn*, p.68.
17   *Letters*, II, 143.
18   Walter Scott, *Rob Roy* with introductory essay and notes by Andrew Lang (London, 1906), author's introduction, pp.xxvi–xxvii.
19   David Daiches, *A Critical History of English Literature* (London, 1960), II, 845.
20   'Sir Walter Scott (1771–1832)', *Uncollected Scottish Criticism*, p.216.
21   *Albyn*, p.28.
22   'A Romantic Poet', *Uncollected Scottish Criticism*, pp.206–7.
23   *The Paradox of Scottish Culture*, p.75.
24   Edwin Muir, *Scott and Scotland* (London, 1936), p.72.
25   Lionel Trilling, *Beyond Culture* (Harmondsworth, 1967), p.54.

26 *Selected Letters of Malcolm Lowry*, eds Harvey Breit and Margerie Bonner Lowry (London, 1967), p.210.

27 *Treatise of Human Nature*, ed L A Selby, Bigge (Oxford, 1896), pp.189–90.

28 Ibid., p.253.

29 'Philosophy and Fiction: The Challenge of David Hume', *Hume and the Enlightenment*, ed W B Todd (Edinburgh, 1974), p.65.

30 Ibid., p.69.

31 Ibid., p.70.

32 *Journal of Tour to Hebrides*, p.326.

33 *London Journal*, p.246.

34 Ibid., p.249.

Bibliography

PRIMARY SOURCES

Blacklock, Thomas, *Poems on Several Occasions* (Glasgow, 1746)

Blair, Hugh, *Critical Dissertation on the Poems of Ossian, Son of Fingal*, 2nd edn (London, 1765)

——*Lectures on Rhetoric and Belles Lettres*, with an introductory essay by the Rev Thomas Dale (London, 1879)

Boswell, James, *London Journal 1762–1763*, with an introduction and notes by Frederick A Pottle (London, 1950)

——*Boswell in Holland 1763–1764*, ed Frederick A Pottle (London, 1952)

——*The Journal of a Tour to Corsica; and Memoirs of Pascal Paoli*, edited with an introduction by Morchard Bishop (London, 1951)

——*Boswell's Column*, Being his Seventy Contributions to 'The London Magazine' under the pseudonym 'The Hypochondriack' from 1777 to 1783, introduction and notes by Margery Bailey (London, 1951)

——*The Journal of a Tour to the Hebrides with Samuel Johnson LL.D.*, Everyman edition, (London and New York, 1909)

——*The Life of Samuel Johnson LL.D.*, ed Mowbray Morris, Globe edn (London, 1914)

——*Letters of James Boswell to the Rev. W. J. Temple*, with an introduction by Thomas Seccombe (London, 1908)

——*Letters*, collected and edited by Chauncey B Tinker (Oxford, 1924)

Burns, Robert, *Life and Works*, ed Robert Chambers, revised by William Wallace, 4 vols (Edinburgh and London, 1896)

——*Poems and Songs*, edited and introduced by James Barke (London and Glasgow, 1955)

——*The Poems and Songs*, ed James Kinsley, 3 vols (Oxford, 1968)

——*Commonplace Book 1783–1785*, edited with an introduction by David Daiches (London, 1965)

——*Letters*, ed J De Lancey Ferguson; 2nd edn, ed G Ross Roy (Oxford, 1985)

Byron, Lord, *Complete Poetical Works*, ed Jerome J McGann (Oxford, 1980)

Carlyle, Alexander, *Anecdotes and Characters of the Times*, ed James Kinsley (London, 1973)

Ferguson, Adam, *An Essay on the History of Civil Society* (London and Edinburgh, 1767)

Fergusson, Robert, *Poems* (Scottish Text Society), ed Matthew P McDiarmid (Edinburgh, 1956)

Home, John, *Douglas*, ed Gerald D Parker (Edinburgh, 1972)

——*Plays*, edited with an introduction by James S Malek (London and New York, 1980)

——*The History of the Rebellion in the year 1745* (London, 1802)

Hume, David, *Treatise of Human Nature*, ed L A Selby-Bigge (Oxford, 1896)

——*Enquiries concerning the Human Understanding and concerning the Principles of Morals*, ed L A Selby-Bigge (Oxford, 1902)

——*Essays Literary, Moral, and Political* (London and New York: Routledge, n.d.)

——*Four Dissertations* (New York, 1970). Facsimile of edition printed for A Millar (London, 1757)

——*The History of England from the Invasion of Julius Caesar to the Revolution in 1688* (London, 1824)

——*Life and Correspondence of David Hume*, ed J Hill Burton (Edinburgh, 1846)

——*Letters*, ed J Y T Grieg, 2 vols (Oxford, 1969)

——*New Letters of David Hume*, eds Raymond Klibansky and Ernest C Mossner (Oxford, 1969)

Hutcheson, Francis, *An Inquiry into the Origins of our Ideas of Beauty and Virtue* (1725). Facsimile editions prepared by Bernhard Fabian (Hildesheim: Georg Olms, 1971)

——*Concerning Moral Good and Evil*, 5th edn (London, 1753)

——*System of Moral Philosophy* (London, 1755)

Kames, Lord (Henry Home), *Elements of Criticism* (1762), with an introduction by Robert Voitle (Hildesheim and New York: Georg Olms Verlag, 1970)

Mackenzie, Henry, *Works*, in 8 vols (Edinburgh 1808)

——*The Man of Feeling*, edited with an introduction by Brian Vickers (London, 1967)

——*Anecdotes and Egotisms*, edited with an introduction by H W Thompson (London, 1927)

——*Letters to Elizabeth Rose of Kilravock*, ed Horst W Drescher (Edinburgh and London, 1967)

——*An Account of the Life and Writings of John Home, Esq.* (Edinburgh, 1822)

Macpherson, James, *Poems of Ossian*, with an introduction by John MacQueen (Edinburgh, 1971). Reprint of *The Poems of Ossian, containing the Poetical Works of James Macpherson*, with notes and illustrations by Malcolm Laing, 2 vols (Edinburgh, 1805)

——*The Life and Letters of James Macpherson*, by Bailey Saunders (London and New York, 1894)

Ramsay, Allan, *The Ever Green: A Collection of Scots Poems* (Glasgow, 1874)

——*Works*, ed A M Kinghorn and A Law (Edinburgh and London, 1970)

Ramsay, Allan and Fergusson, Robert, *Poems*, ed Alexander Manson Kinghorn and Alexander Law (Edinburgh and London, 1974)

Robertson, William, *Works*, 12 vols (London, 1817)

Scott, Sir Walter, *Rob Roy*, with an introductory essay and notes by Andrew Lang (London, 1906)

Smith, Adam, *Lectures on Rhetoric and Belles Lettres*, edited with an introduction and notes by John M Lothian (London, 1963)

——*The Theory of Moral Sentiments*, edited by D D Raphael and A L Macfie (Oxford, 1976)

——*Correspondence*, eds Ernest Campbell Mossner and Ian Simpson Ross (Oxford, 1977)

Smollett, Tobias, *The Adventures of Roderick Random*, edited with an introduction by Paul-Gabriel Boucé (Oxford, 1979)

——*The Adventures of Peregrine Pickle*, edited with an introduction by James L Clifford (London, 1964)

——*The Adventures of Ferdinand Count Fathom*, edited with an introduction by Damian Grant (London, 1971)

——*The Life and Adventures of Sir Launcelot Greaves*, edited with an introduction by David Evans (London, 1973)

——*The Expedition of Humphry Clinker*, edited with an introduction by Lewis M Knapp (London, 1966)

——*Letters*, ed Lewis M Knapp (Oxford, 1970)

Sterne, Laurence, *Tristam Shandy*, edited with an introduction and notes by Ian Campbell Ross (Oxford, 1983)

——*A Sentimental Journey through France and Italy*, ed Graham Petrie, with an introduction by A Alvarez (Harmondsworth, 1967)

——*Letters*, ed Lewis P Curtis (Oxford, 1935)

Thomson, James, *Complete Poetical Works*, edited, with notes, by J Logie Robertson (London, 1908)

——*The Seasons*, ed James Sambrook (Oxford, 1981)

Wilkie, William, *The Epigoniad*, 2nd edn (London: A Millar, 1759)

SECONDARY SOURCES

(a) *Books*

Arnold, Matthew, *The Study of Celtic Literature* (London, 1891)

Barrow, Isaac, *Theological Works* (London, 1830)

Barzun, Jacques, *Classic, Romantic and Modern* (New York, 1961)

Bayley, John, *The Romantic Survival: A Study in Poetic Evolution* (London, 1957)

Beattie, James, *Essays* (London, 1779)

Bewley, Christina, *Muir of Huntershill* (Oxford, 1981)

Blackwell, Thomas, *An Enquiry into the Life and Writings of Homer*, 2nd edn (London, 1736)

Breit, Harvey and Lowry, Margerie Bonner (eds), *Selected Letters of Malcolm Lowry* (London, 1967)

Brown, S C (ed), *Philosophers of the Enlightenment* (Brighton, and Atlantic Highlands, N.J., 1979)

Chapman, Malcolm, *The Gaelic Vision in Scottish Culture* (London and Montreal, 1979)

Cloyd, E L, *James Burnett, Lord Monboddo* (Oxford, 1972)

Coleridge, Samuel T, 'On Humour', Lectures (1818), *Complete Works of Coleridge*, ed W G T Shedd (New York, 1853), IV

Crawford, Thomas, *Burns: A Study of the Poems and Songs* (Edinburgh, 1965)

——*Society and the Lyric: a study of the Song Culture of eighteenth-century Scotland* (Edinburgh, 1979)

Cowden Clarke, C and M, *Recollections of Writers* (London, 1878)

Daiches, David, *A Critical History of English Literature* (London, 1960)

——*The Paradox of Scottish Culture: the Eighteenth Century Experience* (London, 1964)

——*Robert Burns* (Edinburgh, 1966)

——*Charles Edward Stuart* (London, 1973)

——*Literature and Gentility in Scotland* (Edinburgh, 1982)

Davies, Robertson, *The Revels History of Drama in English*, VI (1750–1880) (London, 1975)

Eliot, T S, *On Poetry and Poets* (London, 1957)

Fairchild, Hoxie N, *Religious Trends in English Poetry* (New York and London, 1949)

Foss, Martin, *Symbol and Metaphor in Human Experience* (Princeton, 1949)

Frank, Joseph, *The Widening Gyre: Crisis and Mastery in Modern Literature* (New Brunswick, N.J., 1963)

Galt, John, *Annals of the Parish*, ed James Kinsley (London, 1967)

Goethe, Johann Wolfgang von, *The Sorrows of Young Werther*, trans Catherine Hutter (New York, 1962)

Gombrich, E H, *Art and Illusion: A Study in the Psychology of Representation* (London, 1959)

Graham, H G, *Scottish Men of Letters in the Eighteenth Century* (London, 1901)

Gray, Thomas, *Correspondence*, eds Paget Toynbee and Leonard Whibley (Oxford, 1935)

Grieve, C M, *Albyn, or Scotland and the Future* (London, 1927)

Hart, Francis Russell, *The Scottish Novel: A Critical Survey* (London, 1978)

Hazard, Paul, *European Thought in the Eighteenth Century* (Harmondsworth, 1965)

Hazlitt, William, *Table Talk* (London, 1819)

——*Complete Works*, ed P P Howe (London and Toronto, 1935)

Hook, Andrew, *Scotland and America: A Study of Cultural Relations 1750–1835* (Glasgow and London, 1975)

Jack, R D S and Noble, Andrew (eds), *The Art of Robert Burns* (London and Totowa, N.J., 1982)

Johnson, Samuel, *Johnson on Shakespeare*, ed Arthur Sherbo (New Haven and London, 1968)

——*The Rambler*, eds W J Bate and Albrecht B Strauss (New Haven and London, 1969), *The Yale Edition of the Works of Samuel Johnson*, V

Keats, John, *Letters*, ed Maurice Buxton Forman (London, 1947)

Knight, William Angus, *Lord Monboddo and Some of his Contemporaries* (London, 1900)

Lehmann, William C, *John Millar of Glasgow* (Cambridge, 1960)

Lockhart, John Gibson, *Peter's Letters to his Kinsfolk*, ed William Ruddick (Edinburgh, 1977)

Low, Donald A (ed), *Robert Burns: The Critical Heritage* (London and Boston, 1974)

MacDiarmid, Hugh, *Selected Essays* (London, 1969)

McElroy, Davis D, *Scotland's Age of Improvement: A Survey of Eighteenth-Century Literary Clubs and Societies* (Washington, 1969)

MacQueen, John, *The Enlightenment and Scottish Literature*, vol. I: 'Progress and Poetry' (Edinburgh, 1982)

Millar, J H, *A Literary History of Scotland* (London, 1903)

Miller, Karl (ed), *Memoirs of a Modern Scotland* (London, 1970)

Montgomerie, William, *New Judgments: Robert Burns* (Glasgow, 1947)

Mossner, Ernest C, *The Life of David Hume* (London, 1954)

Muir, Edwin, *Scott and Scotland* (London, 1936)

——*Essays on Literature and Society* (London, 1965)

——*Uncollected Scottish Criticism*, edited with an introduction by Andrew Noble (London and Totowa, New Jersey, 1982)

Peckham, Morse, *The Triumph of Romanticism* (Columbia, S. Carolina, 1970)

Phillipson, Nicholas T, and Mitchison, Rosalind (ed), *Scotland in the age of Improvement* (Edinburgh, 1970)

Power, William, *Literature and Oatmeal: What Literature has meant to Scotland* (London, 1935)

Pritchett, V S, *The Living Novel* (London, 1966)

Ramsay, of Ochtertyre, John, *Scotland and Scotsmen in the Eighteenth Century*, ed Alexander Allardyce (Edinburgh and London, 1888)

Read, Herbert, *Reason and Romanticism* (London, 1926)

Rousseau, G S, *Tobias Smollett: Essays of Two Decades* (Edinburgh, 1982)

Rousseau, Jean-Jacques, *Confessions* (Paris, 1826)

Scott, Sir Walter, 'Essay on the Drama', *Miscellaneous Prose Works* (Edinburgh, 1847), I.

——*The Lives of the Novelists* (London and New York, 1910)

Smart, J S *James Macpherson: An Episode in Literature* (London, 1905)

Smith, G Gregory, *Scottish Literature: Character and Influence* (London, 1919)

Smout, T C, *A History of the Scottish People 1560–1830* (London, 1969)

Speirs, John, *The Scots Literary Tradition* (London, 1962)

Steiner, George, *The Death of Tragedy* (London, 1961)

Tait, A A, *The Landscape Garden in Scotland 1735–1835* (Edinburgh, 1980)

Thompson, Harold W, *A Scottish Man of Feeling* (London and New York, 1931)

Tobin, Terence, *Plays by Scots 1660–1800* (Iowa, 1974)

Trilling, Lionel, *Beyond Culture* (Harmondsworth, 1967)

Wittig, Kurt, *The Scottish Tradition in Literature* (Edinburgh, 1958)

(b) *Articles*

Auden, W H, 'The Poet and the City', *Modern Poets on Modern Poetry*, ed James Scully (London, 1966), pp.175–92

Bentman, Raymond, 'The Romantic Poets and Critics on Robert Burns', *Texas Studies in Literature and Language*, 6 (1964), 104–18

Butt, John, 'The Revival of Scottish Vernacular Poetry in the Eighteenth Century', *From Sensibility to Romanticism: Essays presented to Frederick A. Pottle*, eds F W Hilles and Harold Bloom (New York, 1965), pp.219–37

Carswell, Catherine, 'Robert Burns (1759–1796)', *From Anne to Victoria: Essays by Various Hands*, ed Bonamy Dobrée (London, 1937), pp.405–21

Crane, R S, 'Suggestions toward a Genealogy of the "Man of Feeling"', *ELH*, I, iii (December, 1934), 205–30

Davie, George Elder, 'Hume, Reid, and the Passion for Ideas', *Edinburgh in the Age of Reason*, ed Douglas Young (Edinburgh, 1967), pp.23–39

Eliot, T S, 'Was there a Scottish Literature?', *The Athenaeum* (1 August 1919), 680–1

Emerson, Roger L, 'The Social Composition of Enlightened Scotland: The Select Society of Edinburgh, 1754–1764', *Studies on Voltaire*, vol. 114 (1973), 291–323

Ferguson, J De Lancey, 'Some Aspects of the Burns Legend', *Philological Quarterly*, XI, no. 3 (July 1932), 263–72

Frye, Northrop, 'Towards Defining an Age of Sensibility', *ELH*, vol. 23 (1956), 144–52

Garrett, Don, 'Hume's Self-Doubts about Personal Identity', *Philosophical Review* 90 (3) (1981), 337–58

Humphreys, A R, ' "The Friend of Mankind" (1700–1760)—An Aspect of Eighteenth-Century Sensibility', *RES*, XXIV, 1948 (no. 95, July), 202–19

Kahrl, George, 'Smollett as Caricaturist', *Tobias Smollett: Bicentennial Essays presented to Lewis M. Knapp*, eds G S Rousseau and P-G Boucé (New York, 1971), pp.169–200

Kinsley, James, 'Burns and the Peasantry', *PBA*, LX (1974), 135–53

McGuirk, Carol, 'Augustan Influences on Allan Ramsay', *Studies in Scottish Literature* (16), 97–109

MacLaine, Allan H, 'Radicalism and Conservatism in Burns's *The Jolly Beggars*', *SSL*, 13 (1978), 125–43

Millar, J H, 'Literary Revival in Scotland after the Union', *The Union of 1707: A Survey of Events*, by various writers (Glasgow, 1907), pp.134–42

Muir, Edwin, 'Scott and Tradition', *Towards a New Scotland*, ed J H Whyte (London, 1935), pp.51–4

Phillipson, Nicholas, 'The Scottish Enlightenment', *The Enlightenment in National Context*, eds Roy Porter and Mikulas Teich (Cambridge, 1981), pp.19–40

Ross, Ian, 'Philosophy and Fiction: The Challenge of David Hume', *Hume and the Enlightenment*, ed W B Todd (Edinburgh, 1974), pp.60–71

Scott, M J W, 'Scottish Language in the Poetry of James Thomson', *Neuphilologische Mitteilungen*, 82 (4), 370–85

Stewart, Larry L, 'Ossian, Burke, and the "Joy of Grief"', *ELN*, vol. 15 (1977–8), no. 1 (Sept. 1977), 29–32

Thomas, R George, 'Lord Bute, John Home and Ossian: Two Letters', *MLR*, 51 (1956), 74–5

Trevor-Roper, Hugh, 'The Scottish Enlightenment', *Studies on Voltaire* 58 (1967), 1635–58

Wain, John, 'Alternative Poetry: An Oxford Inaugural Lecture', *Encounter* (June 1974), pp.26–38

Weston, John C, 'Robert Burns's Satire', *Scottish Literary Journal*, I, no. 2 (December 1974), 15–28

Young, Douglas, 'Scotland and Edinburgh in the eighteenth century', *Studies on Voltaire*, 58 (1967), 1967–90

Index

Addison, Joseph   180
Ainslie, Robert   240
Alexander, Wilhelmina   211, 222
Alienation and multiple voice, Scottish experience of   17, 99, 181, 218–9, 244–5, 251, 252–4
American Indian   44, 47, 150, 169
Aristotle   55, 62, 83, 101, 102, 107, 111
Armour, Jean   222, 233, 234
Arnold, Matthew   62–3
Auchinleck, Lord   11, 124, 125, 140
Auden, W H   246
Authorised Version (King James Bible)   10

Bacon, Francis   85
Barke, James   206
Barrow, Isaac   149
Barzun, Jacques   9, 47, 69, 250
Bayley, John   249
Beattie, James   23, 32, 77, 138
   The Minstrel   68, 105, 106, 251
Begbie, Alison   230
Bellow, Saul   253
Bernbaum, Ernest   150
Blacklock, Thomas   11, 72, 90–2, 94, 153
Blackwell, Thomas   55
Blair, Hugh   54, 55, 62, 108, 110, 128, 129, 196
   Critical Dissertation on the Poems of Ossian   68
   Lectures on Rhetoric and Belles Lettres   83
Blair, Robert, *The Grave*   11, 43
Blake, William   209
Bold, Alan (ed), *Tobias Smollett: Author of the First Distinction*   ix
Boris Godunov   250
Boswell, James   1, 3, 6, 7–8, 12, 120–142, 254
   and Corsican freedom   134–7
   and Presbyterianism   122–3
   and Scottish education   122

attitudes to Scottishness   126–8, 133–4
relationship with father   124–5
relationship with Johnson   132–3, 138–41
search for *personae*   128–42
Boswell in Holland   133–4
Boswell's Column ('The Hypochondriack' essays)   137–8
Journal of a Tour to Corsica   134–7
Journal of a Tour to the Hebrides   127, 138–41
Letter to the People of Scotland   125
Life of Samuel Johnson LL.D.   140–1
London Journal   120–4
Braxfield, Lord   11
Brooke, Henry, *The Fool of Quality*   158
Bruce, Michael   153, 183, 195
Brueghel, Pieter the elder   200
Buffon, George Louis Leclerc, Comte de   223
Burns, Gilbert   240
Burns, Robert   2, 3, 8, 10, 17, 18, 28, 30, 35, 37, 41, 47, 61, 62, 69, 81, 94, 96, 124, 129, 145, 156, 164, 181, 183–5, 186–219, 220–46, 251
   and Edinburgh   8, 196, 211, 212, 214, 236
   and Enlightenment thought   190–1, 194–6, 210
   and mock-heroic   206–9, 240
   and older Scottish tradition   201–2
   and religious controversy   189, 193–4, 202
   and rural community   188, 200–3, 207–9
   anticipates Romantics   216–17
   as man of feeling   231–9
   as national bard   211–12
   dramatic element in poetry   190ff.
   language duality   207, 209, 211, 213–4
   life as self-drama   229ff.
   method of song-composition   217